AN INFINITE JOURNE

ENDORSEMENTS

RARELY HAVE I READ A book on sanctification that is simultaneously serious and fresh, at once reflective and accessible. Andy Davis combines analytical astuteness with pastoral passion. Those who think of themselves as Christians but who have no desire to grow in holiness need this book; Christians who want to be increasingly conformed to Christ will cherish this book.

— **DR. D. A. CARSON**
Research Professor of New Testament
Trinity Evangelical Divinity School

WE CAN BE GRATEFUL TO Andy Davis for writing a much needed book on sanctification. The book is biblically grounded but also pastorally warm and wise. Readers who desire to grow in Christ or who long to teach others about spiritual maturity will find this book to be an invaluable resource.

— **DR. THOMAS R. SCHREINER**
James Buchanan Harrison Professor of New Testament
Interpretation and Associate Dean of Scripture and
Interpretation
The Southern Baptist Theological Seminary

AN INFINITE JOURNEY IS A labor of love from the heart of a faithful pastor who dearly loves his people. It is a marvelous treatment of the doctrine of sanctification and a call to grow in Christlikeness. It is biblically grounded, theologically rich, and practical in application. It felt like I was reading a modern Puritan. Do not be hesitant to delve into this treasure because of its size. The precious nuggets of truth that leap from its pages will make the investment a wise one indeed.

— **DR. DANIEL L. AKIN**
President
Southeastern Baptist Theological Seminary

I LOVE ANDY DAVIS' EXTRAORDINARY mind. I love the breadth of his reading. Most of all, I love his terrific understanding of the Christian life and his grasp of the gospel. He is a faithful brother, and this book is a gift to the church.

— **DR. J.D. GREEAR**

Lead Pastor of The Summit Church and author of *Stop Asking Jesus Into Your Heart* and *Gospel: Recovering the Power that Made Christianity Revolutionary*

BESIDES THE BIBLE, IT WOULD be difficult to find any other single resource with more biblically sound, theologically rich, pastorally helpful, and practical insight about Christian growth than this book. Moreover, it's not just a book about progress in Christlikeness, for I know Andy Davis and I can affirm that there's a life of growth in grace behind the book. I recommend it to anyone on the Infinite Journey.

— **DR. DON WHITNEY**

Associate Professor of Biblical Spirituality
Senior Associate Dean for the School of Theology
The Southern Baptist Theological Seminary

AN INFINITE JOURNEY

Growing toward Christlikeness

ANDREW M. DAVIS

AMBASSADOR INTERNATIONAL
GREENVILLE, SOUTH CAROLINA & BELFAST, NORTHERN IRELAND

www.ambassador-international.com

An Infinite Journey

Growing toward Christlikeness

© 2014 by Dr. Andrew M. Davis

Printed in the United States of America

ISBN: 978-1-62020-236-4
eISBN: 978-1-62020-335-4

Cover design and typesetting: Matthew Mulder
E-book conversion: Anna Riebe

AMBASSADOR INTERNATIONAL
Emerald House
427 Wade Hampton Blvd.
Greenville, SC 29609, USA
www.ambassador-international.com

AMBASSADOR BOOKS
The Mount
2 Woodstock Link
Belfast, BT6 8DD, Northern Ireland, UK
www.ambassadormedia.co.uk

The colophon is a trademark of Ambassador

To Christi
It is a joy to journey with you toward mutual Christlikeness!

TABLE OF CONTENTS

FOREWORD

DURING MY TEENAGE YEARS, I became steeped in evangelical revivalism. I often got the impression from pastors and evangelists that salvation more or less equaled justification. From time to time, we learned about sanctification and glorification, but these truths were often assumed more than they were expounded. The real action was in getting saved, which meant being justified by faith in Jesus Christ as one's personal Lord and Savior.

I spent several years trying to nail down the exact moment I had been justified, since I was taught that my assurance of salvation is based almost entirely upon my decision to believe in Jesus for salvation. I often worried that I had not been sincere enough in my faith, because I still struggled with indwelling sin. I prayed some version or other of the "sinner's prayer" dozens of times in an effort to be sure I was really saved. As far as I knew, the Christian life was about getting justified, knowing you were justified, and helping other people get justified.

I was in college when it first dawned upon me that salvation is not a single moment in time, but rather is a spiritual journey. Justification is not an end unto itself—it is the beginning of a spiritual pilgrimage that begins in this life and ultimately ends in the next life. I had been saved by grace through faith (justification), I was being saved as the Holy Spirit conformed me more to the image of my Savior (sanctification), and I would be saved at the last day when I am finally and forever freed from sin, sickness, sorrow, and suffering (glorification). It was liberating to finally understand that "he who began a good work in you will bring it to completion at the day of Jesus Christ" (Phil. 1:6, ESV).

Providentially, my wife and I became a part of the First Baptist Church of Durham, North Carolina in 2005. We had learned of Andy Davis and his ministry at the church from some mutual friends. We wanted a church that emphasized expositional preaching, God's sovereignty in salvation, meaningful church membership, and the importance of evangelism and missions; we found it at FBC Durham. Once we joined the church, we discovered that Andy often speaks of the Christian life as two infinite, interrelated journeys. In the past eight years, my own spirituality has been shaped by the awareness that I am on an inward journey toward sanctification and ultimately glorification, and an outward journey to proclaim the lordship of Jesus Christ here, there, and everywhere.

An Infinite Journey is the fruit of many years of preaching and teaching on the nature of the Christian life, primarily in the context of a local church. I have watched Andy Davis faithfully model the two infinite journeys for the people he shepherds. I have seen this vision of the Christian life shape the spirituality of public school teachers, medical doctors, lawyers, businessmen, stay-at-home mothers, retirees, converted convicts, international graduate students, seminary students and professors, and foreign missionaries. I have become convinced that speaking of two infinite journeys is a helpful and memorable way to describe authentic, biblical Christianity.

I am glad you have decided to read this book; I do not believe you have done so by accident. My prayer is that An Infinite Journey will be a means of sanctifying grace in your own spiritual walk as you continue on the two infinite journeys of the Christian life.

Nathan A. Finn
Elder, First Baptist Church of Durham
Associate Professor, Southeastern Baptist Theological Seminary
October 15, 2013

UNDERSTANDING SALVATION'S INFINITE JOURNEY

CHAPTER 1

AN INFINITE JOURNEY MAPPED OUT

GOD HAS SET BEFORE THE Church of Jesus Christ two infinite journeys. These two journeys have one destination, one ultimate goal, and in the end will prove to have been one and the same journey after all. Before the foundation of the world, God ordained these two journeys for his glory and for the joy of his people. He ordained that the Church would make them, and that the Church would finish them. Both journeys require immense human effort and untold suffering in order to be accomplished. If you are a Christian today, these journeys are your central work, your central means of bringing glory to God. And what are these journeys? 1) The external journey of the worldwide advance of the Kingdom of Jesus Christ to all nations. 2) The internal journey of an individual Christian from being dead in sin to gloriously perfect in Christ.

These two journeys are referred to directly and indirectly in many places in Scripture. They are not always referred to as journeys, but that is what they are. The essential idea of a journey is progress; i.e., advancing gradually to a desired destination. The external journey of the worldwide advance of the Kingdom of Christ—from Jerusalem to the ends of the earth, through the ministry of the gospel—is a gradual process requiring great effort, labor, and suffering. The internal journey of individual, personal salvation—from justification, through sanctification, into glorification—is also a gradual process requiring great effort, labor, and suffering.

Both infinite journeys are displayed in Paul's letter to the Philippians, chapter 1.

1) The external journey of the gospel: *"I want you to know, brothers, that what has happened to me has really served to advance the gospel"* (Philippians 1:12).

2) The internal journey of sanctification: *"Convinced of this, I know that I will remain and continue with you all, for your progress and joy in the faith"* (Philippians 1:25).

Both verses use the same Greek word, prokopē, to speak of "progress" or "advance." This word, used twice, thus speaks of two journeys.

THE EXTERNAL JOURNEY OF GOSPEL ADVANCE

In the first case, Paul wants the persecuted Philippian church to know that his arrest and chains have actually helped the gospel make progress throughout the Praetorian Guard (Philippians 1:13). These elite soldiers were among the finest in the entire Roman empire, the toughest, most loyal, and most dedicated men the emperor had. It seems that Paul may have been chained to some of these Praetorian guardsmen, and had seized the opportunity to proclaim the gospel of Jesus Christ to them one after the other. Undoubtedly Paul's supernatural joy in Christ—despite his dreadful circumstances—must have made quite an impression on many of them, and they gave his message a careful listening. Paul hints that some of them may even have become Christians as a result (note that there are believers in "Caesar's household," Philippians 4:22). What is more, once the rest of the church saw how courageously and joyfully Paul was suffering for Christ, they were now emboldened to share the gospel fearlessly (Philippians 1:14)! Church history shows that, within one generation of Paul, there were Christian churches as far north as wild and forbidding Britain. Could it be that some Praetorian Guards believed Paul's gospel and became even more loyal to Christ than they were to the emperor, and spread the gospel to such distant places?

This is the progress of the gospel that Paul was speaking of: the gradual advance of the Kingdom of Christ through the verbal proclamation of the gospel message. *"Christ is proclaimed, and in that I rejoice"* (verse 18).

This worldwide advance of the gospel is the heroic story of missions, commanded and predicted by the resurrected Christ: *"[Jesus] said to them, 'Thus it is written, that the Christ should suffer and on the third day rise from the dead, and that repentance and forgiveness of sins should be proclaimed in his name to all nations, beginning from Jerusalem'"* (Luke 24:46–47).

The Church has been traveling this journey for almost two thousand years. Since the time when Philippians was written, the gospel has been carried heroically to the most distant parts of the earth's surface. Missionaries have crossed the burning sands of the Arabian Desert, the forbidding slopes of the Karakoram Mountains, the measureless expanses of the Pacific Ocean, and the dangerous wilds of the jungles of Irian Jaya. Martyrs have suffered persecution and died, families have suffered tropical illnesses and died, missionaries have suffered starvation and died, all to accomplish the "advance of the gospel," to make progress along this external journey.

THE INTERNAL JOURNEY OF SANCTIFICATION

The Apostle Paul also mentions the other of our two infinite journeys, in Philippians 1:25 : *"Convinced of this, I know that I will remain and continue with you all, for your **progress** and joy in the faith."*

The issue here is Paul's ongoing concern for the individual Philippian Christians after they have trusted Christ and been baptized. He is immensely concerned about their *"progress and joy in the faith."* Another name for "progress in the faith" is sanctification, the internal journey of gradual growth into Christlikeness. This internal journey is as important to Paul as the external, and that is why he wrote Philippians to begin with. His desire is that his letter will help them make *"progress in the faith,"* and to this end he constantly preaches, teaches, prays, and labors. He is greatly concerned that they become fully mature in Christ, letting the manner of their life be worthy of the gospel of Christ (1:27), responding to persecution with his same joyful attitude (1:28), putting others' needs ahead of their own with the perfect servant heart of Christ (2:1–11), working out their salvation with fear and trembling (2:12–13) as Paul did, by focusing totally on Christ, pressing on toward the goal for the upward call of God in Christ Jesus (3:7–14), and learning to constantly rejoice, trust, think, and be content in Christ (4:4–13).

This internal journey is the personal struggle of each Christian with the world, the flesh, and the devil. It requires a different kind of valor in the face of suffering than does the external journey, but it is the essence of the ongoing saving work of Christ in the individual Christian. This internal journey is a major and constant emphasis in the New Testament. Christ spoke of two roads, a narrow one leading to life and a broad one leading to destruction, and commanded us to *"enter through the narrow gate"* (Matthew 7:13–14). He also taught of the "way" to the Father, saying, *"I am the way. . . . No one comes to the Father except through me* (John 14:6). Christianity itself was originally called "The Way" (Acts 9:2; 19:9, 23; 24:14, 22), indicating this sense of a "way of salvation" (Acts 16:17). The book of Hebrews commands us to *"run with perseverance the race marked out for us"* (Hebrews 12:1), while Paul commanded that we should *"run so as to obtain,"* and said he did not *"run like a man running aimlessly"* (1 Corinthians 9:24, 26). In many of his epistles, he spoke of his own "race" (Acts 20:24, Galatians 2:2), and at the end of his life, he said *"I have finished my race"* (2 Timothy 4:7). All of Peter's and Paul's references to Christian spiritual growth (e.g., 1 Peter 2:2, Colossians 1:10) are allusions to the same issue—the internal journey—using different metaphors.

In the final analysis, these two journeys are really one and the same thing, and they are carried on for the same ultimate goal— the glory of God in the final perfection of the Church. God has ordained that his chosen ones shall most certainly be saved to the uttermost; they shall be resurrected from being *"dead in transgressions and sins"* (Ephesians 2:1) and brought to absolute perfection in Christ. Christ came to *"save his people from their sins"* (Matthew 1:21), and that means to save his chosen ones from everything that sin has done to them. The final end of salvation is total conformity to Christ (Romans 8:29), and he will not stop until each of the elect are brought into this perfection. Thus do the two infinite journeys become one: only when each individual elect of God is 1) brought to personal faith in Christ through the missionary work of the Church (the external journey), and 2) totally glorified in Christ, perfect in body, soul, and spirit in the Kingdom (the internal journey), will the work of God in this world be complete. These two journeys have one goal: *"the praise of his glory"* (Ephesians 1:12, 14).

WHY I CALL THESE JOURNEYS "INFINITE"
The word "infinite" is perhaps misleading, if one gathers from it that we will never reach our destination in these two journeys. The astonishing fact is that perfection is actually guaranteed in both of them! The Church of Jesus Christ will most certainly finish these journeys, and will enjoy the fruit from them forever. Personal perfection cannot be attained in this lifetime, but it will be granted us when we see the Lord. But we will attain the goal of the internal journey, total conformity to Christ.

So why call them "infinite?"[1] Simply because only an infinite power source can accomplish them, and because both will extend to the ends of our lives. Only the infinite power of God can enable the Church to advance the Kingdom of Christ to the end of the earth. As we quoted above, Christ said, *"You will receive **power** when the Holy Spirit comes upon you, and you will be my witnesses in*

Jerusalem, Judea, Samaria, and to the ends of the earth" (Acts 1:8). Paul said it was only by his power which works so mightily in him that he was able to carry on his ministry as apostle to the Gentiles (Colossians 1:28–29, Ephesians 3:7, 1 Corinthians 15:10). Without the infinite power of the Holy Spirit, the gospel message would never make a single convert, and the messengers would give up because of Satan's overwhelming opposition.

In the same way, it takes the infinite power of God and the infinite effectiveness of the ongoing priestly work of Christ to save us *"to the uttermost"* (Hebrews 7:25, ESV). Concerning the infinite power at work in us to complete our salvation, the Apostle Paul prayed specifically that the Ephesian Christians would be able to grasp the magnitude of the power that God is exerting to complete our salvation (see Ephesians 1:18–19). He said that this power was like the working of God's mighty strength in raising Christ from the dead and seating him at his right hand in the heavenly realms. And in the same way, God had raised us up from being dead in our transgressions and sins and will sit us with him in heaven as well. Therefore, sanctification is an infinite journey, because only the infinite power of God can complete it. And only the infinitely powerful priestly ministry of Christ at the right hand of God can keep us from all spiritual harm and enable us to make a single step forward in our sanctification.

Jesus summed it up when he said *"Apart from me, you can do nothing"* (John 15:5). Only with a lively sense of dependence on the infinite power of God will we make progress in these two journeys.

EVANGELICALISM'S NEGLECTED JOURNEY: SANCTIFICATION

The modern evangelical movement has been far more concerned about evangelism than about discipleship. "Bible-believing" churches have seen the church somewhat as a "weekly, stationary evangelistic rally."[2] The success of the church is measured in weekly attendance, finances, and especially in "soul-winning," measured through baptismal statistics. Pastors are measured by their success in attracting an ever-larger congregation. Evangelical denominations continually develop and market new strategies to win the lost. If the person "makes a decision" for Christ, they are quickly baptized and counted in the all-important statistics for reporting success to the outside world. Church-planting missionaries working with unreached people groups are frequently held accountable to report their progress to their superiors in statistical terms; reporting that the people of a ministry are growing in grace and in the knowledge of Christ (2 Peter 3:18) is not easily quantifiable, and therefore not welcome. If people becoming more and more Christlike is "all"(!!) that missionaries have to report, they may be reprimanded for neglecting evangelism!

Of course, if counting baptismal results were ungodly or unimportant, Acts 2:41 would not have told us that three thousand souls were added to the church through baptism. However, Acts 2:42 goes on to tell us that these people *"devoted themselves to the apostles' teaching and fellowship, to the breaking of bread and to prayers,"* and Acts 2:43–47 describes an intense life of full commitment as growing disciples of Jesus Christ. It should be unsettling when evangelical churches constantly have to do "follow-up" to find some of their new "converts" who never attend church. It should be unsettling when statistics show that there is very little difference between the divorce statistics of born-again Christians and those of the surrounding culture. It should be unsettling when there is so little spiritual maturity, so little sacrifice for Christ, so little hunger and thirst for righteousness, so little suffering for his glory.

There are many contributing factors to this present situation, but among them must be a loss of focus on the internal journey of sanctification in the life of the Church. When so much of the church service is geared to being "seeker-sensitive," when Sunday

School classes are totally focused on the visitors, actively seeking to make the lessons basic and simple and avoiding harder biblical content, when there seems no place for the meat of the Word of God in any church meeting or ministry, it should not be surprising that the church is suffering from such profound spiritual immaturity. The Church needs to reclaim a Bible-saturated, Spirit-drenched emphasis on *both* of these infinite journeys, learning that they are absolutely intertwined. It is impossible for the Church to make progress externally to the ends of the earth if there are no Christians mature enough to pay the price to go as missionaries and martyrs. And it is impossible to make genuine progress in sanctification if the people only read good Christian books and stay in classrooms, but refuse to get out into the world as witnesses. These journeys are mutually interdependent: without progress in one, there can be no progress made in the other.

CAPTAIN COOK & WILLIAM CAREY: "EXPECT GREAT THINGS, ATTEMPT GREAT THINGS"

On August 26, 1768, one of the most remarkable men in the history of the British Navy set sail for the Pacific Ocean. His name was Captain James Cook, and his voyage aboard a sturdy refitted coal ship named the *Endeavor* would change the course of history in many ways. The challenging purpose of Cook's expedition was to explore and chart as much of the vast Pacific Ocean as he could.

> As captain of the *Endeavour*, he would sight and survey hundreds of landfalls that no westerner had ever laid eyes on. . . . The most important prize of this and the two subsequent voyages that Cook would make was measured not in territory but in knowledge. Patient and methodical where his predecessors had been hasty and disorganized, he would sweep away myths and illusions on a prodigious scale, and in the end would give to the world a long-sought treasure: **a comprehensive map of the Pacific**.[3]

James Cook's voyages were followed with immense interest back in England, and after his shocking and sensational death in the Hawaiian Islands, his accounts of his voyages flew from British printing presses and made permanent imprints on the imaginations of countless English schoolboys. His astonishing rise from common seaman to ship captain, coupled with his bold and courageous accomplishments of discovery, gave English ambitions new fuel and wider scope. The name of his vessel, the *Endeavor*, matched the slogan on the coat of arms awarded him posthumously by the king of England: "He left nothing unattempted."

One of the schoolboys who thrilled to the accounts of Cook's discoveries was William Carey. His imagination was fired and his ambitions set in motion by reading Cook's *Journals*. His horizons expanded, and his dreams wafted across the seemingly endless expanses of the Pacific. But his ambitions took a completely different turn than he originally expected when he bowed his knee to the kingship of Jesus Christ and took Jesus' yoke upon himself. Once he combined his understanding of the spiritual needs of the natives who lived in these distant lands with the Great Commission of Jesus Christ to take the gospel to the ends of the earth, Carey's ambitions were cast in the same direction as those of the Apostle Paul in Romans 15:20: "*It has always been my ambition to preach the gospel where Christ was not known, so that I would not be building on someone else's foundation.*" By the spring of 1792, Carey had published these convictions in a world-changing pamphlet, *An Enquiry into the Obligations of Christians to Use Means for the Conversion of the Heathens.*

On Wednesday, May 30, 1792, at Friar Lane Baptist Chapel, Nottingham, England, William Carey put this challenge into one of the most influential sermons ever preached in church history, what came to be called a "deathless sermon," based on Isaiah 54:2–3. Speaking to the Northamptonshire Baptist Association, Carey passionately exhorted his Baptist colleagues to: "Expect great things from God, and attempt great things for God." This slogan became a by-word for the modern missionary movement. The idea was simple and powerful: God's eternal plan concerning the worldwide spread of the gospel cannot be thwarted, and therefore it decrees that energetic effort will succeed in accomplishing it. In other words, just because God has determined before the foundation of the world that *"this gospel of the Kingdom will be preached in the whole world as a testimony to all nations"* (Matthew 24:14), doesn't mean that the church should do **nothing**, and just let God do everything. On the contrary, the church will succeed precisely because God has ordained it! Therefore, the church should "use means for the conversion of the heathen" and should "expect great things from God and attempt great things for God." We can expect great things from God because great things are both promised and required for the immense task of worldwide evangelization. We can attempt great things for God because great things will be rewarded by God with success, since they are required for the accomplishment of this infinite journey of worldwide evangelization.

The secular adventuring spirit of Captain James Cook was simply this: bold endeavor for the worldwide spread of the British Empire. "He left nothing unattempted." The spiritual adventuring spirit of William Carey was simply this: bold endeavor for the worldwide spread of Christ's empire. "Expect great things from God, attempt great things for God." Now, what Carey applied to the external journey of worldwide missions, I would like to apply to the internal journey of personal sanctification. I yearn for a generation of Christians who will do the same thing in the internal journey of sanctification, while in no way neglecting the external journey of gospel advance. We need to spare nothing in our efforts to reach as high in personal Christlikeness as Carey reached wide in missionary achievement. We need to take on sin patterns and defeat them by the power of the Spirit. We need to make ambitious resolutions in Scripture memorization and prayer and character development, and see those goals met to the glory of God. We should yearn to reach the end of our days here on earth knowing that we never rested in our efforts to grow to maximum Christlikeness. We should fear lying on our deathbed and groaning, knowing that we let some lust or sin habit rob us of the best years of our lives on earth. What was said of Captain James Cook concerning an immeasurable secular journey must also be said of us concerning our infinite spiritual journey in sanctification: "We left nothing unattempted."

And we should do all this not neglecting in any way the passion of Carey for the external journey of worldwide evangelization. Perish the thought! Actually, we should be ambitious in the internal journey so we can be ever-more fruitful in the external journey. We should always be *"grow[ing] in the grace and knowledge of Christ"* so we can lead as many souls to Christ as he permits. We should run the internal race with perseverance so we can run the external race with eternal fruitfulness: more and more souls for Christ.

TOWARD A COMPREHENSIVE MAP OF SANCTIFICATION

As noted above, one of the main goals of the meticulous and thorough Captain Cook was "a comprehensive map of the Pacific." This map was of immense value to all navigators who followed Cook, for he took the immensity of that body of water and made it accessible on paper. I have a similar goal in the issue of sanctification.

Sanctification is growth into Christlikeness in all areas of life. Conformity to Christ in everything is an overwhelming concept. Thankfully, God has not left us in the dark, for the Bible gives us everything we need to know about what it means. But with every command from Jesus, every exhortation from Paul, every insight from John or precept from Peter, with every example from the

Old Testament that the Holy Spirit presses on our consciences, and with the weight of the Law of God still relevant in the New Covenant, the scope of what it means to be "spiritually mature" grows and grows. After a while, it becomes difficult to have a sense of everything that God wants us to be and do.

This becomes very acute for pastors and other disciple-makers, for such leaders need to know what they are to shoot for in their ministries. As they bring someone new to Christ, they need to have a sense of what the goal is in the spiritual growth of those now entrusted to their care. It is just as significant an issue for parents who are seeking to bring up their children in the "*training and instruction of the Lord*" (Ephesians 6:4). An accurate map of the journey from spiritual immaturity to maturity would be immensely beneficial.

This is one of the lasting appeals of John Bunyan's classic book on sanctification, *Pilgrim's Progress*: it lays out a roadmap from conversion to heaven. And even if it doesn't systematically cover all areas of Christian life, so many are addressed, and with such power, that people have been moved by the English tinker's astonishing masterpiece for over three hundred years.

Another analogy for what I am attempting is found in the introductory volume to the Encyclopedia Britannica. That volume is called a "Propedia," and in it there is a fascinating "Outline of Knowledge." It divides all of human knowledge into ten major categories:

1. Matter and Energy
2. The Earth
3. Life on Earth
4. Human Life
5. Human Society
6. Art
7. Technology
8. Religion

9. The History of Mankind
10. The Branches of Knowledge

Of course, each of these major sections has major subdivisions as well. This kind of arrangement in zoology is called a "taxonomy." In this book, I will attempt a taxonomy of sanctification, seeking to organize—as much as I can, and in clear headings— what the Bible lays on us as reasonable goals for spiritual growth. My goal is to be as thorough as possible without multiplying the length beyond accessibility.

When I was growing up, my mother taught me that the secret to an orderly room was: "a place for everything, and everything in its place." I am seeking to organize the Bible's teachings on sanctification so that there is a place for everything and everything can be put in its place. Final achievement of this goal will elude us, because the inner life is so deep and rich, and the standard of Christlike perfection is so high. Also, many of these areas strongly overlap, so that it's hard to separate, for example, heart desire expressed in prayer, from the action of prayer itself. Yet I believe the effort to sort things out will prove beneficial in stimulating Christian growth.

In this book, I will argue that all of Christian maturity can be found under four major headings: Knowledge, Faith, Character, and Action. Each of these I will break into some major subdivisions, which I will seek to describe and support from Scripture. A "Map of Sanctification," or perhaps better an "Outline of Sanctification," would look like this:

1. Knowledge: Spiritual truth
   a. Factual knowledge gained from God's word
   b. Experiential knowledge gained from living in God's world
2. Faith: Assurance and Conviction of Spiritual Truth
   a. Certainty that Invisible Spiritual Realities are True
   b. Assurance of Things Hoped For

    c. Conviction of Sin

    d. Reliance on Christ as All-Sufficient Savior and Provider

    e. Reception of Spiritual Guidance

3. Character: Internal Nature Conformed to Christ

    a. Affection: Loving What Christ Loves and Hating What Christ Hates

    b. Desire: Yearning for What Christ Yearns for

    c. Will: Choosing What Christ Would Choose

    d. Thought: Having the Mind of Christ

    e. Emotions: Feeling What Christ Would Feel

    f. Virtues: Situational Heart Attributes Conformed to Christ

4. Action: Habitual Obedience

    a. Main Action: Presentation of the Body as a Spiritual Sacrifice

    b. Negative Obedience: Personal holiness/purity

        i. Purity from sin

        ii. Proper handling of sin's occurrence

    c. Positive Obedience: Seven Key Arenas

        i. Worship

        ii. Spiritual Disciplines

        iii. Family

        iv. Ministry to Believers

        v. Mission to Non-Believers

        vi. Stewardship

        vii. Work

Here is a graphical representation of this outline.

A PATHWAY TO CHRISTIAN MATURITY

KNOWLEDGE
FACTUAL AND EXPERIENTIAL
SPIRITUAL INFORMATION

FACTUAL
Gained from the Scripture

EXPERIENTIAL
Gained from living in God's world

Leads To
→

Romans 10:17
So faith comes from hearing, and hearing through the word of Christ.

FAITH
ASSURANCE OF AND COMMIT-
MENT TO SPIRITUAL TRUTH

- Certainty that specific invisible spiritual realities are true
- Assurance that hoped-for specific good thing promised in scripture will certainly come true
- Conviction that specific sin in me, and that God hates it and will judge people for such sins
- Reliance on Christ as all-sufficient savior, refuge, provider, shield
- Reception of spiritual guidance and knowledge

Leads To
↑
Psalms 119:100 I have more understanding than the elders, for I obey your precepts.

Leads To
↓
Ephesians 3:16-17
...that Christ may dwell in your hearts through faith.

ACTION
EXTERNAL LIFESTYLE OF
HABITUAL OBEDIENCE

1. Presentation of Body to God
2. Personal Holiness
3. Seven-fold obedience to God's commands

   1. Worship
   2. Spiritual Disciplines
   3. Family
   4. Ministry to Believers
   5. Mission to Non-Believers
   6. Stewardship
   7. Work

Leads To
←

Matthew 12:23
Either make the tree good and

CHARACTER
INTERNAL NATURE CON-
FORMED TO CHRIST

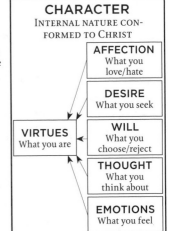

AFFECTION
What you love/hate

DESIRE
What you seek

VIRTUES
What you are

WILL
What you choose/reject

THOUGHT
What you think about

EMOTIONS
What you feel

Furthermore, I will argue that sanctification occurs in a cycle that follows this order: growing knowledge increases faith, increasing faith transforms character, transformed character produces action, and action feeds knowledge. This arrangement of all the various elements of sanctification in their place and order may prove helpful to all Christians seeking to grow, but not knowing where to begin. It may also help parents, pastors, and disciplers in knowing how to work with growing Christians, or missionaries in knowing what to seek in the people who are converting.

BOLD ENDEAVOR IN SANCTIFICATION, UNDERSTANDING THE GREAT COMMISSION

In the end, knowing all of this information will be useless if it doesn't result in actual growth on the part of Christians. This growth happens only by the grace of God, but it also happens with solid effort on our part: *"Therefore, my dear friends, as you have always obeyed—not only in my presence, but now much more in my absence—continue to* **work out your salvation** *with fear and trembling, for it is God who works in you to will and to act according to his good purpose"* (Philippians 2:12–13). I will describe how our efforts, so unwelcome in justification and impossible in glorification, are very much needed in sanctification. And I will urge that, like Captain Cook in his voyages and William Carey in his mission to India, we "leave nothing unattempted." Like Captain Cook's ship, we should be setting out in a bold endeavor for God's glory, in our personal growth into Christlikeness.

Every biblically literate Christian knows that one of the most important passages in the Bible is the so-called Great Commission, which is given at the very end of Matthew's Gospel:

> Then Jesus came to them and said, "All authority in heaven and on earth has been given to me. Therefore go and make disciples of all nations, baptizing them in the name of the Father and of the Son and of the Holy Spirit, and teaching them to obey everything I have commanded you. And surely I am with you always, to the very end of the age. (Matthew 28:18–20)

This one passage of Scripture has been the central motivation for more missionary sermons, books, strategies, and fruit than any other passage in the Bible. However, in an effort to "get people saved" (by which they mean justified, these converts having merely "prayed the sinner's prayer"), they have neglected the fullness of Christ's command. As I will argue in this book, the goal is for the Church to make mature disciples (learners) of Christ: disciples who are taught the fullness of his word and obedience to all of his commands. We shall see that this involves an inherited pattern of right doctrine and right living being used faithfully to help new converts conform to Christ fully, with the goal being comprehensive obedience.

MY GOAL: GOD'S GLORY IN YOUR INSIGHT AND ENCOURAGEMENT

In presenting a thorough description of sanctification with all its component parts, I am seeking to instruct people concerning the fullness of the Bible's teaching on Christlikeness, and to encourage people to strive daily to reach that goal. Once we see all that God expects of us, it will easily become discouraging if not understood properly. It is the great blessing of the gospel that all the elements of our great salvation—justification, sanctification, and glorification—are by grace based wholly on the work of Christ for us and in us. In the end, not one of us will be righteous enough based on our efforts in sanctification to stand before our Holy God. But Christ has already worked at the cross an absolutely perfect righteousness for us, which he has given us in justification, received as a gift simply by faith alone.

Yet God does desire us to make strong efforts to "*grow in grace and the knowledge of Christ*" (2 Peter 3:18). It is my earnest prayer that God will use this book to motivate you to do precisely this, to the glory of God and for your eternal happiness in heaven.

OUR GREAT SALVATION

THE WORD "GREAT" IS THROWN around so casually in our culture that it loses its meaning. In nature, there are the Great Lakes, the Great Barrier Reef, and the great white shark; in history, Alexander the Great and the Great War; in literature, *The Great Gatsby* and *Great Expectations*. Every sports enthusiast likes reading the list of the "100 Greatest Baseball Players of All Time", and Muhammad Ali called himself "The Greatest." Even in commercial life, you can go to Great Clips for a haircut and search on Google to find "great wedding gift ideas" or a "great vacation spot." In many of these cases, the word "great" is an overstatement.

However, when it comes to the salvation Christ has won for us, the word "great" is an understatement! The goal of this chapter is to understand how truly great is our salvation in Christ, and to understand its component parts: regeneration, justification, sanctification, and glorification. More to the point, here we must understand the role of human effort in sanctification, as opposed to its role in regeneration, justification, and glorification. My desire is to call on Christians to put forth supreme effort in the journey of sanctification, of growing in Christ, but to do so knowing the full process of our great salvation. Our great salvation is a complex and marvelous thing, and God calls on us to study it carefully that we may glorify him by it as we should.

WE MUST CONSTANTLY STUDY
OUR GREAT SALVATION

Our salvation is called "great" in Hebrews 2:3: *"how shall we escape if we ignore such a **great** salvation?"* The context in the book of Hebrews is very significant. The author is writing to some Jewish people who had made an initial profession of faith in Christ, but who were wavering in their commitment to Christ, and choosing not to go to church (Hebrews 10:25) because of persecution by the Jewish community. So the entire epistle to the Hebrews is rightly called an "epistle of warning." These Christians were being warned not to drift away (Hebrews 2:1), turn away (Hebrews 3:12), or fall away (Hebrews 6:6) from Christ.

For this reason the author of Hebrews makes this soul-saving demand: *"We must pay more careful attention, therefore, to what we have heard, so that we do not drift away. . . . [H]ow shall we escape if we ignore such a great salvation?"* (Hebrews 2:1–3).

Drifting away from Christ is a painful thing to watch in someone else, and even worse to experience in ourselves. The image in my mind is of a sailboat alongside a dock, with its mooring line just lying loosely on the pier. The gentle ebb and flow of the basically placid sea does not present any immediate threat to the boat, so if you came back in five minutes, you would barely notice that the mooring line had slipped a little. But come back in ten hours, and the changing tide and the consistent bobbing of the boat has caused it to drift away entirely; it is gone. So it is with many who profess faith in Christ. Their initial excitement about the Christian life can soon ebb, and their neglect of the gospel can result in drifting away from Christ. This is why each of us must heed the clear instruction the book of Hebrews gives us to be ever vigilant over our own souls.

The remedy given in Hebrews 2:1 is clear: *"We must pay more careful attention to what we have heard . . . so that we do not drift away."* "What we have heard" is clearly the gospel message itself, and "paying more careful attention" means to study it and attend to it and give our hearts fully to it, so that we can understand its message better and better. The alternative to studying the gospel is that we *"ignore such a great salvation"* (Hebrews 2:3). The word translated *ignore* means to "neglect" or "make light of" our salvation, to treat it lightly as though our very lives did not depend on it. In order to avoid gradually drifting away from Christ, therefore, we need to study the greatness of our salvation, study it carefully and diligently, study it daily. There will never be a time on this earth that we will graduate from the careful study of the gospel, or from needing to believe its message. We will be sitting under its greatness the rest of our lives.

OUR GREAT SALVATION IS UNFATHOMABLE

In 1521, Ferdinand Magellan, in the process of leading the first ships to circumnavigate the globe, attempted to sound the depths of the central Pacific Ocean. He spliced six lengthy lines together and attached them to a cannonball. He lowered the cannon ball until the line ran out—four hundred fathoms, or about 2400 feet. Magellan concluded that the ocean was immeasurably deep—literally "unfathomable." At that place in the Pacific, he would have probably needed as many as fifty such lines spliced together to hit bottom!

Yet when we come to the infinite richness of the gospel, we are like sailors out in a rowboat, pulling pieces of string out of our pockets, splicing them together and trying to find the bottom of the Pacific Ocean. Certainly the Apostle Paul must have felt something like that. In the book of Romans, after writing eleven chapters of the deepest and richest description of gospel doctrine in the Bible, he reacted in wonder and amazement at what God had revealed through him: *"Oh, the depth of the riches of the wisdom and knowledge of God! How unsearchable his judgments, and his paths beyond tracing out!"* (Romans 11:33). Paul is marveling over the doctrinal depths of the gospel, and he states that we can never exhaust its riches or fully plumb its depths. Even still, the effort is essential to our ongoing salvation. Hebrews 2:1 says we must *"pay more careful attention to what we have heard,"* even though it is infinitely deep.

A single verse from the Psalms helps capture how infinite is this gospel: *"My mouth will tell of your righteousness, of your salvation all day long, though I know not its measure"* (Psalm 71:15). The full measure of all God has done to work salvation in one individual life and around the world is beyond calculation. Though we can never fully know the measure of the saving works of God, yet it is richly beneficial and essential to our ongoing salvation to study them all. We cannot know the full measure of our salvation for a variety of reasons:

1. We don't perfectly understand how sinful we were, still are, and will continue to be, until we are glorified.

2. We don't perfectly understand how holy God is and how offensive were our sins against him, how hot and righteous was his wrath against us, and how great was our danger (eternity in hell).

3. We don't perfectly understand how great is our heavenly inheritance, how much joy and blessing awaits us when we are finished being saved, nor do we understand what kind of glory will be revealed to us (the amazing perfection of the New Heaven and New Earth) and in us (for we will shine like the sun).

4. We don't perfectly understand the price that was paid on our behalf, the infinite value of the blood of Christ and of the immense suffering he absorbed in propitiating the wrath of God.

5. We don't perfectly understand the infinite power that is at work in us and around us to guarantee our final perfection in Christ, the completion of our salvation.

6. We don't perfectly understand how much God does for us every day to keep us in the faith—to protect us from the devil, to resist our own fleshly sinful tendencies, to filter out temptations that are too hard for us, to feed and nourish our faith.

7. We don't perfectly understand the human sacrifices that were made along the way in two thousand years of Church history to ensure that we would at some point hear the true and pure gospel.

8. We don't perfectly understand how much of all of these same things God is doing to a countless multitude from every tribe and language and people and nation around the world.

However, though in this world we cannot know the measure of our salvation fully, yet we should study it carefully, get to know it thoroughly, and rejoice in it completely.

THE STAGES OF OUR GREAT SALVATION

God did not intend to give us our salvation all at once, but in parts. Perhaps an illustration of this is found in Jesus' unusual healing of a blind man in Bethsaida, recorded for us in Mark 8:22–25. Jesus spit on the man's eyes, put his hands on him, and then asked him, "Do you see anything?" The man looked up and said, "I see people; they look like trees walking around." Once more, Jesus touched the man's eyes, and his sight was only then perfectly restored.

What a remarkable encounter! There is no other healing like it in the gospels, a healing effected in distinct stages. The question that immediately comes to mind is, "Why?" Certainly we can't imagine that Jesus' first attempt at healing this blind man was somewhat of a failure, so that he had to try again. That would deny Jesus the glory of his divine perfection. There was always a perfect intention in everything Christ did. I believe all of Jesus' miracles were signs of the actual nature of the salvation work he came to do, living pictures in the present physical world of what he intends to do in our souls and in the universe at the end of time.

God has begun a marvelous healing work in us, and we are measurably better than we were before. But he is not done healing us. Now we see people like trees walking around, but when Christ is done with us, we shall see perfectly. The Apostle Paul put it this way: *"Now we see but a poor reflection as in a mirror; then we shall see face to face. Now I know in part; then I shall know fully, even as I am fully known"* (1 Corinthians 13:12).

Thus God wills our salvation to come to us in parts. There are several distinct stages of salvation, each with its own patterns: Stage I) the process of calling/drawing; Stage II) the moment of regeneration, faith, and justification; Stage III) the process of sanctification; Stage IV) the moments of glorification (first of the soul at death, and then of the body at resurrection). For the Christian, the first two stages are over, the third stage is progressing now, and the fourth stage is yet to come. Thus, speaking in terms of time for a Christian in the process of sanctification, we have been saved, (Titus 3:5, Ephesians 2:8), we are being saved, (1 Corinthians 1:18, 1 Peter 1:8–9), and we will be saved (Romans 5:9–10).

The focus of this chapter is understanding human effort (works) in these various stages; human effort achieves nothing positive in Stages I and II, is essential in Stage III, and is unnecessary in Stage IV, as we shall see.

STAGE I: THE PROCESS OF CALLING AND DRAWING

As we have seen, Romans 8:29–30 lays out the order of salvation very plainly: *"For those God foreknew he also predestined to be conformed to the likeness of his Son, that he might be the firstborn among many brothers. And those he predestined, he also **called**; those he **called**, he also justified; those he justified, he also glorified."* Foreknowledge and predestination happen for an individual in the mind of God

before the foundation of the world. But this calling Paul speaks of
is the beginning of God's direct work on an individual, bringing
them to saving faith.

For the elect, this begins at the moment of birth and continues until the moment of regeneration. I believe this calling is the
process Jesus referred to in John 6:44, by which the Sovereign
God draws to himself his elect, using an innumerable array of
methods and means to put one truth after another in place in the
heart of his future children. Jesus said this "drawing" is essential
to salvation, and without it no one will be saved: *"No one can come
to me unless the Father who sent me draws him, and I will raise him up
at the last day"* (John 6:44). The word "draw" in this verse is used
of drawing a sword out of a sheath (John 18:10), dragging in a net
full of fish (John 21:6, 11), and dragging prisoners to the authorities for judgment (Acts 16:19, 21:30; James 2:6). Many have spoken
against the doctrine of "irresistible grace," saying that no one is
"dragged kicking and screaming into the Kingdom." Well, no one
is dragged "kicking and screaming," but we are drawn effectually
by the power of God. So this aspect of the calling is the "drawing"
I am speaking of here.

Some may object to linking the "calling" of Romans 8:29 with
the "drawing" of John 6:44. Some tend to think of "the call" as
effectual immediately in transforming spiritually dead people to
life, and anything before that was not the "calling" of Romans
8:29. However, Jesus spoke of a general calling when he said
"Many are called, but few are chosen." (Matthew 22:14). Thus there
is a calling that is more general and preparatory, and a calling that
is immediately effective. The first aspect of this calling is what I
am linking to the "drawing" of John 6:44.

In this drawing process, one encounter after another shapes
the heart of the lost person, and though in one sense the unregenerate person is indeed "dead in their transgressions and sins"
(Ephesians 2:1), yet they still live in those sins (Ephesians 2:2) day

by day and are experiencing their poisonous effects. Meanwhile, God is putting the pieces together for the moment when at last he will sovereignly give miraculous new life. It reminds me of the tumblers of a combination lock: when the knob is turned to the proper positions in succession, one tumbler after another gets positioned until they are all in place and the lock can be opened. So an encounter with a godly grandmother at age six, with a Sunday school teacher at age eight, with a street corner evangelist at age fourteen, and with a Christian dorm-mate at age eighteen, can all be used by God to prepare the lost person for their eventual conversion at age twenty. The tumblers are all getting put in position step by step, and nothing is lost or wasted. This is the drawing process by which God is calling to the sinner to come to Christ.

At the time that Saul of Tarsus was converted on the road to Damascus, this "Hebrew of Hebrews" began the day still *"breathing out murderous threats against the Lord's disciples"* (Acts 9:1). When Christ appeared to Saul in resurrection glory on the Damascus road, he said, *"Saul, Saul, why do you persecute me? It is hard for you to kick against the goads"* (Acts 26:14). The word *goads* refers to sharp metal spikes put on the plow to keep the ox from kicking back at the master. It explains the wise and powerful way in which Christ worked in Saul's life before his conversion. By that point, the Lord had already put every piece in place: Saul's years of training in the Scriptures, his knowledge of the basic facts of Christ's life, his partial understanding of the gospel preached by men like Stephen, his involvement in the vicious persecution of the Church (including his willing assent to and involvement in the death of Stephen), the powerful sermon Stephen preached (Acts 7), and the winsome way Stephen died. As Saul made his way to Damascus, these things (and many others besides) were spiritual goads, pricking his conscience in an unmistakable direction.

But Saul was "kicking against" these goads, causing himself psychological, emotional, and spiritual pain. Jesus shows amazing compassion for his enemy, saying *"it is hard for you to kick against the goads."* The word *hard* is variously translated "harsh, austere, severe." Whenever a sinner is resisting the calling of God, it creates a certain amount of spiritual pain, and God uses that pain to bring him in the end to Christ.

The goads are God's sovereign actions in a person's life, over perhaps decades of experiences in God's world, and they are used by God to bring the person to Christ in the end. But they alone are insufficient without the preaching of the gospel and the internal regenerating work of the Spirit. These constitute the final aspect of the calling that God does in a human heart. The gospel message of Christ crucified is proclaimed in some manner, the person hears it, and by it the regenerating power of the Holy Spirit creates something that wasn't there before: *"God . . . gives life to the dead and calls things that are not as though they were"* (Romans 4:17). It is similar to the miraculous power of Christ at work in \ when Christ called to him, a dead man buried for four days, *"Lazarus, come forth!"* (John 11:43). The power of Christ went forth in the audible call, producing a supernatural effect—resurrection—and an ability for Lazarus to obey the command to come forth. So it is with the effectual calling of the Spirit in the heart of an elect person at the moment of regeneration: with the audible sound of the gospel comes a new power to respond.

STAGE II: THE MOMENT OF REGENERATION, FAITH, AND JUSTIFICATION

The next elements of salvation all happen instantaneously. In fact, they are so intertwined it becomes very difficult to separate them. Many theological battles have been fought over the order of regeneration and faith in particular. I give logical priority to regeneration over faith because faith is a gift of God, the evidence of God's regenerating work in a previously dead human heart.

REGENERATION

The culmination of the calling of God is the moment of regeneration. God speaks as a Creator-King into nothingness, and creates something that wasn't there before. He does it by the power of the Spirit while the person is hearing the gospel of Christ. The best verse in all of Scripture to explain this moment is 2 Corinthians 4:6: *"For God, who said, "Let light shine out of darkness," made his light shine in our hearts to give us the light of the knowledge of the glory of God in the face of Christ."* This likens our regeneration to the sovereign work of God in creating light in Genesis 1:3. There, God spoke into nothingness and created physical light by the word of his power. In regeneration, God speaks into the spiritual deadness of our hearts and creates a special kind of light that did not exist before: the *"light of the knowledge of the glory of God in the face of Christ."* Christ, as *"the radiance of God's glory and the exact representation of his being"* (Hebrews 1:3), appears glorious, magnificent, attractive, and completely desirable.

This moment of spiritual clarity about Christ occurs in conjunction with the clear proclamation of the gospel: thus the glory of Christ specifically proclaimed in the gospel message of the cross and empty tomb becomes exceedingly attractive. The person is alive to truths to which up until that moment they had been utterly dead. They are made a *"new creation"* (2 Corinthians 5:17) at this moment, *"born again"* by the Spirit of God (John 3:3). Since the light is shining in our hearts, this is the moment in which God removes the *"heart of stone"* and gives instead a *"heart of flesh"* (Ezekiel 11:19, 36:26).

FAITH AND REPENTANCE

This spiritual light described in 2 Corinthians 4:6 shining in the newly-made heart must have a receptor or it cannot be seen. At the moment God causes *"his light to shine in our hearts to give us the light of the knowledge of the glory of God in the face of Christ,"* he creates also the eyesight of the soul, namely faith. Faith is a gift of God (Ephesians 2:8), and it is the capacity to receive what God is freely giving. I call it the eyesight of the soul because, like the eye, it does not create reality, but rather simply receives what comes to it, as the eye receives the light that comes to it from the world. Faith receives the truth of God, as the eye receives the light of the world. At the moment God opens up within the soul the eyesight of faith, Christ then appears to the individual sinner as what he really is: the glorious display of the perfections of God. The soul cleaves to Christ, trusts in Christ's blood, accepts Christ's saving work on its behalf. The Scripture reveals that the word of the gospel is the effective means of faith springing up in the heart: *"so faith comes from hearing, and hearing through the word of Christ"* (Romans 10:17, ESV).

Faith has also a negative side, and that is to see our own wickedness in the pure light of the person of Christ and of the Law of God. We hate our sin and want to be free from it forever. We turn away from wickedness and toward God. This is called "repentance." The close link between repentance and faith can be seen in Jesus' initial preaching of the Kingdom of God: *"The time has come,"* he said. *"The kingdom of God is near. Repent and believe the good news!"* (Mark 1:15). Repentance is an internal change of heart that is inevitably displayed by a change of life that is the beginning of the journey of sanctification. Thus we'll return to it later. Suffice it to say that repentance is part of the gracious work of God in a sinner's heart that is indispensable to the process of salvation. It occurs for the first time as a component of justifying faith at this moment of regeneration.

JUSTIFICATION

The centerpiece of the gospel of grace is this simple truth: sinners are justified by faith alone, apart from works of the Law. Simply by believing the gospel of Jesus Christ a sinner is justified (made righteous) in the sight of God, not by anything he or she can do. The most important text in the whole Bible on this crucial doctrine is Romans 3:21–30. In that vital section of Scripture, Paul asserts that there is a righteousness from God apart from the law which comes through faith in Christ. Every single person on earth has sinned, and every person who is justified in the sight of God is so by faith in Christ alone. God presented Christ as a propitiation for our sins, and every sinner who has faith in Christ is justified by God's grace. This justification by faith precludes all boasting, for no sinner is ever justified by works of the law, but merely by grace through faith.

As Romans chapter 3 teaches, the foundation of our justification is the redeeming work of Christ on the cross, a redemption made in his blood. There Christ paid the righteous penalty due for our sins, fully propitiating the just wrath of God for anyone who believes in him (v. 25). The effectual core of Christ's atoning work is the exchange of our sin (and the guilt that justly goes with it) for his perfect righteousness: *"God made him who had no sin to be sin for us, so that in him we might become the righteousness of God"* (2 Corinthians 5:21). On the basis of our faith alone is this transfer made. Our guilt is laid on Christ, who suffered in our place (Isaiah 53:5–6); Christ's perfect righteousness is imputed to us, and we are declared righteous by our holy Judge.

The doctrine of the imputation of Christ's righteousness to us by faith is under attack in our day[4], but it is taught openly in Romans chapter 4:

> What then shall we say was gained by Abraham, our fore-father according to the flesh? For if Abraham was justified by works, he has something to boast about, but not before God. For what does the Scripture say? "Abraham believed God, and it was counted to him as righteousness." Now to the one who works, his wages are not counted as a gift but as his due. And to the one who does not work but trusts

him who justifies the ungodly, his faith is counted as righteousness. (Romans 4:1-5, ESV)

The key verse is Romans 4:3, quoting Genesis 15:3: *"Abraham believed God, and it was counted to him as righteousness."* The Greek phrase translated *"counted to him"* can also be translated "credited" or "reckoned," and it has a sense of the matter being entirely in the mind of God. In the accounting book of God's appraisal, Abraham was thought of, considered, or reckoned as righteous. What is the source of Abraham's righteousness? 2 Corinthians 5:21 says, *"in him (Christ) we become the righteousness of God."* Paul teaches the same thing in Philippians, stating that he was willing to lose everything in his former way of life *"that I may gain Christ and be found in him, not having a righteousness of my own that comes from the law, but that which is through faith in Christ—the righteousness that comes from God and is by faith"* (Philippians 3:8–9). This righteousness is justification righteousness, imputed to us, credited to our account, reckoned to us in the mind of God by simple faith in Christ.

So in justification, by faith all our guilt is removed from us and laid on Christ, all God's righteous wrath and condemnation are poured out on him as our substitute, and Christ's perfect righteousness is imputed to us. At the instant of saving faith in Christ, God sees us as perfectly righteous in Christ, and he will see us that way for eternity. There is nothing we can do to improve our standing in his eyes, for Christ's perfect righteousness is already ours by faith. All our sins, past, present, and future, are completely forgiven: *"In him we have redemption through his blood, the forgiveness of sins, in accordance with the riches of God's grace"* (Ephesians 1:7).

At this glorious moment of regeneration, faith, and justification, *"every spiritual blessing in Christ"* (Ephesians 1:3) is lavished on the new believer by God's grace. The gift of the indwelling Holy Spirit comes as a seal that we are God's own possession (Ephesians 1:13), and the Spirit begins his essential ministries of conviction of sin (John 16:8), daily guidance (John 16:13), illumination of the Word of God (1 Corinthians 2:10,13), testimony with our spirits that we are children of God (Romans 8:16), and assistance in prayer (Romans 8:26). Before that moment, the Spirit was not indwelling, and now he is and will be forever (John 14:16–17). So also the new believer is adopted as a child of God (John 1:12–13, Romans 8:16) and takes a permanent place in the family of God (John 8:35). Many other blessings flow at this moment as well: reconciliation with God (Romans 5:10–11), spiritual union with Christ (Romans 6:4–5), cleansing of a guilty conscience (Hebrews 9:14), rescue from the dominion of darkness and transfer into the kingdom of Christ (Colossians 1:13). All of these gifts (and others besides) occur at this one moment, and they will never be revoked.

Not one of them comes, however, by human effort or striving. They come by grace through faith apart from works (Ephesians 2:8–9, Titus 3:5). Thus the true believer is eternally secure in the grip of God's sovereign grace. No enemy is powerful enough to snatch Christ's sheep from God's omnipotent hand (John 10:28–30), and Christ will lose none of all that the Father entrusted to him, but will raise all of them up at the last day (John 6:39–40, 44).

With that solid ground under our feet, we can now embrace the progressive part of our salvation: sanctification. But as we labor, struggle, fail, weep, succeed, exult, fall, and rise again in the pursuit of daily holiness, we must keep ever before us these immutable truths: "I am a regenerate, justified believer in Jesus Christ, seen in him as perfectly righteous, adopted into God's family, completely at peace with God, and in that state I will continue until I am finally vindicated on Judgment Day."

STAGE III: THE PROCESS OF SANCTIFICATION

From the moment of justifying faith until the moment of death, we are in the process of sanctification: the infinite, internal journey. Sanctification is a partnership between God and the believer, whereby the believer puts sin to death and brings forth fruit in keeping with repentance.

Sanctification is different than justification. In justification, our effort and works are unnecessary and unwelcome, repugnant to God; in sanctification, they are essential and celebrated, commanded by God. Justification is unchanging, set once for all in the heavens; sanctification is dynamic, constantly changing based in part on our faithfulness or faithlessness to God. Justification inevitably leads to sanctification; without evidence of sanctification, there should be no assurance of justification. There are no degrees of justification: we are either justified or we are not. There are infinite degrees of sanctification, based on how conformed we are to the infinitely high standard of Christ.

The central treatise on sanctification is found in Romans chapters 6 through 8. The basic idea of Romans 6 is that, since we are united with Christ, we have died to sin, and cannot live in it any longer (Romans 6:2–5). Based on that premise, we are told to consider ourselves dead to sin, but alive to God in Christ Jesus (Romans 6:11). And we are to fight to prevent our bodies from being used now as they were in the past, as instruments of sin. Instead, we are to present ourselves to God, and to present the parts of our bodies to him as instruments of righteousness (Romans 6:12–13). In the past, such a presentation of our members to sin brought about ever-increasing habits of wickedness (Romans 6:19). From now on, the same dynamic must be used to produce ever-increasing habits of righteousness (Romans 6:19, 22). New status (dead to sin, alive to God in Christ) should produce new thinking (I am dead to sin, I am alive to God), resulting in a new presentation of the body and its members in service to ever-increasing righteousness.

However, the bitterness of the struggle to walk in holiness in our mortal bodies is clearly highlighted in Romans chapter 7. Many commentators have struggled with Romans 7, wondering if Paul was speaking pre-conversion or post-conversion, or some other more eccentric option. One verse shows us that he is speaking as a converted, justified man, a man with a new status and a new nature when he says, *"as it is, it is **no longer** I myself who do it, but it is sin living in me"* (Romans 7:17). He says it again a few verses later: *"now if I do what I do not want to do, it is **no longer** I who do it, but it is sin living in me that does it"* (Romans 7:20). The words *"no longer"* imply a decisive break with sin that can only have happened in Christ. Therefore, when a Christian sins, he does it as an alien venturing into a foreign land, knowing that it is not his native home.

But through deeply ingrained habits, we still sin. And that is also the purpose of Romans 7—to show us that we will be struggling with sin the rest of our lives. The *"sin living in me"* has built up such strength of habit in the members of this *"body of death"* that we are fighting its pull at every single moment of our lives.

Romans 7:14–25 shows the bitterness of the journey of sanctification. The great Scottish preacher Alexander Whyte said, "Aye, it's a sore fight all the way."[5] Paul describes how much he yearns to do good but cannot seem to carry it out, while at the same time lamenting that the very evil that he would like to kill forever, he actually continues to do! The indwelling sin and indwelling Holy Spirit are in constant warfare against each other, and though the Spirit cannot be conquered and will be victorious in the end, yet the flesh (the old nature with its habits and practices) wins many battles every day, *"for the sinful nature desires what is contrary to the Spirit, and the Spirit what is contrary to the sinful nature. They are in conflict with each other, so that you do not do what you want"* (Galatians 5:17).

That final statement is so telling: we actually never really do what we want, for what we want is always divided between the flesh and the Spirit. We are not wholehearted in anything we choose: we neither sin wholeheartedly nor do we obey Christ wholeheartedly. This anguish caused Paul to cry out, *"What a wretched man I am! Who will rescue me from this body of death?"* (Romans 7:24). His buoyant and triumphant faith motivates his answer to his own question: *"Thanks be to God through our Lord Jesus Christ"* (Romans 7:25). God will rescue us from the body of death through Jesus Christ! But in the meantime, while we live in the mortal body, we struggle bitterly.

Romans chapter 8 speaks of the transcendent power of the indwelling Holy Spirit, and the consistent victory of the Spirit in the life of the true believer. It begins with that triumphant ring of assurance: *"there is therefore now no condemnation for those who are in Christ Jesus"* (Romans 8:1). It ends with another, even more triumphant ring of assurance: *"for I am convinced that neither death nor life, neither angels nor demons, neither the present nor the future, nor any powers, neither height nor depth, nor anything else in all creation, will be able to separate us from the love of God that is in Christ Jesus our Lord"* (Romans 8:38–39).

In between, Paul speaks of the nature of the triumphant work of the Spirit in the life of the true Christian. The Spirit's presence in our lives is the grounds for our assurance that we will not be condemned on Judgment Day. There is a clear contrast between the non-Christian life—dominated by the *"mind of the flesh,"* which cannot please God, cannot obey God, cannot live for God, and cannot love God—and the Christian life, led by the Spirit of God (Romans 8:5–8).

The central act of the Holy Spirit in sanctification is to lead the Christian into battle against sin: *"for if you live according to the flesh you will die, but if by the Spirit you put to death the deeds of the body, you will live. For all who are **led by the Spirit** of God are sons of God* (Romans 8:13–14, ESV); *if you are **led by the Spirit**, you are not under the law"* (Galatians 5:18). Romans 8:13 may be the key verse in the Bible on the Christian's responsibility and victory in the bitter ongoing struggle with sin. The blending of the Spirit's power (*"if by the Spirit"*) and the believer's responsibility (*"you put to death* *the deeds of the body*") is clear. And the stakes couldn't be higher, for the verse contrasts that daily battle with the opening statement, *"if you live according to the flesh you will die,"* then Paul says that only those who are led to put sin to death by the Spirit are truly children of God; the word *for* connecting verse 13 and verse 14 supports this strong conclusion: if you are not led by the Spirit into battle against sin, you are not a child of God.

Unlike justification, sanctification is dependent upon a Christian's constant effort, struggle, faith, and obedience, in conjunction with the power of the indwelling Holy Spirit. Thus sanctification is a mysterious collaboration between the power of God and the efforts of the believer. A vital passage on this collaboration is Philippians 2:12–13: *"continue to work out your salvation with fear and trembling, for it is God who works in you to will and to act according to his good purpose."* The human side of sanctification is intense labor, working out salvation in fear and trembling. It is a serious struggle, a fight against the world, the flesh and the devil, and as far as the believer is faithful in this struggle, he will make good progress in sanctification. Yet he does not struggle alone; rather it is God who is at work in him to will and to do according to God's good purpose. Sanctification is a collaboration, the believer and God working side by side, but with priority given to God's power, apart from which we will certainly fail.

STAGE IV: THE MOMENT(S) OF GLORIFICATION

We come now to the final stage of our great salvation: glorification. Glorification is the gracious act of our sovereign God whereby he instantaneously, perfectly, and eternally conforms justified sinners to Christ in every respect. Unlike sanctification, glorification is not a process in which our efforts and faith are required. It is an instantaneous work of God. It happens in two stages and in two distinct times: at death and at the General Resurrection. At the physical death of believers, they are immediately separated from the *"body of death,"* removed from this present evil age, and brought into the very presence of the Lord. *"We are confident, I say, and willing rather to be absent from the body, and to be present with the Lord"* (2 Corinthians 5:8, KJV). At that moment, they are made perfect: spiritually, mentally, emotionally, volitionally. All of the internal aspects of our being will be perfectly conformed to Christ, and we will be like him.

Hebrews chapter 12 speaks of a heavenly Mount Zion in which we come *"to the assembly of the firstborn who are enrolled in heaven, and to God, the judge of all, and to **the spirits of the righteous** made perfect"* (Hebrews 12:23, ESV). The phrase *"the spirits of the righteous made perfect"* is extremely revealing. They are *"spirits"* (meaning they have no bodies) and they were righteous by faith in Christ while they lived, but now *"made perfect"* in the heavenly realms. Their hearts are totally conformed to Christ. Now they simply await the resurrection of the body in order to be finally and fully saved. No one but Christ has a resurrection body, and all these departed saints await the final act of their salvation and their glorification. They wait for perfection in heaven, as Hebrews 11 makes plain: *"these were all commended for their faith, yet none of them received what had been promised. God had planned something better for us so that only together with us would they be made perfect"* (Hebrews 11:39–40).

Meanwhile, we await the same thing here on earth—the redemption of the body, which is the final act of our salvation. *"[W]e ourselves, who have the firstfruits of the Spirit, groan inwardly as we wait eagerly for our adoption as sons, the redemption of our bodies. For in this hope we were saved. But hope that is seen is no hope at all. Who hopes for what he already has? But if we hope for what we do not yet have, we wait for it patiently"* (Romans 8:23–25). These resurrection bodies will be totally conformed to Christ's, and will be glorious: *"But our citizenship is in heaven. And we eagerly await a Savior from there, the Lord Jesus Christ, who, by the power that enables him to bring everything under his control, will transform our lowly bodies so that they will be like his glorious body"* (Philippians 3:20–21); *then the righteous will shine like the sun in the kingdom of their Father"* (Matthew 13:43). The glory of the resurrection body is described in these terms by the Apostle Paul in 1 Corinthians 15:

> There are heavenly bodies and earthly bodies, but the glory of the heavenly is of one kind, and the glory of the earthly is of another. There is one glory of the sun, and another glory of the moon, and another glory of the stars; for star differs from star in glory. So is it with the resurrection of the dead. What is sown is perishable; what is raised is imperishable. It is sown in dishonor; it is raised in glory. It is sown in weakness; it is raised in power. It is sown a natural body; it is raised a spiritual body. If there is a natural body, there is also a spiritual body. (1 Corinthians 15:40–44)

Notice the incredible contrasts Paul draws between the mortal body and the resurrection body: the mortal body is perishable, in that worms and bacteria and other scavengers feed on it and destroy it in the grave; the resurrection body is imperishable, since death no longer has any power over it; the mortal body is sown (buried) in dishonor, because it is the righteous penalty for being sinners in Adam and in action; it is raised in glory, shining radiantly like the sun; the mortal body is sown in weakness, paralyzed by death and powerless to do anything; the resurrection body will be characterized by power; the mortal body is natural, the resurrection body is a "spiritual body," which we cannot fully comprehend.

This is the end of glorification and of the entire salvation process: total conformity to Christ in spirit, body, mind, emotions, will, everything. And not just for one individual, but for all the elect, those whom God chose from the foundation of the world to be his adopted children.

SUMMARY

In this chapter we have looked at the great salvation God is giving us in Christ. We have seen the need to study it carefully for the rest of our lives, to protect ourselves from drifting away from Christ. We have discussed the impossibility of knowing the full measure of our salvation, but have noted that that should only encourage us to study it the more deeply. We have seen that God intends to give us this full salvation in stages, working it out over time in our lives and even beyond death until it has been fully achieved for us and for all of God's elect. We have studied the elements of this great salvation: progressive work in us prior to conversion (drawing/calling); instantaneous work in us at conversion (regeneration, effectual calling, faith, repentance, justification, indwelling of the Holy Spirit, adoption, union with Christ, freedom from the law, rescue from Satan's dark kingdom); progressive work in us after conversion (sanctification); instantaneous work in us after death (glorification).

On this solid foundation we are now free to zero in on sanctification, so that we can know how we are to grow up in our salvation. We can do this without misunderstanding how our toilsome labors in our own salvation relates to the finished work of Christ on the cross and our perfect standing in justification righteousness in God's sight.

For this great salvation, we ought to be on our faces daily, with tears of gratitude to Almighty God for crafting such a plan, and to Christ, for shedding his precious blood to purchase it for us, and to the Holy Spirit, for so powerfully applying it to us. To God alone be the glory!

CHAPTER 3

GRAPHING CHRISTIAN PROGRESS

ON SEPTEMBER 15, 1982, A new concept in newspapers hit the stands for the first time. *USA Today* was the brainchild of Allen Neuharth, CEO of the Garnett Company, and it had a distinctive look unmatched by any other major national newspaper. One of the characteristics that defined the *USA Today* look was the use of colorful charts and graphs to capture a huge amount of information in a small space. While these visuals could tend to oversimplify complex issues, they also had the advantage of communicating concepts quickly and memorably.

There may be nothing in life as complicated as the unfolding of a Christian's sanctification day by day. The intense struggle with sin, the complexities of daily life in a modern, fast-paced world, and the staggering quantity of commands God has given us make the ups and downs of the Christian life impossible to capture perfectly. Yet despite all of this, in this chapter I desire to present an array of sanctification charts to capture the variety of experiences that the people of God have in sanctification. The purpose of this is to give a general sense of how sanctification can work, and how it does work differently in different people.

WARNINGS ABOUT THE USE
OF THESE GRAPHS

This chapter will present a different way of charting the journey of sanctification. Like a map, it uses simple symbols to describe much more complex things. Like Bunyan's allegory, it pieces together various aspects of biblical doctrine and practical experience to describe what sanctification may be like for various Christians. The various charts I present here are meant to be suggestive of aspects of the sanctification journey. Taken together, they are meant to teach aspects of success and failure in the Christian life—what to seek, and what to avoid.

The charts follow patterns much more familiar in the world of mathematicians and scientists, and therefore not everyone will readily embrace them. However, their lessons may still be plain even to those who prefer a more literary or artistic presentation. Some may never really be able to embrace such an "engineering" graph of the Christian life. To them I heartily recommend John Bunyan's *Pilgrim's Progress* as a more artistic way of charting our Christian progress.

These charts may be useful in your understanding of the path of sanctification. Or they may cause damage if misunderstood or misapplied. Therefore some warnings about them are in order.

1). WE CANNOT KNOW OUR OWN CHART PERFECTLY.

Only God knows our actual progress in him: how great it is, how quickly it proceeds. He does not choose to give us daily sanctification reports like the New York Stock Exchange or the NASDAQ. The days we may feel are our best may be viewed quite differently by God's perfect eye. Similarly, some of the days we may feel are our worst, God may have seen a humility and brokenness in our "failures" that was greatly pleasing to him. So, we cannot know perfectly how we are doing at any given time. The reason we cannot perfectly draw our own charts is because every person has blind spots and cannot look upon their own life with the perspective of God, or even with the possibly somewhat-objective perspective of an outside human observer. Strong proof of this is the statement made by the apostle Paul in his first epistle to the Corinthians. In 1 Corinthians 4 Paul writes, *"I care very little if I am judged by you or by any human court; indeed, I do not even judge myself."* Paul claims here to not judge his own standing before God. Another way of putting it for our purposes here is that he could not accurately draw out his own chart. In essence, Paul declares that neither he nor his audience can judge him properly, but God alone.

2). THE CHARTS ARE MERELY SUGGESTIVE.

The charts have details that are meant to be suggestive of progress either toward or away from Christ. The actual size and shape of the curves, their jags and troughs, are merely suggestive. By looking at these shapes, we are meant to learn aspects of backsliding, spiritual growth, repentance, etc. But the actual shape, size, and ordering of these charts cannot be relied on with mathematical accuracy, despite their apparent precision.

3). NO ONE CHART WILL PERFECTLY DESCRIBE ANY HUMAN SPIRITUAL EXPERIENCE.

The charts have titles that are meant to suggest certain patterns of sanctification that Church history and present experience have revealed. The titles are meant to be helpful, but no one chart will perfectly describe any human spiritual experience. Life goes on for so many years that we may bear aspects of each of these charts at different times. All of us will be a complex hybrid of these kinds of curves.

4). THE CHARTS ARE OVERLY SIMPLISTIC.

A number of years ago, a fad called "biorhythms" was sweeping the country. The theory was that all of human behavior could be predicted based on three sinusoidal curves of varying frequencies: the physical cycle (lasting twenty-three days), the emotional cycle (lasting twenty-eight days), and the intellectual cycle (lasting thirty-three days). Whole books of analysis were published describing what kind of day you could have if your physical and your emotional cycles were both positive and ascending, but your intellectual cycle was negative and descending, etc. As I look back on it now, it is laughable to think that all of human behavior could be so simply captured.

So it is with these charts. At any given moment, there could be twenty different themes going on in my life. My actions could be diligent, my motives pure, my outward demeanor kind and gentle, but my mind could be distracted and my heart anxious about an upcoming encounter or trial. No one line on a chart can accurately represent how much I am like Christ at that moment. So also while I am praying, or watching a ballgame on TV, or fixing a broken chair, can any one line accurately capture the totality of my heart as it compares with Christ? Of course not. Again, the charts are merely meant to be suggestive of the overall trends that are possible in the Christian life.

5). THE CHARTS ARE NOT MEANT TO GIVE COMFORT TO THE LOST OR THE HABITUALLY, WILLFULLY SINFUL.

One of the great dangers in these charts is that people living in habitual sin will somehow locate themselves in this or that chart, take comfort and false assurance from the chart, and go on living in sin. May it never be! God never intends anyone to feel comfortable about sin, and it is possible to use these charts to misdiagnose your situation.

Some time ago, the concept of the "carnal Christian" became popular among some evangelical groups. The basic idea was that someone could be saved, and yet living no differently than an unbeliever day after day. In their lives there would be no hunger and thirst for righteousness, no patterns of obedience, little or no prayer or Bible reading, spotty church attendance, coupled with a love for the world, and a worldly mindset hostile to the Christian faith. Yet, because these people had "prayed the sinner's prayer" or gone forward at a Billy Graham rally, or "asked Jesus into their hearts" at a youth camp, they were supposedly Christians. This shallow idea of conversion was coupled with the biblical concept of "once saved, always saved," and a poisonous concoction resulted. Once that concoction was downed, the person became seriously ill with spiritual self-deception. The end of that road is hell. If anything gives you complacent comfort in a sinful lifestyle, it is a devilish component of the problem.

6). THE CHARTS ARE NOT TO SCALE.

Since the goal of the Christian life is absolute perfection in Christ, no one should ever think that we ever make it fifty percent or seventy-five percent of the journey to perfection. Perhaps if the real scale were shown, no one's chart of "progress" would even be visible, compared to the standard of Christ. After all, is a man standing on the top platform of a park ranger's fire observation tower on the summit of a mountain closer to the sun than a man lying down on a cot in the valley below? Of course he is, but the part of the journey (from the valley all the way to the sun) that the man on the tower has made is such a tiny the percentage of the total journey that one can barely calculate it. This is an infinite journey we are on, and we will never have any cause to boast in our own progress, but only in the perfection that Christ alone earned and that Christ alone can give.

THE BASIC COMPONENTS OF
THE CHARTS DESCRIBED

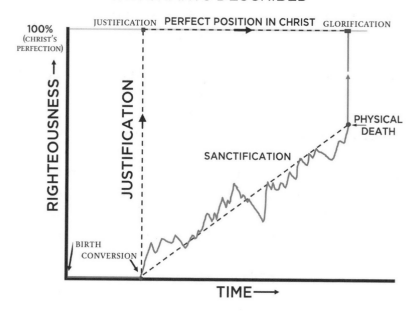

THE RIGHTEOUSNESS AXIS

The y-axis (vertical) of the chart is the "Righteousness Axis." Righteousness could be defined as conformity to God's standard, or conformity to Christ: Christlikeness. The Bible teaches us that there are two types of righteousness; imputed and practical. Imputed righteousness is Christ's perfect righteousness, imputed or credited to our account by faith at the moment of justification. Practical righteousness is our actual, daily heart obedience to God's laws. Martin Luther wrote about this distinction in a book entitled *Two Kinds of Righteousness* (1519):

> There are two kinds of righteousness. . . . The first is alien righteousness, that is the righteousness of another, instilled from without. This is the righteousness of Christ by which he justifies though faith, as it is written in I Cor. 1:30: "whom God made our wisdom, our righteousness and

sanctification and redemption." . . . This is an infinite righteousness, and one that swallows up all sins in a moment, for it is impossible that sin should exist in Christ. On the contrary, he who trusts in Christ exists in Christ; he is one with Christ, having the same righteousness as he.[6]

Luther's concept of *alien righteousness* is the same thing that I refer to as positional or imputed righteousness. It is all righteousness that comes to us from outside ourselves—from Christ to us. It is the same righteousness Paul speaks of in Phil 3:9: *"not having a righteousness of my own that comes from the law, but that which is through faith in Christ—the righteousness that comes from God and is by faith."* In every moment of our Christian life we are seen in Christ's perfect righteousness, and it is in that security that we work out our salvation. Once justified, we cannot improve our position before the Father. He could not love us more. We could not be more reconciled to him. We could not be more secure in our salvation. All these realities are the good fruits of justification.

Second, there is practical righteousness, or as Luther called it, proper righteousness. It is not righteousness that we work out alone, but with and as a result of the first righteousness given to us by Christ. Luther writes:

> The second kind of righteousness is our proper righteousness, not because we alone work it, but because we work with that first and alien righteousness. This is that manner of life spent profitably in good works, in the first place, in slaying the flesh and crucifying the desires with respect to the self, of which we read in Gal. 5:24, "And those who belong to Christ Jesus have crucified the flesh with its passions and desires."[7]

In the charts, the one hundred percent righteousness line represents Christ's perfect righteousness. At the moment of justification by faith, all the charts show a dotted line going up to the one hundred percent level and continuing to the end of life and beyond. This represents perfect righteousness, imputed to the believer by faith in Christ. The other line, the one that goes up and down and does in fact look like a Dow Jones or NASDAQ chart, represents our daily struggle with practical righteousness: with moment-by-moment obedience to the Law of God in the power of the Holy Spirit, as well as occasional lapses into sin.

THE TIME AXIS

The x-axis (horizontal) of the chart represents time as it passes through a person's life. Time represents opportunity. Time is not just a matter of the earth spinning on its axis or orbiting around the sun, but it is the unfolding of God's redemptive plan. Salvation unfolding is the purpose of time, and therefore time gives opportunity for individuals to make progress in that redemptive plan. As Christians, we should think of time as opportunity to grow in righteousness.

According to Hebrews 3:7–8, **today** is the only time available for making spiritual progress: "*So, as the Holy Spirit says: 'Today, if you hear his voice, do not harden your hearts'*" (Hebrews 3:7–8); "*therefore God again set a certain day, calling it Today, when a long time later he spoke through David, as was said before: 'Today, if you hear his voice, do not harden your hearts'*" (Hebrews 4:7).

Tiny threads of time are the warp and woof of God's redemptive tapestry: a series of todays, used well or poorly. God has ordained that the physical universe be composed of atoms, so also has God ordained that history be composed of moments. Personal and world history is an accumulation of todays, and how they were spent. At death, our window of opportunity will be closed, our time on earth finished. We can no longer store up treasure in heaven. We can no longer lead people to Christ. We can no longer suffer gladly for Christ. The time for all these things will be past. The call to every Christian is to make the most of this short segment of time, to make every day count for eternity.

FROM BIRTH TO REGENERATION

On each chart, the line representing the segment of time from a person's physical birth to their new birth, or regeneration in Christ, is flat zero. This line is flat zero to represent the fact that—outside of Christ—they have no good works at all. They have made no progress toward holiness. Though a person may display some good actions as a result of common grace, none of these works will count as righteousness on the final judgment day. Before salvation all people are in rebellion against God, and all their works are done in this rebellion. There is no such thing as weighing a lost person's good works against their bad works to see which one is greater. Before justification all the works of a lost person are done in sin and in rebellion toward God. Thus the scale is completely slanted toward the non-Christian's destruction.

This is not harsh, but biblical. Romans 14:23 states very clearly that *"everything that does not come from faith is sin."* The unbeliever has no faith, so everything they do is done in sin. Romans 3:10–11 expresses the same concept: *"there is no one righteous, not even one; there is no one who understands, no one who seeks God."* Many more Scriptures could be multiplied to support this concept, but the Bible is clear that all those who reject the salvation of God are completely wicked—dead in their transgressions and sins (Ephesians 2:1). From this state of being, salvation by works is impossible, because there are no good works to be justified by—they simply don't exist! Salvation can only come through the righteousness of Christ being given by faith.

AT REBIRTH: JUSTIFICATION BY FAITH IN CHRIST

At the moment of justification, the perfect righteousness of Christ is immediately imputed to the believer's standing before

God, and the result is perfect righteousness. This is displayed by the dotted line that ascends instantly to the one hundred percent level, Christ's perfect righteousness. At that same moment, the line of practical daily righteousness sets out on its journey toward making daily behavior match this perfect standing in Christ.

FROM JUSTIFICATION TO DEATH

This is where the human involvement in sanctification makes the charts different from one another. These differences are as varied as the number of Christians on earth, but some general trends can be described. The line itself, as already mentioned, represents practical daily righteousness. This is our daily obedience, imitation of Christ, godliness, etc. When the line is going up toward the top of the chart, we are making progress, growing in grace and in the knowledge of Jesus Christ (2 Peter 3:18). When the line is going down, we are in disobedience, sinning in some way. We desire to make the line go up as fast as possible.

The "up" designation is supportable from Scripture: "*I press on toward the goal for the prize of the **upward** call of God in Christ Jesus*" (Philippians 3:14, ESV). So also the "down" designation as well, for Christ says to the church at Ephesus: "*Yet I hold this against you: You have forsaken your first love. Remember the **height from which you have fallen**! Repent and do the things you did at first*" (Revelation 2:4–5). From these two verses (and others) we have a sense of upward progress being good, and downward regression being bad. The word "backsliding" in Jeremiah (2:19, 8:5, 14:7, etc.) implies a turning away from God, and since Godwardness is generally presented as the "*upward*" call, we have a sense of willful transgression as a backsliding down the treacherous side of a mountain.

When I was a high school student, I ran cross-country track. Occasionally, we would go for workouts to the nearby New England Sand and Gravel Company sandpit, where we would run up huge hills made of nothing but sand. It was a grueling workout, because it forced the runners to make steady, hard progress upward. As soon as you slowed down, you slid down. So it is with sanctification—at any given moment, we can either continue to pursue the *"upward call of God in Christ Jesus,"* or we can turn away from it. All *"turning away"* is represented in these charts as a downturn in the sanctification line, an upside-down "V". So also, all repentance causes a downturn to turn back up again, making progress again toward the one hundred percent line. Thus all repentance is represented by the sanctification line making a right-side-up "V."

The rates of progress or of backsliding are conjectural; some make progress at a much faster rate than others. Perhaps they have immersed themselves in the Bible, or have spent the summer on a daily street evangelism task force in the inner city. They will say later, "I never grew so much as that summer!" Their line will have made rapid progress during that time. In the same way, not all sinful lapses have an equal impact on the sanctification line. Some sins are bigger than others, and make a more lasting impact on the soul.

The general trend of the normal line is upward, since God is completing the good work he began in us. The Holy Spirit is working, the Bible is having its impact, the progress is steadily upward, though maybe not as much as we would like. If there is absolutely no growth, the person is not justified, for Romans chapters 5–8 teach that true justification is always followed by sanctification. Without *some* progress in practical holiness, we are still dead in our transgressions and sins. There is a practical holiness that results from our Spirit-led efforts that is essential to our salvation: *"make every effort to live in peace with all men and to be holy; without holiness no one will see the Lord"* (Hebrews 12:14).

AT DEATH

At death, the person's soul is separated from their physical body and is immediately with the Lord (2 Corinthians 5:8). At that moment, the soul is instantly made perfect, one hundred percent righteous in actuality, just as they were seen by God in Christ all their lives from justification to that moment. This is glorification. As we've noted, Hebrews 12:23 speaks of the inhabitants of the heavenly Zion as *"the spirits of righteous men made perfect."* Disembodied perfected spirits are presently with the Lord, and so will all dead Christians be until the great resurrection day, when the body will be as conformed to Christ's resurrection body as the soul was conformed to Christ's perfect soul. In this condition of perfect glorification, we will spend eternity.

VARIETIES OF SANCTIFICATION CURVES

1). CONSISTENT ABUNDANT FRUITFULNESS:

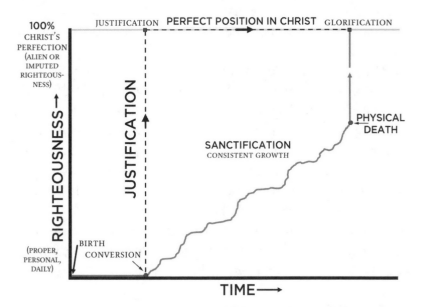

This is the chart that is most challenging for the average Christian to look at, since we really don't measure up to it!

However, there are some people whose Christian lives have, for the most part, been characterized by steady growth with very little regression. They are consistently about the Master's business, and they bring much fruit into the Kingdom. They are not tripped up by gross sins, and though they may struggle with a variety of sins, those sins are hard to see on the outside. In the Bible, people like Joseph and Daniel are examples of those who hardly ever can be seen to sin, and who bear great fruit for God through sacrificial servanthood. Even their enemies testify about their godliness. This kind of chart is a goal for us to aim at for the rest of our lives.

2). LATE BLOOMER:

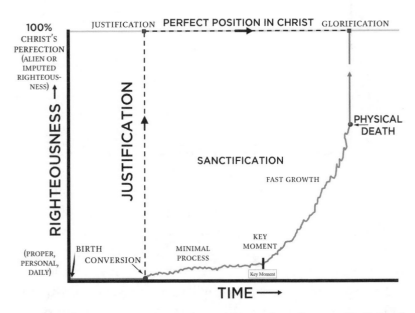

This chart represents a person who makes slow and minimal progress in their Christian life after conversion, until a key moment occurs that changes everything. Perhaps it is the death of a loved one, a serious illness, a conference, a mission trip, the reading of a great Christian book on sanctification, a new pastor coming to church, or a mature Christian taking this person under his wing and helping him to grow. It could be a combination of many of these kinds of factors and others. In any case, this key moment serves as a line of demarcation in their Christian experience. From that time on, such a person makes remarkable progress until death.

3). THE THIEF ON THE CROSS:

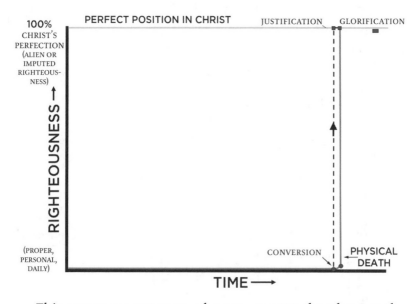

This represents someone who was converted perhaps at the very end of their life. In one way, this graph is a picture of great triumph, a trophy of the grace of God even to a persistent sinner. But in another sense, this graph is a picture of a great tragedy. The line from birth to conversion represents almost all of their earthly life, so this person will have almost no fruit to show. In John Piper's book, *Don't Waste Your Life,* he tells the story of a man who had for years stubbornly resisted family members who sought to lead him to Christ. Finally, when Piper's father, who was a traveling evangelist, came to town, the Spirit moved on this tough sinner's heart, and he at last yielded and was marvelously saved. But in the church, amid all the joyful noise of celebration came the sound of bitter lament: "I've wasted it! I've wasted it!!" It was the man himself, lamenting the waste of the majority of his life in selfishness and sin.[8] So the conversion of a man or woman near the very end of life is a great triumph of the sovereign grace of God, but also a great tragedy of the scarcity of fruit that life will have to show.

Note, however, that there is still *some* fruit in this person's life, some tiny progress made upwards in practical righteousness. The thief on the cross shows a tremendous amount of grace in the few lines he has in the Bible. In Luke 23:42 he shows amazing faith in seeing—in the dying Jesus—a Savior who will come later in a Kingdom. Also note the boldness and courage he has in confronting his sinning friend who was reviling Christ: *"But the other criminal rebuked him. 'Don't you fear God,' he said, 'since you are under the same sentence?'"* (Luke 23:40). And note the humility he has in confessing his own sinfulness to his friend: *"We are punished justly, for we are getting what our deeds deserve"* (Luke 23:41). Note the faith he has in seeing Christ's innocence: *"but this man has done nothing wrong"* (Luke 23:41). And finally, note this spiritual beggar (Matthew 5:3) asking boldly for a place in the coming Kingdom he knows he doesn't deserve: *"Jesus, remember me when you come into your kingdom"* (Luke 23:42). With nothing in his hands to commend him, he asks for a place in the eternal Kingdom, and it is granted to him. He also clearly showed faith in both Jesus' resurrection and in his own. In just a short time, with hands and feet pinned motionless by the crucifying nails, this faith-filled thief still brings forth abundant fruit at the very end of his life with his mouth. His statement stand as a river of encouragement to both sinner and evangelist alike that, while there is still breath, there is still time.

4). RESTORED FROM GREAT SIN:

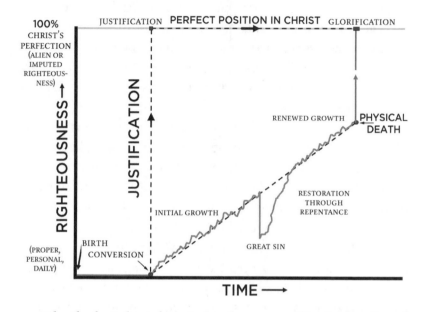

Like the last chart, here is another story of both tragedy and triumph. This is perhaps the chart of someone like King David, whose sin with Bathsheba devastated a chunk of his life, rendering him almost spiritually paralyzed. But by the grace of God, he repented, humbled himself under God's mighty hand, allowed the appropriate disciplines to wash him painfully clean, and resumed his growth in the Lord. This is also the story of Simon Peter, whose boastful self-reliance was shattered the night he denied the Lord three times, but whose status as the leader of the apostles was restored graciously by Christ (John 21). It is the story of some pastors I know who had to leave their ministries because of sexual immorality, but who were restored to fruitfulness (if not to the pastoral ministry itself) by the love of Christ and the forgiveness of spouses, family members, and church members. It is the hope of anyone who has already fallen into great sin, that there can be great mercy and great forgiveness, and great fruitfulness after the restoration. It is also the great fear of any who have not yet fallen into sin, and who seek to avoid all the pain and wasted time that it would bring.

Note that the fall is deep, and the time it takes to recover is long, not instantaneous. One friend commenting on this chart said it should show a series of smaller falls leading up to it, because these great falls usually have smaller dress rehearsals before they occur. That is true, and a worthwhile observation, but it doesn't always have to be the case.

5). FORSAKEN FIRST LOVE:

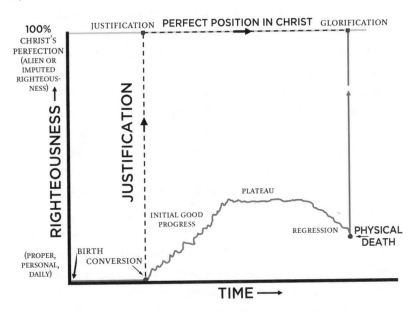

This chart shows three basic stages: initial good progress in the Lord, plateau in which things get stale, and then regression, the fruit of forsaking the first love. It is given as a warning.

Here is another tragedy in the Christian life, referred to in Revelation 2. In that chapter, the glorified Christ has written personalized letters to each of the seven churches in Asia Minor to whom John will send the book of Revelation. To the church in Ephesus, Christ has a number of good things to say: they are faithful doctrinally, have tested false teachers and exposed them, have persevered, have labored for Christ, and have not grown weary through all their toilsome labor. But Christ also says this, very painfully to this church:

> Yet I hold this against you: You have forsaken your first love. Remember the height from which you have fallen! Repent and do the things you did at first. If you do not repent, I will come to you and remove your lampstand from its place. (Revelation 2:4–5)

Though there is much conjecture on what it means that they had "forsaken their first love," most commentators think it has to do with the intensity of their affection for Christ himself. Their worship is a little cold, their hearts are not so filled with joy at his sacrifice for them. They were not doing certain things they had done at first, perhaps including times of extended worship and corporate prayer. Their love for Christ had grown dim. Even worse, this was the result of a conscious choice on their part, no accident. Jesus said, "*You have **forsaken** your first love.*" They decided, perhaps a little at a time, to love something else more than they loved Jesus.

The remedy is clear: remember, repent, and do. Remember the height from which you have fallen. (We already mentioned this concept earlier in the chapter). This refers to their high level of sanctification, of their love for Christ. Remember the way it was in the earlier days. This reminds me of God's forlorn appeal to wandering Israel:

> I remember the devotion of your youth, how as a bride you loved me and followed me through the desert, through a land not sown. Israel was holy to the Lord, the firstfruits of his harvest; all who devoured her were held guilty, and disaster overtook them, declares the Lord. Hear the word of the Lord, O house of Jacob, all you clans of the house

of Israel. This is what the Lord says: "What fault did your fathers find in me, that they strayed so far from me? They followed worthless idols and became worthless themselves." (Jeremiah 2:2–5)

How sad it is when this happens to us as Christians! And how difficult is it to face the waning of our hot affections for Christ. Many remember their college years, times spent in campus groups in all-night prayer meetings or doing bold evangelistic outreaches. What a painful question the Lord asks Israel when he says, "*What fault did your fathers find in me, that they strayed so far from me?*" The decision to stray from hot affection in the Lord is no accident. It is usually a matter of idolatry, finding greater pleasure in created things rather than the Creator. So the first remedy is: "*Remember the height from which you have fallen.*" The second remedy is: "*Repent.*" Face your sin honestly and own up to it. Turn away from it as wickedness, and bring forth fruit in keeping with repentance. This is the third remedy: "*Do the things you did at first.*" Fill your time with sweet times of love and devotion with Christ, not with worldly pursuits. Sing praise songs with joy in your heart. Spend an hour in prayer . . . then do it again. Allow Christ to up your cold heart in him.

6). MIRED IN MEDIOCRITY:

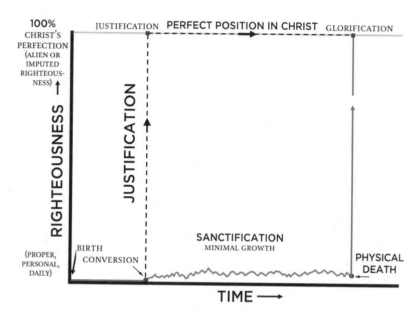

This may be the scariest chart of all, for two reasons. First, I think it describes the state of many Christians in American churches today. Second, I think people who live this kind of a Christian life should have no firm assurance of their salvation. The fruit in their lives is so minimal, they should be strongly questioning whether they have even been born again at all.

We can see from the outside, given this chart, that the person really is regenerated by the Spirit: they have Christ's perfect righteousness imputed to them, and we can see they are spiritually alive, since there is some movement in the sanctification chart. yet since we cannot know for certain what our own chart is, I think this person lives a life very little different from that of his other moral, non-church-going neighbors. The big desire here is that this person would repent, shake off the doldrums, stop settling for mediocrity in the Christian life, and "expect great things from God, attempt great things for God." Then their chart will look like the Late Bloomer chart described earlier!

7). ULTIMATE DISCIPLINE FOR SIN:

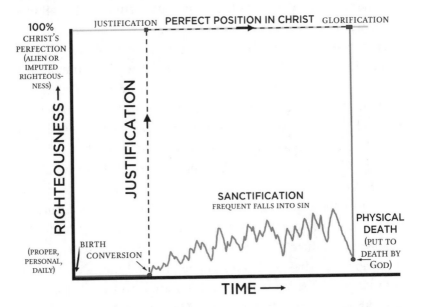

This is a chart that is probably lived out much more frequently than we may ever know about on this side of eternity. Christians die every day, but God never sends an angel down with a scroll saying, "Hear ye, hear ye! Be it known to all citizens of the Kingdom of Christ that this man has been put to death because of a long-standing pattern of secret sin. The Lord patiently waited for him to repent, but he would not. Now the Lord has graciously taken him from this life, both to spare him further sin and to spare the Church further corruption. Be warned all citizens of the Kingdom, take it to heart, and repent!" But yet, I believe that the Lord does, in fact, put some of his children to sleep (death) because of sin. So it was in Corinth, as some were eating and drinking judgment on themselves by frivolously partaking in the Lord's Supper, without reverently perceiving the Body and Blood of Christ: *"for anyone who*

eats and drinks without recognizing the body of the Lord eats and drinks judgment on himself. That is why many among you are weak and sick, and a number of you have fallen asleep" (1 Corinthians 11:29–30). This is a stern response on the part of the Lord, but he is free to do it any time he chooses, in order to keep the Church from being polluted.

A clearer example is the case of Ananias and Sapphira, who, during the era of the Church when so many were selling property and laying it at the apostles' feet so it could be distributed to anyone who had need (Acts 4:32–37), decided to test the Holy Spirit. They sold a piece of property, but kept back part of the money for themselves. They then lied to the Lord in front of the whole congregation; each separately and, in turn, each fell dead (Acts 5:7–10). The Apostle Peter clearly ascribed their deaths to the direct action of God the Holy Spirit.

This is the seriousness of sin, and it also serves as a warning to all of us. If we dabble in sin, the Lord has the right to discipline us for it immediately, without being accused of injustice. Note in the graph that the Christian has been up and down in his walk with Christ for some time before God put him to death. There were, in fact, many "dress rehearsals" of this sin, and God could have taken the sinner out immediately, if he had so willed. But even in the case of a wicked woman named Jezebel in the church in Thyatira, God says, *"I have given her time to repent of her immorality, but she is unwilling"* (Revelation 2:21). Therefore, all of us are warned to avoid sin and to be pure in our secret lives, lest this should happen to us.

SUMMARY

These eight graphs, the basic curve and the seven special cases, are merely suggestive of the variety of experiences that Christians may have in the progress of their sanctification. Honestly, our curves are immeasurably more complicated than these simple graphs depicted here. We could probably do a graph for individual areas of sanctification such as personal prayer, Bible reading, kindness to our spouses, faithfulness in evangelism, attitude during suffering, purity in battling lust, humility, etc. A composite curve is something only God could do. But the curves may well serve a useful purpose in stimulating us to growth and warning us against sin.

KNOWLEDGE

A PATHWAY TO CHRISTIAN MATURITY

KNOWLEDGE
FACTUAL AND EXPERIENTIAL
SPIRITUAL INFORMATION

FACTUAL
Gained from the Scripture

EXPERIENTIAL
Gained from living in God's world

FAITH
ASSURANCE OF AND COMMIT-
MENT TO SPIRITUAL TRUTH

- Certainty that specific invisible spiritual realities are true
- Assurance that hoped-for specific good thing promised in scripture will certainly come true
- Conviction that specific sin in me, and that God hates it and will judge people for such sins
- Reliance on Christ as all-sufficient savior, refuge, provider, shield
- Reception of spiritual guidance and knowledge

ACTION
EXTERNAL LIFESTYLE OF
HABITUAL OBEDIENCE

1. Presentation of Body to God
2. Personal Holiness
3. Seven-fold obedience to God's commands

   1. Worship
   2. Spiritual Disciplines
   3. Family
   4. Ministry to Believers
   5. Mission to Non-Believers
   6. Stewardship
   7. Work

CHARACTER
INTERNAL NATURE CON-
FORMED TO CHRIST

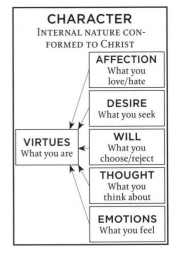

AFFECTION
What you love/hate

DESIRE
What you seek

VIRTUES
What you are

WILL
What you choose/reject

THOUGHT
What you think about

EMOTIONS
What you feel

SECTION INTRODUCTION: KNOWLEDGE

THE HUMAN BRAIN IS THE most complex and astonishing creation of God in the physical universe. King David, marveling at God's creation of his own body said, *"I praise you because I am fearfully and wonderfully made"* (Psalm 139:14). Nothing in the physical universe is more fearfully and wonderfully made than the human brain. Medical science tells us that the average human brain has one hundred billion neurons. To put that immense number in perspective, researchers estimate that the Amazonian rain forest stretches 2.7 million square miles and has one hundred billion trees. Thus, the human brain has as many neurons as there are trees in the vast, steamy jungles of the entire Amazon jungle!

The brain is the center of memory, mood, instinct, will, emotion, decision, and all bodily functions. It is the seat of individuality and personal history—we train our brains with every experience we go through in life. Our powers of interpretation and reason are centered in the brain, and here the five senses— sight, sound, touch, smell, taste—constantly deliver their packets of information for analysis.

So it is here, in the human brain, that the battle of salvation is fought. In discussing our spiritual warfare against Satan, Paul said: *"for though we live in the world, we do not wage war as the world does. The weapons we fight with are not the weapons of the world. On the contrary, they have divine power to demolish strongholds. We demolish **arguments** and every pretension that sets itself up against the **knowledge** of God, and we take captive every **thought** to make it obedient to*

Christ" (2 Corinthians 10:3–5). Note my three highlighted words: *arguments* (meaning concepts, as in a debate), *knowledge,* and *thought.* The human brain is the prize ground over which God and Satan have waged their infinitely unequal war.

KNOWING GOD VS. KNOWING ABOUT GOD

In this section, I will be arguing that factual information gained from Scripture and experiential information gained by living are both foundational to the sanctification process. But they are not the totality of our salvation. Jesus defined eternal life in this way: *"Now this is eternal life: that they may **know** you, the only true God, and Jesus Christ, whom you have sent"* (John 17:3). To live eternally means to know God and Christ. This "knowing" must be a fearsome, deep, and infinite thing, if it the very reason why Christ died. And it must go beyond merely knowing facts about God or having experiences that teach us things about God.

This "knowing" of God and of Christ was the entire focus of Paul's drive in life as well: *"I count everything as loss because of the surpassing worth of **knowing** Christ Jesus my Lord"* (Philippians 3:8). Paul clearly wants far more than just facts about Christ or experiences that teach him about Christ. But he is constantly seeking those as well, both for himself and for the disciples he is training.

In heaven, when we will see God face to face (Revelation 22:4), when we shall know as fully as we are fully known (1 Corinthians 13:12), when we will no longer need anyone to teach us anything about God, for God himself will finish his New Covenant decree (Hebrews 8:11), when all of that is consummated and we are perfectly one with the Father and the Son (John 17:23), then our "knowing" of God will be infinitely more than all we can ask or imagine in this life. Will we then know facts and have experiences with God? Yes, of course, for relationship between persons is impossible without facts and shared experiences. So "knowing

God" is intimately connected with, but goes infinitely beyond, factual and experiential knowledge.

However, because knowing about God factually and experientially is essential to the "knowing" that Christ prayed for in John 17:3, it is infinitely worthwhile to pursue it here on earth. Just because eternal life is more than knowing facts from the Bible and from experience, this doesn't mean we shouldn't pursue—with every fiber of our being!—knowledge of God and experiences with God. I believe that without pursuing that kind of lower knowledge, we'll never attain the final knowledge in heaven, because it is of the essence of the salvation God is working in us to press after all the knowledge there is of God and of Christ.

TWO BASIC PATTERNS OF DISCIPLESHIP: FACTUAL AND EXPERIENTIAL

During his controversy with the Pharisees, who were trying to trap him over paying taxes to the Romans, Jesus used the fact that Caesar's portrait was imprinted on the coin to solve the problem: *"Give to Caesar what is Caesar's, and to God what is God's"* (Matthew 22:21). But how were Caesar's portrait and inscription imprinted on that coin? In the ancient world, coins were manufactured by a punch and die set. There were two dies, one for the head (obverse) side of the coin, one for the tail (reverse) side. The dies were inscribed with the negative of any image the coin maker wanted imprinted on the coin, and were made of extremely hard metal. The coin started as a blank disc of softer metal, and was put on the anvil on top of the obverse die. The reverse die was embedded in a hammer that struck the blank disc. At the same time that the reverse die smashed into the blank on the top side of the coin, the obverse did the same on the bottom. The softer metal of the blank coin "smooshed" into the markings on the dies, and the coin was thus struck with its characteristic image. This is how Caesar's portrait and inscription were imprinted on the denarius Jesus held up to make his point.

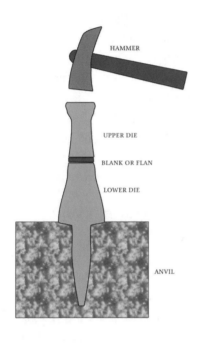

Now obviously one of the keys to coin manufacture was repeatability—every coin had to look the same when it was finished. To attain this goal, the die metal had to be much harder than the blank coin, so the coin's metal conformed to the die rather than the other way around. Every single coin had the exact same image of Caesar on it. This is a picture of sanctification, for God the Father wants to conform all of us to his Son: *"for those God foreknew he also predestined to be **conformed to the likeness** of his Son, that he might be the firstborn among many brothers"* (Romans 8:29).

Amazingly, God has designed a two-fold "die system" to conform us to Christ. The Greek word for the die struck on the blank coin was *tupos,* and it is used in two key places in the New Testament, in both places translated by the word "pattern":

> Sound doctrine: *What you heard from me, keep as the **pattern** of sound teaching, with faith and love in Christ Jesus* (2 Timothy 1:13).

> Godly lifestyle: *Join with others in following my example, brothers, and take note of those who live according to the **pattern** we gave you* (Philippians 3:17).

By means of these two "dies," God intends to make every one of us conform to Christ. The pattern of sound teaching conforms us in our thinking, and the pattern of sound living conforms us in our actions. We are not to be innovators, inventing a new kind of disciple every generation. Each disciple of Jesus Christ is to follow with absolute conformity the pattern of sound doctrine handed down from the apostles. So also each disciple of Christ is to live a holy lifestyle in a certain pattern as well, including certain features as separation from the world, spiritual disciplines (Bible study and prayer), godly relationships, pure speech, faithful stewardship, etc.

Now these two patterns also conform to the two types of knowledge we are presenting here. The pattern of sound teaching comes to us in words, in spiritual facts which are taught in the Bible. The pattern of sound living comes to us in the Scripture as well, but it also comes by imitating godly role models. Discipleship is carried on in the church by godly disciplemakers, mature Christians, who teach right doctrine and exemplify right living.

By these two powerful patterns of knowledge—factual and experiential—God intends to shape us in Christ's image. Thus knowledge is the beginning of sanctification. Let's find out how.

CHAPTER 4

FACTUAL KNOWLEDGE

"ROME WASN'T BUILT IN A day." This old proverb makes a simple but profound point: anything worth building is going to take time and patience in order to build it properly. It flies in the face of our age of instant gratification, where our technology has conditioned us to expect to receive whatever we're seeking immediately. We can program speed dial numbers on our cell phones to cut down the time of dialing the phone number. By our smartphones and websites, we can know immediately if a tsunami has hit Indonesia or an economic summit has convened in Europe. We can even turn a rebellious teen into a cheerfully compliant one in less than five minutes, if the recent radio ad of a secular child psychologist is true! We have been trained toward impatience by our lightning-quick information age.

But Rome wasn't built in a day. The small village on the Tiber took three centuries to gain ascendancy over the Etruscans and the other tribes in the central Italian peninsula. Then, methodically, Rome's glory grew and grew. A river of building materials flowed in and massive building projects began to reach for the sky; for example, the system of eleven aqueducts that supplied the city's million inhabitants with fresh mountain water year-round took almost five hundred years to complete. Each succeeding emperor had a vision not only for the advance of the empire's boundaries, but also for the glory of the city of Rome itself.

In like manner (but for infinitely more glorious and eternal purposes), God desires to build a City of Truth in the heart of all his children. This City of Truth will also be erected brick by brick; that is, line by line of Scripture, precept by precept, truth by truth, over years of time spent in his Word and his world. Theological truths, in all their depth and breadth, take years to be established and rise to completed form in the human heart, resulting in an increasingly mature worldview by which the Christian understands everything that happens to him in this world, and by which he lives his life.

THE BUILDING MATERIALS: BIBLICAL FACTS

- In the beginning, God created the heavens and the earth (Genesis 1:1).
- Abraham believed the Lord, and the Lord credited to him as righteousness (Genesis 15:6).
- The sons of Issachar were Tola, Puah, Jashub and Shimron—four in all (1 Chronicles 7:1).
- Christ died for our sins according to the Scriptures, . . . he was buried, . . . he was raised on the third day according to the Scriptures (1 Corinthians 15:3–4).
- Those who accepted Peter's message were baptized, and about three thousand were added to their number that day (Acts 2:41).
- We must all appear before the judgment seat of Christ, that each one may receive what is due him for the things done while in the body, whether good or bad (2 Corinthians 5:10).
- Christ is coming with the clouds, and every eye will see him, even those who pierced him, and all tribes of the earth will wail on account of him (Revelation 1:7).

Above are seven texts from the Bible. Each one is a nugget of gold ore extracted from the inexhaustible mine of spiritual information, and each one makes its own contribution to the growing City of Truth inside the minds of believers. From these verses, for example, we can know that God made the universe, how Abraham was justified by faith, who the sons of Issachar were, what are the basic facts of the gospel message of Christ, how the Church grew on the day of Pentecost, what Judgment Day will hold for each one of us, and some aspects of the future coming of Christ. That is not all these verses teach, but these facts flow from a simple reading and pondering of the texts of Scripture listed above. And these facts are not all equally vital to the Christian life, but they are all equally true, and they have all been deemed useful by the God who inspired the Bible.

Altogether, the Bible contains over 31,000 verses, and over 775,000 words in an average English translation. That is an incalculable treasure trove of spiritual truth, given us by the goodness of our loving God. And although not every spiritual fact is equally significant, yet *"all Scripture is God-breathed and useful"* (2 Timothy 3:16). We may not perceive how knowing the names of Issachar's four sons could possibly make a difference in our lives, but yet we know God speaks no worthless words. From such facts as these, a limitless abundance of material is mined for the City of Truth.

God calls us on a lifetime journey of discovery in the vast world of the biblical text. There are sixty-six books to be learned, hundreds of people and place names, overlapping chronologies, unfolding history, deepening themes. Some passages tell us what to do quite directly: *"Do everything without complaining or arguing"* (Philippians 2:14). Others, like Isaiah's oracles against the nations in Isaiah 13–23, seem far removed from our daily lives. We are not permitted to discard any passage as irrelevant (2 Timothy 3:16); all passages are given to lead us to maturity. Fact after fact, truth after truth, all are given by an infinitely wise God.

FACTS COMBINING AND RECOMBINING

Factual knowledge gained from the Bible is indispensable to our Christian life and growth: facts about God, Christ, creation, humanity, and all other topics are the raw materials from which our minds craft the fired bricks, dressed stone, and carved timbers from which God's City of Truth is built. But raw biblical data must be arranged in connection with other scriptural truths to accomplish spiritual maturity.

God has ordained that the whole physical universe should be constructed from tiny things called atoms. The 118 elements (types of atoms) of the periodic table comprise all the basic building blocks of every single physical thing in creation. These same 118 elements combine in countless configurations to make all the myriad molecules that comprise our bodily organs, and all physical matter. The study of how these atoms combine and recombine is called chemistry. The study of how Bible facts combine and recombine is called theology.

Every modern metropolis has vast interconnections and interdependent systems. Every city needs power, water, drainage, transportation, communication, and other systems. These systems must interconnect well for the city to be functional and prosperous. In the same manner, the City of Truth is established on a vast array of interconnecting biblical themes, the depth of which is unfathomable—far more unfathomable than the Pacific Ocean, and even than the entire universe itself.)These interconnections have traditionally been traced out in human works known as systematic theology (the study of the Bible's doctrines topically), biblical theology (the study of the Bible's unfolding truth across the eras of biblical history), and historic theology (the study of the Bible's doctrines across the eras of Church history). Though not every Christian will study theology formally, yet the system of truth arising in the heart must be biblical. This growing theology is the truth system from which we live every day.

Perhaps the most significant example of these interconnections is the doctrine of the Trinity. This doctrine is not taught in any one text of Scripture, and the word "Trinity" never appears in the Bible. Rather, it arises from a combination of three different doctrines, each rooted in their own series of what are called "proof texts": 1) that there is one God and only one God; 2) that this one God has eternally existed in three persons, each of them distinct from each other; 3) that these three persons (Father, Son, Holy Spirit) are equally God. Each of these ideas is rooted in Scripture, arising from the pages of the Bible by the rules of human language and a right use of reason. Therefore, it is right to call the doctrine of the Trinity "the word of God."

From these interconnections the City of Truth rises brick by brick, building by building, avenue by avenue, statue by statue, aqueduct by aqueduct, within the heart of a believer. From these things also a whole life is transformed, gradually, over years, by the Word of God.

A RIVER ROCK VS. A FOREST ROCK

In the woods of New Hampshire, near the beautiful Kancamagus River, I once had a picnic with some friends. We were talking about the transforming power of the word of God on the mind. I dug out a small rock from the forest floor and took it to the river, where I fished out another rock of similar size. I asked them to look at the two rocks and compare them. Someone said, "One of the rocks is covered with dirt, but the other one is clean." So I crouched down and swished the dirty rock in the river for ten seconds or so. It came out wet and clean of all dirt. Again, I asked them to compare the two rocks. They took them and looked at them carefully. Another of the guys said, "The river rock is smooth and shiny, but the forest rock has all kinds of sharp edges." New Hampshire is the Granite State, and this rock had crystalline peaks all over, hard as granite. I asked, "How do we transform the forest rock into a river rock?" The answer was simple: put it in the river. But for how long? Well, perhaps a century or so! A hundred years of river water gently flowing over the surface of the forest rock, carrying small granules of sand as a mild abrasive, would transform that jagged rock, and make it as smooth and shiny as the other. The patient activity of the Kancamagus River would do the work.

So it is with the transformation of a Christian from immaturity to maturity. Some dirt particles (sin habits) get washed off immediately after conversion, but the rest of the change is more difficult. Transformation only comes by immersing the mind in the word of God, allowing it to wash over our thoughts, until gradually we have learned to think as Christ does. And this is precisely what Paul is commanding us to do in Romans 12:1-2.

BE TRANSFORMED BY THE RENEWING OF YOUR MIND: ROMANS 12:1-2

After writing eleven magnificent chapters of deep theology unfolding the gospel of Jesus Christ, Paul spends the last five chapters applying that doctrine to the transformation of Christians. He begins with these key verses:

> Therefore, I urge you, brothers, in view of God's mercy, to offer your bodies as living sacrifices, holy and pleasing to God—this is your spiritual act of worship. Do not conform any longer to the pattern of this world, but be transformed by the renewing of your mind. Then you will be able to test and approve what God's will is—his good, pleasing and perfect will. (Romans 12:1-2)

The first and most important act of worship a Christian can do is present his body to God as a living sacrifice. Having established the pattern of right worship, he turns to the only way by which all Christians will actually present their bodies in constant worship: mental transformation. Life in this world is dynamic, and we are not going to stay the same, no matter what. We are either going to be increasingly transformed into Christlikeness, or we are going to be increasingly conformed to the world's corrupted image.

But how does that happen? Romans 12:2 tells us very plainly: we are to be *"transformed by the renewing of our minds."* What is the renewing of our minds? The concept here is *"making things new,"* and the same root word is used of all the **new** things that God works to bring about full salvation: Jesus pours *"new wine into new wine skins"* (Matthew 9:17), Jesus' blood is the blood of a *"new covenant"* (Luke 22:20), Jesus gives us a *"new commandment, to love one another,"* we ourselves are a *"new creation"* (2 Corinthians 5:17, Galatians 6:15), there will be a *"new heavens and new earth,"* (2 Peter 3:13), for Jesus is *"making everything new."* (Revelation 21:5). In the same manner, we are to train our brains to think in new ways, patterned after Christ and after all the new things he is doing and will do in our salvation.

How is our mind to be thus renewed? It is only by consistent immersion in the word of God. It is the unique role of the written word of God, as illuminated and applied by the indwelling Spirit, to change the way we think, and therefore the way we live. As we've already noted, the human mind is the battleground between the Spirit and Satan, and between the Spirit and the flesh. It is this very thing—the sinful human mind—that God has judged, says Romans 1:28: *"furthermore, since they did not think it worthwhile to retain the knowledge of God, he gave them over to a depraved mind, to do what ought not to be done."* People rejected the knowledge of God as worthless, so God gave their minds over to depravity. The outworking of this depraved mind is seen plainly in what follows in Romans chapter 1: *"They have become filled with every kind of wickedness, evil, greed and depravity. They are full of envy, murder, strife, deceit and malice. They are gossips, slanderers, God-haters, insolent, arrogant and boastful; they invent ways of doing evil; they disobey their parents; they are senseless, faithless, heartless, ruthless"* (Romans 1:29–31). A depraved mind leads to a depraved life. A transformed mind leads to a transformed life.

The old pattern of evil thinking leading to evil living is plain. *"So I tell you this, and insist on it in the Lord, that you must no longer **live** as the Gentiles do, in the futility of their **thinking**"* (Ephesians 4:17). But at conversion, everything changes. We are "new creations" in Christ (2 Corinthians 5:17), and have been given the "mind of Christ" (1 Corinthians 2:16). Also, God has spoken into our hearts a new kind of knowledge: *"for God, who said, 'Let light shine out of darkness,' made his light shine in our hearts to give us the light of the knowledge of the glory of God in the face of Christ"* (2 Corinthians 4:6). At the moment of regeneration, God hides in our inner beings a treasure of incalculable value: the *"light of the knowledge of the glory of God in the face of Christ."* It is amazing to note what Paul says next about the location of this treasure. *"But we have this treasure in jars of clay to show that this all-surpassing power is from God and not from us"* (2 Corinthians 4:7). It is in *"jars of clay"* that God chose to store this infinite treasure. And more specifically, we know that this knowledge is not kept in the leg, or in the wrist, or in the pancreas, or the liver, and not even in the "heart," properly speaking. It is kept in the brain. Thus, the brain is a "jar of clay," part of the mortal body which must be transformed to serve Christ fully.

CHRIST OPENED THEIR MINDS TO UNDERSTAND THE SCRIPTURES

The brain of the Christian, then, must be transformed by a constant renewing process, and then the whole body and life will follow. Thanks be to God, Christ has power directly over the human brain to make it new. He does this, in particular, by opening it to the word of God. After rising from the dead, Jesus appeared to his disciples to "offer many convincing proofs" that he was alive (Acts 1:3). The central, lasting evidence he gave them was to show them that his death and resurrection had been written in the Scriptures centuries before any of it happened: *He said to them, "This is what I told you while I was still with you: Everything must be fulfilled that is written about me in the Law of Moses, the Prophets and the Psalms."* (Luke 24:44). But this clear teaching will only fall on blind eyes and deaf ears if God doesn't undo the work of Satan, who *"has blinded the minds of unbelievers, so that they cannot see the light of the gospel of the glory of Christ, who is the image of God"* (2 Corinthians 4:4). So Jesus at that moment did a miracle—he worked directly in their brains so they could understand the Scriptures he was teaching them. *"Then he opened their minds so they could understand the Scriptures"* (Luke 24:45).

This is the great engine of sanctification, the driving force behind the transformation of your entire life to the glory of God. Here you will find all the power you need to be holy and to be eternally fruitful to the glory of God. This is the power behind it all: *"he opened their minds so they could understand the Scriptures."* Without this, we are blind, and we will fall into the ditch. But with this direct work of Christ on our minds by the power of the Spirit, we will be transformed from glory into glory, until we are fully conformed to the image of Christ.

SCRIPTURE THE ALPHA AND OMEGA OF FAITH IN CHRIST

It is the Scripture which God has given to enable us to know Christ, and through him to know the salvation he alone can give us. Scripture holds the preeminent place in the salvation plan of God. Apart from Scripture, we know literally nothing about Jesus Christ, and apart from Christ we are lost. According to Romans 1:19–20, God ordained to give some "pre-evangelism" in the beauty of creation. Thus from a magnificent sunset, or a spectacular snow-capped mountain peak, or an elegantly soaring eagle, or a breeching whale, we can discern the hand of a wise and loving Creator.

But Christ cannot be so discerned. That God has linked Christ and the Scripture together intimately can be seen from the way John calls him the "Word" (John 1:1, 14). This title is underscored by the astonishing frequency with which Jesus quoted Scripture, and with which Old Testament Scriptures were fulfilled in Jesus.

However, strong evidence of the link between Scripture and our faith in Christ is found in the magnificent account of Christ's resurrection in John chapter 20. John begins the chapter by describing the experience he and Peter had at the empty tomb that fateful morning:

> Then Simon Peter, who was behind him, arrived and went into the tomb. He saw the strips of linen lying there, as well as the burial cloth that had been around Jesus' head. The cloth was folded up by itself, separate from the linen. Finally the other disciple, who had reached the tomb first, also went inside. He saw and believed. (They still did not understand from Scripture that Jesus had to rise from the dead.) (John 20:6–9)

John's statement about Scripture in verse 9 explains his statement in verse 8: "*He saw and believed.*" It seems as though John is almost apologizing for his need for physical evidence of Jesus' resurrection. He knew that the true ground and sustaining power of faith in the resurrection for every believer is Scripture alone, not physical experience.

Later in that same chapter, Jesus will gently rebuke doubting Thomas' lack of faith apart from sensory input. Thomas had said, "*Unless I see the nail marks in his hands and put my finger where the nails were, and put my hand into his side, I will not believe it*" (John 20:25). Because he was an apostle and therefore was to serve as an eyewitness of the resurrection, Jesus granted his request, giving him sensory evidence of his resurrection. "*Then he said to Thomas, 'Put your finger here; see my hands. Reach out your hand and put it into my side. Stop doubting and believe'*" (John 20:27). Thomas responded with the clearest affirmation of faith in the Bible: "*My Lord and my God!*" (John 20:28). Then Jesus spoke his word of correction to

Thomas (and of eternal blessing on believers to the ends of the earth and the end of time): *"Because you have seen me, you have believed; blessed are those who have not seen and yet have believed"* (John 20:29). Throughout all the intervening twenty centuries of human history, every single person who has come to believe that Jesus is Lord and God, and that he died for their sins and rose again bodily from the dead, stands under this eternal word of blessing, spoken by the very mouth of Christ.

But here we find the reason for John's explanatory statement about his own faith in John 20:8: he *"saw and believed."* He saw the physical evidence of Jesus' resurrection—the stone removed from the entrance, the grave-clothes lying set in their position, the head covering folded up by itself. The physical evidence screamed, "Resurrection!" But John knew full well that believers' faith in Christ needs to rest on something else: the Scriptures. Hence he adds, *"they still did not understand from Scripture that Jesus had to rise from the dead"* (John 20:9).

The physical evidence was vital for the eyewitnesses to note and later to commit to writing in Scripture. But no other generation would have their same access to that empty tomb. None of us gets to tour the empty gravesite and touch the linens. Even John, in later years, if his faith may have wavered and flickered through Satan's onslaughts, could not have revived and strengthened his faith by a physical tour of the tomb. Scripture alone is the hot coal bed, and the Spirit alone the bellows breath that can take the lukewarm iron of our faith and reheat it red-hot again.

God has ordained that we will come to know Christ, believe in him, and grow up to maturity in him in one way alone, by the testimony of Scripture. Thus Scripture's testimony to the person and work of Christ is indispensable to our faith. It is for this very reason that Paul links hearing the word of God to faith in Christ: *"so faith comes from hearing, and hearing through the word of Christ"* (Romans 10:17). Faith finds its genesis in the hearing of the word of God. But faith in Christ also finds its ongoing existence, nurture, strength, growth, and health in the same *word of Christ.* The Scripture is both the Alpha and the Omega of faith in Christ, and every letter in between. No believer can maintain a healthy and growing faith in Christ without constant nourishment in the word of God.

THE VINE AND THE BRANCHES: "REMAIN IN MY WORD"

A similar point emerges from the teaching Jesus gave his disciples the night before he was crucified: they would continue to live spiritually only if they continued to live in him and in his words.

> I am the vine; you are the branches. If a man remains in me and I in him, he will bear much fruit; apart from me you can do nothing. If anyone does not remain in me, he is like a branch that is thrown away and withers; such branches are picked up, thrown into the fire and burned. If you remain in me and my words remain in you, ask whatever you wish, and it will be given you. This is to my Father's glory, that you bear much fruit, showing yourselves to be my disciples. (John 15:5–8)

This poignant image is essential for understanding both sanctification and the role of Scripture's testimony to Christ for spiritual life, health, and growth. Simply put, Jesus is saying "Live constantly in me, and do it by allowing my words to live in your mind and by obeying what they command. If you do this, you will bear eternal fruit, proving that you are really one of my disciples."

Every branch of the vine is attached to the vine and nourished by it through microscopic tubules. These tubules carry life-sustaining sap—nutrients and water—which are essential to the ongoing life, health, growth, and fruitfulness of the branch. If that connection is severed, the branch will die. In no believer can that connection ever be completely severed; God's sovereign power will not allow it to happen. But it is essential for each disciple to understand their need for "remain" in the vine, to stay in close connection with Christ. And Christ ministers his life, love, and presence by means of his words (v. 7), the Scripture.

THE NEED FOR CONSTANT REMINDING

In 1920, a fourteen-year-old farm boy was plowing a field in Utah. As he moved up and down across the acres, plowing in one straight line after another, he began to think about his hobby, electronics, and in the mind of this boy-genius sprang an idea that has affected America deeply. The boy's name was Philo Farnsworth, and within seven years, he had invented the basics of modern television. Amazingly, the television Farnsworth invented was based on the principle of endless repetition; the standard television screen was a glass tube coated with phosphorescent material that glowed when struck with a stream of electrons; as soon as the stream of electrons moved on, the phosphor in one spot began to fade. It had to be refreshed constantly. The television painted the screen with a stream of electrons thirty times per second in the pattern of the plowing of a field, line upon line, endlessly refreshing the phosphor so it wouldn't fade.

This principle of repetition to restore what has faded is somewhat how our memories work, and somewhat how our character is formed. Because of the fall into sin, our brains have significant weaknesses. For the issue of sanctification, none is more damaging than our tendency to forget the good things we've learned. Constant repetition is necessary to keep past scriptural truth always in the forefront of our minds. It is not the case that every time we read the Bible or hear a good sermon we learn something entirely new, nor is that necessary. Sometimes, all that's required is to be reminded of past insights. Paul said that constant reminders acted as a "safeguard" for Christians (Philippians 3:1), and Peter made reminding his disciples of past truths in which they were well-established a centerpiece of his ministry (2 Peter 1:12–13). This is especially true in the issue of the fundamental, central facts of the gospel itself, which we will never outgrow.

WISE FOR SALVATION THROUGH FAITH IN CHRIST JESUS

For this reason Paul exhorts Timothy to continue immersing himself in Scripture, though he was already a solid Christian with a pastoral ministry, who was consistently teaching and preaching to a flock: *"But as for you, **continue in what you have learned** and have become convinced of, because you know those from whom you learned it, and how from infancy you have known the holy Scriptures, which are able to make you wise for salvation through faith in Christ Jesus"* (2 Timothy 3:14–15).

The salvation journey is a process that is not completed in this life. Therefore, as long as we live in this world, we must continue to saturate our minds in Scripture. Paul says the Scriptures are *"able to make you wise for salvation through faith in Christ Jesus"* (v. 15). As we have seen, salvation is a process that continues through various stages until it is complete in glory. Sanctification was the stage Timothy was in at the moment Paul wrote to him. He wasn't done with salvation, therefore he wasn't done with Scripture. For this reason Paul urges him to *"continue in what you have learned."* In other words, keep feeding on the very Scriptures that initially brought you to faith in Christ. The Scriptures alone possess the power to make us *"wise for salvation through faith in Christ Jesus."* Wisdom is a disposition of the heart fed by knowledge through faith. The truths of Scripture are the food of faith, and faith produces wisdom for ongoing salvation.

THE MINISTRY OF THE WORD
PRODUCES MATURITY

What Paul counsels for Timothy he opens up to the whole church in Ephesians chapter 4, concerning the ultimate purpose of the ministry of the word of God. There Paul is talking about spiritual gifts, and the different roles that various people play in the Church. Though the Church is completely united, yet different gifts and roles have been given to each of us (Ephesians 4:7). Paul highlights here the spiritually gifted men who present the word of God to the people: apostles, prophets, evangelists, pastors, and teachers. And what is the ultimate goal of this ministry? Paul makes it very plain: *"to prepare God's people for works of service, so that the body of Christ may be built up until we all reach unity in the faith and in the knowledge of the Son of God and become mature, attaining to the whole measure of the fullness of Christ"* (Ephesians 4:12–13). In other words, the ministry of the word of God primes the pump for all the other ministries in the Church, and all of them working together produce the spiritual maturity that is the goal of sanctification.

Paul's description of that maturity focuses primarily on doctrinal knowledge resulting in maturity in the face of false teaching: *"Then we will no longer be infants, tossed back and forth by the waves, and blown here and there by every wind of teaching and by the cunning and craftiness of men in their deceitful scheming. Instead, speaking the truth in love, we will in all things grow up into him who is the Head, that is, Christ"* (Ephesians 4:14–15). Immature people are easily swayed by false teaching, but mature people instead "speak the truth (i.e. right doctrine) in love (i.e. right character)", and by doing this more and more, we make progress in the internal journey to Christlikeness.

Thus the most vital need for a church is godly evangelists, pastors, and teachers, who minister the word of God to bring people from spiritual darkness to ever-increasing light, ever-increasing knowledge of Christ. The faithful ministry of the word of God is essential to the ongoing growth of the church to spiritual maturity. Pastors should heed this well, and faithfully preach the whole Bible to their people.

PAUL'S PRAYERS FOR THE MATURITY OF THE CHURCHES

Paul's remarkably rich prayers for the sanctification of growing Christians are more evidence for the central role of knowledge in the Christian life. For example, as Paul brings the precious believers in Ephesus before the throne of grace, his eye is on the infinite journey still ahead of them. He desires that their salvation would be finally completed, that they may be *"holy and blameless in [God's] sight"* (Ephesians 1:4), living in the very presence of God in heaven. To this end, he prays for their knowledge so they will make bold progress in sanctification, rather than being defeated by Satan's deceptions.

> I keep asking that the God of our Lord Jesus Christ, the glorious Father, may give you the Spirit of wisdom and revelation, so that you may **know** him better. I pray also that the eyes of your heart may be enlightened in order that you may **know** the hope to which he has called you, the riches of his glorious inheritance in the saints, and his incomparably great power for us who believe. (Ephesians 1:15–19)

So what does Paul pray for? In a word, he prays for **knowledge**. Paul makes one basic request on their behalf, and then adds three related requests to it. He prays that God would, by his Spirit, reveal himself to the Ephesians so that they would **know** him better. He desires that knowing God would fill their existence with all of his richness, so that they would yearn to be like him, love him, and serve him. **Knowledge** of God is the foundation to all of that. But Paul goes beyond this to add three related topics to their spiritual education. Paul prays that the *"eyes of their hearts would be* *enlightened,"* an amazing phrase referring to the effects of the Holy Spirit of God, the *"Spirit of wisdom and revelation,"* moving within our hearts giving us an internal vision of spiritual realities. Paul is praying for the eyesight of the soul to be sharpened through knowledge: *"in order that you may* **know** . . . *"* (v. 18). Knowledge of what? Three things in particular: 1) the hope to which God has called them; 2) the riches of their glorious inheritance in the saints; 3) God's incomparably great power at work in them and around them. Paul wants them to be supernaturally expectant of an infinitely glorious future in heaven—a future of seeing God himself in glorified resurrection bodies in a perfect world (the "hope of their calling," Romans 8:18–24). He wants them to have a sense of the richness of their inheritance, which they will enjoy with all the saints. And he wants them to be overwhelmed with a sense of the infinite power of God at work to be sure they **will** inherit all these things. So in all of this, Paul is praying for their spiritual **knowledge**.

Several other examples of Paul's prayer life show this same focus on knowledge:

- Ephesians 3:14–19: praying for the saints to grasp (comprehend) the infinite dimensions of God's love for them in Christ;
- Philippians 1:9–11: praying for their love to grow in knowledge and depth of insight, resulting discernment, purity, and righteousness;
- Colossians 1:9–12: praying for God to fill them with the knowledge of his will through wisdom and understanding, resulting in a life pleasing to him in every way.

Paul's rich prayers in his epistles give us a sense of the importance he placed on spiritual knowledge in the sanctification of the beloved churches he was helping to grow. His example should also affect our prayer lives as well: we should be praying these things for ourselves, our churches, our loved ones, and missionary works around the world. It should also empower the right esteem of a healthy teaching ministry in the church, for Paul inevitably coupled his descriptions of his prayer life with more teaching content as well. Paul's prayer life, coupled with his amazing teaching ministry, is clear evidence of the importance of spiritual knowledge in sanctification.

"HEAD KNOWLEDGE" VS. "HEART KNOWLEDGE"

"I grew up in a Christian home," said the young lady who was sharing her testimony at an evening church service, "and I learned a lot about the Bible. But it was all head knowledge, not heart knowledge. It wasn't until all that head knowledge moved down to my heart that my life began to change." I watched as she pointed from her head to the center of her chest, to represent the movement of this knowledge, almost like the journey food travels through the esophagus to the stomach. As I listened to that, I realized how many times I'd heard that distinction: head knowledge vs. heart knowledge. In many cases, it seemed like head knowledge was the enemy and heart knowledge the friend of true spiritual life. The longer that distinction was pressed in that manner, head knowledge seemed to be denigrated, almost an obstacle to truly walking with Christ.

Now there is a valid issue people are seeking to address here. It is possible to know something of the Bible and still remain unconverted or disobedient. As a matter of fact, there are many Bible scholars who diligently study the Bible (as did the Pharisees of Jesus' day), but who refuse to come to Christ that they might have life (cf. John 5:39–40). I have heard some highly intelligent scholars at secular institutions who teach courses on comparative world religions and "the Bible as literature," who know facts about the Bible that many Christians do not know. But they remain "dead in their transgressions and sins" (Ephesians 2:1).

Many passages warn against knowing spiritual facts but refusing to believe, love, and obey the truth. The demons of James 2:19 know that there is one God, and they shudder; the apostates of Hebrews 10:26–31 and 2 Peter 2:20–22 have heard the full gospel, lived it for a while and rejected it, and are worse off for having known the truth; and Christians whose obedience to the Master lags behind their knowledge of his will are warned that the more they know, the more they will be punished if they disobey (Luke 12:47–48). All of these passages, and many more like them, warn Christians against knowing but not believing, loving, or obeying the truth: head-knowledge that is not heart-knowledge.

Even Paul, who spent most of his ministry teaching and preaching rich spiritual facts to build up the knowledge of the churches, said, *"Knowledge puffs up, but love builds up. The man who thinks he knows something does not yet know as he ought to know"* (1 Corinthians 8:1–2). The issue there, however, was not that head-knowledge is a bad thing and heart-knowledge a good thing. Rather it was that more mature Corinthian Christians, who knew that food sacrificed to idols was just food, were flaunting that knowledge and harming their fellow Christians. They also were arrogantly assuming that they had nothing more to learn. But any idea that Paul is denigrating head-knowledge would be foolish and harmful.

All in all, "head knowledge" vs. "heart knowledge" is a somewhat artificial distinction, and the disparaging of head knowledge can be damaging to our ongoing growth. We *must* keep growing in knowledge or we will cease making progress in the Christian life. All of that knowledge begins as head knowledge, concepts understood by the mind, before anything else can occur. And we must have as much of that head knowledge as possible. But woe to us if, through unbelief, we do not allow that knowledge to transform us into the image of Christ and change the way we live our lives.

SUMMARY

The constant accumulation and renewal of scriptural knowledge in our minds is absolutely essential to the journey from spiritual immaturity to maturity. Having a wealth of biblical knowledge does not guarantee spiritual maturity, but progress toward maturity is impossible without accurate knowledge of the Word of God. The constant flow of biblical truth sustains faith, transforms character, and results in the godly life that God has commanded of all his children.

CHAPTER 5

EXPERIENTIAL KNOWLEDGE

JOHN CALVIN CALLED THE PHYSICAL universe "the theater of God's glory."[9] As we look in wonder at the uncountable starry host of the Milky Way, the snow-capped grandeur of the Rocky Mountains, the purples and reds of a sunset over the Grand Canyon, or the thunder of crashing waves on the seashore after a severe storm, we have a sense of the greatness and majesty of God. God has put his glory on display in the physical world.

In a similar way, God has unfolded his wisdom and attributes in redemptive history, by his sovereign control of events in daily life all around the world. Thus the physical universe and unfolding human events are both vital sources of spiritual information. They are together not just the "theater of God's glory," but the university for Christian maturity. A spiritually mature person does not just have a vast array of biblical facts stored up in their head, but also a wide variety of spiritual experiences in God's world which have shaped their minds and helped them grow. Thus there are two vital sources of the knowledge that leads to godliness: God's word and God's world. There is factual knowledge and there is also experiential knowledge.

Now it is clear—from the emphasis I have put in the previous chapter on the indispensable role of the Bible for progress in the internal journey—that I put the priority on Scripture over experience, simply because Scripture speaks with a clearer voice than does experience. Many have "spiritual experiences" that they subsequently interpret a certain way and are misled. Scripture stands over all private experiences and interprets them. It is a dangerous thing to trust experience in the absence of a solid base of biblical knowledge: going astray is a certainty in that case.

SCRIPTURE'S LANGUAGE IS BASED ON EXPERIENCE

However, apart from life in this world, Scripture itself is unintelligible. Scripture is written in human language, and all human language is absorbed primarily through experience. From infancy, a child is taught his mother tongue (probably even by his mother): nouns, verbs, adjectives, grammar, syntax, all of them learned in daily life. Experience comes first, and language follows. A child can live in the world for eighteen months or more before 'speaking a single word. But that entire time, that child is learning about God's world through experience.

For example, long before learning the Apostle Paul's command, *"Be completely humble and gentle; be patient, bearing with one another in love"* (Ephesians 4:2), a child has a vast storehouse of experiential data on what humility, gentleness, patience, and love look like. The child can recall the many times his mother cradled him in her arms when he was crying, and gently, tenderly cared for his skinned knee or some hurt feelings. Apart from that ever-growing storehouse of experiential data, Paul's command would be literally unintelligible. Paul openly appeals to this storehouse of life experience when he wrote to the Thessalonian Christians, *"we were gentle among you, like a nursing mother taking care of her own children"* (1 Thessalonians 2:7, ESV). That experience is common all over the world—a nursing mother tenderly caring for the needs of her infant. Paul appealed to it to remind the Thessalonian Christians of how he had been among them.

REAL LIFE CONTINUES TO ILLUMINATE SCRIPTURE

That storehouse continues to grow long after conversion, well into the adult years of Christian development. We meet people in God's Kingdom who are both humble and prideful, both gentle and harsh, both patient and impatient, both loving and unloving. So our knowledge base is being constantly augmented. Some role models step forward and become powerful examples to us of all godly traits; so also, bad role models are noted. We remember specific encounters with all these people, both painful and pleasant, and these encounters help us understand the Scripture.

Furthermore, we see *ourselves* behaving in all of these ways: sometimes obedient to Paul's command in Ephesians 4:2, sometimes disobedient. Real life gives meaning to the words on which Scripture depends, and Scripture in turn interprets real life experiences. When we have learned sufficiently what gentleness and patience look like in daily life, what they look like in a facial expression or in body language, then the command from God through Paul stands over daily life behavior and judges it: "That was gentleness! Good! Do it all the more!" or "At that moment you were impatient and harsh. That was sin. Repent!" So it is with all the words used in Scripture. Each of them must have a data base of life experience behind them, or they will be unintelligible to us.

Every day that we live in this world, expands our life experiences and makes us more and more ready to understand the all-sufficient Scripture. It is the Scripture that sanctifies, but it does its work in the context of an ever-growing storehouse of experience.

DAILY LIFE EXPERIENCE IS CAPTURED IN SCRIPTURE'S TEACHINGS

Scriptural knowledge doesn't compete with the experiential, but rather relies on it. Christ consistently used common life experiences to make his points. His parables skillfully used everyday experience to teach spiritual truths. Many of them began with the words, *"The Kingdom of Heaven is like"*: a man who sowed good seed in his field, but at night an enemy came and sowed weeds among the wheat (Matthew 13:24); a mustard seed planted in a garden (Matthew 13:31); yeast that a woman took and mixed throughout dough (Matthew 13:33); treasure hidden in a field (Matthew 13:44); a merchant looking for fine pearls (Matthew 13:45); a net thrown into the sea, that gathered all kinds of fish (Matthew 13:47); a king who wanted to settle accounts with his servants (Matthew 18:23); a landowner who went out early in the morning to hire men to work in his vineyard (Matthew 20:1); a king who prepared a wedding banquet for his son (Matthew 22:2); ten virgins who took oil in their lamps and went out to meet the bridegroom (Matthew 25:1). These examples could be multiplied at much greater length. Jesus consistently appealed to various realms of experience to make his spiritual points: physical creation—"see how the lilies of the field grow," observation of natural tendencies—"they don't labor or spin," and history—"yet I tell you that not even Solomon in all his splendor was dressed like one of these" (Matthew 6:28–29).

Jesus openly discussed this at one point with Nicodemus, when he'd been using an enhanced analogy to lift Nicodemus' understanding of spiritual truth to a higher level. Jesus told him, *"You must be born again"* in order to enter the Kingdom of Heaven (John 3:3,7). Nicodemus knew what it meant to be born, but he'd never heard of being "born again." Jesus was using a common earthly experience in an entirely new way, to speak to this man's heart about his spiritual need. Nicodemus could not follow Jesus into the new mental territory, but instead stayed close to home and so turned Jesus' words into foolishness: *"How can a man be born when he is old?" Nicodemus asked. "Surely he cannot enter a second time into his mother's womb to be born!"* (John 3:4). Jesus later addressed Nicodemus's unwillingness to allow earthly language to be stretched, in order to instruct us on heavenly realities: *"I have spoken to you of earthly things and you do not believe; how then will you believe if I speak of heavenly things?"* (John 3:12). "Speaking of earthly things" is teaching that uses earthly experiences to teach us spiritual truths, and no one did it better than Jesus. But all of Scripture relies on life experience to make spiritual truth intelligible.

BIBLICAL EXAMPLES OF LEARNING BY EXPERIENCE

There are some lessons we must live through in order to learn. Some things just cannot be fully explained in a book, but only learned by experience. The Bible is full of examples of the people of God learning by experience. Let's look at four in particular:

1. MOSES' ARMS LIFTED IN PRAYER

The first example comes from the amazing experience Moses had in praying over the Israelites as they fought a battle against the Amalekites, during the Exodus from Egypt to the Promised Land:

> The Amalekites came and attacked the Israelites at Rephidim. Moses said to Joshua, "Choose some of our men and go out to fight the Amalekites. Tomorrow I will stand on top of the hill with the staff of God in my hands." So Joshua fought the Amalekites as Moses had ordered, and Moses, Aaron and Hur went to the top of the hill. As long as Moses held up his hands, the Israelites were winning, but whenever he lowered his hands, the Amalekites were winning. When Moses' hands grew tired, they took a stone and put it under him and he sat on it. Aaron and Hur held his hands up—one on one side, one on the other—so that his hands remained steady till sunset. So Joshua overcame the Amalekite army with the sword. (Exodus 17:8–13)

It is very helpful for us to picture in detail what was happening that day, in order to see how this experiential knowledge impressed itself on Moses. As Moses stood on the mountain overlooking the battlefield and started to pray with uplifted hands, the Lord blessed Joshua and the Israelite army with obvious success. Then, after a period of time, Moses felt the fatigue in his arms building, and he decided to take a break. While he was taking his break, he noticed that Israel began to lose the battle. Alarmed, he stood up and lifted his arms again in prayer. The tide turned in Israel's favor, and Joshua rallied the men toward victory. Perhaps at least one more time Moses had to go through this cycle, until he learned by experience the lesson God was teaching him: that prayer is indispensable to the victory that God desires for his people. Having learned that lesson by experience, Moses then contrived to have Aaron and Hur get him a stone to sit on, while they supported his weary arms in the uplifted position, so that Joshua could finish the victory completely.

I think George Mueller learned his confidence in prayer in the exact same way—by experience. Here was a man whom God used to care for the daily needs of over ten thousand orphans, a man accustomed to getting down on his knees and trusting God for one immediate need after another. This was a man who kept an accurate journal recording over fifty thousand specific answers to prayer! One experience after another of God's faithfulness led him to a level of confidence in prayer that can scarcely be measured.

2. ISRAEL HUMBLED AND TRAINED IN THE DESERT:

During their forty years in the desert, God trained the Israelites as a father trains his son. He gave them forty years of discipline mixed with blessings. It is especially interesting how God led the nation, step by step through their journey, with a pillar of cloud and fire:

> On the day the tabernacle, the Tent of the Testimony, was set up, the cloud covered it. From evening till morning the cloud above the tabernacle looked like fire. That is how

it continued to be; the cloud covered it, and at night it looked like fire. Whenever the cloud lifted from above the Tent, the Israelites set out; wherever the cloud settled, the Israelites encamped. At the Lord's command the Israelites set out, and at his command they encamped. As long as the cloud stayed over the tabernacle, they remained in camp. When the cloud remained over the tabernacle a long time, the Israelites obeyed the Lord's order and did not set out. Sometimes the cloud was over the tabernacle only a few days; at the Lord's command they would encamp, and then at his command they would set out. Sometimes the cloud stayed only from evening till morning, and when it lifted in the morning, they set out. Whether by day or by night, whenever the cloud lifted, they set out. Whether the cloud stayed over the tabernacle for two days or a month or a year, the Israelites would remain in camp and not set out; but when it lifted, they would set out. At the Lord's command they encamped, and at the Lord's command they set out. They obeyed the Lord's order, in accordance with his command through Moses. (Numbers 9:15–23)

This pattern disciplined the Israelites to follow the Lord their God, and not make a move unless the Lord commanded it. It gave the church a timeless picture of total dependence on God and submission to his leadership. They learned by experience to look to the pillar in order to determine whether or not they were to move. And the Lord did not follow any predictable pattern, but the dictates of his own inscrutable wisdom: sometimes the pillar would stay in a place only from evening till morning; other times it might stay as much as a year or more. Whatever the Lord willed, they did.

The same lesson was taught concerning their daily bread. The manna came from heaven as a daily miracle. They were trained to look to God not only for physical direction from day to day for their travels, but also for their very sustenance itself. The manna had its own special rules: they were only to gather enough for one day, and they learned that any manna saved overnight would quickly swarm with maggots. They also learned by experience that this rule was relaxed for the Sabbath, for God commanded them to collect a double portion for the Sabbath, so they would not have to labor for their food on the Sabbath. When they sinfully went out to collect food on the first Sabbath after these regulations had been established, there was none on the ground. So the Israelites learned a vital lesson: *"He humbled you, causing you to hunger and then feeding you with manna, which neither you nor your fathers had known, to teach you that man does not live on bread alone but on every word that comes from the mouth of the Lord"* (Deuteronomy 8:3).

The lesson, "Man does not live on bread alone but on every word that comes from the mouth of God," is vital even for today. Israel lived or died by God's word, by what God provided or didn't provide, by what God commanded or forbade. Israel was trained to look to God's mouth and follow his words as though their very lives depended more on God's words from his mouth than from God's provision from his hand. Word preceded and superseded bread. And this God taught Israel by experience . . . forty years of it!

3. PAUL AND CONTENTMENT

At the end of his letter to the Philippians, the Apostle Paul said that he'd learned a precious secret in the Christian life: "I know what it is to be in need, and I know what it is to have plenty. I have learned the secret of being content in any and every situation, whether well fed or hungry, whether living in plenty or in want" (Philippians 4:12). The secret of Christian contentment is a treasure beyond the value of any earthly wealth. In his classic story *The Count of Monte Cristo*, Alexander Dumas wrote of a vast treasure hidden in a cave on the Mediterranean island of Monte Cristo. The hero in the story, Edmund Dantes, found this treasure by following a secret map he'd received from an aged fellow prisoner, named the Abbe Faria. This map led Dantes to a treasure box filled with a thousand gold ingots (each weighing two to three pounds), rare jewels, diamonds and coins—worth over 13 million francs—and he was instantly a rich man.

However, the wealth Edmund Dantes acquired by the whispered secret of Abbe Faria is nothing compared to the secret the aged Apostle Paul wanted to bequeath to the Philippian church, his children in the faith. For as Paul said in another place, *"godliness with contentment is great gain"* (1 Timothy 6:6). The real treasure is contentment, and it is of such great value that the Puritan writer Jeremiah Burroughs called it *The Rare Jewel of Christian Contentment.* The secret of Christian contentment in "any and every situation" can only be learned by experience, by walking with Christ through all circumstances. The answer to the question, "What is the secret of Christian contentment?" is perhaps unsatisfying to an immature Christian: *"I can do everything through him who gives me strength"* (Philippians 4:13). That person might say, "Of course, I know that that's the right answer. But I am still frequently discontent, both in times of plenty and in times of want." Not until that person learns by personal experience how Christ gives strength for Christian contentment in any and every situation will they be mature in this vital area.

Paul walked with Christ through more and varied circumstances than many of us can possibly imagine, many of them extremely painful:

> Five times I received from the Jews the forty lashes minus one. Three times I was beaten with rods, once I was stoned, three times I was shipwrecked, I spent a night and a day in the open sea, I have been constantly on the move. I have been in danger from rivers, in danger from bandits, in danger from my own countrymen, in danger from Gentiles; in danger in the city, in danger in the country, in danger at sea; and in danger from false brothers. I have labored and

toiled and have often gone without sleep; I have known hunger and thirst and have often gone without food; I have been cold and naked. (2 Corinthians 11:24–27)

These overwhelming trials put Paul in a position again and again to learn what he said was the secret of contentment: *"I can do everything through him who gives me strength."* The secret, hidden strength of Christ so powerfully working through him in his ministry (Colossians 1:29) also increasingly gave Paul a supernatural contentment in any and every situation. But he had to learn it by experience.

4. PETER AND GENTILE BELIEVERS

Peter was a Jew, and from childhood he'd been trained to stay physically separate from Gentiles, lest he be spiritually defiled. Jews were not allowed to go into Gentile homes and eat with them, nor to be in close contact with Gentiles in any way. Peter acted on this training even after Gentiles started to come into the church, and Paul had to rebuke him for his hypocrisy (Galatians 2:11). How, then, did Peter come to the point of being able to accept Gentiles as spiritually clean in the sight of God? It took a supernatural vision, amazing providential occurrences, and the pouring out of the Holy Spirit in a visible, powerful way on Gentiles to convince him, to teach him a lesson no book could fully drive home.

The full story is told in Acts 10, of how an angel appeared to a Roman centurion named Cornelius and told him to send to Joppa for a man named Peter, who would bring a message by which he and all his family would be saved from their sins. Immediately Cornelius sent some men as messengers. Just before they arrived at the home where Peter was staying, Peter had a vision. This vision was of a large sheet being let down to earth by its four corners, and it contained all kinds of "unclean" animals, which Jews had been forbidden by the Law of Moses from eating. Peter heard a loud voice from heaven, "Get up Peter, kill and eat." Peter answered with shock, "Never, Lord! I have never eaten anything impure or unclean." Then the voice from heaven answered a second time, "Do not call anything impure that God has made clean." This happened three times, and then it was all taken up to heaven again.

While Peter was thinking about this mysterious lesson, at that exact moment, the men sent from Cornelius arrived, and the Holy Spirit told Peter to have no fear about going with them. After they explained why they were there, Peter returned with them to Caesarea. After arriving at Cornelius's house, he went in without hesitation and found a large assembly of Gentiles waiting to hear the word of the gospel. At that moment, the light dawned on Peter and he understood the purpose of the vision of the "unclean" animals and of the whole mission on which the Spirit had sent him: "*I now realize how true it is that God does not show favoritism but accepts men from every nation who fear him and do what is right*" (Acts 10:34–35). The expression "I now realize" means the truth of the lesson had seized him suddenly, that he had put two and two together. The truth that God could accept the Gentiles if they were cleansed by faith was absolutely sealed when, after Peter had preached the gospel of Jesus Christ, the Holy Spirit fell on these Gentiles in the same way he had come on the church at Pentecost.

Peter repeated the lessons he had learned by experience at the Jerusalem council on circumcision in Acts 15. The meeting had been called to deal with the question of whether or not it was necessary for Gentile converts to be circumcised and required to obey the Law of Moses. Here, like a good schoolboy, Peter recited the very lessons he had learned that time concerning the large sheet and Cornelius:

> Peter got up and addressed them: "Brothers, you know that some time ago God made a choice among you that the Gentiles might hear from my lips the message of the gospel and believe. God, who knows the heart, showed that he accepted them by giving the Holy Spirit to them, just as

he did to us. He made no distinction between us and them, for he purified their hearts by faith. Now then, why do you try to test God by putting on the necks of the disciples a yoke that neither we nor our fathers have been able to bear? No! We believe it is through the grace of our Lord Jesus that we are saved, just as they are." (Acts 15:7–11)

This lesson Peter learned by a series of experiences. None of these lessons came from a book, but they corroborated biblical teaching about the New Covenant and about Christ's words declaring all foods clean. Experiential learning was essential to the gospel advance.

DAILY LESSONS IN GOD'S LOVE

One of the most vital lessons God teaches us by experience is how much he loves us, and how completely he cares for our needs. The doctrine of providence—God's sovereign control over daily life events—is taught many texts of Scripture. Here are just two examples:

- Are not two sparrows sold for a penny? Yet not one of them will fall to the ground apart from the will of your Father (Matthew 10:29).
- The lot is cast into the lap, but its every decision is from the Lord (Proverbs 16:33).

A mature Christian has a much more developed sense than does an immature Christian of God's active control over daily life, and especially of his provision for his children. King David relates this lifetime of experience in a single verse: "*I was young and now I am old, yet I have never seen the righteous forsaken or their children begging bread*" (Psalm 37:25). Simply by living year after year under God's providential care, especially when trained by Scripture in what to look for, we will have a clear vision of God's power and love directed for the good of his chosen people.

DISCIPLINE FOR SIN: LEARNING
BY BITTER EXPERIENCE

Another vital form of knowledge gained by experience is God's loving discipline of his sinning children. This kind of knowledge can only be gained in daily life. It does not come from reading the Bible or hearing good preaching. Hebrews 12 teaches this plainly:

> In your struggle against sin, you have not yet resisted to the point of shedding your blood. And you have forgotten that word of encouragement that addresses you as sons: "My son, do not make light of the Lord's discipline, and do not lose heart when he rebukes you, because the Lord disciplines those he loves, and he punishes everyone he accepts as a son." Endure hardship as discipline; God is treating you as sons. For what son is not disciplined by his father? . . . Our fathers disciplined us for a little while as they thought best; but God disciplines us for our good, that we may share in his holiness. No discipline seems pleasant at the time, but painful. Later on, however, it produces a harvest of righteousness and peace for those who have been trained by it. (Hebrews 12:5–11)

This kind of discipline is something God does in the lives of sinning Christians to chasten them and train them not to sin. It could be any form of hardship or affliction: physical illness (for that person or for a loved one), financial hardship, loss of a precious possession, relational difficulties with others, loss of a cherished dream, etc. By living through that painful experience, the Christian is trained to hate sin and to fear God. We can clearly see the pain King David went through after committing adultery with Bathsheba—unremitting trouble in his family life with Amnon, Tamar, Absalom, and others. We can also see the pain Peter went through when the Lord looked at him, as the rooster crowed right after Peter had denied Jesus a third time, and how

Peter as a result went outside and wept bitterly (Luke 22:61–62). We learn *about* discipline factually by reading the Bible, but we *are* disciplined experientially when the Lord deals with us painfully and wisely in our sins.

SUFFERING: THE GRADUATE SCHOOL OF SPIRITUAL EXPERIENCE

In several key passages in the New Testament, suffering is clearly linked to the process of spiritual maturation. In fact, the statements are so strong that it seems that it is impossible to grow up to maturity without enrolling in suffering as the graduate school of spiritual experience. These verses clinch forever the point I'm generally making here in this chapter: acquiring knowledge by experience is essential to our spiritual growth.

The first passage is James 1: *"Consider it pure joy, my brothers, whenever you face trials of many kinds, because you know that the testing of your faith develops perseverance. Perseverance must finish its work so that you may be mature and complete, not lacking anything"* (James 1:2–3). Here James tells Christians not merely to accept trials stoically, but to consider them "pure joy." Why? Because of knowledge! "Because you know that. . . " Being well-trained factually can help you learn experientially. But the focus here is on experiential knowledge, and based on this passage, without "trials of many kinds" we will be the opposite of what verse 3 tells us; instead we will be immature, incomplete, lacking something. Thus, in order to grow to full maturity, we must have trials.

The second key passage is Romans 5, in which Paul is unfolding the grounds of our full assurance of justification: *"Not only so, but we also rejoice in our sufferings, because we know that suffering produces perseverance; perseverance, character; and character, hope"* (Romans 5:3–4). Once again, Scripture is encouraging us to have a supernatural reaction to suffering. We are to rejoice in it, because we have been instructed by factual knowledge gained in the Scripture, that suffering is forever linked to the development of proven character. The Greek word translated "character" means "something which has been tested and revealed as genuine." Only by the testing of our faith will our character be developed and our heart be transformed, so that who we really are is revealed. In the parable of the Seed and the Soils, it was only when the sun came up and plants were scorched (trouble or persecution because of the word) that the rocky soil plants were exposed as false believers, with no genuine root system in Christ (Matthew 13:6, 20–21). Trouble in the Christian life that actually causes us to become stronger in our faith is a cause of great assurance of the genuineness of our faith. And according to Romans 5:4, proven character results in greater hope.

Again and again, church history has borne out the truth of this scriptural theme: great suffering produces great fruit in the lives of true Christians. Paul's joyful suffering in the Philippian jail, his long *résumé* of sufferings (2 Corinthians 11:23–27), his learning by suffering not to rely on himself but on God (2 Corinthians 1:8–9)—these lessons have been repeated again and again in the lives of those who came after him. The blood of martyrs was seed for the church, said Tertullian. How did he know that? Both from Scripture and from experience. Foxe's *Book of Martyrs* celebrated the suffering that the church had to undergo to protect the true gospel. A subplot of that glorious record is the effect of the suffering on those who were enduring it. By the time they died, they were prepared for heaven in ways hard to imagine. Adoniram Judson's immense sufferings in Burma—the death of two wives and several children, his imprisonment, persecution, the loss of possessions, the long delay before seeing any fruit from his labors—produced not only thousands of genuine converts, but also a genuine deepening of his own faith and spiritual maturity.

SUMMARY AND CONCLUSION

In these two chapters, we have seen the foundational role that knowledge plays in the infinite journey of internal conformity to Christ. The knowledge of which I speak is of two types: factual and experiential. Factual knowledge is gained from Scripture, experiential knowledge is gained from living under the Spirit in God's world. Factual knowledge consists of a limitless series of insights from texts of Scripture, which the Holy Spirit connects together to build a "City of Truth," brick by brick, within our minds. This City of Truth is that which shapes our world view, which governs our every decision and the overall purposes of our lives. The series of insights from Scripture comes into our minds in a variety of ways: by reading, meditating on, and memorizing the Bible ourselves; by hearing good preaching; reading good Christian literature; having godly, Scripture-saturated conversations with other Christians; etc. Experiential knowledge is gained by a daily lifestyle in God's world, as God providentially directs our paths. Each encounter, when interpreted by the Holy Spirit and by the existing City of Truth within us, adds to that growing City and prepares us for future service to him. Opening ourselves (under the leadership of the Spirit) to new experiences in serving Christ greatly accelerates our experiential intake, as much as increasing our memorization of and meditation on Scripture increases our factual intake. If we choose to go out witnessing, or to serve food in an inner-city mission center, or to try a three-day fasting and prayer experiment, we expose ourselves to God in new ways; and we grow faster. And if God allows us to endure suffering, perhaps through disciplining us for our sin or perhaps just through the providence of a serious illness entering the family, we will grow even faster.

So, my closing appeal to you is this: grow up by knowledge! Develop an insatiable appetite for the Word of God and then follow where it leads. As you do, watch for the Lord to lead you into ever-increasingly challenging circumstances to train you for his glory. This knowledge primes the pump for all following steps in Christian sanctification. Knowledge feeds faith, which transforms character, which produces actions. Those actions in turn increase knowledge all the more. And in this way you will "grow up into him who is the head, even Christ" (Ephesians 4:15).

FAITH

A PATHWAY TO CHRISTIAN MATURITY

KNOWLEDGE
FACTUAL AND EXPERIENTIAL
SPIRITUAL INFORMATION

FACTUAL
Gained from the Scripture

EXPERIENTIAL
Gained from living in God's world

FAITH
ASSURANCE OF AND COMMIT-
MENT TO SPIRITUAL TRUTH

- Certainty that specific invisible spiritual realities are true
- Assurance that hoped-for specific good thing promised in scripture will certainly come true
- Conviction that specific sin in me, and that God hates it and will judge people for such sins
- Reliance on Christ as all-sufficient savior, refuge, provider, shield
- Reception of spiritual guidance and knowledge

ACTION
EXTERNAL LIFESTYLE OF
HABITUAL OBEDIENCE

1. Presentation of Body to God
2. Personal Holiness
3. Seven-fold obedience to God's commands

   1. Worship
   2. Spiritual Disciplines
   3. Family
   4. Ministry to Believers
   5. Mission to Non-Believers
   6. Stewardship
   7. Work

CHARACTER
INTERNAL NATURE CON-
FORMED TO CHRIST

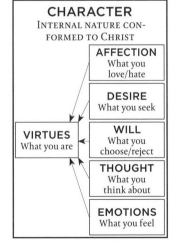

AFFECTION
What you love/hate

DESIRE
What you seek

VIRTUES
What you are

WILL
What you choose/reject

THOUGHT
What you think about

EMOTIONS
What you feel

SECTION INTRODUCTION: FAITH

WITH HIS HEART BEATING WILDLY, the young man looked out from the house at the hills surrounding Dothan, scarcely believing what he was seeing. Somehow in the night, a massive force of Aramean soldiers had snuck in and taken position around the city. They even had horses and chariots, and images of fleeing in terror and being cut down by a skilled charioteer brought instant terror to his mind. He ran back into the house and summoned the seer, frantically describing the scene to the man of God. "O, my lord, what shall we do?" he exclaimed. There seemed to be no escape. Elisha surveyed the scene with the practiced eye of faith, and calmly turned to the young man. "Don't be afraid," the prophet answered. "Those who are with us are more than those who are with them." The young man was bewildered; it seemed like thousands against two. But his eyes betrayed him. There was more in reality than could be seen by the natural eye.

The kind prophet, spiritual mentor to this young man's growing faith, turned to the Lord, the author and perfecter of faith: "O Lord, open his eyes so he may see." Suddenly, the young man could see what had always been there but had been invisible to his unaided eyes—the hills filled with horses and chariots of fire, all around Elisha. The human army, which a moment ago looked terrifyingly formidable, suddenly shrank into laughable nothingness. Elisha's mature faith enabled him to see in the spiritual realm what the young man's physical eyes could only see in the physical. Those horses and chariots of fire were not produced by

Elisha's faith—they were there whether Elisha believed or not. But by faith Elisha perceived their presence before the young man could see a thing.

As we've already noted, faith is the eyesight of the human soul. Faith has the unique power under God to receive from him spiritual truth. It is gifted with the ability to perceive who God is and what he is doing in the world. Like the eye, faith does not create reality, but instead passively receives information from the true nature of things. Many people emphasize faith wrongly, as though by faith we can compel God to do something he is not willing to do, or to create something out of nothing (as if we were gods ourselves).[10] But rather, faith is a passive faculty of the soul by which God communicates spiritual realities, and through which he can pour into the believer all the good gifts his love and his wisdom have determined to give. God has ordained faith to play the central role in our justification, as we've already seen in the chapter on our great salvation: *"Therefore, since we have been justified through faith, we have peace with God through our Lord Jesus Christ"* (Romans 5:1). A faith sufficient for our justification is imparted to the human soul as an act of God's grace, enabling us to receive full forgiveness in Christ. In its immature stage, it is well-pleasing to God and is fully equal to the role of justifying the wicked.

However, like every living thing in God's creation, faith is designed to grow. The growth of our faith is essential to our ongoing sanctification. The purpose of this section is to define and describe faith, and to unfold its attributes when it is fully mature as a worthy goal for Christians to strive for.

THE FIVE ELEMENTS OF FAITH

In this section, we will see that faith is comprised of five elements:

- The certainty of invisible, spiritual realities: past, present and future;
- The assurance of things hoped for, both in this world and the next;
- The conviction of personal sin;
- Active reliance on Christ as all-sufficient Savior, provider, and protector;
- Reception of spiritual guidance.

CHAPTER 6

CERTAINTY OF INVISIBLE SPIRITUAL REALITIES

THE ESSENCE OF FAITH IS that it operates on invisible things. Paul's statement, *"We walk by faith, not by sight"* (2 Corinthians 5:7, ESV), directly contrasts faith and sight. So does Hebrews 11:1, which says, *"Now faith is the assurance of things hoped for, the conviction of things* **not seen"** (NASB), and 2 Corinthians 4:18, *"So we fix our eyes not on what is seen, but on what is* **unseen**. *For what is seen is temporary, but what is* **unseen** *is eternal."*

Faith does not operate on things that are visible, just as eyesight is not employed to hear a violin solo or taste a succulent peach. Faith is designed to perceive invisible realities, and press the certainty of them to the human soul. Since we are justified only by faith (Romans 3:28), and since when Christ returns with the clouds *"every eye will see him, even those who pierced him"* (Revelation 1:7), the urgency of today is underscored. Now, today, while it is still the era of faith, when Christ has not yet revealed himself in his Second Coming glory, each unbeliever must exercise faith in Christ for the full forgiveness of sins.

Faith operates in three vital invisible realms: the past as recorded in Scripture; the present invisible spiritual world which exists around us right now; and the future as promised in Scripture by God the Savior or threatened in Scripture by God the Judge. None of these three realms can be seen by the eye; truths from each must come by faith in Scripture's statements about them.

REALM #1: THE PAST AS
RECORDED BY SCRIPTURE

Ours is an historical faith; it is concerned with the acts of Almighty God in history. The Bible begins with a statement of historical fact: *"In the beginning, God created the heavens and the earth"* (Genesis 1:1). It is faith that accepts this first step of history: *"By faith we understand that the universe was formed at God's command, so that what is seen was not made out of what was visible"* (Hebrews 11:3). From that first act of God, a march of "Redemptive History" began that we can only perceive properly by faith. The events of Redemptive History, including the Flood, the patriarchs, the Exodus from Egypt, the establishment of the nation of Israel in the Promised Land under the Old Covenant, the acts of the kings of the Jews, the words and deeds of the prophets, the exile to Babylon, and the restoration from exile all point toward a consummation of the ages in the coming of Christ. Christ's own birth, sinless life, miracles, teachings, atoning death, and bodily resurrection are matters of the historical record. We cannot see any of them with our eyes, but must simply accept by faith that the Bible's historical record is true.

This issue is most powerfully connected to the gospel message, and especially to Christ's resurrection from the dead. And the history really matters, as Paul pointed out: *"If Christ has not been raised, your faith is futile; you are still in your sins"* (1 Corinthians 15:17). Our faith would be futile, Paul says, unless our faith is connected to the historical record of Christ's life as preached in the gospel and recorded in Scripture. All generations who lived after the eyewitnesses to Christ's resurrection must accept it by Scripture alone, or they will never believe. *"He told them, "This is what is written: The Christ will suffer and rise from the dead on the third day, and repentance and forgiveness of sins will be preached in his name to all nations, beginning at Jerusalem"* (Luke 24:46–47). If we don't believe the Scripture's accounting of history, we will be lost forever. Faith operates in this first invisible realm—the past—before any of the others, for here is the gospel: *"For what I received I passed on to you as of first importance: that Christ died for our sins according to the Scriptures, that he was buried, that he was raised on the third day according to the Scriptures"* (1 Corinthians 15:3–4).

REALM #2: THE PRESENT INVISIBLE SPIRITUAL WORLD

Just as in the days of Elisha, we are surrounded—at every moment—by an invisible spiritual world. Above all, this world contains God himself. When the Apostle John was invited to pass through a doorway into heaven to see a glimpse of the present spiritual realm, the first thing he saw was a throne, and someone sitting on it (Revelation 4:1–2). This throne and the one sitting on it are the central reality of the universe, though we cannot see it with our eyes, but can only receive it by faith. A spiritually mature person constantly lives to please this invisible God, has an intense and lively sense of living in the presence of God, and an increasing sense of caring only for the esteem of God. This rising certainty of the invisible God is essential to faith, and essential to a life well-pleasing to God: *"And without faith it is impossible to please God, because anyone who comes to him* **must believe that he exists** *and that he rewards those who earnestly seek him"* (Hebrews 11:6).

God is not visible unless he reveals himself, for God has no physical matter from which light can reflect and enter our eyes. God can reveal himself in *"unapproachable light"* (1 Timothy 6:6) if he so chooses, but *God is spirit* (John 4:24), meaning he cannot be seen by the human eye in the normal way. God is at the center of the invisible spiritual realm: *"Now to the King eternal, immortal,* **invisible***, the only God, be honor and glory for ever and ever. Amen"* (1 Timothy 1:17); *"but when you pray, go into your room, close the door and pray to your Father, who is* **unseen***. Then your Father, who sees what is done in secret, will reward you"* (Matthew 6:6); *by faith [Moses]* *left Egypt, not fearing the king's anger; he persevered because he saw* **him who is invisible** (Hebrews 11:27).

Furthermore, it is by faith alone that we believe in God the Son, Jesus Christ, who was dead but is now alive, risen from the dead and seated at the right hand of God. *"Though* **you have not seen him**, *you love him; and even though* **you do not see him now**, *you* **believe** *in him and are filled with an inexpressible and glorious joy, for you are receiving the goal of your faith, the salvation of your souls* (1 Peter 1:8,9). By faith we have a lively sense of our spiritual union with Christ, that he is alive inside us moment by moment by the power of the indwelling Spirit.

By faith also we accept the person and work of the Holy Spirit, who is invisibly moving powerfully to accomplish God's work all over the world. Just as we've never seen the wind but have seen what the wind does, so it is with people born by the Spirit (John 3:8). By faith alone we can perceive the Spirit's existence and actions in the world.

Therefore, by faith we accept the reality of the Triune God, Father, Son, and Holy Spirit, eternally existing as one God, perfectly united, powerfully acting in harmony one with another. This being, God, fills our hearts to overflowing, even as we acknowledge that *"heaven, even the highest heavens cannot contain him"* (1 Kings 8:27).

The invisible spiritual world also contains angels, demons and other spiritual beings, in various orders and arrangements of power (such that they are called "rulers, authorities, powers, and forces" in Ephesians 6:12, "thrones" in Colossians 1:16, "cherubim" in 73 places in the Old Testament, "seraphim" in Isaiah 6, and "living creatures" in Ezekiel and Revelation). It is commonplace for believers to go their entire lives without seeing a single visible manifestation of any of these spiritual beings, yet we are totally convinced they are there. These are the very things denied by the liberal theologians of Jesus' day, the Sadducees: *"The Sadducees say that there is no resurrection, and that there are neither angels nor spirits"* (Acts 23:8).

Many Western Christians tend to live in a strange kind of practical denial of these mid-level spiritual beings. Missiologist Paul Hiebert wrote a remarkable article describing this problem for Western missionaries operating in third world countries in which there is a lively sense of the spiritual world around us, of angels and demons, and of the influence these beings have on daily life. The author called it "The Flaw of the Excluded Middle,"[11] saying that biblical Christians certainly accept the highest order of existence, God Almighty, the invisible being upon his throne; and we accept the lower order of being, the physical world that surrounds us daily. But we practically deny the significance of the middle order of being, angels and demons, and their impact on daily life.

A spiritually mature person has no trouble accepting the angelic encounters in the book of Daniel. In Daniel 10, he described a terrifying encounter on the banks of the Tigris River with a supernatural being of astounding glory, whose body was like chrysolite, his face like lightning, his eyes like flaming torches, his arms and legs like burnished bronze, and his voice like the sound of a multitude (Daniel 10:5–8). Spiritually mature people accept these beings as real, though they may have never seen one—simply because Scripture testifies so plainly to their existence. We also believe that angels are continually acting as ministering spirits, sent to serve those who will inherit salvation (Hebrews 1:14).

We believe that there are incredibly powerful evil beings as well, arranged in terrifying array against the people of God. We believe that there is a ruler of all demons named Satan, or the devil (Revelation 12:9), who is extremely powerful and who lives to oppose the Kingdom of Christ and to afflict God's people. Ephesians 6 speaks very plainly of these varying orders of Satan's demonic realm: *"our struggle is not against flesh and blood, but against the rulers, against the authorities, against the powers of this dark world and against the spiritual forces of evil in the heavenly realms"* (Ephesians 6:12). Though we do not fully understand the different levels of power and organization of Satan's kingdom in the heavenly realms, yet we believe they exist, and we respect their power. We are not arrogant toward them or making some boastful slanderous accusation against them, but we entrust ourselves to the infinitely greater power of Christ. As Luther put it in his hymn, "A Mighty Fortress is Our God":

> For still our ancient foe doth seek to work us woe
> His craft and power are great, and armed with cruel hate
> On earth is not his equal.
> Did we in our own strength confide, our striving would be losing
> Were not the right man on our side, the man of God's own choosing.
> Dost ask who that may be? Christ Jesus, it is he
> Lord Sabaoth his name, from age to age the same,
> And he must win the battle.

The existence and effect of Satan and his dark kingdom is something we Christians accept by faith. We cannot usually feel them or sense them in any way with our five senses. However, I believe with all my heart that if we endured a single day without divine protection from Satan (usually unnoticed by us), it would be unquestionably the worst day of our lives. And if God willed that for one day Satan and his demons could not influence us in the slightest way, it would feel like heaven on earth. In this way the invisible spiritual forces in the heavenly realms are like the 14.7 pounds per square inch of atmospheric pressure that is constantly pressing on our skin. This is considerable pressure, but we are so used to it that much of the time we forget about its presence. But when we ascend to 30,000 feet in a Boeing 747, and the cabin pressure is stabilizing, we feel it most acutely in our ears.

So it is with the spiritual realms. I have "felt" a Satanic presence much more powerfully in specific places than others: at an abortion clinic in Brookline, Massachusetts, where I was involved in a prolife ministry; while dealing with a voodoo priest in Haiti; while preaching the gospel in India; while talking to a witch in Salem on Halloween. Though I could never prove the presence of demons by means of laboratory techniques, I believe with all of my heart that they were there, opposing the work of God.

Finally, we also accept by faith that the souls of departed Christians are living in the presence of the Lord at this present time. The book of Hebrews speaks of the heavenly Mount Zion, where dwell *"the spirits of righteous men made perfect"* (Hebrews 12:23). On the other hand, by faith we also recognize that the souls of unbelieving sinners are presently experiencing torment in hell, as the rich man does in Jesus' parable (Luke 16:22–24).

All these present spiritual realities—the Triune God, a heavenly realm, angels, demons, righteous human spirits in heavenly bliss and wicked human spirits in hellish torment—are described in Scripture. Not one of them can be proven by the most advanced empirical scientific research techniques, or discerned in any way by our five senses. Yet, spiritually mature people wholeheartedly embrace the existence of these invisible spiritual realities as they are taught in Scripture. This is the second of the three invisible realms in which faith operates: the present spiritual world.

REALM #3: THE FUTURE AS PROMISED OR THREATENED IN SCRIPTURE

The third invisible realm in which, according to Scripture, faith operates is the future, both in this world and the next. It is a world of blessings based on the promises of God, or curses based on the warnings of God. It includes the certainty of the advance of the gospel, of "wars and rumors of wars," of the Antichrist, of the Second Coming of Christ, of Judgment Day, and of an eternal heaven and hell. This future realm will be developed more fully in the next two subsections, which discuss the assurance of things hoped for, and the conviction of things not seen. However, let me just say this: when we read the promises of God, we accept them as written in the blood of Christ; when we read the warnings of God, they are intensely real to us; when we read of the future New Heaven and New Earth, we accept it as though we could see it with our eyes; and when we read of the torments of hell, we accept that they are real, and we fear hell and are deeply concerned for those whose sins are leading them to suffer there eternally.

CHAPTER 7

ASSURANCE OF THINGS HOPED FOR

AS I WRITE THIS CHAPTER, I am sitting on a balcony of a hotel near Thun, Switzerland, overlooking the peaceful Thunersee Lake. Sailboats glide by silently, hundreds of feet below my gaze, in the cobalt-blue waters of this resort lake. To my left are the majestic, snow-capped Alpine peaks comprising the glacier village near Grindelwald, dominated by the ominously towering north face of the Eiger, the brooding craggy profile of the Wetterhorn, and the awe-inspiring Mönch and Jungfrau peaks, two of the highest in all of Europe. The natural beauty here is breathtaking, yet one thought dominates my mind: this beauty is nothing compared to the New Earth that God will make! For God promised the perfection of the earth as part of the final act of human salvation: *"In keeping with his promise we are* **looking forward** *to a new heaven and a new earth, the home of righteousness"* (2 Peter 3:13). "Looking forward," said Peter. It is a disposition of the soul that is intrinsic to saving faith. As a matter of fact, yearning for future blessings of all sorts based on the promises of God is of the essence of faith, and is greatly honoring to God.

A KEY DEFINITION OF FAITH: HEBREWS 11:1

The author of the letter to the Hebrews defined faith as including looking forward: *"Now faith is the assurance of things hoped for"* (Hebrews 11:1, NASB). The "assurance of things hoped for" is a settled confidence that God will bring about all the good things he has promised to us in Christ. The word *assurance* in Hebrews 11:1 is translated "substance" in the KJV. The Greek word behind it has to do with the reality that supports something, or its essential nature. The word translated literally means something which "stands under" something else and gives it support, like a foundation. So, the "assurance of things hoped for" is the sense of absolute certainty of the promises of God. It is that which "stands under" the subjective experience of hope—of joy in an unseen future reality—and gives it all the support it needs.

Faith feeds a forward-looking disposition; it causes a Christian to be happy, strong, and confident no matter what earthly circumstances are currently going on. A Christian going through great suffering is confident that these sufferings are merely preparing us for *"a glory that far outweighs them all"* (2 Corinthians 4:17). A Christian experiencing great earthly success and blessing is grounded in the knowledge that no blessing on earth compares with the future heavenly blessings that are coming. An aging Christian does not need to be melancholy at the passing of time, because, no matter how great our happiness up to this point, **all**— not just some!—of our best possessions, our best experiences, and our best relationships are yet to come. We yearn for the future!

Faith looks forward to "things hoped for" in two invisible future realms: 1) future things in this present age; 2) future things in the age to come. The "things hoped for" are based on the promises of God. Again, these promises are of two types: 1) those things which are absolutely certain, but which haven't happened yet; 2) those things which are generally consistent with the character of God and which give a basis for confidence in specific earthly circumstances, but which may or may not turn out exactly the way the believer hopes they will.

THINGS HOPED FOR IN THE PRESENT AGE

Faith is especially bold in the presence of Almighty God when it comes to his promises. This holy boldness gives great energy to the saints in prayer and great perseverance in action. Puritan Thomas Manton, speaking of persistent prayer based on the promises of God said, "Show him his writing; God is tender of his word."[12] This is the faith of the persistent widow (Luke 18:1–5) who keeps coming and coming until she receives what she wants. It would be impertinence were it not based on the promises and character of God.

EARTHLY CERTAINTIES

God's promises for ongoing provision and protection in the Christian life are appropriated by faith. By faith, we are absolutely certain that God *"will never leave us or forsake us"* (Hebrews 13:5). By faith, we are confident that, if we seek first God's Kingdom and his righteousness, food and clothing sufficient for our needs will be provided for us (Matthew 6:33). By faith we trust that God *"will not allow us to be tempted beyond what we can bear, but with the temptation will make a way of escape so that we can bear up under it"* (1 Corinthians 10:13). By faith, we can know that *"he who began a good work in* [us]*"* will most certainly *"carry it on to completion"* (Philippians 1:6), with the end result that Christ will not lose any of all the people God has given him (John 6:39). Thus we can be confident in Christ that he will maintain our faith and protect our salvation to the end of our days.

GENERAL PROMISES

However, along with these certainties come some things that are consistent with the promises of God and that we hope for with good confidence, yet we allow his will to be done in the matter, without losing confidence in God or in the promises of God. Prayers offered in faith for sick people are in this category. James 5:15 promises that *"the prayer offered in faith will make the sick person well; the Lord will raise him up."* Faith finds its resting place in promises such as this at those trying times; indeed faith can be rooted nowhere else than in the promises of God. But a faith-filled person also knows that God may, in his good judgment, choose to take a loved one home after such an illness. And if he does, he has not broken a promise, for the real "raising up" the Lord will do to heal the sick person will happen through the resurrection of the body.

Therefore, all the prayers offered for specific lost people to be saved, for money to be raised by a certain date to meet a timely need, for a struggling marriage to be healed, or an evangelistic outreach to result in multiple baptisms—all such specific prayers (and countless others like it) can be made with ever-increasing faith based on the general promises of God. But the specific answers to these on a case by case basis can be "No" without our faith dimming in the least.

George Mueller may have been the most spectacularly successful prayer warrior in church history.[13] His life verse was Psalm 81:10: *"I am the Lord your God, who brought you up out of Egypt. Open wide your mouth and I will fill it."* Based on this one promise from God, Mueller sought the throne of grace again and again to meet the temporal needs of over ten thousand orphans, in his lifetime. He recorded over fifty thousand specific answers to prayer, frequently for money, food, or clothing. Each of these answers came within the framework of general promises made, and though God was not bound in any specific case to act the way Mueller requested, yet at the end of such a lifetime of answered prayers, how mighty was Mueller's faith!

BUOYANT IN SUFFERING

However, Hebrews 11 records both remarkable deliverances and astonishing earthly suffering for "heroes of faith." A mature faith can accept whatever God gives, because it is confident that, as the old hymn puts it, "whate'er my God ordains is right."[14] We see a shocking turn from remarkable deliverances to remarkable courage under suffering in Hebrews 11:35: "*Women received back their dead, raised to life again. Others were tortured and refused to be released, so that they might gain a better resurrection.*" Faith leads both to great triumphs in life and to great courage in the midst of acute suffering.

Because of this, it was by faith in the promises of Christ that William Wilberforce was able to lead a twenty-seven year fight against slavery in England. This man faced one setback after another in those years, yet he never gave up. One of his greatest personal traits during that arduous journey was a personal buoyancy that was astonishing to his enemies: "It is necessary to watch him as he is blessed with a very sufficient quantity of that enthusiastic spirit, which so far from yielding that it grows more vigorous with blows."[15] Wilberforce was like a buoyant cork, which enemies could not keep down. What was the source of his resilience over the years? It was nothing less than faith in the power of Christ to win in the end.

This cork-like buoyancy in an earthly struggle for Kingdom advancement has been seen again and again in the servants of Christ, from great missionaries like Adoniram Judson and John Paton, to reformers like Martin Luther and John Calvin, to persecuted pastors like John Bunyan and Charles Simeon, to evangelists like George Whitefield and D.L. Moody, to the bloody parade of martyrs who faced the tyrant's vicious lash in every generation of church history. All of them were buoyed not only by a hope for heaven when they died, but for a hope for the success of their cause on earth. They believed that efforts made in the external journey of worldwide gospel advance would be successful because God had in some sense promised that success. That faith, that "assurance of things hoped for," drove them past appalling obstacles to "expect great things from God and attempt great things for God," as William Carey said.

In the same way, any significant progress made in the internal journey of sanctification must be made based on an assurance of things hoped for. We must believe that efforts made in Scripture memorization, improving of prayer life, increase of passion in worship, transformation of personal character defects (such as irritability, selfishness, laziness, lack of compassion, lust, and procrastination), and the addition of new habits of obedience (such as evangelism, financial generosity, service to the needy) will be ultimately successful and richly rewarded by God, because *"God is at work in you both to will and to work for his good pleasure"* (Philippians 2:13, NASB). Faith is the assurance of those hoped-for goals and aspirations in this life. Without it, we would quickly give up.

THINGS HOPED FOR IN THE AGE TO COME

Even sweeter to the Christian, however, is the confidence we have that the age to come, the New Heaven and New Earth, will be infinitely and eternally satisfying to us, and that we will most certainly live there and enjoy their pleasures and beauties forever. Heavenly hopes are better than earthly hopes, because they are eternal, not temporary. It is a good thing to hope for the money to build an orphanage; it is a better thing to hope for a place in the Father's house (John 14:2). It is a good thing to hope for acceptance to a career position as a missionary to Muslims; it is a better thing to hope to join a multitude greater than anyone can count, from every tribe and language and people and nation, standing around the throne of Christ in perfect and eternal joy (Revelation 7:9). It is a good thing to hope that a godly woman will be your spouse and with her to raise a family to the glory of God; it will be an even better thing to sit with her in radiant white clothing as part of the Bride of Christ at the wedding feast of the Lamb in glory (Revelation 19:7–9).

CERTAINTY OF FINAL SALVATION

By faith, we trust that God will enable us to survive the rigors of Judgment Day, when our whole lives will stand open for God's assessment. By faith, we earnestly hope to be delivered from God's wrath (Romans 5:9, 1 Thessalonians 1:10), to have our spirits made perfectly pure (Hebrews 12:23, 1 John 3:2), to be raised in resurrection bodies (Philippians 3:11, 21; 1 Corinthians 15:12–58), and to be welcomed (2 Peter 1:11) into the New Heaven and the New Earth, which Peter calls the "home of righteousness" (2 Peter 3:13).

HEAVENLY REWARDS

By faith, we expect to be rewarded for earthly service, for earthly suffering, for earthly seeds planted in hope that never seemed to come to fruition while we observed them. It is this forward looking aspect of faith that enabled Paul and Silas to sing in the Philippian jail after being beaten. Jesus told them *"rejoice and be glad, because great is your reward in heaven"* (Matthew 5:12). It was looking forward to the reward that enabled Moses to despise the alluring treasures and pleasures of Egypt, and to instead choose disgrace with the people of God for the sake of Christ (Hebrews 11:26). It is looking forward to the reward that enables Christians to give lavishly to the poor who can never repay:

> When you give a luncheon or dinner, do not invite your friends, your brothers or relatives, or your rich neighbors; if you do, they may invite you back and so you will be repaid. But when you give a banquet, invite the poor, the crippled, the lame, the blind, and you will be blessed. Although they cannot repay you, you will be repaid at the resurrection of the righteous. (Luke 14:12–14)

Only faith enables us to do such seemingly foolish things with our time, energy, and money, investing in eternity when it seems like nothing will come of it.

A healthy theology of rewards is of the essence of faith. As we have already noted, Hebrews 11:6 makes faith in rewards essential to pleasing God: *"And without faith it is impossible to please God, because anyone who comes to him must believe that he exists and **that he rewards those who earnestly seek him**."* In other words, we cannot please God if we don't believe in rewards! We are supposed to live our lives in this world as though the ledger sheet is *supposed* to be imbalanced, that the reason for our suffering and the effects of our seed-planting, and the results of our gifts to the poor, are all hidden and seemingly unrequited. We are supposed to expect to be repaid only *"at the resurrection of the righteous"* (Luke 14:14).

And what is the reward? Hebrews 11:6 says that God rewards those who **seek him**. So, all their lives, these faith-filled pilgrims lived to seek God, to know God, to be in God's presence, to please God. It was God they wanted, and it will be God they receive. After Abram refused to be enriched by the King of Sodom after the victory of Genesis 14, God appeared to him and gave him this delightful promise: *"After this, the word of the Lord came to Abram in a vision: "Do not be afraid, Abram. I am your shield, your very great reward"* (Genesis 15:1). God himself will be our reward!

But I believe it goes beyond this. I believe God will specifically reward each and every act done by faith for his glory. If we give secretly to the needy, expecting only God to notice, he will reward it (Matthew 6:3–4). If we go into our room, close the door, and pray to our Father who is unseen, then our Father who sees what is done in secret will reward us (Matthew 6:6). If we fast secretly for the glory of God and the advance of his Kingdom, God himself will reward it (Matthew 6:17–18). If we give even a cup of cold water to one of Christ's servants to help him in his ministry, we will never lose our reward (Matthew 10:42). When Jesus comes in his Father's glory with all the angels, he will reward each person according to what he has done (Matthew 16:27). To believe in future rewards for present suffering and service is absolutely required in order to please God. If we say, "I don't need any reward; for me it is enough to make God happy," we might think we are being humble, but we are actually being arrogant. God intends us to live daily for the rewards, and to store up as many of them as possible for the future (Matthew 6:19–20).

The rewards will be of such a nature that they will increase our love for God and our contact with God. They will not be idols which we cherish and seek apart from him. Therefore, I think a key insight into rewards is given in 1 Corinthians 4 and Matthew 25:

> Therefore judge nothing before the appointed time; wait till the Lord comes. He will bring to light what is hidden in darkness and will expose the motives of men's hearts. At that time each will receive his **praise from God**. (1 Corinthians 4:5)

> His master said to him, "Well done, good and faithful servant. You have been faithful over a little; I will set you over much. **Enter into the joy of your master**." (Matthew 25:21, ESV)

The reward is praise from God: that God would actually praise us and commend us and speak words of blessing on us in specific and detailed ways based on what we have done. He may also give us tokens or emblems of that praise (some people call them "crowns," based on 1 Thessalonians 2:19, 2 Timothy 4:8, James 1:12, Revelation 2:10, 3:11, 4:4, and 4:10) as our permanent possessions in the New Heaven and New Earth. But the essence of the reward is the joy in the relationship: my heavenly Father is pleased with me!

Perhaps it works like this: on a given Tuesday evening, you decided to skip dinner and pray for a specific unreached people group to hear the gospel; you poured out your heart in prayer for that people based on information you got from www.joshuaproject.net; you pleaded with God to bring his elect from that unreached people group to faith in Christ; you never prayed for them again, but merely entrusted that evening to God. You never saw the results of your prayer, but in heaven, God was well-pleased by your faith and your service; he had great joy in it, and now at last on Judgment Day, he says "Enter into the joy of your master—well done, you good and faithful servant." His joy in your service that Tuesday evening becomes an openly shared joy between the two of you for eternity. What better reward could there be?

HAPPY JUST TO BE THERE

Faith also looks forward simply to living forever in the New Heaven and the New Earth. Just being there! This looking forward to heaven is a major theme of Hebrews 11. In Hebrews 11:8–10, the author describes the faith of Abraham, who lived in tents like a stranger in the Promised Land, feeding his hopes day by day on a promise both of a country and a city that was yet in the future: "*For he was looking forward to the city with foundations, whose architect and builder is God*" (Hebrews 11:10). In verses 13–16, the author sums up the faith of all the Patriarchs and their descendants with the repeated assessment that they were "seeing and welcoming at a distance," "looking forward to," and "longing for" a better country: a heavenly one, and one they could finally call their own. Essential to this forward-looking, hope-filled disposition is a relative scorn of earthly attractions and sufferings. These faith heroes confessed that they were "aliens and strangers" on the earth.

The author of Hebrews completes his description of this forward-looking disposition of faith in a remarkable way, saying, "*Therefore, God is not ashamed to be called their God, for he has prepared a city for them*" (Hebrews 11:16). This is absolutely astonishing for us to meditate upon! Every last one of them and every last one of us have sinned and fallen short of the glory of God. Even worse, we have from time to time acted ashamed of God in this present evil age. Yet such is the value of faith in the sight of God that he is not ashamed in any way to be associated with people such as us, "to be called [our] God." He has prepared for us a place in which he will dwell in intimate contact with us, face to face, and *"he will be their God and [we] will be his people"* (Revelation 21:3).

SCOURING SCRIPTURE FOR DETAILS

Faith scours Scripture for details of that future world, the "New Heaven and New Earth" which is the "treasure hidden in the field" (Matthew 13:44) and the "pearl of great value" (Matthew 13:45–46). Scripture reveals much about that future treasure:

- It will be a place of infinite joy and pleasure, in intimate, eternal, face to face fellowship with God the Father, Son, and Holy Spirit.
- It contains both a city and a country: the New Jerusalem and the New Earth.
- The New Jerusalem will be immense, a place of perfect union between heaven and earth, a place under no threat but whose gates stand open constantly for the rich blessing of the nations to be brought within her walls.
- The New Earth itself will be physical, a perfect world to be explored, developed, and cared for, and ravishingly beautiful.
- We will be perfectly conformed to Christ in every way: physically, mentally, emotionally, spiritually, and volitionally.
- There will be some kind of feasting there, and we will eat food as Christ did in his resurrection body.
- There will be work, and positions of responsibility and authority, though no jealousy of those over us or domination of those under us.
- We will have eternal possessions on the New Earth, our inheritance.
- We will enjoy perfect fellowship with people from every nation and language, and from every era of Redemptive History.

These are the ultimate things we hope for, and faith is the foundation of our confidence that all these riches will be ours in the future.[16]

Therefore, a spiritually mature person will delight in the "things hoped for" with an ever-growing faith, seizing every promise in Christ and cherishing them. Such a person will live with an ever-increasing focus on heaven: filled with hope, and buoyantly joyful and confident, as God works out his sovereign plan for our eternal bliss and his infinite glory. That Christian will "expect great things from God and attempt great things for God" in both the internal journey of sanctification and the external journey of Kingdom advance. There can be no more secure, joyful, and hope-filled people on earth than mature Christians, as faith fills our hearts with a sense of how great are the things that God has planned for those who love him.

CHAPTER 8

CONVICTION OF THINGS NOT SEEN

FAITH HAS BOTH A POSITIVE and negative aspect. We just finished describing the positive aspect of faith: assurance of things hoped for. But Hebrews 11:1 gives the negative aspect as well: conviction of things not seen. As we've seen, those things we hope for are attractive to us, appealing, magnetic to our hearts. But faith also warns us of the dire effects of sin. Faith makes the wrath of God real and powerful in our hearts before the day of God's wrath, when his righteous judgment is revealed (Romans 2:5). To unbelievers, that day remains hidden, unseen, and so often rejected. But to believers, the day that we will all stand before the Judgment Seat of Christ giving an account for every careless word we've spoken (Matthew 12:36) is powerfully real. These fearful and negative things become more vivid in the heart of a believer by a growing faith.

FAITH IS A TWO-SIDED COIN

John Newton understood the negative aspect of saving faith when he wrote the lyrics to *Amazing Grace*: "'Twas grace that taught my heart to fear, and grace my fears relieved." Grace moves in the hearts of the elect when they hear the gospel fully proclaimed, including the dire threat of hell if they refuse to repent and believe. Grace kindles faith in the elect, and that faith is a coin with two sides: assurance of things hoped for (e.g., full pardon for sins, adoption into the family of God, a rich, warm welcome from God into heaven), and conviction of things not seen (e.g., a detailed record of sins committed, a deep knowledge of indwelling sin still remaining, a raging inferno of wrath awaiting all the unsaved).

This two-sided coin of faith, its sweet attractive side ("assurance of things hoped for") and its fearful negative side ("conviction of things not seen"), continues to develop more and more as the Christian matures. There will come a time when faith will become sight and will no longer be needed: its positive side will become our eternal inheritance, and its negative side will become obsolete with the destruction of the world, the flesh, and the devil. But in the meantime, while these enemies continue their brutal assault on our souls, the negative aspect of faith is essential to our protection and spiritual progress.

"CONVICTION" IN HEBREWS 11:1

Before we proceed, it is necessary to establish carefully the negative aspect of faith found in Hebrews 11:1. This is especially vital because many of the English translations of this key verse do not pick up the proper sense of the critical word which the New American Standard Bible translates as "conviction." The KJV gives us this rendering of Hebrews 11:1: *"Now faith is the substance of things hoped for, the **evidence** of things not seen."* Evidence? It is as though faith is what proves to us, like evidence in a trial, the reality of invisible things. This word "evidence" gives us the sense that it is by faith that the soul gathers convincing proof that the invisible world is real. The NIV has it this way: *"Now faith is being sure of what we hope for and certain of what we do not see."* Again, it seems as though the translators felt that both halves of Hebrews 11:1 were saying essentially the same thing—faith is the means by which invisible things become certain to the soul. However, the ESV and RSV are identical to the NASB: *"Now faith is the assurance of things hoped for, the **conviction** of things not seen."*

What, then, is the Greek word behind the translation, "conviction?" And how should we understand it? The Greek word is [*greek*]. A careful study of the seventeen times the related verbal forms of this Greek word appears in the New Testament, along with another solitary noun use in 2 Timothy 3:16, gives a strong certitude that this word in Hebrews 11:1 means "a rebuke for sin." The word has to do with producing evidence of sin to bring about a sense of conviction necessary for repentance. The sting of conviction for sin is what the New Testament has in mind when the word is employed. Look at the following texts which employ this word (highlighted below, either in noun or verb form).

- 2 Timothy 3:16   All Scripture is inspired by God and profitable for teaching, for **reproof**, for correction, for training in righteousness. *[NASB]*
- Matthew 18:15   If your brother sins, go and **show him his fault** in private; if he listens to you, you have won your brother.
- Luke 3:19   But when Herod the tetrarch was **reprimanded** by him because of Herodias, his brother's wife, and because of all the wicked things which Herod had done, Herod also added this to them all: he locked John up in prison. *[NASB]*
- John 3:20   Everyone who does evil hates the light, and will not come into the light for fear that his deeds will be **exposed**.
- John 8:46   Which one of you **convicts** Me of sin? If I speak truth, why do you not believe Me? *[NASB]*
- John 16:8   When he (the Holy Spirit) comes, he will **convict** the world of guilt in regard to sin and righteousness and judgment.
- Revelation 3:19   Those whom I love I **rebuke** and discipline. So be earnest, and repent.

What, then, is the Greek word behind the translation, "conviction?" And how should we understand it? The noun is *elegxos*, used only once in the New Testament. But a careful study of the seventeen times the related verbal form of this word (*elegxo*) appears in the New Testament, along with a related noun (*elegmon*) in 2 Timothy 3:16, gives a strong certitude that this word in Hebrews 11:1 means "rebuke for sin." *"And you have forgotten that word of encouragement that addresses you as sons: 'My son, do not make light of the Lord's discipline, and do not lose heart when he* **rebukes** *you'"* (Hebrews 12:5). The idea here is that God lovingly rebukes all of his adopted children, whenever they need it. One of the great ministries of the indwelling Holy Spirit in the life of a genuine believer is that of potent conviction of sin where needed, especially by means of the rebuking power of the Scripture (2 Timothy 3:16) and the ministry of other believers. In Matthew 18:15 above, believers are commanded to confront other brothers and sisters in Christ concerning sin. In that process, they are to go privately and produce evidence (proof) of the sin and seek to bring the person to repentance.[17]

WHY CONVICTION IS ESSENTIAL
TO ONGOING SALVATION

Faith's work of conviction will sadly be needed as long as "sin living in us" (Romans 7:17) continues to work its havoc. It is something God promises to keep doing for us as long we live in this world. In our struggle against sin (Hebrews 12:4), our loving Lord knows we need all the help we can get. Since the essence of our journey of sanctification is putting sin to death by the Spirit, the ongoing conviction that specific sins are in us is indispensable. Usually, the gentle, quiet voice of the Spirit while we are reading a text of Scripture or listening to a faithful sermon is sufficient. Then we are confronted with the evidence of our sin and we readily repent. The text stands in front of us like Nathan did in front of sinful and unrepentant King David, pointing the finger and saying, "You are the man!" (2 Samuel 12:7). If we judge ourselves strenuously, we will not need any further disciplinary action by our loving Father (1 Corinthians 11:31). Sometimes however, if we are blind to indwelling sin, he will need to increase his chastising work on us, in order to bring us to repentance (Hebrews 12:4–11). Either way, this "conviction of things not seen" is part of God's loving work in our lives, and faith is the channel by which this work is done. Jesus reminds sinners in Laodicea of his personal zeal to get his whip and cleanse his church of wickedness: *"Those whom I love I* **rebuke** *and discipline. So be earnest, and repent"* (Revelation 3:19).

THINGS NOT SEEN

Now what does it mean, "conviction of **things not seen**"? The author uses a similar phrase a few verses later in Hebrews 11:7 in describing Noah's faith. *"By faith Noah, when warned about* **things not yet seen**, *in holy fear built an ark to save his family. By his faith he condemned the world and became heir of the righteousness that comes by faith"* (Hebrews 11:7). The "things not yet seen" were the events surrounding the coming flood that would consume the world of men in a watery display of the fierce wrath of God. By faith, Noah took the warning of the coming flood very seriously, and acted accordingly. The warning produced in Noah's heart a "holy fear" which resulted in powerful actions, everything needed to save his family in the ark. Every piece of lumber sawn in two, every nail driven, every stroke of the brush with tar, was motivated by Noah's faith in "things not yet seen" (the impending flood).

Thus, "things not seen" should be understood as anything from the three invisible realms in which faith operates—past, present, or future—that produces shame for sin, fear of God's judgment, and resultant repentance. Past "things not seen" could be Israel's sins during the Exodus that Paul used to warn the Corinthian church (1 Corinthians 10:1–11), or David's sin with Bathsheba (2

Samuel 11). Present "things not seen" could be God's pure eyes, "too pure to look on evil" (Habakkuk 1:13); or the six-winged seraphim, who cover their faces and feet, and who cry aloud continually, "Holy, holy, holy is the Lord Almighty" (Isaiah 6:2–3); or the sense of the surrounding "great cloud of witnesses" (Hebrews 12:1), the holy men and women of God who have finished their race of salvation and are in the heavenly Mount Zion waiting for us to complete ours. Future "things not seen" could be the terrors of the coming wrath of God and of the torments of hell, which both Jesus (Matthew 5:29–30) and Paul (Ephesians 5:6, Colossians 3:6) employed to warn believers away from sin; or Judgment Day, when we will have to give an account for "things done in the body, whether good or bad." (2 Corinthians 5:10). Anything from these three invisible realms that God uses to bring about sight of sin, sorrow for sin, confession of sin, shame for sin, hatred of sin, and turning from sin[18] may be what the author of Hebrews had in mind when he spoke of the "conviction of things not seen."

Therefore, a spiritually mature person will fully expect this convicting process to be going on regularly in his/her life. Such a person will not bridle with pride when someone confronts him with evidence of his sin, but will be grateful for it and humbly accept it: *"Let a righteous man strike me—it is a kindness; let him rebuke me—it is oil on my head. My head will not refuse it"* (Psalm 141:5). When such a person reads accounts of the sins of the Israelites or of some evil king in the Bible, he will bow humbly and say, *"Search me, O God, and know my heart; test me and know my anxious thoughts. See if there is any offensive way in me, and lead me in the way everlasting"* (Psalm 139:23–24).

This negative aspect of faith—a constant sense of reproach for our sinfulness—is essential to keep us characterized by "a broken spirit, a broken and contrite heart" that God will not despise (Psalm 51:17). It keeps us humble, like the tax collector who would not look up to heaven but beat his breast and said *"God have mercy on me, a sinner"* (Luke 18:13). Faith keeps us moving in the arduous journey of sanctification, for the essence of the journey is detecting, hating, and turning from our own sin.

CHAPTER 9

RELIANCE ON CHRIST

FAITH ENABLES THE SOUL TO rest securely in God, as if serenely standing on the walls of a mighty fortress and, looking out over a vast, besieging army, having no anxiety about the outcome. As John Newton put it in the hymn, "Glorious Things of Thee Are Spoken,"

> On the rock of ages founded,
> What can shake thy sure repose?
> With salvation's walls surrounded,
> Thou may'st smile at all thy foes.

That confident smile by the soul that trusts in Jesus is greatly glorifying to God Almighty. He yearns to work it in us, and to have us smile at any foe that assails our souls. He yearns to take the same faith in Christ that justified us, and teach us to extend it to any trouble we may face in the two infinite journeys of sanctification and service that will take us through the remainder of our days here on earth.

That we need a refuge is intrinsic to the universe in which we live. Since the entrance of evil into this world by Satan's rebellion and Adam's fall, we live in constant danger. However, we sinful humans have a consistent tendency to build our own refuges, brick by brick, and to put trust in those refuges, or, conversely, to allow our hearts to flutter in the anxiety and terror that insecurity produces. Having seen the threat, we either seek to meet it ourselves and trust in our own provisions, or we fear that the threat cannot be met, and so we cry aloud in faithless despair. In either condition, we sin greatly against God and dishonor his name.

Just as there is no greater threat than damnation on Judgment Day, so there is no greater salvation, refuge, or provision than the finished work of Jesus Christ on the cross. God is greatly glorified by his children, who, seeing the threat of sin, flee to Christ for refuge. Therefore, a spiritually mature man or woman has learned from Scripture and experience to place full confidence in Christ as all-sufficient Savior, Refuge, and Provider. The settled, peaceful condition of the soul that results from this active trust, no matter the circumstances, is greatly glorifying to God.

TRUE RELIANCE VS. FALSE RELIANCE

One of the central lessons of the Old Testament was to teach Israel to rely on God, and God alone. In order to establish a pure reliance on God for all things, God had to strip Israel of all false hopes, all faulty foundations, and all sinful alliances. Therefore the Old Testament gives positive commands and examples of rightly trusting in the Lord, but it also puts on plain display the wide variety of false hopes which polluted the souls of God's chosen people.

In the book of Proverbs, the Lord commanded his people, *"Trust in the Lord with all your heart and lean not on your own understanding; in all your ways acknowledge him, and he will make your paths straight"* (Proverbs 3:5–6). The Hebrew word translated "trust" is a rich one, used in a variety of ways in the Old Testament. It has to do with security and peace, and it is frequently translated that way: *"Follow my decrees and be careful to obey my laws, and you will live **safely** in the land. Then the land will yield its fruit, and you will eat your fill and live there in **safety**"* (Leviticus 25:18–19). The image is of a peaceful countryside in which God's people live in peace and quietness of heart, untroubled by danger, all their needs met. Scripture displays this trust again and again:

- I will lie down and sleep in peace, for you alone, O Lord, make me dwell in safety (Psalm 4:8).
- To you, O Lord, I lift up my soul; in you I trust, O my God. Do not let me be put to shame, nor let my enemies triumph over me (Psalm 25:1–2).
- Though an army besiege me, my heart will not fear; though war break out against me, even then will I be confident (Psalm 27:3).
- You will keep in perfect peace him whose mind is steadfast, because he trusts in you. Trust in the Lord forever, for the Lord, the Lord, is the Rock eternal (Isaiah 26:3–4).

POSITIVE AND NEGATIVE EXAMPLES

So in these Old Testament passages we have multiple commands to trust in the Lord. God also puts before us multiple examples of those who trusted fully in his name and were powerfully delivered from their enemies, and also those who trusted in something other than the Lord, and as a result were destroyed. These stories of the successes and failures of God's people are encouragements and warnings to us who have fled to Christ for refuge.

LESSONS OF GOD THE SAVIOR

In moving Israel out of bondage in Egypt to the Promised Land, God began to teach this central lesson: *Trust in the Lord with all of your heart.* God put his omnipotence on display in the ten plagues with which he judged the gods of Egypt and the mighty power of Pharaoh. Egypt trusted in their gods and in Pharaoh to save them, and both failed utterly. This display came to a climax when Israel was trapped by the Red Sea with no possible escape, and Pharaoh had encircled them with the mightiest army on the face of the earth. Israel cried out to the Lord, who spoke through Moses saying, *"The Lord will fight for you; you need only to be still"* (Exodus 14:14). After Israel safely crossed the Red Sea, with the water like a great wall to the left and the right, and the mighty Egyptian army was subsequently drowned, then the nation had a solid basis for trusting in the Lord forever: *"And when the Israelites saw the great power the Lord displayed against the Egyptians, the people feared the Lord and* **put their trust in him** *and in Moses his servant"* (Exodus 14:31).

LESSONS OF GOD THE PROVIDER

But God was not through teaching the lesson of faith. Not only would God be their Savior and Deliverer, but he would also be their Provider as well. So the Lord used their own natural rhythms of hunger and thirst to teach them a central lesson— God will supply all your needs according to the infinite bounty of his storehouse. By providing bread from heaven every day, water from a rock, daily guidance in the pillar of cloud and fire, and by miraculously preventing their shoes from wearing out, God taught Israel to look to him for everything they would need in life (Deuteronomy 8:1–4). So in the Exodus, God taught these two basic lessons of faith: I am your Savior from all danger and I am your Provider for all needs.

THE ENEMY OF FAITH—SELF-RELIANCE

But as soon as the time came for Israel to enter the Promised Land, they forgot God. They turned to the idol which competes with God above all others: self-reliance. Moses sent out twelve spies to explore the land of Canaan which God had promised to give them. The land they saw was delightfully rich. However, the spies also brought a disease back from their exploration: the filthy virus of unbelief. Ten of the twelve spies spread a bad report about the land. They spoke of the giant Anakites in the land, while they themselves shrank in their own estimation: *"We seemed like grasshoppers in our own eyes, and we looked the same to them"* (Numbers

13:33). This drained courage from the hearts of the Israelites, who then murmured against God and wanted to go back to Egypt.

The Israelites' focus was completely on their own military prowess, and they rightly came up short in that assessment. But they sinned in this self-focus and their resultant despair. God judged their faithlessness: *"In spite of this, **you did not trust** in the Lord your God, who went ahead of you on your journey, in fire by night and in a cloud by day, to search out places for you to camp and to show you the way you should go"* (Deuteronomy 1:32–33). God took this failure to trust in him as the greatest of sins, and their punishment was extremely severe—God declared through Moses that they would wander around in the desert for forty years, until every one of that sinful generation who did not trust in him died.

But then the people rebelled again. Stunned by Moses' words and by God's declaration of their punishment, they did an about-face and, looking inward again at their own military prowess, they put on their armor, *"thinking it easy to go up to into the hill country"* (Deuteronomy 1:41). It was just the other side of the same coin: self-reliance. Self-reliance that looks inward and fails to find the necessary resources to meet the threat results in *despair*. But self-reliance that looks inward and actually finds the necessary resources to meet the threat results in *arrogance*. Israel clearly displayed both of the results of self-reliance. Despair and arrogance are merely two sides of the same coin. But God despises the coin itself: **self-reliance**. For the rest of Israel's history, God fought their self-reliance. And for the rest of our lives on earth, God will fight our self-reliance as well.

MULTIPLE FALSE TRUSTS

There are many other false refuges in which people put their trust, and at some point or other, Israel leaned on them all. People can rely on their own understanding (Proverbs 3:5), physical strength or personal wisdom (Jeremiah 9:23), material wealth (Proverbs 18:11), the fortifications of a well-built city wall (Deuteronomy 28:52), chariots and horses (Psalm 20:7), self-righteousness (Ezekiel 33:13), and worst of all, idols (Isaiah 42:17). God has rejected each of these, and judges all who trust in them.

FALSE ALLIANCES

Again and again, Israel was tempted to trust in something other than the Lord. A common substitute for reliance on the Lord was the military alliance with a pagan power. Frequently, some faithless king of the Jews would be confronted with a terrifying military situation and, instead of falling on his face before God and trusting in his power, the king would send envoys with treasure to another foreign power to form an alliance. In Isaiah chapter 7, wicked King Ahaz, when faced with a terrifying enemy, made a fatal mistake: he turned to Assyria and asked for military assistance. Assyria agreed, invaded, and then took over the whole country!

Once it became clear that Assyria was not a savior but an even bigger threat, Israel turned to Egypt to make another sinful alliance. Isaiah 31 addresses that wretched attempt: *"Woe to those who go down to Egypt for help, who **rely** on horses, who **trust** in the multitude of their chariots and in the great strength of their horsemen, but do not **look to** the Holy One of Israel, or seek help from the Lord"* (Isaiah 31:1). The same issue was working here: "Who are you relying on? Who is your hope? Who is your confidence?" The Hebrew word translated "look to" means to gaze upon, to focus upon, to regard steadily, as a child looks to his mother for food, as a servant looks to his master for provision and guidance, as a soldier looks to his commanding officer for leadership. This is the look of faith, the look of trust, the look of reliance; it was meant to be given to God alone, but here was Israel giving it to Egypt!

EXAMPLES OF TRUST

Of course, Israel didn't always fail the lesson of trust. Under godly leadership, occasionally the Jews openly trusted in the Lord and won great victories against overwhelming odds. King Asa, faced with an army of over a million Cushites prayed, *"Lord, there is no one like you to help the powerless against the mighty. Help us, O Lord our God, for **we rely on** you, and in your name we have come against this vast army"* (2 Chronicles 14:11). And God delivered Israel. King Jehoshaphat, faced with a vast army of Moabites and Ammonites, prayed: *"We have no power to face this vast army that is attacking us. We do not know what to do, but **our eyes are upon you"*** (2 Chronicles 20:12). Again, God delivered Israel. Many such examples exist.

But perhaps no story in Israel's history teaches so fully the issue of trust and reliance as the story of godly King Hezekiah's encounter with Assyria's arrogant emperor, Sennacherib, and his equally arrogant field commander. This story is so powerful, it is recounted three times in Scripture: Isaiah 36–37, 2 Kings 18–19, and 2 Chronicles 32. In those five chapters, the same Hebrew word for "trust" seen in Proverbs 3:5 is used twenty times. It is the greatest concentrated lesson on trust in the history of Israel's kings.

When the Assyrian army stood at the walls of Jerusalem, the arrogant, idol-worshiping field commander of the Assyrian army put his finger on the issue with exceptional clarity: *"Tell Hezekiah, 'This is what the great king, the king of Assyria, says: "On what are you basing this confidence of yours?"'"* (Isaiah 36:4). That's it! What is the source of your confidence? What is the foundation of your hope as you face the future? The field commander went on to make it as picturesque as possible: *"You say you have strategy and military strength—but you speak only empty words. **On whom are you depending**, that you rebel against me? Look now, **you are depending** on Egypt, that splintered reed of a staff, which pierces a man's hand and wounds him if he leans on it! Such is Pharaoh king of Egypt to all who **depend** on him"* (Isaiah 36:5–6). What an image: a weak man, leaning, putting his entire weight on a staff that proves unequal to the task. It splinters, it pierces his hand, and he falls to the ground in agony, clutching a bloody hand. The splintered reed is an unreliable, unreasonable basis of support, and it ends up destroying you in the end. That is the experience of any person who relies on anything but God, and it was spoken by an arrogant pagan warrior!

But Hezekiah knew what to do when faced with an impossible situation: he turned to the Lord in humility, fasting, and weeping, and he spread the matter before God in prayer (Isaiah 37:14–20). Hezekiah had no other stratagem, nowhere else to turn. Assyria had conquered every other nation they had invaded, and no one had ever been able to stand against them. Furthermore, the King of Assyria had already conquered most of Judah itself. At that moment, King Hezekiah could do nothing but turn to the living God and beg for salvation. From his faith, Hezekiah derived unshakable strength, and he in turn strengthened his people: *"Be strong and courageous, be not afraid nor dismayed for the king of Assyria, nor for all the multitude that is with him: for there be more with us than with him: With him is an arm of flesh; but with us is the Lord our God to help us, and to fight our battles."* **And the people rested themselves upon** *the words of Hezekiah king of Judah* (2 Chronicles 32:7–8, KJV). Note how Hezekiah's words became the resting place for his people; they leaned on Hezekiah's words as the firm basis for their own confidence. Salvation could come from no other place than Almighty God. And salvation came, to the glory of God! The angel of the Lord came from heaven and killed 185,000 Assyrian soldiers in one night.

All of these military encounters taught one clear lesson: *"Trust in the Lord with all your heart"* (Proverbs 3:5): not on your military prowess, or the size of your army, or your powerful ally, or your wealth, or anything else (see Psalm 33:16–22).

The question remains before us as well: What are you relying on? What are you resting yourself upon? What do you use to comfort yourself when you consider an uncertain and even terrifying future? When sick, do you think of the excellent hospital near your home, or do you trust in Christ? When seeking a job, do you trust in your extensive education and varied work experience, or do you trust in Christ? When restless and yearning for satisfaction, do you turn to the world, or to Christ? And ultimately, when you are struggling with besetting sin, do you use willpower or some other technique, or do you trust in Christ?

CHRIST: ALL-SUFFICIENT SAVIOR FROM SIN

This is precisely what the Holy Spirit seeks to work in a desperate sinner who has come to realize that he has nowhere else to turn. The finished work of Christ on the cross is the only foundation on which our souls can rest. Samson asked to be put near the two pillars on which the entire temple of Dagon rested (Judges 16:29). When Samson toppled these pillars, the entire structure came crashing down. Faith recognizes that Christ alone is the pillar and foundation of the soul's hopes. So therefore, *"if Christ has not been raised, your faith is futile; you are still in your sins"* (1 Corinthians 15:17). Christ is everything; faith can have no other resting place.

The issue here is one of total reliance, of placing your entire weight in one place. When I served as a missionary in Japan, my wife and I and our two young children went to visit an ancient vine footbridge in the remote Iya Valley on the island of Shikoku. This historic bridge was famous throughout the region, hundreds of years old, made of twisted vines, and supporting the weight of people who dared to travel across it on foot over a deep ravine. My wife took one look at that flimsy-looking bridge, swaying under the weight of others who were venturing across as we watching, and she declared that she wanted no part of it. It was perhaps fifty feet above the rocky river, and it had slats of wood as the footpath by which a traveler would seek to make it to the other side. The slats were separated by several inches, and you could see between them all the way down to the river below.

I read the signs about the bridge and learned how long it had been there and how many people crossed it every year. I watched others cross it successfully. I felt the main vine cables that fixed the bridge to the side of the ravine. And I decided to trust that bridge with my life and the life of my son, Nathaniel. As I held his hand, we took a courageous first step onto the swaying bridge and an even more courageous second step. Now we had entrusted our entire weight to this ancient vine bridge. With no further deliberation, we made our way to the other side.

That is an illustration of faith in Christ. Like the vine bridge, Christ alone must support my entire weight, my soul's state before Almighty God. And faith in Christ means having no additional means of support . . . just Christ alone. If I rig myself up with a rappelling rope and harness while crossing the vine bridge, I am really not trusting in the bridge to support me. The hymn "Come Ye Sinners, Poor and Needy" captures this element of faith with striking vividness:

> Lo, the incarnate God, ascended,
> Pleads the merit of his blood:
> **Venture on him, venture wholly,**
> **Let no other trust intrude!**

> I will arise and go to Jesus,
> He will embrace me in his arms;
> In the arms of my dear Savior,
> O there are ten thousand charms.

Saving faith involves "venturing out" onto Christ, venturing "wholly," entrusting our eternal well-being in his trustworthy hands. It also involves a certain jealous protectiveness over that venturing: "Let no other trust intrude." Like another man wanting oddly to join in the passionate embrace of a husband and wife, so would any other trust than Christ be an intrusion.

As we have already seen, the most common intruder in the embrace between the soul and the Savior is self-reliance, especially self-righteousness. Paul forever rejects this in forceful language in Philippians 3. After listing his Jewish credentials as a reasonable basis for "confidence in the flesh" (i.e. religious self-confidence), he turns his back on anything but Christ:

> But whatever was to my profit I now consider loss for the sake of Christ. What is more, I consider everything a loss compared to the surpassing greatness of knowing Christ Jesus my Lord, for whose sake I have lost all things. I consider them rubbish, that I may gain Christ and be found in him, **not having a righteousness of my own** that comes from the law, but that which is through faith in Christ—the righteousness that comes from God and is by faith. (Philippians 3:7–9)

By faith, we confidently rest on Christ alone as Savior from the wrath of God. We recognize that his righteousness is the only perfect righteousness which can survive the scrutiny of Judgment Day. And we continue to rest in that, secure from all of Satan's foul accusations, for the rest of our lives.

CHRIST AS ALL-SUFFICIENT PROVIDER FOR THE TWO JOURNEYS

As we must entirely rely on Christ for the beginning of the Christian life, so we must rely on him alone for the completion of it: *"Let us fix our eyes on Jesus, the author and perfecter of our faith, who for the joy set before him endured the cross, scorning its shame, and sat down at the right hand of the throne of God"* (Hebrews 12:2). Jesus is faith's "author," the one who pioneered it, who spoke it into existence from nothingness, the one who wrote its first lines on the blank pages of our soul. Jesus is also faith's perfecter, the One who will complete the work he began in us. Jesus claims primacy over every portion of faith's journey: *"I am the Alpha and the Omega, the First and the Last, the Beginning and the End"* (Revelation 22:13). Therefore, we must continue in the development of our growing faith in the same way in which our faith first came into existence. Having been justified by faith in Christ, we must be sanctified also by faith in Christ.

This is a vital lesson: sanctification must proceed along the same principle by which we first began. The Galatian Christians were being deceived by false teachers who advocated that daily submission to the Laws of Moses were essential to completing the salvation process. Paul passionately rejected that mixing of human fleshly effort with simple faith in Christ: *"Are you so foolish? Having begun by the Spirit, are you now being perfected by the flesh?"* (Galatians 3:3, ESV). We cannot advance one step in sanctification, we cannot make one move toward Christlike perfection, by unaided fleshly striving. Rather, by faith-filled reliance on Christ moment by moment, we will grow up into him who is the Head: *"Therefore, as you received Christ Jesus the Lord, so walk in him, rooted and built up in him and established in the faith, just as you were taught, abounding in thanksgiving"* (Colossians 2:6–7). *"As you received Christ Jesus as Lord, so* [i.e., in the exact same manner] *walk in him. . . ."* It is only by full reliance on Christ as Savior, from all aspects of sin, that we will finish our internal journey.

What is true of the internal journey of sanctification is also true of the external journey of Kingdom advance. The Kingdom cannot advance one step by unaided human effort. Therefore God raised up examples in church history of men and women whose faith in the all-sufficient God to meet every need for their ministries shines in the darkness of human self-reliance still. Hudson Taylor, the great missionary to China's inland regions, trained himself before he even left for China to rely on Christ alone through prayer. The key question was this: could Taylor learn to move man, through God, by prayer alone? So Taylor resolved to keep his needs hidden from men, and instead to seek what he needed from God alone, through faith-filled prayer. To Taylor, this was the proving ground for his faith, to see if God really was calling him to reach the teeming millions of China with the gospel:

> To me it was a very grave matter . . . to contemplate going out to China, far from all human aid, there to depend upon the living God alone for protection, supplies, and help of every kind. I felt that one's spiritual muscles required strengthening for such an undertaking. . . . When I get out to China . . . I shall have no claim on anyone for anything. My only claim will be on God. How important to learn, before leaving England, to move man through prayer alone.[19]

Taylor's astonishing ministry in China, the founding and growth of the China Inland Mission by faith alone, apart from human stratagems, was a trailblazing moment in the history of missions, and the beginning of the "faith missions" movement. It was by faith alone that Taylor recruited an army of laborers and a river of funds for the movement. On whom was Taylor relying? For his whole life, for both the internal journey of sanctification and the external journey of Kingdom advance, he was relying on Christ alone.

So also an anecdote from Charles Spurgeon's life serves to illustrate this point. His preaching ministry was the sensation of England, and week after week, people were coming from great distances to hear him. He decided to build the Metropolitan Tabernacle to house the huge numbers who yearned to hear the word of God preached with such transforming power. As the money for the project was being raised, a wealthy benefactor approached Spurgeon privately and promised him twenty thousand pounds for the completion of the project if the funds should fail to come in by the needed time. A friend who was aware of the secret offer said to Spurgeon brightly, "Isn't it easier to trust God for the rest of the money now?" Spurgeon answer, "Not at all; it's easier to trust the twenty thousand pounds!"[20]

CHRIST CONSTANTLY SUPPLIES OUR FAITH

God gave us our faith to begin with, and only God through Christ can keep it alive. The night before Christ died, Simon Peter was full of confidence in himself and his own ability to remain faithful to Christ. Jesus warned Peter of Satan's impending attack, and taught him to trust in God and in Christ's intercessory ministry for the very survival of Peter's faith: *"Simon, Simon, Satan has asked to sift you as wheat. But I have prayed for you, Simon, that your faith may not fail. And when you have turned back, strengthen your brothers"* (Luke 22:31–32). This is the essence of Christ's ongoing intercessory ministry on our behalf: That our faith may not fail.

So Hebrews tells us that our Great High Priest Jesus constantly intercedes for us: *"Consequently, he is able to save to the uttermost those who draw near to God through him, since he always lives to make intercession for them"* (Hebrews 7:25, ESV). The verse states that by constantly interceding for us, Christ is able to save us "to the uttermost." I take this to mean that Christ's constant intercession for us is absolutely essential in order to finish our salvation. Luke 22:32 teaches us the topic of that intercession: that our faith may not fail under Satanic assault. If you believe in Jesus for even one more day, it will be because God sustained your faith through Christ.

In his magnificent allegory of the Christian life, *Pilgrim's Progress*, John Bunyan did a masterful job of portraying our ongoing reliance on Christ's ministry for the maintenance of the work of grace in our soul. Christian, the allegorical pilgrim who is making his way to the Celestial City, stops at Interpreter's house, where he is trained and prepared for his journey. Interpreter acts out little vignettes to teach many vital spiritual lessons. The "Fire Burning Against the Wall" was one of the most striking:

Then I saw in my dream that the Interpreter took Christian by the hand, and led him into a place where was a fire burning against a wall, and one standing by it, always casting much water upon it, to quench it; yet did the fire burn higher and hotter.

Then said Christian, What means this?

The Interpreter answered, This fire is the work of grace that is wrought in the heart; he that casts water upon it, to extinguish and put it out, is the Devil; but in that thou seest the fire notwithstanding burn higher and hotter, thou shalt also see the reason of that. So he had him about to the backside of the wall, where he saw a man with a vessel of oil in his hand, of which he did also continually cast, but secretly, into the fire.

Then said Christian, What means this?

The Interpreter answered, This is Christ, who continually, with the oil of his grace, maintains the work already begun in the heart: by the means of which, notwithstanding what the devil can do, the souls of his people prove gracious still. And in that thou sawest that the man stood behind the wall to maintain the fire, that is to teach thee that it is hard for the tempted to see how this work of grace is maintained in the soul.[21]

By this we can see how much we are totally dependent upon Christ for everything, even for believing in him for one more day. We will endure all of Satan's temptations and assaults, we will persevere in the faith despite the onslaught of worldly enticements, we will continue to run the race of faith despite the besetting load of indwelling sin, and we will do all of this only by the mighty power of God through Christ working in us to will and to do according to his good pleasure. Therefore, to God alone be the glory for the completion of our salvation!

SUMMARY

A spiritually mature person has a developed sense of total reliance on Christ, having learned to rely on Christ alone for all provision for the two infinite journeys. Such a person knows—to the very depth of his being—that all the resources for each step traveled must come from Christ alone. Therefore, the more we mature in Christ, the more aware we will be of this total dependence, the more violently we will reject false supports as unwelcome intrusions, and the more aware we will be of our tendency toward self-reliance. As a result, we will be prepared to display total reliance on Christ by our daily actions, such as prayer for wisdom and assistance.

CHAPTER 10

RECEPTION OF SPIRITUAL GUIDANCE

RECENTLY I RECEIVED A VERY useful gift from a friend: a navigation system for my car. It has a global positioning sensor (GPS) which uses communication with triangulating satellites to tell it where it is on the surface of the earth. It also has an extensive database of every highway, boulevard, avenue, street, road, way, lane, bypass, etc., in the country. Finally, it has software that enables it constantly to evaluate the best directions for getting from where I am to where I want to be.

God has set before us two infinite journeys: the internal journey of sanctification and the external journey of worldwide disciple-making. Both journeys have the same destination: total conformity to Christ for God's elect. But what guidance system has God given us to make these journeys? We know that Christ **is** the journey: *"I am the way, and the truth and the life. No one comes to the Father except through me"* (John 14:6). But what of the details, and the left and right turns along the way?

GUIDANCE IN THE INTERNAL JOURNEY

In addition to the map display screen, that I can look at if I choose to, the GPS navigation system actually has the capability to speak to me as I drive, telling me in a metallic female computer voice, "Sharp right turn onto Route 98 in one minute." Isaiah prophesied a day when the highway of holiness would be established in our hearts and the navigation system would be activated to guide us along it: *"And a highway will be there; it will be called the Way of Holiness. The unclean will not journey on it; it will be for those who walk in that Way; wicked fools will not go about on it"* (Isaiah 35:8). *"Whether you turn to the right or to the left, your ears will hear a voice behind you, saying, 'This is the way; walk in it'"* (Isaiah 30:21). Jesus is revealing in John 14:6 that he is the "Way of Holiness." The gift of the indwelling Holy Spirit is our navigation system, for Romans 8:13–14 teaches us that those who are led by the Spirit to put sin to death are the children of God. Moment by moment, the Spirit speaks to the heart of a child of God, saying "This is the way, walk in it."

Faith is the means by which we receive the guidance of the Spirit through the twists and turns of life in the physical world, so that we continue to make progress on both journeys. There is a delightful promise of intimacy with Christ that any true Christian can recognize and identify—the ability of Christ, the Good Shepherd, to speak to his sheep in a way they will understand: *"My sheep listen to my voice; I know them, and they follow me"* (John 10:27). I believe that this intimate relationship is secured for us by the power of the indwelling Holy Spirit. He is, in fact, the "Spirit of Christ" speaking in us (Romans 8:9). By this, we can know that we are Christians, as we hear and obey the Good Shepherd's voice.

This kind of guidance was both demonstrated and promised in the Old Testament. It was clearly displayed in the pillar of cloud and of fire that led Israel through the wilderness, the visible manifestation God's guidance. David felt God's guidance personally, as reflected in Psalm 23: *"The Lord is my shepherd, I shall not be in want. He makes me lie down in green pastures, **he leads me** beside quiet waters, he restores my soul. **He guides me** in paths of righteousness for his name's sake"* (Psalm 23:1–3).

In the internal journey, it is especially in "paths of righteousness" that the Lord leads us, warning us from temptations, protecting us from evil, guiding us to spiritual mentors or churches or good books that will help us grow in grace and in the knowledge of Christ. The world is full of pitfalls, traps, and snares that Satan would lay for us. Yet as Paul says, *"we are not unaware of his schemes"* (2 Corinthians 2:11). How are we so aware of the devil's schemes? The Lord warns us and guides us safely through them, showing us the "way of escape" that he has sovereignly guaranteed will always be available for us: *"No temptation has overtaken you that is not common to man. God is faithful, and he will not let you be tempted beyond your ability, but with the temptation he will also provide the **way of escape**, that you may be able to endure it"* (1 Corinthians 10:13, ESV).

GUIDANCE IN THE EXTERNAL JOURNEY

In the external journey of Kingdom advance, God guides us by giving us insight into the best, most fruitful paths of service for his glory. David again sets us a good example for this as well. David's seeking of guidance from the Lord for specific direction in his life was a powerful evidence that David was "a man after God's own heart" (1 Samuel 13:14), in direct contrast to King Saul, who preceded him. Saul did what was right in his own eyes, and did not inquire of the Lord for guidance. On the rare occasion when he did ask, the Lord would not answer him (1 Samuel 14:36). In fact, the dark epitaph of Saul's wicked reign was written starkly: *"Saul died because he was unfaithful to the Lord; he did not keep the word of the Lord and even consulted a medium for guidance, and **did not inquire of the Lord**. So the Lord put him to death and turned the kingdom over to David son of Jesse"* (1 Chronicles 10:13–14).

But David inquired daily of the Lord, even asking specific guidance for his movements, and God answered him clearly. God told him to attack the Philistines who were raiding the threshing floors at Keilah (1 Samuel 23:1–5), and to pursue an Amalekite raiding party who had kidnapped his family (1 Samuel 30:8). There is clear indication that David made such inquiries frequently, and that God gave him constant guidance (1 Samuel 22:15). One of the most remarkable of these occasions was the time that God even gave David specific battle instructions, telling him to circle around behind the Philistines in the Valley of Rephaim (2 Samuel 5:22–25).

So also in the New Testament, the Lord gives specific strategic guidance to his servants again and again in the book of Acts, for the purpose of the external journey of worldwide gospel advance. For example, in Acts 8, Philip is guided to a certain desert road by an angel of the Lord, and then to a specific chariot there by the indwelling Spirit, resulting in a prime witnessing opportunity with the Ethiopian eunuch (Acts 8:26–29). This same guidance completely enveloped the life and ministry of Paul from the moment of his conversion until the end of his life. The Lord gave Ananias detailed directions to go to the house of Judas on Straight Street, and to baptize Saul of Tarsus (Acts 9:11). By then, the Lord was already telling Saul (Paul) step by step how he was to minister in order to advance the gospel. He would give him that kind of guidance for the rest of his life. The Holy Spirit clearly guided the church at Antioch to set apart Paul and Barnabas, and to send them on their first missionary journey (Acts 13:2–4). On Paul's next journey, the Spirit led Paul and Silas forcefully west toward Europe rather than east toward Asia:

> Paul and his companions traveled throughout the region of Phrygia and Galatia, having been kept by the Holy Spirit from preaching the word in the province of Asia. When they came to the border of Mysia, they tried to enter Bithynia, but the Spirit of Jesus would not allow them to. So they passed by Mysia and went down to Troas. During the night Paul had a vision of a man of Macedonia standing and begging him, "Come over to Macedonia and help us." After Paul had seen the vision, we got ready at once to

leave for Macedonia, concluding that God had called us to preach the gospel to them. (Acts 16:6–10)

In some cases, Christ gave his guidance merely to encourage Paul and to keep him going in the ministry. It is easy to think of Paul as some kind of ministry robot, a machine perfectly programmed to do the will of Christ and to suffer anything cheerfully. But Paul hurt like any of us, wrestled with fears, had to overcome discouragement, and struggled to keep going in the face of Satanic opposition. Like anyone else, he needed encouragement in order to keep going and not give up. The Lord did this a number of times for Paul.

- [In Corinth] One night the Lord spoke to Paul in a vision: "Do not be afraid; keep on speaking, do not be silent. For I am with you, and no one is going to attack and harm you, because I have many people in this city." So Paul stayed for a year and a half, teaching them the word of God. (Acts 18:9–11)

- [During Paul's trial in Jerusalem] The following night the Lord stood near Paul and said, "Take courage! As you have testified about me in Jerusalem, so you must also testify in Rome." (Acts 23:11)

- [Paul speaking to shipmates during the storm] Last night an angel of the God whose I am and whom I serve stood beside me and said, "Do not be afraid, Paul. You must stand trial before Caesar; and God has graciously given you the lives of all who sail with you." So keep up your courage, men, for I have faith in God that it will happen just as he told me. (Acts 27:23–25)

- [During Paul's trial in Rome before Caesar] At my first defense, no one came to my support, but everyone deserted me. May it not be held against them. But the Lord stood at my side and gave me strength, so that through me the message might be fully proclaimed and all the Gentiles might hear it. And I was delivered from the lion's mouth. (2 Timothy 4:16–17)

COMMON FORMS OF GUIDANCE

Such dramatic communications from the Lord to his servants— by means of supernatural visions, dreams, angelic visitations and the like—are clearly not the norm (nor were they for the Apostles). More commonly, the Lord speaks to us as he did to Elijah in the cave on Horeb, in a "still, small voice" (1 Kings 19:12, KJV). These quiet impressions from the Lord may have to do with personal spiritual growth (internal journey) or missionary strategy (external journey), or other vital details of our spiritual health and fruitfulness. Such impressions must be tested by the Word of God, for no private impression can ever take priority over Scripture. Furthermore, it is good to test them by the elders of the local church and by the Body of Christ in general. But to reject them altogether is dangerous.

James even strongly urges us that a lively faith will seek wisdom and guidance from the Lord:

> If any of you lacks wisdom, he should ask God, who gives generously to all without finding fault, and it will be given to him. But when he asks, he must believe and not doubt, because he who doubts is like a wave of the sea, blown and tossed by the wind. That man should not think he will receive anything from the Lord; he is a double-minded man, unstable in all he does. (James 1:5–8)

This is God's usual way of giving guidance to his children: by the Spirit, by prayer, by the Scripture, or in a still, small voice.

A BURDEN FROM THE LORD

Throughout the history of the church, the Lord's choicest servants have been able to gain vital guidance from the Lord in prayer. By this means, they received a burden or calling for a specific work that then governed the whole direction of their lives. For the apostle Paul, it was clear: *"I consider my life worth nothing to me, if only I may finish the race and complete the task the Lord Jesus has given me—the task of testifying to the gospel of God's grace"* (Acts 20:24). Other messages of guidance clarified Paul's "race": *"I am the apostle to the Gentiles"* (Romans 11:13); *"It has always been my ambition to preach the gospel where Christ was not known, so that I would not be building on someone else's foundation"* (Romans 15:20). These insights formed the direction of Paul's life; they were his calling.

Others have had similar callings and burdens: Martin Luther for the reformation of the church; John Calvin for the systematic teaching of the Bible; William Tyndale for the translation of the Bible into English; George Whitefield for open-air field preaching of the new birth (preaching that became a pattern for all mass evangelism to follow); William Carey for the "heathen" of Asia; William Wilberforce for the abolition of slavery; Hudson Taylor for the vast unreached millions of the inland regions of China. These burdens were communicated directly to their souls and became a powerful calling on their whole lives. In church life today, a young man may feel a calling to become a pastor: *"Here is a trustworthy saying: If anyone sets his heart on being an overseer, he desires a noble task"* (1 Timothy 3:1). Others may feel a calling to the mission field, even to a specific region or people group. This sense is a strong form of guidance from the Lord, and every Christian should seek the Lord for it.

SPIRITUAL GIFTS SUITABLE FOR THE CALLING

Along with a life calling, God gives spiritual gifts suitable for the task. It is by paths of service that are manifestly blessed, by the encouragement of the Body of Christ, as well as by the internal testimony of the Spirit, that individual Christians are able to discern and develop God's special gifting for them for his service.

The doctrine of spiritual gifts is laid out in greatest detail in 1 Corinthians 12–14, as well as in Ephesians 4 and Romans 12. But it is in Romans 12:1–8 especially that Paul tells us how we are to discern what our own gifts are, and it is by specific guidance we receive through faith. According to this passage, a Christian must first totally consecrate himself, body and soul, to the service of God (v. 1), then be transformed by the renewing of their mind (v. 2), and then test and approve God's will for their lives (v. 3). This is done by thinking about yourself soberly by faith (v. 4), understanding the various possible patterns for service in the Lord's body (vv. 4–8), and using the gifts he has blessed you with to serve the body (vv. 6–8). Only by the particular guidance of the Lord in daily life, having been trained by the Scripture and affirmed by the church, can individual Christians identify their spiritual gifts and the patterns of life service best suited for them.

PROVIDENTIAL SIGNS FOR ENCOURAGEMENT

God controls all events of heaven and earth. Sometimes he gives providential occurrences that greatly confirm his leading. While it is wrong to seek these as a prerequisite for obeying Christ, yet it is also wrong to deny that the Lord gives them occasionally as an encouragement to his servants who are boldly taking chances for his glory.

My first mission trip occurred in the summer of 1986, when a group of college and seminary students went to Kenya to minister with local pastors and missionaries there. As a good number of people from our small Baptist church were committed to going, I knew about the trip but had never remotely considered going myself, since I would have had to quit my job to do it. It was a ten-week trip, and I was working full time as an engineer, having graduated from M.I.T. two years previously.

However, God used a young woman named Kim to challenge me concerning the trip. The conversation went something like this:

Kim: "A lot of us are going on a mission trip to Kenya this summer."

Andy: "I know. I'll be praying for you."

Kim: "Have you thought about going yourself?"

Andy (laughing): "No . . . I'd have to quit my job!"

Kim: "Have you prayed about it?"

Andy: "No."

Kim: "Well, you shouldn't act like you know without asking him. It's not your life, you know!"

Kim's boldness shocked me, and I agreed to pray about it (still never intending to go.) As a matter of fact, I forgot about my promise to pray about it until the next week. I was having my quiet time, and the Lord brought the whole issue to my memory. I went through the formality of asking, "Lord, do you want me to quit my job, and go on a ten-week mission trip to Kenya?" Never in all my life did I have such a clear sense of guidance from the Lord as at that moment. "Absolutely!" was the answer I sensed from my loving Savior. "Then what should I do when I get back?" "Enroll in seminary full time and earn your master of divinity degree." I obeyed that calling from the Lord, and my life has never been the same.

Soon after that, I confronted the issue of financial support for the trip. I was not eager to ask people for the money I would need, so I decided simply to pay for the trip out of my savings. But a trusted Christian friend advised me that raising support would be good for my faith: a good testing ground for my calling to go on the trip. He couldn't have been more right. So I decided to give to others my money that I would have spent on the trip, and to raise my own needs through prayer, and by contacting churches and individuals. I contacted my former church, Grace Chapel in Lexington, and asked for funds. They were very interested in the trip, and said they would get back to me. In the meantime, I gave away my own money anonymously, through cashier's checks. One person was having a particularly difficult time raising money, so I prayed about an amount to give him: a much larger amount than usual. In prayer, I felt the Lord urging me to give not only a large amount, but an odd amount. I don't recall what it was, but it was not divisible by ten or five as such checks usually are. After putting the cashier's check directly in his mailbox, I went home. The next day I received a check from Grace Chapel for the exact amount I'd just put in my friend's mailbox! It was an astonishing moment for me, since that odd amount was a secret, known only to me. Well, known only to me and to the Lord!

Curious about why Grace Chapel had designated that odd amount for my support, I contacted the minister of missions with whom I'd been communicating. He laughed, and said it came from an assessment of my needs, the number of other students they were supporting, and the amount of money they had available. The amount of their check to me was simply the random result of this arithmetic. I think it was heavenly arithmetic, for it served as a direct confirmation to me that I'd chosen the right path for my life (quitting my engineering job) and the right way of going about it (trusting God in prayer to meet my needs). I sank to my knees in worship; it was one of the holiest moments of my life.

DIRECT GUIDANCE FROM THE SCRIPTURE

For all of this discussion of spiritual impressions, however, first place must be given to the most significant form of direct, spiritual guidance the Lord gives to his people: by means of the Spirit's illumination, and the application of Scripture directly to our hearts. This is the greatest, clearest, most certain, and most common form of communication from the mind of God to the minds of his servants. Perhaps no passage speaks as clearly to this kind of "speaking" that the Lord does as Hebrews 3:7-8: "*So, as the Holy Spirit says: 'Today, if you hear his voice, do not harden your hearts'*" (Hebrews 3:7-8). This passage is so vital in our daily experience of guidance from the Lord that it bears careful consideration.

In Hebrews 3:7–4:11, the author does an extended meditation on Psalm 95, applying it to the dire situation in which these Jewish people who had made a profession of faith in Christ now found themselves, as they were tempted to turn away from Christ. Psalm 95 itself is a meditation by King David on the failure of the Jews to believe God and to trust him enough to enter the Promised Land.

The author to the Hebrews focuses on David's psalm, written almost one thousand years before, which itself meditated on the failure of their ancestors four or five centuries before that. The main lesson David gleaned from his meditation was, *"Today, if you hear his voice, do not harden your heart."* The author to the Hebrews highlights every aspect of this statement in his extended meditation in Hebrews 3:7–4:11, but he especially develops a theology of *Today*. *Today* in Paul's text means "right now"; "the time in which you are currently living, deciding, and acting." *Today* is the only time in which we can possibly serve God, obey God, love God, follow God. We can learn from yesterday and we can prepare for tomorrow. But we cannot obey God yesterday or tomorrow. *Today* is all we have, and it is all we will ever have in this world. The tapestry of our lives will be woven with one strand after another from the spool called *Today*; so what we do with today is everything.

And the center of our life is hearing God speak to us *today*. As the Jews learned in the desert that *"Man does not live on bread alone, but on every word that comes from the mouth of God"* (Deuteronomy 8:3), so also the author to the Hebrews wanted these Jewish followers of Jesus to learn to live moment by moment on the word of God. It was precisely for this reason that he ended his extended meditation on Psalm 95 with these words: *"For the word of God is living and active. Sharper than any double-edged sword, it penetrates even to dividing soul and spirit, joints and marrow; it judges the thoughts and attitudes of the heart"* (Hebrews 4:12).

Note carefully, therefore, how the author introduces his meditation on Psalm 95: *"so, as the Holy Spirit says, 'Today, if you hear his voice*'" (Hebrews 3:7). Notice that King David is not mentioned here at all, though he is definitely mentioned in Hebrews 4 as the author of Psalm 95. But here, David's authorship is not the issue. What matters is that it is the **Holy Spirit** who speaks Psalm 95 to us *today*. And note carefully the tense of the verb: "*as the Holy Spirit says*." Not *said*, but *says*. This is essential to the very next clause, "*Today, if you hear his voice*." It is not David's voice, but the voice of the Holy Spirit that we must hear. And according to Hebrews 3:7, God speaks to us by the Holy Spirit via the means of texts of Scripture.

So, if you want to hear God speak to you today, sit down and read the Bible, doing so in total reliance on the Holy Spirit. This makes the accumulation of the spiritual knowledge we spoke of in the Knowledge section a living, breathing communication from the eternal God. The words are no longer dead black marks on a white page. Rather, it is the "living and active" word of God (Hebrews 4:12), it is Christ speaking to his sheep, it is the Holy Spirit guiding us in the two infinite journeys, it is "everything we need for life and godliness" (2 Peter 1:3).

So the key issue of faith is this: as believers in our Lord Jesus Christ, we have bowed our stiff necks and have taken his kingly yoke on us (Matthew 11:28–30); therefore these are not idle words for us, they are our life (Deuteronomy 32:47), and we must obey them completely. Therefore the message of Psalm 95 and Hebrews 3:7–4:11 is clear: "*Today, if you hear his voice, **do not harden your hearts**.*" Obey what he says! Cherish the fact that he speaks to you! Show you cherish it by doing whatever he commands!

OBEDIENCE PROMOTES UNDERSTANDING

The more faithfully we obey his voice in Scripture, the more clearly we will hear him speak to us in the future. "I obey, therefore I understand" is a key link in the Knowledge-Faith-Character-Action quartet that makes it an upward cycle to maturity:

"I have more understanding than the elders, for I obey your precepts"
(Psalm 119:100). A powerful spiritual encounter with the living God
is awaiting all true believers every time they open the Scripture.
Thus do we pray, *"Open my eyes that I may see wonderful things in
your law"* (Psalm 119:18), and even more, *"Incline my heart to your testimonies"* (Psalm 119:36). The heart has an "inclination," a tendency
toward or away from something, as we will see in the Character
section of this book. The Psalmist is asking God to transform his
heart toward obedience to his commands.

The key moment of our entire Christian lives is that moment
when the Spirit speaks to our hearts by the Scripture. If we soften
our hearts, yield, obey, and follow, we will grow. If we harden our
hearts, resist, rebel, and turn away, we will stop growing. Nothing
could be more vital than to hear Jesus, our Good Shepherd, speak
to us, his sheep; to recognize his voice in the pages of the Holy
Bible; and to get up and follow him.

A critical Scripture on this form of guidance is John 14:21.
There, Jesus says: *"Whoever has my commands and obeys them, he is
the one who loves me. He who loves me will be loved by my Father, and
I too will love him and show myself to him."* Note the steps Jesus says
we must follow.

We must first *have* his commands. That is, we must know what
he has told us. We do this by reading and learning the Bible.

Next, we must *love* Christ.

Finally, we must *obey* his commands. (Love logically comes
before obedience, since the obedience proves the love.)

If we do these things, Christ *promises* us that we will *experience* the love of the Father and the Son, including greater self-dis-
closure by himself. Christ says, "I will show myself to him." This
means greater revelation from him, and a closer, more intimate
relationship with him. Obedience leads to relationship, and from
this relationship we will come to know him and his will better.

GOD REVEALS HIS PLANS TO THE OBEDIENT

Part of that intimacy is that Christ will show more of his mysterious plans, even on a detailed level, to a very obedient servant. In this way, the more obedient we are, the more detailed and fruitful will be our prayer life. We will begin praying and laboring for details of Christ's sovereign plan that others may not see. The most famous example of this from church history is the amazing account of George Mueller and the fog:

> In August of 1877, George Mueller and his wife were traveling on the steamship *Sardinian* for an important ministry appointment in the United States. Suddenly the ship ran into a dense fog bank off the coast of Newfoundland. For twenty-four hours, the captain stood on the bridge, waiting for some glimmer of opening in the fog so they could proceed. Suddenly something happened that changed his life forever: seventy-two year-old George Mueller appeared on the bridge! "Captain, I have come to tell you I must be in Quebec by Saturday afternoon." "It is impossible," replied the captain. "Very well," said Mueller, "if your ship cannot take me, God will find some other way—I have never broken an engagement for fifty-two years. Let us go down into the chart-room and pray." The captain wondered which lunatic asylum Mueller had come from. "Mr. Mueller, do you realize how dense this fog is?" "No, my eye is not on the density of the fog, but on the living God, who controls every circumstance of my life." Mueller then knelt down and prayed simply. When he had finished the captain was about to pray, but Mueller put his hand on his shoulder, and told him not to: "First, you do not believe he will; and second, I believe he has, and there is no need whatever for you to pray about it!" The captain looked at Mueller in amazement. "Captain," he continued, "I have known my Lord for fifty-two years, and there has never

been a single day that I have failed to get an audience with the King. Get up, captain, and open the door. You will find that the fog is gone." The captain walked across to the door and opened it. The fog had lifted.[22]

Jesus was "showing himself" to George Mueller in ways he doesn't to other, less faithful servants. The greater our obedience, the more of himself and his plans Christ will show. Christ intended to move the fog; he told Mueller of it in that prayer time, so that Mueller's joy and confidence in prayer would increase. Faith doesn't create the blessing, it merely receives it—just as the eye doesn't create the splendor of a lush, green mountain valley, it merely receives it.

Thus we see that an ever-maturing faith will produce a greater and greater sense of what the Father is doing, so that we can be fruitfully involved in it. In this way, our prayer lives and patterns of service will be maximally fruitful. Jesus put it this way: *"I no longer call you servants, because a servant does not know his master's business. Instead, I have called you friends, for everything that I learned from my Father I have made known to you. You did not choose me, but I chose you and appointed you to go and bear fruit—fruit that will last. Then the Father will give you whatever you ask in my name"* (John 15:15–16). Having said this, however, we must still leave the final answer for all our prayers to God. He alone knows the best outcome for all the complex human circumstances we may pray about in life.

THE SPIRIT LEADS US INTO BATTLE

The most significant form of guidance in the two journeys is the Holy Spirit's leadership into battle. In the internal journey, the Holy Spirit leads us into battle within our own souls, to vicious struggle with indwelling sin. If we are not following his lead into that battle, we are not children of God: *"For if you live according to the sinful nature, you will die; but if by the Spirit you put to death the misdeeds of the body, you will live, because those who are **led by** the Spirit* *of God are sons of God"* (Romans 8:13–14). In the external journey, the Holy Spirit leads us into battle in Satan's dark world, to rescue the perishing through the advancement of the Gospel of Jesus Christ. If we are not following his lead into that battle, we are scattering while he is gathering: *"He who is not with me is against me, and he who does not gather with me scatters"* (Matthew 12:30).

Be not deceived! These two infinite journeys are the issue of our lives. And to these twin journeys Christ leads us through the Spirit and through the Scripture every single day. Day after day, then, we are to sit at Christ's feet in our daily quiet times and get our instructions: the day's marching orders. Our orders must have something to do with the warfare of the internal and external journeys, or we are not hearing him properly: *"So, as the Holy Spirit says: "Today, if you hear his voice, do not harden your hearts"* (Hebrews 3:7–8).

SUMMARY

A spiritually mature man or woman receives consistent guidance from Christ through the Holy Spirit. The Good Shepherd speaks, and his sheep hear his voice clearly. Through consistent patterns of costly obedience, spiritually mature servants of Christ are increasingly able to recognize Christ's guidance. They actively seek it in prayer and he gives it to them, following his lead in both the internal journey of sanctification and the external journey of worldwide Kingdom advance. They are clearly instructed and warned about sin, are strongly aware of Satan's immediate schemes, and take the evasive action Christ opens up for them. They put themselves in the path of wisdom, and follow his lead to go to this church or that service or read such and such a book for maximum spiritual growth. They also seek for and receive guidance concerning ministry and service for Christ, both on a grand scale (an overall life calling, and the spiritual gifts needed for that calling) and on a detailed scale (to go to this city rather than that one, or speak to this person on the airplane about Christ, or invest in publishing equipment to print Bibles and tracts, etc.). They receive specific encouragement from the Lord to keep going in ministry. Finally, they receive daily guidance and encouragement from the Lord, primarily through the Spirit's illumination and application of Scripture to their eager and willing hearts.

CHARACTER

A PATHWAY TO CHRISTIAN MATURITY

KNOWLEDGE
FACTUAL AND EXPERIENTIAL
SPIRITUAL INFORMATION

FACTUAL
Gained from the Scripture

EXPERIENTIAL
Gained from living in God's world

FAITH
ASSURANCE OF AND COMMIT-
MENT TO SPIRITUAL TRUTH

- Certainty that specific invisible spiritual realities are true
- Assurance that hoped-for specific good thing promised in scripture will certainly come true
- Conviction that specific sin in me, and that God hates it and will judge people for such sins
- Reliance on Christ as all-sufficient savior, refuge, provider, shield
- Reception of spiritual guidance and knowledge

ACTION
EXTERNAL LIFESTYLE OF
HABITUAL OBEDIENCE

1. Presentation of Body to God
2. Personal Holiness
3. Seven-fold obedience to God's commands

   1. Worship
   2. Spiritual Disciplines
   3. Family
   4. Ministry to Believers
   5. Mission to Non-Believers
   6. Stewardship
   7. Work

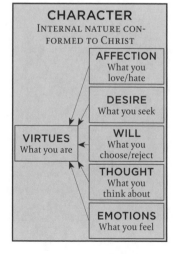

CHARACTER
INTERNAL NATURE CON-
FORMED TO CHRIST

AFFECTION
What you love/hate

DESIRE
What you seek

VIRTUES
What you are

WILL
What you choose/reject

THOUGHT
What you think about

EMOTIONS
What you feel

SECTION INTRODUCTION: CHARACTER

THE STORY IS TOLD IN Russia of a magnificent deception during the reign of Empress Catherine II, crafted by her minister Grigori Aleksandrovich Potemkin during her visit to the Crimea in 1787. Potemkin had led the military campaign in the Crimea and had been victorious, but the spoils seemed hardly worth the effort. The region was underdeveloped and would have been disappointing to the empress. According to the story, the shrewd Potemkin had hollow facades of villages erected along the Dnieper River, in order to dazzle the eyes of the Empress and her court as they drifted past on their royal barges. His purpose was to make the region look far more attractive than it really was, and so enhance his reputation in the empress' eyes.

Now whether the story is true or not is a matter of historical debate. But it serves to illustrate an important aspect of fallen human nature. We are experts at erecting facades to make ourselves appear better than we really are. Like Potemkin, we attempt to impress others by a sham, a deception, a ruse, because it is far easier to achieve the goal of the esteem of others through a hollow appearance than through the reality of genuine godliness. Of course, Potemkin's ruse, if it ever really happened, would have been a great dishonor to the empress. She would have been pathetically poor in her discernment if she couldn't have sniffed out the fake villages with only a small amount of keen observation. How much, then, do we dishonor God by thinking he will be pleased with anything less than genuine piety, with anything less than a heart truly transformed into Christlikeness?

True Christianity is a matter of the heart. The heart is the true nature of the person, the true inner self. When God sent Samuel to anoint one of the sons of Jesse as king, God did not tell him initially which son he had chosen. When the firstborn, Eliab, came and stood in front of Samuel, Samuel was truly impressed by his appearance, his outward bearing. *"But the Lord said to Samuel, 'Do not consider his appearance or his height, for I have rejected him. The Lord does not look at the things man looks at. Man looks at the outward appearance, but the Lord looks at the heart'"* (1 Samuel 16:7).

God revealed to sinful King Saul that he had sought "a man after his own heart" (1 Samuel 13:14). The Hebrew word translated "after" means "in conformity with"; that is, a man who loves what God loves and hates what he hates, who desires what he desires and will choose what God would have him choose, a man who will gladly carry out his will for Israel and not follow his own ways (as King Saul had done). That man was David, the best example in the Old Testament of a man with a heart after God.

But God's focus on heart religion was most clearly revealed in the person and teaching of his only begotten Son, Jesus Christ. In the Sermon on the Mount, Jesus said *"Blessed are the pure in heart, for they will see God"* (Matthew 5:8). Jesus then immediately used the Law of Moses to probe the depths of the human heart as no teacher ever had before. It was not enough not to murder, said Jesus; if any man is angry with his brother in his heart, he is in danger of the fire of hell. It was not enough not to commit adultery with your body, said Jesus; if any man looks at a woman lustfully, he has already committed adultery with her in his heart. It was not enough to give alms to the poor, or to pray or fast; what matters far more is your heart's motive for each of these. Such good works, said Jesus, should be done as a secret act of devotion to God, who will reward each one. We should not desire the fool's gold of human praise for pious deeds, but we should daily store up in heaven the true treasure of God's esteem and his future praise: *"for where your treasure is, there your heart will be also"* (Matthew 6:21). Thus it is clear that Jesus Christ is after the heart, the true self, the inner person. Purity of heart is the goal of true religion.

But according to Jeremiah, the heart is precisely where the problem lies: *"The heart is deceitful above all things and beyond cure. Who can understand it?"* (Jeremiah 17:9). Furthermore, Jeremiah despaired of any possibility of evil humans choosing a radical transformation by sheer willpower or by any other contrivance: *"Can the Ethiopian change his skin or the leopard its spots? Neither can you do good who are accustomed to doing evil"* (Jeremiah 13:23).

So God desires purity in the human heart, and only the pure in heart will see him. But our hearts are naturally wicked and deceitful, and we cannot make any radical change in our own hearts. This is precisely why we need Christ. The saving work of Christ is a deep work of genuine transformation of the human being. It is no Potemkin village; no sham; no show. Jesus' delight is in true godliness, worked by his own sovereign power, in the heart of a human being: *"Behold, you delight in truth in the inward being, and you teach me wisdom in the secret heart"* (Psalm 51:6, ESV). Satan masquerades as an angel of light, and his servants masquerade as servants of righteousness (2 Corinthians 11:14–15). Judas Iscariot deceived the other eleven apostles for years, concerning his genuine status before Jesus. But a true Christian is a supernatural work of God, transformed from the inside out. The promise of the New Covenant is of a radical transformation: *"I will sprinkle clean water on you, and you will be clean; I will cleanse you from all your impurities and from all your idols. I will give you a new heart and put a new spirit in you; I will remove from you your heart of stone and give you a heart of flesh. And I will put my Spirit in you and move you to follow my decrees and be careful to keep my laws"* (Ezekiel 36:25–27).

God delights in the perfection of his Son. From eternity past, the Father has been gazing into the magnificent face of his only begotten Son, and delighting in what he sees, for Christ is *"the image of the invisible God, the firstborn over all creation"* (Colossians 1:15). The love of the Father for the Son blazes brighter and hotter than all the stars in the universe combined. It is infinite. Therefore God's deepest desire in salvation is to replicate within each of us, in a mysterious and marvelous way, the image of Christ: *"For those God foreknew he also predestined to be conformed to the likeness of his Son, that he might be the firstborn among many brothers"* (Romans 8:29). The work of sanctification, therefore, is a work of radical transformation, of working in us what is pleasing to him, of creating us to be like what he has already decreed that we are: the righteousness of Christ. In justification, God declares us positionally righteous in Christ; in sanctification, God works within our character the righteousness he has already credited to our account; in glorification, God completes that work so that we will be perfectly conformed to Christ.

The purpose of this section is to describe the various aspects of character presented in the Bible that God is seeking to work within us. I desire to describe major categories of character, and to flesh them out in detail, so we can have a developed sense of what kind of people we ought to be, as we wait for the consummation of the age (2 Peter 3:11). The Apostle Paul called on the Ephesian Christians to live up to the calling which they—and we—have received (Ephesians 4:1). That calling is nothing less than perfection, flowing from perfectly transformed hearts. Though we have seen that perfection is impossible in this life, yet Christlike perfection in character and action should be the goal of every Christian, every day.

FIVE AREAS OF CHRISTIAN CHARACTER

Christian character is an internal nature conformed to Christ in five different areas, resulting in a variety of virtues.

1	Affection	What you love and what you hate
2	Desire	What you seek
3	Will	What you choose and what you reject
4	Thought	What you think
5	Emotion	What you feel

Virtues	What you are

The first five add up at any given moment to the sixth; virtues are descriptors of various states of being, of which many are listed in Scripture. Since Christ is the standard, we should think of this list of virtues in the following manner: Christian character is 1) loving what Christ loves and hating what Christ hates; 2) desiring what Christ would desire; 3) choosing what Christ would choose and rejecting what Christ would reject; 4) having the mind of Christ, so thinking his thoughts; 5) feeling what Christ would feel; 6) being what Christ is in his nature. Having listed them generally, let us now delve into them carefully and specifically.

CHAPTER 11

AFFECTION—WHAT YOU LOVE AND WHAT YOU HATE

OF ALL THE HUNDREDS OF commandments given by God, Jesus chose this one as the first and greatest: *"Love the Lord your God with all your heart and with all your soul and with all your mind"* (Matthew 22:37). According to Jesus, love is the greatest measure of a soul, and its truest indicator.

Therefore, the reason God loves Jesus so much is that Jesus so perfectly loves what God loves and so perfectly hates what God hates: *"You have loved righteousness and hated wickedness; therefore God, your God, has set you above your companions by anointing you with the oil of joy"* (Hebrews 1:9). Here God the Father speaks his eternal affection for his Son, and declares precisely why he loves him so much, and precisely why God will see to it that Christ's throne will last forever and ever: **because** Christ has *"loved righteousness and hated wickedness,"* **for this reason** God sets Jesus Christ infinitely above all other human beings.

Christlike character, then, must conform to this standard. It is a matter both of what we love and what we hate. We must not merely **be** righteous, we must **love** righteousness itself, whether in ourselves or in others, ultimately in God above all else. We must not merely avoid wickedness, we must **hate** wickedness itself, whether in ourselves or in others, in the world, in Satan and his

203

demons, wherever it may be found. Our growth in sanctification is an ever-increasing intensification of this love and this hatred.

INSIGHTS FROM EDWARDS

It was Jonathan Edwards more than anyone else who zeroed in on this dual nature of true religion. The central thesis of Edwards's *Treatise on Religious Affections* is that true religion in great part consists in holy affections. According to Edwards, affections are the sensible exercises of the soul toward anything in the universe, either in approving or disapproving of that thing. This approval or disapproval is a matter of the heart, and it varies in degree, from pure, absolute hatred, to dislike, to perfect indifference, to like, to pure, absolute love. Remarkably, Edwards asserts that the soul does all of this approving and disapproving based on its own nature, and over that nature we have no control. We cannot choose as an act of the will to love something we have hated, or vice-versa.

THE NUMBER LINE OF AFFECTION

Being somewhat mathematically inclined, personally I see Edwards's insight most clearly in terms of a number line, from negative infinity, through zero, to positive infinity. I then assign values to topics or issues on this number line of affection:

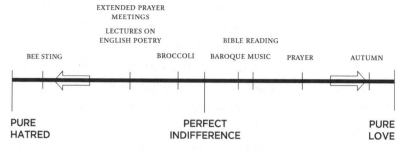

AFFECTION

If I assembled at random a focus group of one hundred people, and chose one hundred different items taken from the *Encyclopedia Britannica*, and had the focus group place all the items on the scale of affection, from negative infinity (absolute hatred) through zero (perfect indifference) to positive infinity (absolute love), it might be a challenge for them to differ between something at +100 and something at +150. But they would certainly be able to place all hundred items somewhere on the line, either on the positive or negative side; and the point would be made. Some possible items for assessment might be the Statute of Liberty, broccoli, the French Revolution, silk, bee stings, lectures on English poetry, Abraham Lincoln, marathons, AIDS, steak cooked rare, steak cooked well-done, Genghis Khan, rancid milk, autumn, baroque music, etc. The human soul has the ability to perceive each of these things, assess them, and be either attracted to or repulsed by them, either strongly or weakly. Obviously, knowledge is essential to this perceiving ability. There are many items in the *Encyclopedia Britannica* of which I and many others have absolutely no knowledge whatsoever, so they remain at zero (perfect indifference). However, the more we know about something, the clearer becomes our inclination toward—or repulsion from—that thing.

Now, what does God command us above all other things? To love him with all our heart, soul, mind, and strength. That means that God should be furthest to the right on our graph of affections. Each Christian should love God more than anything else in the universe. But do you? Do I? This is the question that stands over us every day of our lives. The essence of idolatry is to have greater affection for any created thing over the Creator. This is the sinful exchange which the human race made in Adam and has continued to make every day, right up to the present moment: *"They exchanged the truth of God for a lie, and worshiped and served created things rather than the Creator—who is forever praised. Amen"* (Romans 1:25).

MASSIVE REARRANGEMENT
AT REGENERATION

Apart from the regenerating work of the Holy Spirit, every single person on the face of the earth is an idolater. All people are created to place their ultimate affection on something; to love something; to live for something. The miracle of the New Birth is that a huge number of items of the number line of affection get instantly rearranged—things we used to love, we now hate, and things we used to hate, we now love. The work of sanctification is to continue to rearrange our affections until we love more and more what Christ loves, and hate more and more what Christ hates.

Before conversion, we loved some things that Christ saw as wicked. Perhaps a sinner might delight in pornography, in off-color humor, in drugs or alcohol, in being greedy or selfish, or in the feeling of power that comes when you put someone down in public or slander them behind their backs. Along with that delight came a whole array of idolatries: of good gifts from God that we loved too much, or indulged in to excess or unlawfully. Perhaps love of sex, food, entertainment, hobbies, travel, ease, sleep, earthly luxuries, etc. We didn't just do sin, we delighted in it, and we approved of it in others (Romans 1:32). We were among those *"who delight in doing wrong and rejoice in the perverseness of evil"* (Proverbs 2:14). Proverbs diagnoses our condition well: *"A fool finds pleasure in evil conduct"* (Proverbs 10:23). We had a positive affection for evil things, an "inclination" toward evil, in Edwards's language.

Also before conversion, the things of God were repulsive to us in varying degrees. Bible reading was boring, good preaching was offensive, Christian conversation was annoying, Christian books dull, worship repulsive. Therefore, for many non-Christians, church attendance was the farthest thing from their mind, either a complete waste of time or downright disgusting. For other non-Christians, the situation was more complicated than that. Trained and brought up to go to church, they went for impure reasons: to meet people of the opposite sex, to make business acquaintances, to feel good about themselves, to appear righteous to some human audience, etc. But the actual things of God—righteousness, justice, purity, holiness, the majesty of the person of God himself—these things were not attractive to them, perhaps even secretly repulsive.

HOSTILITY TO CHRIST TRANSFORMED TO ULTIMATE AFFECTION

At the center of this hostility to the holy things of God was enmity against Christ and his work on the cross. God wisely set up the cross as an offensive stumbling block to anyone but those in whom the grace of God has worked regeneration. The image of a dead Jewish man, bloody and grotesque, hanging from a wooden cross, naturally creates nothing but revulsion in the natural mind: *"He was despised and rejected by men, a man of sorrows, and familiar with suffering. Like one from whom men hide their faces he was despised, and we esteemed him not"* (Isaiah 53:2–3). "Despised and rejected by men": that phrase sums up our natural response to Christ crucified. He is a "stumbling block" to Jews, a "laughing stock" to Gentiles (1 Corinthians 1:23), and all people naturally turn away from such a figure. The natural mind does its work: it appraises Christ crucified, and then has a vigorous disaffection for him. We reject Christ!

But by the miracle of the Spirit's work in our hearts, what had before been repulsive suddenly becomes incredibly beautiful, alluring, and attractive. The cross of Christ is, for us who are being saved, *"the power of God and the wisdom of God"* (1 Corinthians 1:24). We might also add that the cross is the beauty and majesty and glory of God, all concentrated like pure white light, then diffracted like a prism into all of God's glorious colorful attributes. The more we, like Isaac Watts, "survey the wondrous cross on which the prince of glory died," the more of God's attributes we see there. What was at -10,000 on our number line of affection becomes an instant +10,000 or more. And that is a miracle! For no human being has the power over their own heart to cause it to love what they used to hate, and to hate what they used to love.

But God has such power, and this is precisely the light that he causes to shine in our hearts: *"For God, who said, "Let light shine out of darkness," made his light shine in our hearts to give us the light of the knowledge of the glory of God in the face of Christ"* (2 Corinthians 4:6).

Amazingly, Jesus knew that it would be the ugly depiction of his death that would in the end be attractive to his sheep: *"But I, when I am lifted up from the earth, will draw all men to myself"* (John 12:32). The word "draw" there is the same word Christ used in John 6:44 to speak of the Father's secret work in the hearts of his elect: *"No one can come to me unless the Father who sent me **draws** him; and I will raise him up at the last day."* This is a positive attraction within the hearts of the elect, made possible only by the massive and miraculous rearrangement that happens in their hearts at regeneration; what was repulsive has now become infinitely attractive, and we are effectively drawn to Christ by his death.

NEW CREATION MEANS NEW AFFECTIONS

With this central rearrangement of Christ going from repulsive to attractive comes a correspondingly massive rearrangement across the board. It is moving day, and the moving never stops: *"Therefore, if any man is in Christ, he is a new creature; the old things passed away; behold, new things have come"* (2 Corinthians 5:17). Everything begins to look new. There is a sudden internal desire to please Christ, to be like Christ. Almost immediately, like newborn babies we crave the pure milk of the word, so that by it we may grow up in our salvation, now that we have tasted that the Lord is good (1 Peter 2:2). Where did that craving come from? From the work of the Spirit in our newly made hearts! We now **want** the Word of God, yearn for it, delight in it. We begin to hear our Good Shepherd's voice in the preaching and reading of the word, and we love it.

A whole new set of loves begins to take root: prayer, Christian fellowship, Spirit-led worship, good deeds done to others, etc. We have instantly acquired a strong taste for things we used to hate. And the more we grow, the more these tastes will develop, and new avenues will be opened up in our hearts. I began to delight in church history because these heroes of the faith were my brothers and sisters in Christ, and because by faith they accomplished incredible things for the glory of God. It made me want to be like them. I loved missionary biographies, martyrs' stories, accounts of the Reformation, and of revivals blessed by God. I began to delight in the feeling I got when meeting Christians from other races or ethnic backgrounds, and discovering that they were truly brothers and sisters with whom I had immense affinity, because of our common faith in Christ.

SANCTIFICATION: LOVING THE LIGHT MORE AND MORE

As we develop in Christian maturity, we see the Spirit prod these loves, developing them more and more. The level of love we have at the moment of conversion was just meant to be the starting point: *"Now about brotherly love we do not need to write to you, for you yourselves have been taught by God to love each other. And in fact, you do love all the brothers throughout Macedonia. Yet we urge you, brothers, to do so **more and more**"* (1 Thessalonians 4:9–10); *"And this is my prayer: that your love may abound **more and more** in knowledge and depth of insight"* (Philippians 1:9); *"We ought always to thank God for you, brothers, and rightly so, because your faith is growing **more and more**, and the love every one of you has for each other is **increasing**"* (2 Thessalonians 1:3). God, through the Spirit, is pushing these loves to become more and more developed, more and more intense.

Unfortunately, the flesh constantly opposes this movement, and Satan and the world conspire with the flesh to dampen our love for Christ and the things of God. Sadly, some Christians can turn away from their initial love, the early motions of their passion for Christ: *"I remember the devotion of your youth, how as a bride you loved me and followed me through the desert, through a land not sown"* (Jeremiah 2:2); *"Yet I hold this against you: You have forsaken your first love"* (Revelation 2:4). It is against this dampening action of sin, the dowsing of our love for Christ, that the Spirit must constantly battle all the years of our sanctification.

A WHOLE SERIES OF NEW LOVES

The positive work of sanctification, then, is to love what Christ loves, and more and more intensely as time goes on. What are these things? Ephesians 5:12 says we should *"find out what pleases the Lord."* The Bible is the best library for that research, for in it, again and again, God tells us what he loves. A true Christian loves these things as well:

- Above all, loving God himself, above any created thing (Matthew 22:37)
- Cherishing Christ, his only begotten Son, in whom God delights (Matthew 3:17; 12:18)
- Loving all human beings, created in the image of God (Matthew 22:39)
- Especially loving other Christians, brothers and sisters in Christ (Psalm 16:3, 1 John 3:14)
- Loving the poor and needy (Psalm 146:7–9)
- Delighting in God's creation, the world he made for the display of his glory ((Psalm 104:31)
- Loving God's promises, plans, will, and purposes (Psalm 40:8, 119:140)
- Loving our own weaknesses and trials, as they keep us humble (2 Corinthians 12:10), as well as suffering and adversity (James 1:2–4)
- And many others besides . . .

Our God is a delighted and delightful being. He is not merely loving, he is Love itself (1 John 4:8, 16). His love cannot be measured, and it is a matter of Christian growth to gain an ever-increasing sense of what he loves and how much he loves it, and then to be filled to overflowing with his love (Ephesians 3:18–19). This is the core of true Christian character: love.

A WHOLE SERIES OF NEW HATREDS AS WELL

However, the transformation of our hearts is not merely positive: loving what Christ loves. We are also instantly transformed and equipped to hate what Christ hates: *"Let those who love the Lord hate evil"* (Psalm 97:10). I cannot both love the Lord and embrace the virus that has spread destruction throughout his beautiful universe: *"To fear the Lord is to hate evil"* (Proverbs 8:13); *"Love must be sincere. **Hate what is evil**; cling to what is good"* (Romans 12:9). For our love to be sincere, we must hate what God hates.

God is a passionate being, and God's emotions are perfect. Hell is a measure of God's passionate hatred of sin. So also is the world-wide flood of Noah and the outpouring of fire and brimstone on Sodom and Gomorrah. So also, and above all else, is the display of his wrath poured out on his own Son on the cross. For this reason, Paul responds so passionately to the question, "Shall we go on sinning that grace may increase?" His answer is a resounding, *"May it never be!"* Or *"By no means!"* Or *"God forbid!"* (Romans 6:1–2) A mild reaction to sin is as inconceivable as a mild reaction on the part of a husband to some criminal who is attacking his wife.

When Christ saw the money-changers and corrupt religionists making huge profits from the sacrificial system in the temple, he sat down and patiently wove together a whip from cords. Then he poured out his wrath on those sinners, overturning their tables, driving away their animals, and shouting "How dare you turn my Father's house into a marketplace, a den of thieves?!" A healthy

Christian, developing in sanctification, will have an increasingly passionate reaction to evil.

So that we may know and imitate his heart, God frequently lists specific sins that he hates. These include:

- idolatrous worship (Deuteronomy 12:31, 16:22),
- hypocritical worship (Amos 5:21, Isaiah 1:13–14),
- haughty eyes, a lying tongue, hands that shed innocent blood, a heart that devises wicked schemes, feet that are quick to rush into evil, a false witness who pours out lies, and a man who stirs up dissension among brothers (Proverbs 6:16–19),
- pride and arrogance (Proverbs 8:13),
- robbery and iniquity (Isaiah 61:8),
- the evil world system (James 4:4).

God expects his people not only to hate these sins but to fight against them, to expose them, and to purify the church from them. If his people tolerate sin, Christ will judge them (Revelation 2:20). America is a country which increasingly prides itself on being open-minded and tolerant, and in a pluralist and free society such as ours, Christians must tolerate some degree of wickedness in public society (such as false religions, for example). But the problem comes when God's own people do not recognize evil for what it is, and do not have the same passionate reaction to it that God does.

SUMMARY

In summary, the core of Christian character is LOVE: love of what Christ loves, and hatred of what Christ hates. At regeneration, every Christian receives a massive transformation of the heart such that many things they used to love, they now hate, and many things they used to hate, they now love; all things have been reassessed in the light of the knowledge of the glory of God in the face of Christ. A spiritually mature man or woman sees that the intensification and development of their affections are being increasingly conformed to Christ's.

CHAPTER 12

DESIRE—WHAT YOU SEEK

THE CHRISTIAN LIFE ON THIS earth is a life of deep longing, since so many of the promises of God are as yet unfulfilled. Paul says *"if we hope for what we do not yet have, we wait for it patiently"* (Romans 8:25). Yes, a Christian waits patiently. But a Christian also waits with intense longing, with deep desire. A strong desire for God and for his gifts characterizes a spiritually mature heart.

OUR DESIRES PATTERNED AFTER GOD'S

In this life of desire, we display the image of God, for our God also longs and desires as well. God's perfect plan, formed by his infinite wisdom before the creation of the world, sets the course for his desires. His omnipotent right hand moves in space and time to achieve all that his heart desires. He will continue to desire and to achieve those desires until the end of time. For example, David reveals that God desires our integrity, our godly character, which is the focus of this chapter: *"Surely **you desire** truth in the inner parts; you teach me wisdom in the inmost place"* (Psalm 51:6). Job noted that God's desires govern his actions: *"But he is unchangeable, and who can turn him back? What he **desires**, that he does"* (Job 23:13, ESV). In Psalm 132, God very clearly reveals his own desires, using a word that reflects passion:

> For the Lord has chosen Zion, he has **desired** it for his dwelling: "This is my resting place forever and ever; here I will sit enthroned, for I have **desired** it—I will bless her

with abundant provisions; her poor will I satisfy with food. I will clothe her priests with salvation, and her saints will ever sing for joy. Here I will make a horn grow for David and set up a lamp for my anointed one. I will clothe his enemies with shame, but the crown on his head will be resplendent." (Psalm 132:13–18)

This Psalm reflects the yearning that God has to save his people and to settle them in the New Heaven and New Earth, with the throne of his Anointed One (Christ) in their midst. This is the central longing of his soul: the glory of his Son in the final salvation of his people.

Christ told us that the Father seeks true spiritual worshipers, and that this seeking is the center of what he is doing in the world: *"Yet a time is coming and has now come when the true worshipers will worship the Father in spirit and truth, for they are the kind of worshipers **the Father seeks**. God is spirit, and his worshipers must worship in spirit and in truth"* (John 4:23–24). This passionate longing of God for people who will worship him in spirit and in truth drives his sovereign plan, and thus all history.

CHRIST ALSO DESIRES AND SEEKS

Since Christ is the perfect image of his Father, and he is the One whom the Father sent to accomplish his desire, it is not at all surprising that Christ himself spoke of his own seeking and his own longings. The central desire of Christ's life was to do the will of God: *"I desire to do your will, O my God; your law is within my heart"* (Psalm 40:7–8; see Hebrews 10:5). The burning mission of his life was also one of desire: to seek wandering sinners, and to delight when they repented and came home. After Zacchaeus's marvelous conversion, Jesus summed up his entire life work in terms of desire: *"The Son of Man came to seek and to save what was lost"* (Luke 19:10).

So also, the night before Jesus was crucified, as he sat down with his beloved disciples to partake of the Passover meal, he expressed his desire to eat with them, not only on earth but also in heaven: *"I have eagerly desired to eat this Passover with you before I suffer. For I tell you, I will not eat it again until it finds fulfillment in the kingdom of God"* (Luke 22:15–16).

To be conformed to Christ means to live a life of passionate desire—above all, desiring to do the will of God and to seek the lost, so we may dwell with them and Christ in heaven forever.

DESIRE DESCRIBES THE SOUL

The desires of the heart are an excellent indicator of the condition of the soul, and holy desires mark the nature of the converted soul. No one made this clearer than Henry Scougal in his timeless classic, *The Life of God in the Soul of Man*. This one book changed George Whitefield's life and has been used mightily in the hearts of many others. Scougal's profound statement is this: "The worth and excellency of a soul is to be measured by the object of its desires." If we desire worthless things, it shows something about the excellence of our souls. Conversely, if the object of our desire is something great, noble, and virtuous, that also speaks of the excellence of our souls.

Along these same lines, John Piper writes:

> The heart is a desire factory. The human heart produces desires as fire produces heat. As surely as sparks fly upward, the heart pumps out desire after desire for a happier future. The condition of the heart is appraised by the kinds of desires that hold sway. Or, to put it another way, the state of the heart is shown by the things that satisfy its desires. If it is satisfied with mean and ugly things, it is a mean and ugly heart. If it is satisfied with God, it is a godly heart.[23]

So the question before us now is simply this: what do you want?

THE CONSTANT BATTLE WITH EVIL DESIRES

Before conversion, our hearts were set on unholy desires. We longed for earthly pleasures and success, for the praise of people and the satisfaction of the flesh. We lived our daily lives *"gratifying the cravings of our sinful nature and following its desires and thoughts"* (Ephesians 2:3). The desires for evil things are frequently called lusts, and a brief list of three lusts sums up Satan's daily menu of temptation with which he ensnares the world: *"the lust of the eyes, the lust of the flesh, and the boastful pride of life"* (1 John 2:16). These three simple yearnings have ensnared every generation of humanity since the fall of Adam.

James tells us that these desires are the origin of sin: a yearning for something not granted by God. It is in the first motions of desire that sin is conceived within the human heart: *"Each person is tempted when he is lured and enticed by his own desire. Then desire when it has conceived gives birth to sin, and sin when it is fully grown brings forth death"* (James 1:14–15). Therefore, a Christian is constantly battling to root out not only bad actions, but also the bad desires that gave them birth. The greatest nemesis of our Christian lives is that, even after conversion, the same evil desires continue to plague us, to battle us every step of the way (Galatians 5:16–17).

YEARNING FOR GOD ABOVE ALL THINGS

After conversion, however, God sets within our hearts a yearning for the highest blessings in the universe. And there is no higher blessing than intimacy with God himself. So a Christian yearns for God, for the face of God, for the presence of God, for a touch from God, for a taste of God. And once we have tasted of his presence, nothing else in the universe can compare with him.

In Psalm 73, the Psalmist overcame his jealousy of the prosperous wicked by considering a treasure greater than anything else in the universe: God himself. The Psalmist poured out the rekindled desire in his heart in words that few have ever matched. Even now, they bring me to tears:

> When my heart was grieved and my spirit embittered, I was senseless and ignorant; I was a brute beast before you. Yet I am always with you; you hold me by my right hand. You guide me with your counsel, and afterward you will take me into glory. **Whom have I in heaven but you? And earth has nothing I desire besides you**. My flesh and my heart may fail, but God is the strength of my heart and my portion forever. (Psalm 73:21–26)

This longing for God has always characterized the heart of the truly converted. It was in Moses' heart when he cried out on Mount Sinai, *"Please show me your glory!"* (Exodus 33:18), and it was in David's heart when he said, *"One thing I ask of the Lord, this is what I seek: that I may dwell in the house of the Lord all the days of my life, to gaze upon the beauty of the Lord and to seek him in his temple"* (Psalm 27:4).

After the coming of Christ into their lives, the redeemed have learned to seek the presence of God by seeking Christ. A yearning for Christ is a yearning for God himself. Therefore, the central desire of the Apostle Paul's life was to know Christ. Compared to that, all other profits and advantages shrank into relative nothingness:

> But whatever was to my profit I now consider loss for the sake of Christ. What is more, I consider everything a loss compared to the surpassing greatness of knowing Christ Jesus my Lord, for whose sake I have lost all things. I consider them rubbish, that I may gain Christ and be found in him, not having a righteousness of my own that comes from the law, but that which is through faith in Christ—the righteousness that comes from God and is by faith. **I want to know Christ,** and the power of his resurrection, and the fellowship of sharing in his sufferings, becoming like him

in his death, and so, somehow, to attain to the resurrection from the dead. (Philippians 3:7–11)

The desire to know Christ better drove Paul day after day. He had tasted the glory of Christ briefly on the road to Damascus, and it left him both deeply satisfied and insatiably thirsty.

SEEKING GOD'S FACE NOW, BY THE SPIRIT

It is the unique ministry of the Holy Spirit to pour out the love of God into our hearts (Romans 5:5), and to testify with our spirits that we are children of God (Romans 8:16). The Spirit frequently does this by moving us to seek God's outpoured affection in prayer, like a child seeking something good from her father. Jesus taught us about prayer in Luke chapter 11, and he surprises us by saying that we should ask him for "the Holy Spirit":

> Which of you fathers, if your son asks for a fish, will give him a snake instead? Or if he asks for an egg, will give him a scorpion? If you then, though you are evil, know how to give good gifts to your children, how much more will your Father in heaven give the Holy Spirit to those who ask him! (Luke 11:11–13)

I think this means that we should be asking the Father to pour out his love into our hearts by the Holy Spirit, that we might be able to better grasp the infinite dimensions of the Father's love for us in Christ, so that we might be filled to the measure of all the fullness of God.

Martyn Lloyd-Jones wrote an entire book, *Joy Unspeakable*, about the astonishing ways that God has gifted his people with these foretastes of heaven, and about how essential they are for full empowerment in the gospel ministry. He cited Puritan Thomas Goodwin's description of this kind of spiritual experience of God's love:

[Goodwin] describes a man and his little child, his son walking down the road and they are walking hand in hand. And the child knows he is the child of his father, and he knows that the father loves him, and he rejoices in that, and he is happy in it. There is no uncertainty about it at all. But suddenly the father, moved by some impulse, takes hold of that child and picks him up, fondles him in his arms, kisses him, embraces him, showers his love upon him and then he puts him down again, and they go on walking together.[24]

Lloyd-Jones then went on to cite numerous testimonies from church history of the way that others have experienced this love from God. One example of this was D.L. Moody. Lloyd-Jones introduced Moody's testimony by saying that he'd had a good ministry, a useful one up to that point, but that he felt something was deeply missing:

I began to cry as never before, for a greater blessing from God. The hunger increased; I really felt that I did not want to live any longer. I kept on crying all the time that God would fill me with his Spirit. Well, one day in the city of New York—oh! What a day! I cannot describe it, I seldom refer to it. It is almost too sacred an experience to name. Paul had an experience of which he never spoke for fourteen years. I can only say, God revealed himself to me, and I had such an experience of his love that I had to ask him to stay his hand.[25]

Lloyd-Jones says that this experience was so powerful that Moody felt almost physically crushed by it. He also says that from that point forward, Moody went on to preach as a dynamic evangelist whose ministry changed the lives of hundreds of thousands.

The message of Lloyd-Jones's book concerning this extraordinary blessing, the experience of the face of God, is best summed up in this exhortation by Thomas Goodwin: "Sue him for it! Sue him for it! Ask him for it! Don't give up!"[26] Therefore, every Christian should consistently be seeking as much of an experience of the face of God in this life as he will give us. The Scriptures indicate that he yearns to give more of himself here and now than we seem to want to ask him for.

HUNGERING AND THIRSTING AFTER RIGHTEOUSNESS

We will never attain perfection in this world. The power of indwelling sin is too great. But one of the greatest indicators of the New Birth is the deep yearning we have for perfect righteousness. The nature of the regenerate life here on earth is not so much characterized by Christlikeness as by a yearning after Christlikeness, which when fed properly drives the Christian to greater and greater conformity to the Savior—the internal journey of sanctification.

With one benediction in the Sermon on the Mount, Jesus gave immense hope to all of us who struggle bitterly with sin. Jesus said, *"Blessed are those who hunger and thirst for righteousness, for they will be satisfied"* (Matthew 5:6, ESV). All converted people live in a mysterious and temporary state, being indwelt both by sin and by the Holy Spirit. We who live with the indwelling Spirit are consistently convicted about our sinfulness, and we cry out with Paul, *"What a wretched man I am! Who will rescue me from this body of death?"* (Romans 7:24). We know we are not righteous in our daily lives, but every Christian has a deep yearning for righteousness. We want to be like Christ! We desire to be holy! This is the "homing beacon" of our souls; it was implanted in us at conversion, and it drives us on through the suffering of sanctification until our souls are perfected in glorification.

This hunger and thirst for righteousness feeds an increasing hatred of our own sinfulness, a crying out against it. We long for the day when we will be delivered to sin no more. We long for the day when our affections, desires, will, thoughts, and emotions will perfectly conform to Christ. We rage against the sluggishness of our hearts to love Christ and to sacrifice for him. These holy desires were implanted in the soul at regeneration, and they are fed by patterns of faith-induced obedience. They protect the soul from sin, and they guide the ambitions of our lives.

YEARNING FOR THE CONSUMMATION OF CHRIST'S KINGDOM

Along with seeking God himself and our own righteousness, a Christian should also yearn for the consummation of Christ's kingdom in heaven and on earth. This yearning produces the will and the actions that have accomplished such a glorious advance of the church from those first days recorded in the book of Acts. It should organize all our efforts, so that we are not seeking merely to feed our bodies with food and our flesh with pleasure. God has rescued us from a lifestyle dominated by meeting temporary needs and building tiny, pathetic empires that will someday be no more than dust in the wind. *"Seek first his Kingdom and his righteousness,"* Jesus exhorts us in Matthew 6:33. This is the governing drive of the external journey. This is what we should seek and what we should desire: we want to see Christ enthroned, praised, honored, and glorified for who he is and for what he did at Calvary. God the Father has a passionate yearning to see Christ enthroned and glorified, for he said to his Son, *"Ask of me, and I will make the nations your inheritance, the ends of the earth your possession"* (Psalm 2:8), and *"Sit at my right hand until I make your enemies a footstool for your feet"* (Psalm 110:1). A Christian, re-created in the image of God, has the same deep desire. So, in the Lord's Prayer, we express our deep desire: *"Your Kingdom come, your will be done, on earth as it is in heaven"* (Matthew 6:10).

For us, however, it is not enough that it happen. We want to *see* it, to *experience* it, to *partake* of it! In this, again, we are patterned after Christ, for he expressed a deep longing to his Father in his high priestly prayer of John 17:

> Father, **I want** those you have given me to be with me where I am, and to see my glory, the glory you have given me because you loved me before the creation of the world. (John 17:24)

This is the central desire that motivated Christ to save us, and that keeps motivating him to finish to the uttermost our salvation. In his great love for us, he wants to give us the greatest gift he can give. And that is to be with him and to see his glory. This is what Christ deeply desires for us, and we, in his image, deeply desire it as well.

PRAYER: DESIRE STOKED WHITE-HOT

If the driving force of sanctification is desire, it is beneficial for us to see desires for godly things grow stronger within us. But the sluggishness of our hearts is a scandal. In C.S. Lewis's sermon "The Weight of Glory," he criticizes the weakness of our desires:

> If we consider the unblushing promises of reward and the staggering nature of the rewards promised in the Gospels, it would seem that Our Lord finds our desires not too strong but too weak. We are half-hearted creatures, fooling about with drink and sex and ambition when infinite joy is offered to us, like an ignorant child who wants to go on making mud pies in a slum because he cannot imagine what is meant by the offer of a holiday at the sea. We are far too easily pleased.[27]

That is a stirring thought, that we are too easily pleased. That must be extended to include everything that God wants us to desire: His face, his Kingdom, his righteousness, our holiness, our children's salvation, the conversion of unreached people groups, etc. In all of these areas, we are far too easily pleased, our desires far too weak.

Hence the gift of prayer. True prayer accomplishes many things, but one of its greatest purposes is the intensification of our own desires after the things of God. Some time ago, I took my family to visit Colonial Williamsburg to experience life in the 18th century. My favorite shop is the blacksmith's, where burly men make horseshoes, shovels, nails, and other useful implements out of iron. I love watching these men pull on the large, leather bellows to fire up the coal bed for their work; the seething, hissing coals are fed a powerful stream of air and so become even hotter. The blacksmith then sticks a piece of black iron, flat and cold, into the coals. A minute later he pulls it out, white-hot, soft and ready to be pounded into shape.

So it is with prayer. The longer we stay in the presence of the Almighty by the power of the Spirit, the more our hearts are heated by his purposes and his will, and the more his desires become our desires. Heated up by prayer, we become soft and malleable to God's purposes. This process is greatly assisted by providence and by our own obedience, for the more we invest in the answer to our prayers, the more our hearts will desire what God wills. But prayer is the furnace, the coal bed by which our hearts are heated up from their black coldness toward the things of God to desire what we didn't care about before: His pleasure, his presence, his face, his glory, our neighbors, the salvation of lost people, relief for the poor, improvement in marriages, establishment of fruitful ministries, etc.

AMBITION: DESIRE FOCUSED

The greatest desires of a human heart are those that control the direction of one's life, that organize the efforts of one's years.

These desires are called ambitions. Ordinarily we equate ambition with a self-worshiping drive to build an empire for our own glory, like that of Alexander the Great, or of a young executive who is advancing up the corporate ladder by skillful, Machiavellian use of office politics. But ambition in itself is neither a good thing nor a bad thing: it is simply desire focused. If the thing desired is a good thing, then the ambition is good. Otherwise it is not.

What, then, is the place of ambition in the Christian life? Ambition calls forth immense and varied efforts, strategies, sacrifices, resources, and actions. When it is harnessed to drive us along the tracks laid down in Scripture for the two infinite journeys, ambition is a gift from God, given by faith as a "calling," as was mentioned earlier. And I believe it is godly to have ambition for God's glory in the two infinite journeys: to be ambitious to grow into Christlikeness and to advance Christ's Kingdom as much and as quickly as possible here on earth is a good thing. And frankly, I think it is wrong to have either no ambition or weak ambitions in this area. As William Carey said, "Expect great things from God, attempt great things for God." That is ambition, and it is a good thing.

The Apostle Paul had two great ambitions in life. His central ambition, in every minute of his life, was that God would be pleased with his actions and choices: *"Therefore we also have as our ambition, whether at home or absent, to be pleasing to him"* (2 Corinthians 5:9). That was the overriding desire of his life every moment, to please the Lord. But Paul had another ambition: *"It has always been my ambition to preach the gospel where Christ was not known, so that I would not be building on someone else's foundation"* (Romans 15:20). The Greek word translated "ambition" literally means a "love of honor," and Paul deeply desired the honor of taking the gospel to uncharted territories, including Spain (Romans 15:24). This desire drove his life, and though there's no evidence that he ever reached Spain, yet Paul's godly ambition resulted in countless thousands of people entering into the Kingdom.

Whatever specific ministries God may lay on the heart of one of his children, a yearning for glory in the Kingdom will drive a whole lifetime of achievement by the power of the Spirit. Note the ambition behind Paul's general characterization of the kind of life that attains heaven:

> To those who by persistence in doing good seek glory, honor and immortality, he will give eternal life. But for those who are self-seeking and who reject the truth and follow evil, there will be wrath and anger. (Romans 2:7–8)

Only those people "seeking [i.e., yearning for, desiring, driving for, ambitious for] glory, honor and immortality" will receive eternal life. This seeking for glory is our own glorification in heaven,[28] received as a gift from God by his grace. This is not the "self-seeking" of verse 8, but it is seeking glory, honor, and immortality from the hand of the only One who can give it—Jesus Christ. It is not wrong to earnestly desire what God has declared that he will give to those who persistently seek it by doing good, by building the Kingdom.

SUMMARY: WHAT THE GODLY SEEK

Having laid the foundation for the existence of strong, godly desires within the heart of a mature Christian, it is beneficial to present a brief list of things which the godly are shown in Scripture to be seeking:

- God himself above all things (Deuteronomy 4:29, Psalm 27:4)
- Jesus Christ whom he sent (Philippians 3:10–11)
- God's Glory, Name, Renown (Isaiah 26:8)
- Christ's Kingdom (Matthew 6:33)
- Righteousness (Matthew 5:6)
- Personal holiness (Hebrews 12:14)
- Wisdom and Understanding (Proverbs 2:3–6).
- Refuge and Protection (Psalm 61:4)

- Heaven; "Things above" (Colossians 3:1, Philippians 1:23)
- God's word (Psalm 119:45, Jeremiah 15:16)
- God's will (Psalm 40:8)
- The good of others, especially in eternity (Philippians 4:17)
- The lost (Romans 10:1)
- Peace with others (1 Peter 3:10, Hebrews 12:14)
- Glory, honor, immortality (Romans 2:7).
- Justice and relief for the oppressed and needy (Isaiah 1:17)

Thus the spiritually mature have strong desires, not weak. In sanctification, they have learned to battle evil desires which wage war against their souls, and to feed the central desire of their lives: the face of God. They have kindled within themselves a hunger and thirst for their own righteousness and that of all the elect of God. Thus they have stimulated a deep desire for the advancement of the Kingdom of God to the ends of the earth, and have learned to set their desires for the consummation of the age in the New Heaven and the New Earth. A spiritually mature heart is therefore filled with powerful desires, kept white-hot by Scripture and prayer.

CHAPTER 13

WILL—WHAT YOU CHOOSE AND WHAT YOU REJECT

THE NATURE OF THE HUMAN will—the ability to make choices—has been the focal point of millennia of philosophical and theological wrangling. It is beyond the scope of this chapter to probe the depths of the will to the level that, for example, Jonathan Edwards did in his classic, *On the Freedom of the Will.*[29] Simply put, my central message is this: a spiritually mature Christian is characterized by a will that conforms to that of Christ, because they have learned by faith to choose what God wills.

THE WILL IS THE SERVANT OF THE HEART

The foundational insight Edwards gives us in his work is that the will is a servant of the heart, of the true nature. The idea of a "free" will, as though it were a loose cannon untethered to anything in the soul, but tossed back and forth in some random, irrational pattern by the waves of circumstances, is false and unbiblical. Rather, the will takes the affections and desires of the heart and translates them by choices into the actions of the body. The will never makes a single choice apart from what the heart perceives, loves, and desires.

Human will is complex in that it is based on the two faculties of the soul that Edwards clarified in his *Treatise on Religious Affections*: perception and inclination. When the heart faces a decision, it weighs the matter internally based on perception of all the issues it perceives are involved, and based also on its relative inclination or disinclination of all those issues. There are always an array of pluses and minuses in every decision, and this is all the more true the more momentous the decision is. What the heart loves and what the heart hates play the central role in the will, because in the end the will chooses what the heart most delights in and desires.

FREE WILL A SLAVE

The consistent example of Israel in the Old Testament was of the perversity of the human will, of a people **unwilling** to love, obey, and serve God. Through unbelief, the Jews refused to enter the Promised Land: *"But you were unwilling to go up; you rebelled against the command of the Lord your God"* (Deuteronomy 1:26). Isaiah testified about them, *"These are rebellious people, deceitful children, children unwilling to listen to the Lord's instruction"* (Isaiah 30:9).

This unwillingness came to a head when God sent his Son into the world. His own people refused to accept him, but rejected him and conspired to kill him: *"He came to that which was his own, but his own did not receive him"* (John 1:11). Jesus spoke of this directly to his Jewish opponents: *"you are unwilling to come to Me so that you may have life"* (John 5:40). This tragic unwillingness by the Jews came to a head in Jesus' seven-fold woe spoken over the leaders of his people, culminating in his bitter lament over their refusal to come to him: *"O Jerusalem, Jerusalem, you who kill the prophets and stone those sent to you, how often I have longed to gather your children together, as a hen gathers her chicks under her wings, but you were not willing"* (Matthew 23:37).

The natural human will, left to itself, would never choose Christ—not in a million years. It is for this reason that Paul revealed that salvation does not ultimately come down to human choice: *"So then it depends not on human will or exertion, but on God, who has mercy"* (Romans 9:16).

THE CHOICE OF LAZARUS

The miracle of the New Birth in Christ is that spiritual truths become suddenly clear, and dead hearts come alive to act wisely based on those truths. And the clearest truth of all is that it's better to be with Jesus than dead in sin! A good example of the right exercise of the human will is seen plainly in the account of the resurrection of Lazarus in John chapter 11. Lazarus was buried in a cold, stone tomb, perhaps with the corpses of his ancestors. Jesus ordered the stone removed, then gave Lazarus a simple command: *"Lazarus, come out!"* (John 11:43). It was a command only a living person could obey, but with the command came the power to obey. Now Lazarus was confronted with a choice, as all of us are every moment of the day: he could either obey Christ's command, or disobey. However, the issue had been greatly clarified by Christ and was as straightforward as all of our decisions should be. Either Lazarus could disobey and stay wrapped in grave clothes in the cold, dark tomb, or he could obey and come out, have the grave clothes removed, and be with Jesus, to celebrate the greatest miracle of his ministry with a great banquet. It was corpses and darkness vs. Jesus and sunlight. With the matter so clarified, Lazarus did what one billion out of one billion people in his circumstance would have done: he chose to obey Jesus' command and come out. Imagine the resurrected Lazarus answering Christ's command petulantly, "No, I won't come out, and you can't make me!" how ridiculous.

The resurrection of Lazarus is a physical picture of the miracle of the New Birth. And at its core is the giving of a new heart, as Ezekiel prophesied: *"I will give you a new heart and put a new spirit in you; I will remove from you your heart of stone and give you a heart of flesh. And I will put my Spirit in you and move you to follow my decrees and be careful to keep my laws"* (Ezekiel 36:26–27). By that new heart we can see spiritual choices as clearly as Lazarus saw his physical choice.

Frankly, in the end, all of our decisions should be this clear. At every moment, there is a will of God for us, as we are constrained by the commands of God in Scripture. Our decisions should be as clear, since they are informed by Scripture, experience, faith (a sense of God's presence, a yearning for reward, a fear of sin, a reliance on Christ, a sense of immediate guidance by the Spirit), affection (loving what God loves and hating what God hates), and desire (yearning for God's glory in the fulfillment of his promises). If we could only see every decision from heaven's perspective, we would never go astray.

A BITTER STRUGGLE FOR CONTROL

But sadly, it's not always as clear as this, is it? Sometimes insanity sets in and we choose death rather than life. In Romans 7, Paul reveals the bitter struggle for control going on constantly in the Christian between the flesh and the Spirit. Here it seems that the will acts contrary to the regenerate nature. The regenerate nature loves righteousness, desires it and ought to choose it. But Paul seems something else going on inside his heart: *"I do not understand what I do. For what I want to do I do not do, but what I hate I do"* (Romans 7:15). Paul probed deeper, speaking of good desires that he, for some reason never chose to do: *"I have the desire to do what is good, but I cannot carry it out"* (Romans 7:18). When Paul acknowledges that he does what he hates, he admits a certain dual nature within us, the presence of "sin living in me." *"As it is, it is no longer I myself who do it, but it is sin living in me"* (Romans 7:17). Indwelling sin loves what God hates and sometimes, through deception, hijacks the will to achieve actions that the new nature knows very well are evil and will result in suffering and sadness. These dual centers of control within the Christian use the will to achieve very different types of actions. For this reason, the infinite journey of sanctification is a constant warfare, not a leisurely stroll.

IMITATING CHRIST IN GETHSEMANE

Ultimately only Christ can save us in this battle; his Spirit within us enables us daily to follow his example for us. Throughout his life, Christ's food was to do the will of the Father (John 4:34), but this commitment came to a head in Gethsemane. Christ's willful act of denying himself for the glory of God and the salvation of his sheep was the most courageous act in history, and the ultimate paradigm for the proper exercise of the human will at any moment.

What happened at Gethsemane? It is an infinite mystery, yet some aspects are clear. When Christ entered Gethsemane, he knew exactly what was going to happen—he would most certainly die on the cross as a ransom for sinners. But apparently there was still a dimension of knowing that was withheld from Jesus by his loving heavenly Father. All of this comes from a meditation on one word in Mark's gospel, which the KJV accurately translates: *"And he taketh with him Peter and James and John, and began to be **sore amazed**, and to be very heavy"* (Mark 14:33, KJV). The word "amazed" stops us in our tracks! In some sense, Christ was amazed at the cross in Gethsemane. The same word is used of the crowd's reaction to Jesus' ministry (Mark 9:15) and to the Apostles' healing of the lame beggar (Acts 3:11). It is translated in those places "astonished," and it implies a sense of wonder, as if seeing something they'd never seen before.

Now how does that apply to Jesus in Gethsemane? I believe that when Christ began to pray, God revealed to him in an immeasurably more vivid way what it would be like to die on the cross as a substitute for his sheep, drinking the cup of God's wrath poured out full strength. The revelation occurred within Christ himself, within his mind, and it shocked him. It was akin to the difference between seeing a grainy black and white photo of the Grand

Canyon, and seeing an IMAX movie of a helicopter ride through the Grand Canyon. The impression on the soul is much livelier, causing a much more intense reaction. As Christ began to pray, God turned up the intensity in Christ's mind of what it would be like to drink the cup of his wrath, to absorb the lightning bolt of his indignation, to go through hell in our place, as our substitute. And it literally knocked Jesus to the ground and so increased the pressure in his body that blood began to flow from his sweat pores and fell in great drops to the ground (Luke 22:44).

The Father did this, I believe, to give Christ the ability to make a more informed choice as to whether or not he would go through with their plan. The Father had refrained from doing it sooner, because the level of suffering would have been too great for Jesus' human body to bear for any length of time.

But now comes the most heroic moment in human history: *"Going a little farther, he fell with his face to the ground and prayed, "My Father, if it is possible, may this cup be taken from me. **Yet not as I will, but as you will**"* (Matthew 26:39). At this moment, Jesus put his own will completely under the will of his Father. At this moment, he overturned the wretched choice Adam had made in the Garden of Eden, and all the wretched choices God's elect have made in their willful sinning since Adam's first sin. Here Christ showed the proper use of our human will: to do the will of the Father. Thus, Christ concluded his prayer time with these stirring words: *"My Father, if it is not possible for this cup to be taken away unless I drink it, may your will be done"* (Matthew 26:42).

"Not my will, but yours be done." This is the pattern for the free exercise of a healed human will for the rest of time. Christians are not robots. Rather, we are those who are freed from bondage to sin, who increasingly realize that God's ways are ultimately delightful and bring forth good fruit.

Following Edwards' insights, the human will makes its choices based on perception and inclination. By faith we learn to subjugate our own immediate perceptions to the revealed will of God. In effect we are saying, "Not my perception, but your word is true." By faith, the inclination of the heart is to please the Father, not the self: "Not myself be pleased, but may you be pleased." By faith, the true perception (i.e. the Father's) becomes ours. By faith the true pleasure (i.e. the Father's) also becomes ours. So the Father's will becomes ours.

In this way we can understand Christ's choice in Gethsemane. He was *pleased* to lay down his life; it was a free choice that he made. He did it for joy, for pleasure: *"Let us fix our eyes on Jesus, the author and perfecter of our faith, who for the joy set before him endured the cross, scorning its shame, and sat down at the right hand of the throne of God"* (Hebrews 12:2). Christ knew by faith that the Father's will would produce infinite joy and blessing. So by faith he chose it. Christ is our paradigm in the exercise of free choice for the rest of our lives.

CHOOSING EVEN SUFFERING
FOR GREATER PLEASURE

A spiritually mature person, like Jesus, accepts that pain and suffering are an intrinsic part of this sin-cursed world, but that ultimate pleasure still exists and can be ours. However, by faith we accept that ultimate pleasure can be ours only in one place: in the New Heaven and the New Earth, at the completion of God's redemptive plan. By faith we accept that forward-looking stance, as we have already mentioned. Then we choose to do what is **not** apparently in our own immediate best interests, even to the loss of every single earthly advantage and to the "gaining" of much earthly pain. We choose to *"deny ourselves, take up our cross daily and follow Christ"* (Matthew 16:24). We choose this, though it seems utterly foolish to unbelievers. We choose this, because we are really choosing infinitely greater and more lasting pleasure in the next age.

So the will of the mature Christian behaves exactly like the will of the most hedonistic pagan: in both cases we do what is most to our pleasure and the least to our pain; we choose whatever our understanding presents to us as the greatest good. But the difference is that, by faith, we trust that God's way is best, even if it brings great temporary pain. Thus, the more a Christian grows, the more readily we learn to say "Not my will, but yours be done." And yet, just as in the case of Christ, we are using our wills! We are willing what God is willing; we are at last in harmony with the Father who sits on the throne of the universe. We are in part fulfilling our own petition, "Your Kingdom come, your will be done on earth as it is in heaven."

WEIGHING DECISIONS PROPERLY

We make many choices in life: real choices. God is not a "body-snatcher" who turns us into scary zombies who, with blank looks on our faces, "do the right thing." Rather our will follows our affections and desires, as they are rightly informed by Scripture and experience, and as they are empowered by faith.

Edwards, in his treatise on free will, said that we make all choices based on what seems most pleasing to us at that time. He also said that we can have stronger or weaker impressions of things at the moment of choice. For example, a man eating a succulent piece of fruit has a much livelier sense of the sweetness and pleasure of the fruit while he is eating it than he will an hour or a week after finishing it. The choice to keep eating that fruit is greatly empowered by the immediacy of the sensation of pleasure which is made so strongly to his mind.[30]

In the same way, it is the role of the Holy Spirit to use the Scripture to make the invisible spiritual world—especially the presence of God—very immediate to our minds. It is the role of faith to accept these things as true, immediately true, piercingly true. It is the role of affection to love what knowledge and faith have pressed home to the mind. It is the role of desire to yearn for the good things that will come from a right choice. And then, at last, it is the role of the will to move the body to act as according to the highest good. God's way has a tremendous advantage in that it is intrinsically good, beautiful, fruitful. Sin's way is intrinsically evil, ugly, destructive. The Holy Spirit, through the Scripture and experience, works to make these things clear to us at the moment of choice.

If I chose, at random, a pedestrian from the streets of New York and persuaded him to take part in a taste test, and sat him down at a beautifully decorated table in a fine restaurant and placed before him two dishes, one with his favorite meal (perhaps a T-bone steak, baked potato, and a tossed salad) and one with a pile of reeking cow manure, which would he choose? Would there be any point in praising him or acting surprised at his choice? Choice is not worth talking about when the issues are so clear. But frankly, God's will is always more delicious, nutritious, satisfying, and pleasing than any meal, and sin is more disgusting, disease-ridden, damaging, and repulsive than any plate of manure. It is a bizarre feature of sin that it can disguise itself so well, masquerading as something wonderful, and that it can somehow cloak the will of God in filthy garments, as though God were some villain seeking to plunder your house and throw you on a torture rack. It is the unique role of the Holy Spirit, through the training of the mind in Scripture and by experience, through the strengthening of faith, to help us see these things as they really are, not merely as they appear to be.

SUMMARY

A mature Christian has learned by faith to follow consistently the example of Christ by saying to God, "Not my will, but yours be done." The foundation of the right exercise of the will is the new heart that God put in at conversion. By that new heart, the will of the mature Christian makes its choices based on an ever-increasing database of scriptural and experiential knowledge, empowered by faith in the presence and promises of God, and in line with the affections and desires of his new heart. Though insanity occasionally sets in and the sinful nature hijacks the will by causing the mind to focus on the immediate pleasure of sin and forgetting the consequences of that sin and the far greater and more lasting pleasures of righteousness, yet the mature Christian is enabled more and more to choose as Christ did in Gethsemane, saying "Not my will, but yours be done."

CHAPTER 14

THOUGHT—WHAT YOU THINK

WE HAVE ALREADY DISCUSSED THE marvels of the human brain, with its complex neural connections. We have talked about the Holy Spirit's work in using Scripture to erect a "City of Truth" within our hearts, brick by brick. In this section, as we are discussing mature Christian character, I want to speak more about what we choose to think about, and how we choose to think. These aspects of the thought-life of the Christian go a long way to determining the character of the person.

OUR PREVIOUSLY DARKENED MINDS

Let us begin by understanding what God has already done in our minds in saving us, and how radically he has transformed our thinking process. The Scripture has some very shocking things to say about the thought-life of the unbeliever. In the days of Noah before the flood, *The Lord saw how great man's wickedness on the earth had become, and that every inclination of the thoughts of his heart was only evil all the time* (Genesis 6:5). The flood of water that covered the surface of the earth and cleansed it temporarily from man's sin did not reach into the secret recesses of man's brain and cleanse them from evil, however. It wasn't long before the same patterns of evil thinking returned.

No one has so accurately described the darkness of the unregenerate mind as has the Apostle Paul. In all of Paul's writings, the contrast between what our minds used to be and what they are now in Christ has never been more clearly depicted than in Romans 8:5–9:

> For those who live according to the flesh set their minds on the things of the flesh, but those who live according to the Spirit set their minds on the things of the Spirit. To set the mind on the flesh is death, but to set the mind on the Spirit is life and peace. For the mind that is set on the flesh is hostile to God, for it does not submit to God's law; indeed, it cannot. Those who are in the flesh cannot please God. You, however, are not in the flesh but in the Spirit, if in fact the Spirit of God dwells in you. Anyone who does not have the Spirit of Christ does not belong to him. (Romans 8:5–9, ESV)

According to this vital passage, there are two realms we can live in: "in the flesh" and "in the Spirit." The key difference between our lives before being born again and those we live now is our mind-set. The unregenerate mind is set on fleshly things, on earthly appetites and drives. The outcome of that kind of life is death: present spiritual death lived in the world and future eternal death in hell. The life of the Spirit is characterized by a mind set on the things of the Spirit, resulting in a present life of peace and fruitfulness, and future eternal life in heaven. Therefore, the mind-set is the most critical factor in discerning whether or not we have been regenerated, whether or not we are Christians.

From this basic distinction come four aspects of the Christian thought-life that are worthy of discussion: repentance, reckoning, meditation, and wisdom.

REPENTANCE

On October 31, 1517, an Augustinian monk named Martin Luther hammered on the door of the Wittenberg Castle, posting ninety-five theses for a debate that would change the course of history. The first of these theses addressed the issue of repentance:

1. When our Lord and Master Jesus Christ said, "Repent," he willed the entire life of believers to be one of repentance.

It was entirely appropriate for Luther to begin with repentance, for that is exactly where Jesus Christ began with his preaching ministry: *"From that time on Jesus began to preach, 'Repent, for the kingdom of heaven is near'"* (Matthew 4:17). The word *repent* means literally "to re-think," or to change your mind based on new convictions. You have already thought a certain way and have seen the bitter fruit of your faulty thinking; therefore, you repent; you change your mind.

Luther rightly perceived that repentance was not merely a converting grace, but it was something that we would need to continue for the rest of our lives. The City of Truth is not erected on bare ground. Rather, it is built on the smoldering ruins of a past City of Falsehood. We have only begun to think like Christ, and only begun to see the truth. Old patterns of thinking must be repudiated one at a time, and some of them repudiated repeatedly, as the depth of their roots becomes more and more apparent.

So a Christian may repent five times in one hour, even while he goes on a simple trip to the supermarket:

- In the parking lot, another driver takes a convenient parking place that he had picked out for himself; he gets mad and says something under his breath; the Spirit convicts him and he repents, thinking "Why should I have that spot and not him?" He happily chooses another parking spot.
- He begins shopping, and notices an older woman struggling to get a shopping cart out from the stack of carts, but he walks by her and into the store. The Spirit convicts him of his self-focus, and he repents, thinking "She needs my help." He turns around and pulls out a cart for her.

- He walks through the junk food aisle and picks up two bags of his favorite junk food; the Spirit convicts him, reminding him that he intended to lose weight by adjusting his diet; he repents, thinking "I don't need these." He puts them back.
- He walks by the greeting card section, vaguely remembering that his mother's birthday is coming up in two weeks. He thinks, "I'll get a card next week." The Spirit convicts him of his procrastination, and he repents, thinking, "I'm here now. Why presume I'll get another chance?" He picks out a card.
- He waits in the checkout line, near another shopper. The idea of witnessing for Christ pops in his mind but he suppresses it in fear; the Spirit convicts him and he repents saying, "Christ commanded us to be his witnesses." He shares the gospel with the shopper.

These patterns of wrong thinking, and many others, are consistently confronted by the Spirit, using texts of Scripture or painful experiences to reveal the flaws. As Jesus said to the sinful church at Laodicea, *"Those whom I love I rebuke and discipline. So be earnest, and repent"* (Revelation 3:19). It is a mark of the love of God in Christ that he rebukes our faulty thinking and calls on us to repent from it.

RECKONING

This is one of the most vital words in the Christian life, for it is by reckoning Christ's righteousness as our own that God can think of us as perfectly righteous. *"Abraham believed God, and it was **reckoned** to him as righteousness"* (Romans 4:3, RSV). In his own mind, by his own perspective, God chooses to see us as righteous by our faith in Christ, despite the obvious contrary appearance. Christians are to imitate God in various arenas of reckoning, or considering. This aspect of a Christian's thought-life has to do with considering things to be a certain way, though they may readily appear to be very different.

A more popular word for the way someone "reckons" or considers each of these issues and applies that reckoning is "attitude." Attitude comes from a prior reckoning being applied to specific situations, resulting in a certain inward demeanor, with corresponding emotions. We frequently speak of someone's cheerful attitude in hard work, or someone's bad attitude toward authority. A Christian seeks to think about each issue of life as Christ would, and take upon himself a Christlike attitude in each of those arenas.

There are many new thought patterns a Christian spends a lifetime learning. The following is a brief list of the reckoning or considering a Christian has to do. In each case it runs contrary to our old, self-serving way of thinking, and to what our natural senses may be telling us:

- We are to consider ourselves dead to sin but alive to God in Christ Jesus (Romans 6:11).
- We are to consider our present sufferings as not worth comparing with future glory (Romans 8:18), light and momentary (2 Corinthians 4:17), and essential to our salvation. Thus we are to consider it pure joy when they come upon us (James 1:2–4).
- We are to consider ourselves as sheep for the slaughter for the cause of Christ, since that's how God sees us (Romans 8:36).
- We are to consider our daily lives, gifts, money, possessions as not truly ours, but fair game for the advance of the gospel (Acts 20:24, 4:32).
- We are to consider anything we get in this life as better than we deserve (Luke 23:41, 1 Corinthians 15:9).
- We are to consider our weaknesses as strengths in the development of our humble reliance on Christ (2 Corinthians 12:9–10).
- We are to consider others as better than ourselves (Philippians 2:3).

None of these thought patterns is natural to us, and many may seem contrary to reason. But because we trust in the Word of God, we reckon them all (and many other such things) as true concerning us. They govern our attitudes in daily life.

MEDITATION

By meditation, I generally refer to whatever it is we dwell upon, whatever it is that captivates our conscious thought life. The baseball fan marinates his mind in baseball statistics and stories about his favorite players. The soap opera watcher follows the unfolding story line faithfully, and is captivated by the various characters and what is happening to them. The young ambitious lawyer in a prestigious firm is fantasizing daily about what it will take to become a partner in the firm, to obtain a corner office, to be praised and paid accordingly. A young lady who has just met the guy she thinks she will marry spends the whole day dreaming about him, thinking about the next time they can get together; perhaps he's spending his whole time thinking the same thoughts about her.

What we cherish the most is what governs our thought-lives. Jesus put it this way: *"For where your treasure is, there your heart will be also"* (Matthew 6:21). God created the mind to find its ultimate satisfaction in himself. We are to think about him more than we think about anything else. Certainly he created a rich and varied universe, filled with other creatures that variously reflect his glory, and we are to think about them as well. But we are to do so *in relation to him*, in other words, knowing that all things came from him, are sustained by him, and will someday go back to him (Romans 11:36).

Immature Christians may think they cannot control their thought lives, but the Scriptures clearly command us to do precisely that: *"Finally, brothers, whatever is true, whatever is noble, whatever is right, whatever is pure, whatever is lovely, whatever is admirable—if anything is excellent or praiseworthy—think about such things"* (Philippians 4:8). These are the positive things that are to take up our conscious thought-life. We are instructed to think about the *truth*: Jesus is the truth, God's word is truth, and from Christ and the Bible come a seemingly limitless stream of truths about which we can meditate. We should ponder what is *noble*—things that are solemn, stately, majestic, lofty. Our thoughts are not to be lowly, in the gutter, despicable. We are to meditate on what is *right*: those things that line up with the righteousness of God, with his perfect holiness. We are to reflect on whatever is *pure*, especially the perfect purity of heaven, the purity of light, the purity which we will have when glorified. We are to ponder whatever is *lovely*, literally those things that evoke feelings of love and holy pleasure: the beauty of the earth or of a wife's face or a child's voice; especially the beauty of the New Heaven and New Earth (Revelation 21–22). We are to set our minds on whatever is *admirable*—worthy of praise.

This list should filter out pollution from our minds. A water filter is designed to purify water by membranes which allow water molecules to pass through, but which trap particulates and chemicals which foul the water. A good filtration system can result in water that is close to one hundred percent pure. This one verse, Philippians 4:8, serves as an admirable filtration system for our thought-life. Negatively, we are not to allow anything wicked to take root in our thoughts. As Jesus said in the Sermon on the Mount, *"Blessed are the pure in heart, for they will see God"* (Matthew 5:8). Later in that magnificent sermon, Jesus exposed the heart in relation to the Law: we can murder our brother in our heart by anger, we can commit adultery against our wives simply by imagining it in our minds (Matthew 5:22, 28). Therefore, we must not allow our minds to dwell on these kinds of thoughts.

Since our thought-life is so vital, we must carefully monitor anything we put into our minds. The smallest thought can be the beginning of a tragic course of action, as the old saying goes:

Sow a thought, reap an action
Sow an action, reap a habit
Sow a habit, reap a character
Sow a character, reap a destiny.[31]

So, we must fight against evil in the mind, not allowing Satan to put thoughts in our hearts that are not "true, noble, right, pure, lovely, admirable, excellent, or praiseworthy." A mature Christian is very careful about what he watches on TV, what websites he visits on the internet, what movies he sees, what magazines or books he reads, what company he keeps, what music he listens to. If anything comes into our mind that has the tendency to pull it away from holiness, it must be cut off, even if it's as precious as our right eye or right hand (Matthew 5:29–30).

MEDITATION ON SCRIPTURE

Few things are as fruitful and productive as a consistent pattern of meditation on Scripture, for by filling our minds with verses, we automatically push out impurity. This kind of meditation is simply deep, repetitive thinking on passages of Scripture, mulling them over in our minds to draw out the full truth, connecting them to other truths, applying them deeply to our own lives. Psalm 1 speaks of the blessedness of the man who constantly meditates on the word of God, likening him to a tree planted by streams of water, constantly fruitful (Psalm 1:2–3).

The discipline of Scripture memorization greatly enhances this meditation process, for the constant repetition of verses necessary in order to commit them to heart is itself a form of meditation: *I have hidden your word in my heart that I might not sin against you*" (Psalm 119: 11). The benefits of meditation on and memorization of Scripture I will cover in the *Action* section of this book. But suffice it to say at this point, that a person who is constantly repeating Paul's words in Romans 8 (because he is memorizing that chapter) is thinking about "whatever is true, noble, right, pure, lovely, admirable, excellent, and praiseworthy."

WISDOM

Scripturally there is an incredibly close connection between knowledge and wisdom: *"The fear of the Lord is the beginning of knowledge, but fools despise wisdom and discipline"* (Proverbs 1:7). The distinction I make between knowledge and wisdom is the disposition of the soul toward the spiritual knowledge that Scripture and experience produce. The wise heart not only discerns the way of the Lord, but also delights in it and chooses it.

Perhaps the primary passage in the Bible on the distinction between knowledge and wisdom is Proverbs 2:1–11:

> My son, if you accept my words and store up my commands within you, turning your ear to wisdom and applying your heart to understanding, and if you call out for insight and cry aloud for understanding, and if you look for it as for silver and search for it as for hidden treasure, then you will understand the fear of the Lord and find the knowledge of God. For the Lord gives wisdom, and from his mouth come knowledge and understanding. He holds victory in store for the upright, he is a shield to those whose walk is blameless, for he guards the course of the just and protects the way of his faithful ones. Then you will understand what is right and just and fair—every good path. For wisdom will enter your heart, and knowledge will be pleasant to your soul. Discretion will protect you, and understanding will guard you. (Proverbs 2:1–11)

Crucial principles emerge from this passage:

- Gaining wisdom and understanding comes only through diligent study of the word of God. (v. 1)
- A deep yearning for insight must be coupled with fervent prayer. (v. 3)
- The focus of this study is, first and foremost, the fear of the Lord and the understanding of God—if that is established, everything else in life will fall into place. (v. 5)
- Wisdom and understanding both come as gifts from the Lord, which he gives to those who genuinely and fervently seek them. (v. 6)
- The result of wisdom and understanding is practical holiness, the discernment of every good path. (vv. 7–10)

Now comes the key distinction between knowledge and wisdom: *knowledge* is knowing who the Lord is and what is every good path; *wisdom* is delighting in the Lord and every good path, and choosing them daily: *"For wisdom will enter your heart, and knowledge will be pleasant to your soul"* (Proverbs 2:10).

Spiritual knowledge is broad, covering everything from history to law to genealogies to poetry, etc. All of it tends toward the production of wisdom in the heart. But wisdom is specifically the delight in and choosing of the best path to achieve the glory of God in both internal and external journeys. A spiritually mature person is wise, therefore, and this wisdom is practical and woven together in everyday life. The topics of wisdom are as practical and as many as are the issues of daily life: sexual purity, care for the body, the proper handling of wealth, the finding of a godly spouse, the training of children, the use and abuse of speech, business ethics, proper relationship to government officials, dealing well with neighbors, protection from corrupt so-called "friends," the giving and receiving of rebukes, etc. A spiritually mature person has an ever-increasing storehouse of wisdom with which to navigate the often bewildering paths that unfold before him.

SUMMARY

God desires deeply that the thought-life of the Christian be glorifying to him. At conversion, God has given us the *"mind of Christ"* (1 Corinthians 2:16), which means we have the ability now to think like Jesus in every situation in which we find ourselves. In order to do this, however, we must constantly be repenting of past evil thought patterns. We must reckon certain things to be true, even though it feels like they're not; and this reckoning should display itself in our attitudes toward everything we face. We must meditate on whatever is true, noble, right, pure, lovely, and admirable, and kill every thought that's not. As a means to that end, we should learn the discipline of constant meditation on—and memorization of—Scripture. Finally, we should pursue the wisdom of delighting in God's ways. This is a thought-life that glorifies God.

CHAPTER 15

EMOTION—WHAT YOU FEEL

IN ANCIENT GREECE, THE STOICS posited a god who was utterly devoid of all passion, a pure thinking machine. Desiring to be like this god whom they honored, they strove to strip themselves of all human passions, responding with equal calm to both positive and negative circumstances. They despised the weakness of human emotions, and sought to ascend to a level of pure thought. However, the Stoics worshiped a false god, an idol of their own imagination.

THE EMOTIONAL GOD OF THE BIBLE

The God of the Bible is an intensely passionate being. He delights in his creation and in his works; he rejoices, he mourns, he gets angry, he pours out his wrath, he is jealous, he laughs, and above all these, he is compassionate for his people, feeling what they feel. Many Scriptures testify to this:

- God expresses joy: *The Lord your God is with you, he is mighty to save. He will take great delight in you, he will quiet you with his love, he will rejoice over you with singing.* (Zephaniah 3:17)
- God expresses compassion: *As a father has compassion on his children, so the Lord has compassion on those who fear him.* (Psalm 103:13)
- God expresses wrath: *God is a righteous judge, a God who expresses his wrath every day.* (Psalm 7:11)

- God expresses grief: *The Lord was grieved that he had made man on the earth, and his heart was filled with pain.* (Genesis 6:6)

These verses, in partnership with many others, reveal that God is an emotional being. Human emotions, therefore, are a reflection of God's nature as an emotional being. Unlike our emotions, however, God's emotions are perfect, a reflection of his nature, his mind, his purposes, his will, his plans. God is never surprised by circumstances nor overwhelmed by unforeseen events; therefore, he cannot be trapped into some emotional display from which he must later repent. Quite the contrary, God sometimes rationally defers his emotion until the proper time: *"For my own name's sake I delay my wrath; for the sake of my praise I hold it back from you, so as not to cut you off"* (Isaiah 48:9). God knows when it is the right time to get angry, and often times he waits, even in the face of great wickedness. God is never overpowered by emotions like we are; his emotions are always a wise part of his plan.

And most delightfully for us, God rejoices exceedingly when a single sinner repents from sin and returns to him, as Jesus tells us in Luke 15:10. It is the Father who does the rejoicing, and he does it in the presence of the angels so they can see his joy.

THE EMOTIONAL LIFE OF CHRIST

The clearest display of the perfect emotional life of God, however, is seen in the person of our Savior, Jesus Christ. In this as in all things, he is our example.[32] By far, the most common emotion Jesus displayed was compassion for suffering people. He was filled with compassion for a man with leprosy (Mark 1:40–41); he had compassion on hungry, harassed, helpless crowds (Matthew 9:36, 15:32); his heart went out to a widow burying her only son, and he told her "Don't cry." (Luke 7:11–13). Jesus knit his heart to the griefs of his people, and their suffering moved him deeply and emotionally.

But compassion for the suffering was not his only emotion. He was moved by love for specific people in certain circumstances (Mark 10:21). He felt joy in the Holy Spirit over the success of the seventy-two whom he sent out to do miracles and to preach the gospel (Luke 10:21). He felt a pure, holy anger over the abuse of the temple sacrificial system when he cleansed the temple (John 2:15–16). And most significantly of all, he displayed a wide range of deep emotions before raising Lazarus from the dead: gladness (John 11:14–15), sorrow (John 11:35), and most mysteriously of all, a totally submerged rage at death itself (John 11:38). Clearly, Jesus had a rich, full emotional life, and his emotions are a pattern for the healthy emotions of all Christian people.

THE EMOTIONAL LIFE OF A CHRISTIAN

By contrast, our emotional life is not as pure as was Jesus', and our emotions frequently lead us astray. Our emotions are frequently controlled by our sin nature, and so we react directly out of habit and through faithlessness. Almost every emotional state one can imagine is exemplified in Scripture, and many times the Scripture represents the emotions *themselves* as wrong. Part of spiritual maturity is to recognize how frequently our emotions are out of step with spiritual reality as revealed in Scripture, and to use the truth to bring them back in line.

Spiritually mature emotions are constrained by the Word of God and controlled by the Spirit. Many people think that we cannot control our emotions, but the Bible reveals the opposite. One of the most emotional stories in the Bible is that of Joseph and his brothers. It is a story filled with hatred, love, jealousy, and joy. At the climactic moment of his reunion with his treacherous brothers, Joseph felt a river of emotions. Genesis 43:30–31 states, *"Deeply moved at the sight of his brother, Joseph hurried out and looked for a place to weep. He went into his private room and wept there. After he had washed his face, he came out and, **controlling himself**, said, "'Serve* *the food.'"* Joseph's emotions here are not sinful, but it should be noted that they could be controlled for the greater good.

A significant part of spiritual maturity is having our emotions constrained by our new nature in Christ, through our understanding of God's word and his plans. There must be emotional balance, not excess, on either side: lack of appropriate emotion can be evidence of a hard heart as much as excessive, unbridled, ignorant, or ungodly emotions are evidence of an immature heart. Frankly, both extremes are evidence of spiritual immaturity. No matter where you may place yourself on this emotional spectrum, there is some measure of healing that needs to occur. If you can encounter a fellow Christian who is going through a wrenching time of life and feel no compassion toward him or her, your heart is hard. If you do not reach out with compassion at that time, you commit a sin. But, on the other hand, if you are prone to excessive grief over the smallest difficulties of life, there is a problem in the other direction. Christians, then, must learn to control their emotions by the power of the Spirit through the transformation of the Word of God.

FIVE KEY EMOTIONS

The mature Christian displays a wide array of emotions, just as a non-Christian does. However, our emotions are conformed to Christ and informed by the word of God. It is impossible to survey all the emotional states and their shades of passion that are appropriate for a Christian. However, some major emotions are worthy of a closer look: joy, sorrow, fear, compassion, and zeal. Having analyzed these by Scripture, we will finish this section by speaking of the correction of faulty emotions.

JOY

Our God is a happy being: *"Our God is in heaven; he does whatever pleases him"* (Psalm 115:3). Salvation, therefore, is an entrance into a joy that cannot fully be described in words: *"Enter into the joy of your master"* (Matthew 25:21). Our joy comes from knowing God through Christ, and from knowing that God is going to give us infinitely of himself for eternity. Since we have such a foundation for joy in this present world that cannot be shaken, Paul commands us repeatedly to rejoice in the Lord (Philippians 2:18, 3:1, 4:4). Joy comes most powerfully as a fruit of the indwelling Spirit (Galatians 5:22).

It is a great display of the presence of Almighty God when we can rejoice openly in him during times of suffering. Therefore, a supernatural joy in all circumstances is a tremendously attractive evangelistic force in our depressed and hopeless world. When, after having been beaten publicly and thrown into the Philippian jail, Paul and Silas sang hymns of praise at midnight, all the listening prisoners could see the supernatural power of the gospel. The Philippian jailer and his family were saved as a result of that power (Acts 16:23–34).

If, therefore, we can rejoice in times of suffering, how much more should we rejoice always? It is fine to rejoice when good things happen, when good times occur, as long as we are not deluded into thinking of those things as the solid foundation of our joy: *"When times are good, be happy; but when times are bad, consider: God has made the one as well as the other"* (Ecclesiastes 7:14). But since our citizenship is in heaven (Philippians 3:20), and since our treasure is in heaven (Matthew 6:20), then our hearts should be in heaven as well (Colossians 3:1–4). And if so, our joy will be a spring of life welling up inside of us, from which we can drink whenever we are thirsty. Conversely, a joyless Christian is a contradiction in terms, a great dishonor to the Lord. Seventeenth century Anglican bishop Jeremy Taylor put it powerfully, "God threatens terrible things if we will not be happy!"[33]

SORROW

One of the strangest elements of the Christian's emotional life is the consistent conjoining of joy and sorrow. The Apostle Paul described himself and his fellow laborers in the gospel as *"sorrowful, yet always rejoicing"* (2 Corinthians 6:10). This is perhaps best understood in the light of redemption, in seeing life through the lens of Christ's cross. Jesus, *"for the joy set before him, endured the cross, scorning its shame"* (Hebrews 12:2). There is a future joy that makes all the present suffering worthwhile, especially if one understands the suffering as essential and necessary to the journey of sanctification. Thus, in this world, a mature Christian should always be joyful. And in this world, a mature Christian should sometimes be sorrowful.

There is an appropriate sorrow over the damage of sin, primarily in our own hearts and lives, but also in the lives of others and in the world generally. A Christian must be sorrowful over his own personal sin. Without this godly sorrow over sin, genuine repentance cannot occur. As noted above, the Puritan writer Thomas Watson listed six elements of genuine repentance: sight of sin, sorrow for sin, confession of sin, shame for sin, hatred of sin, and turning from sin.[34] Concerning sorrow for sin, Watson writes:

> A woman may as well expect to have a child without pangs as one can have repentance without sorrow. He that can believe without doubting, suspect his faith; he that can repent without sorrowing, suspect his repentance. . . . A true penitent labors to work his heart into a sorrowing frame. He blesses God when he can weep; he is glad of a rainy day, for he knows that it is a repentance he will have no cause to repent of. Though the bread of sorrow be bitter to the taste, yet it strengthens the heart. This sorrow for sin is not superficial: it is a holy agony. It is called in Scripture a breaking of the heart.[35]

Since sin is so heinous, such a vicious enemy and a virulent foe, it is absolutely healthy and reasonable for us to respond emotionally to it. Thus does Scripture command weeping and mourning over sin. James gives a command which modern, fun-loving Christians have a hard time even comprehending, never mind obeying: *"Grieve, mourn and wail. Change your laughter to mourning and your joy to gloom"* (James 4:9). In context, James is calling on Christians to do this before a holy God when they perceive worldliness, double-mindedness, and the pollution of sin within them. Then the only remedy is grief over the sin, and humbling oneself in the presence of a merciful God, that he may lift us up in due time. Much of the worldliness of the church, I believe, is due to the fact that we do not obey this prescription.

However, we are not only to be grieving for our own sins. There is an ocean of sin all around us every single day. Therefore, the Psalmist says *"Streams of tears flow from my eyes, for your law is not obeyed"* (Psalm 119:136). A mature Christian will be increasingly grieved by the sin he sees around him and by all the damage it does. He will be offended by it, disgusted by it, vexed by it.

The ultimate expression of this grief is the agony a mature Christian feels over the spiritually lost, as they careen down the road to hell. Just as Jesus wept over Jerusalem and lamented their lostness (Luke 19:41), so also Paul bitterly grieved over the lost condition of most of his Jewish countrymen, even to the point of being willing to exchange his salvation for theirs, if it were possible. He said *"I have great sorrow and unceasing anguish in my heart"* for the lost among the Jews (Romans 9:1–4). Paul also related agony over lost Gentiles whose god is their stomach, speaking, he says, *"with tears"* (Philippians 3:18–19) William Carey frequently employed a shoe-leather globe to instruct people in England concerning the "heathen" who had yet to hear the gospel; his passion was evident as he cried out with tears in anguish to those who would listen, "These are all pagans! Pagans!!"[36]

COMPASSION

Compassion is love's commitment to feel what someone else is feeling, whatever it may be. It is commanded of Christians for one another in several places: *"Rejoice with those who rejoice; mourn with those who mourn"* (Romans 12:15); *"Finally, all of you, live in harmony with one another; be sympathetic, love as brothers, be compassionate and humble"* (1 Peter 3:8). It is displayed invariably in physical actions, depending on the circumstances: weeping, laughter, an arm around someone's shoulders, jumping up and down and clapping, visiting someone in prison or in the hospital, etc. Apart from genuine compassion, all those actions will be stripped of love and become empty, perhaps even harmful counterfeits. Rather, Paul said *"Love must be sincere"* (Romans 12:9), literally "unhypocritical, unfeigned." The only way that can happen is when we genuinely marry our hearts to the joy or misery of another human being.

In the parable of the Good Samaritan, the actions of the priest and Levite who passed by the wounded man on the road to Jericho reveal that the common state of the human heart towards the suffering of others is cold indifference (Luke 10:31–32). We can't be bothered; we don't care. But since, as we've seen, compassion was Jesus' most common emotion, it will also be the nature of a mature Christian. We "rejoice with those who rejoice" in a selfless manner, free from jealousy over their blessings. We "mourn with those who mourn" because we know from experience the bitterness of suffering and can easily relate to another's suffering. This will move us to action in service to others.

FEAR

When God gave the Ten Commandments to Israel, everything he did to set the stage was designed to bring terror to the hearts of his people: the days of consecration, the command not to venture on the mountain lest they die, the earthquake, the dark cloud, the smoke and fire billowing from Mount Sinai like a furnace, the loud voice. Then God said an astonishing thing to his trembling people through Moses: *"Do not be afraid. God has come to test you, so that the fear of God will be with you to keep you from sinning"* (Exodus 20:20). Everything God had been doing for three days had been to make certain the people of God feared him. All of it was calculated, planned, and accomplished to bring about fear. But once that fear was established, God commanded "Do not fear!" In effect, God's message to his beloved people in Exodus 20:20 is this: fear me properly, and you need fear nothing else for the rest of your life. The converse is true as well: if you don't fear me, you have reason to fear everything else in life. Thus, a Christian should have no fear of men (Isaiah 51:7), or of any earthly consequences of faithfulness to God. But if we sin, we have reason to fear God.

The fear of the Lord is an abiding part of the healthy Christian life. Solomon said it is the beginning of wisdom: *"The fear of the Lord is the beginning of wisdom, and knowledge of the Holy One is understanding"* (Proverbs 9:10). So also in the New Testament, Jesus said that we were to fear God, and not to fear men, even in the midst of intense persecution: *"Do not be afraid of those who kill the body but cannot kill the soul. Rather, be afraid of the One who can destroy both soul and body in hell"* (Matthew 10:28). Human hearts are prone to fear: anxieties over food and clothing (Matthew 6:31), fear of human opinion (Proverbs 29:25), and above all, fear of death (Hebrews 2:15). Fear of the Lord has the power to free us from every other fear in life. It enables martyrs like John Hus to go to the stake singing hymns.

Christ's blood and righteousness should make us very bold in the presence of our heavenly Father, able to venture into the holy of holies with supernatural confidence, expecting fully to be welcomed by a God who is fully reconciled to us (Hebrews 10:19–22). To approach God with anything less than full confidence in Christ is to dishonor the blood of Christ and misunderstand our justification by faith alone.

But there must still remain a holy fear of God that stands as a partner to faith, protecting us from sin while we live in this world. Thus Paul commands us to *"work out your salvation with fear and trembling"* (Philippians 2:12), and calls on us to *"cleanse ourselves from all defilement of flesh and spirit, perfecting holiness in the fear of God"* (2 Corinthians 7:1). These two verses clearly teach us that the journey of sanctification is one we walk in the fear of the Lord. A mature Christian should walk in this holy fear every day of his life.

ZEAL

Christians are also commanded to have zeal, and zeal is a highly emotional state; it is a burning drive and desire to see God glorified, Christ exalted, sinners converted, and the Kingdom of Heaven finally come. We have already spoken of desire in this chapter. Zeal is desire on fire. Christ's zeal came forth when he cleansed the temple. John, writing his account of that event, applied Psalm 69:9 to explain what was happening inside Jesus: *"His disciples remembered that it is written: 'Zeal for your house will consume me'"* (John 2:17).

In the same way, Christians are to be filled with zeal for God's glory and for God's people: *"Never be lacking in zeal, but keep your spiritual fervor, serving the Lord"* (Romans 12:11). The image is one of a pot bubbling up, ready to boil over. God deliver us all from spiritual lethargy, from spiritual deadness! O that we would not be like the lukewarm Laodicean church, neither hot nor cold, whom the Lord desired to spew from his mouth (Revelation 3:16)!

CORRECTING FAULTY EMOTIONS

We have seen that the mature Christian life involves an increasingly healthy display of many emotions: among these are joy, sorrow, compassion, fear, and zeal. These godly emotions will arise by the Spirit in conjunction with the truths of Scripture and God's purposes, as revealed in daily life. However, just as important as the development of appropriate and godly emotions is the correction of faulty emotions, and the control of emotionalism, lest we trust or follow our unstable feelings more than the unchanging truth of God's word. The Bible has a great deal to say about the correction of faulty emotions, since our emotions are so frequently ruled by the flesh and not by the Spirit:

- Corrected from sinful anger: (Jonah 4:9–11, James 1:21)
- Corrected from faithless sadness: (John 20:13, 15)
- Corrected from discouragement: (Psalm 42:5, Luke 24:25)
- Corrected from sinful fear: (John 14:27, Psalm 56:4)
- Corrected from anxiety: (Matthew 6:25–34, Philippians 4:6–7)
- Corrected from sinful joy: (Isaiah 22:12–14, James 4:9–10)
- Corrected from lack of shame over sin: (Jeremiah 6:15)
- Corrected from lack of Christian affection: (2 Corinthians 6:11–13)

These emotional states are faulty because they are based on a wrong way of looking at the world. In every case, the remedy is to take the scriptural truth that applies, and then use it to correct the false viewpoint.

PREACHING TO YOURSELF

So, if we find ourselves in a pattern of wrong emotions, or if we feel we are being hindered from whole-hearted Christian obedience by wrong emotions, how can we rectify the situation? Perhaps the clearest example of a person laboring to correct his own faulty emotional state is found in Psalms 42–43:

> Why are you downcast, O my soul? Why so disturbed within me? Put your hope in God, for I will yet praise him, my Savior and my God. (Psalm 42:5–6)

The Psalmist is having a conversation with his soul. He is confronting himself concerning his own discouragement, because he is aware that his emotions are out of sync with his beliefs about God. In the same way, when our emotions are out of step with spiritual reality, we must preach to ourselves, and we must purposefully remember God.[37]

SUMMARY

Because our heavenly Father is an emotional being, and because our perfect pattern, Jesus, displayed perfect emotions, a healthy emotional life is part of spiritual maturity. This includes such wide-ranging emotions as joy, sorrow, fear, compassion, and zeal. The indwelling Spirit works these emotions in us as appropriate, healing us from the extremes of either emotional deadness or of emotionalism. He teaches us to address faulty emotions with Scripture, especially training us to preach truth to our hearts until our emotions are rightly aligned with those of Christ.

CHAPTER 16

VIRTUES—WHAT YOU ARE

THUS FAR, WE HAVE SEEN five major aspects of the Christian character: affection, desire, will, thought, and emotion. All of these work together to produce various character traits, depending on the situation. These character traits are sometimes called "virtues." Like the attributes of God, these virtues describe a person's nature: who he or she is. The virtues are the fruit of our affections, desires, will, thoughts, and emotions, not additional to them. At any given moment, they summarize the prevailing state of our soul.

Scripture gives many descriptions of positive Christian virtues. Perhaps the most famous list of Christian virtues is found in Galatians 5:22–23: *"the fruit of the Spirit is love, joy, peace, patience, kindness, goodness, faithfulness, gentleness and self-control."* This is what the Holy Spirit produces in us as we abide in Christ. This list is not exhaustive, however, by any means, for other passages of Scripture add to our understanding of what kind of person we should be. The Sermon on the Mount (Matthew 5) extends the list of virtues: poor in spirit, mourning (over sin), meek, merciful, hungering and thirsting for righteousness, pure in heart. Other passages in the epistles add many others as well: compassion, forgiveness (Ephesians 4:32); sympathy, humility (1 Peter 3:8); submissiveness (Ephesians 5:21, 1 Peter 5:5); being peace-loving, considerate, impartial, sincere (James 3:17).

It isn't long before one gets the sense that an exhaustive list of character traits from Scripture would be very difficult to assemble. If one adds the historical accounts in which virtuous character is displayed without being named, other traits such as courage, boldness, confidence, etc., could be added. Bible stories do not give a moral at the end, like one of Aesop's fables, but as Bible stories are read, a sense of godly virtue and character develops. This is a major part of the purpose of Old Testament history. Through these accounts we see how Boaz dealt gently with Ruth, how Esther responded courageously in approaching King Xerxes, how Moses boldly dealt with Pharaoh's hardened responses, and many more. The stories were recorded, in part, so that we might be encouraged by people who lived virtuous lives in the face of adversity. Also, we should be warned by those who lived wicked lives so we do not follow in their same path to destruction. Do not allow yourself to go the way of faithless King Saul, who did not consult God. Do not open the door to adultery, as David did. Do not lie about money (or anything), as did Ananias and Sapphira.

1 Corinthians 10:11 states, *"These things happened to them as examples and were written down as warnings for us, on whom the fulfillment of the ages has come."* On a more positive note Romans 15:4 says, *"For everything that was written in the past was written to teach us, so that through endurance and the encouragement of the Scriptures we might have hope."* From biblical narratives we learn positive and negative character traits, and we are motivated to emulate or avoid each trait.

These Christian virtues which flow from various passages of Scripture are like the beautiful colors of the spectrum, and we are the prism by which this character of Christ is revealed to the world. These traits really are expected of us as Christians, all the time, by the power of the indwelling Spirit, as often as each one is required by the circumstances. And these are just the positive traits! We could just as easily assemble a negative list, since very frequently in Scripture, in the very passages in which we are commanded "Be this!", we are also commanded "Don't be that!" For example: *"Do nothing out of selfish ambition or vain conceit, but in humility consider others better than yourselves"* (Philippians 2:3). Or again,

> Love **is** patient, love **is** kind. It **does not** envy, it **does not** boast, it **is not** proud. It **is not** rude, it **is not** self-seeking, it **is not** easily angered, it keeps **no record of wrongs**. Love **does not** delight in evil **but** rejoices with the truth. It **always** protects, **always** trusts, **always** hopes, **always** perseveres. Love **never** fails. (1 Corinthians 13:4–8)

This famous passage of Scripture goes back and forth between positive and negative character traits.

It is significant that 1 Corinthians chapter 13 describes love in such sweeping terms. In the end, love is the best summary of the Christian virtues: *"And over all these virtues put on love, which binds them all together in perfect unity"* (Colossians 3:14). Love best captures all the positive and negative traits that God is calling us to display. Therefore it is not surprising that all the Law and the Prophets hang on these two commandments: *"Love the Lord your God with all your heart and with all your soul and with all your mind"*; and *"Love your neighbor as yourself"* (Matthew 22:37, 39). If a long list of biblical virtues is too daunting to assimilate, too scary to absorb, then we should just concentrate on these two greatest commandments.

However, the Scripture does give more detail that that, and to honor the wisdom of God in giving us a full revelation of human virtues and vices, it may be beneficial to list in alphabetical order some of the positive virtues that Scripture commands, enjoins, displays, or exemplifies, as well as the negative character traits that Scripture forbids, discourages, rebukes, or holds up as a warning.

A THOROUGH LIST OF VIRTUES TO
WHICH CHRISTIANS ARE CALLED

Depending on the circumstances, Christians are called to be:

Alert – Bold – Cheerful – Committed – Compassionate – Content – Courageous – Determined – Devoted – Devout – Diligent – Discerning – Disciplined – Faithful – Forgiving – Friendly – Generous – Gentle – Genuine – Giving – Glad – Godly – Good – Gracious – Holy – Honorable – Hopeful – Hospitable – Humble – Joyful – Just – Kind – Long-suffering – Loving – Meek – Merciful – Modest – Mournful – Obedient – Orderly – Patient – Peaceful – Poor in Spirit – Praising – Prayerful – Prudent – Pure – Purposeful – Quiet – Reasonable – Relentless – Repentant – Respectful – Restful – Reverent – Sacrificial – Satisfied (in God) – Serious – Sincere – Single-minded – Sober-minded – Steadfast – Strong – Submissive – Sympathetic – Temperate – Thankful – Trusting – Truthful – Understanding – Vigilant – Watchful – Willing – Wise – Worshipful – Worthy – Yielded – Zealous.

A mature Christian is not called to be all these things all the time, but rather these virtues are more like tools in a "character toolbox" that are called for as certain situations may come upon you. When the situation calls for boldness, you must be bold. When the situation calls for compassion, you must be compassionate. If the situation calls for gentleness and one shows boldness, then one is deficient in character at that moment! For example, if your wife is crying over some distressing news from her hometown, and you respond with joy or zeal, your wife will not have been ministered to. The indwelling Spirit is the skillful craftsman who knows how to pull from your "character toolbox" whatever virtue the situation calls for. Much of the Spirit's training of a person's responses comes by experience.

A THOROUGH LIST OF TRAITS WHICH CHRISTIANS ARE CALLED TO REJECT

Christians are called **not** to be:

(Sinfully)Angry–Anxious–Complaining–Covetous–Deceitful – Deceived – Disobedient – Disorderly – Disputing – Double-minded – Doubting – Dull – Embittered – Envying – Foolish – Greedy – Hypocritical – Ignorant – Immoral – Impenitent – Impure – Insolent – Insubordinate – Jealous – Lawless – Lazy – Lukewarm – Lustful – Mocking – Murmuring – Pleasure-loving – Prideful – Quarrelsome – Quick-tempered – Rebellious –Restless – Scornful – Selfish – Self-willed – Sensual – Shameful – Slothful – Sorrowful – Spiteful – Stiff-necked – Stupid – Timid – Unbelieving – Uncharitable – Unclean – Unrepentant – Unruly – Unstable – Unthankful – Unwilling – Vain – Vengeful – Violent – Weary – Willful.

Again, this list is not exhaustive, and many of these words need explaining. A beneficial project would be to find the best single scriptural text to support each of the character traits listed (both the positive and the negative). But the simple listing of the words makes two points. First, it's pretty obvious that the positive traits are deeply desirable and should be sought and developed by growing Christians, while the negative states of the human heart described above are to be rejected by a mature Christian. Thus the work of sanctification is therefore both positive and negative. Second, the quest for perfect character will be ongoing until the day we die.

ENCOURAGEMENT FOR THOSE FEELING "UNDER THE PILE"

It's easy to look at these two lists, both positive and negative, and quickly feel overwhelmed, crushed, or discouraged. It becomes clear from examining lists of this magnitude that perfection will elude us in the Christian life. Even if we were to focus on one virtue closely—patience, for instance—and seek to be as much like Christ in that one area for a week, we would still find our-selves falling woefully short of perfection. We could set out on a Monday morning and seek to be as patient as Jesus was in every encounter, but just let us be forced to deal with a person we find exceptionally irritating, and we quickly lose our composure. Perhaps a snappish answer, or maybe just an impatient sigh, and our patience is gone. And that's just one virtue. How much more overwhelming are all of these put together!

However, here is where we need to go back to our original look at salvation, and remember that at no time do we stand be-fore God in **our** sanctification righteousness, but always only in Christ's perfect righteousness, imputed to us simply by faith the moment we first believed. We should remind ourselves that per-fect virtue **was** achieved once in this life: by Jesus Christ. And that is precisely the righteousness credited to our account by faith. Also, we should still seek Christlike perfection by faith every sin-gle moment, because God has commanded these things of us, and the more Christlike we can become, the better we will advance Christ's Kingdom and the more we will glorify God. Finally, we should understand that these virtues are precisely what the Holy Spirit works in us by his power when we seek him humbly and ask him to fill us. This is why in Galatians 5:22 they are called the "fruit of the Spirit."

ACTION

A PATHWAY TO CHRISTIAN MATURITY

KNOWLEDGE
FACTUAL AND EXPERIENTIAL SPIRITUAL INFORMATION

FACTUAL
Gained from the Scripture

EXPERINTIAL
Gained from living in God's world

FAITH
ASSURANCE OF AND COMMITMENT TO SPIRITUAL TRUTH

- Certainty that specific invisible spiritual realities are true
- Assurance that hoped-for specific good thing promised in scripture will certainly come true
- Conviction that specific sin in me, and that God hates it and will judge people for such sins
- Reliance on Christ as all-sufficient savior, refuge, provider, shield
- Reception of spiritual guidance and knowledge

ACTION
EXTERNAL LIFESTYLE OF HABITUAL OBEDIENCE

1. Presentation of Body to God
2. Personal Holiness
3. Seven-fold obedience to God's commands

   1. Worship
   2. Spiritual Disciplines
   3. Family
   4. Ministry to Believers
   5. Mission to Non-Believers
   6. Stewardship
   7. Work

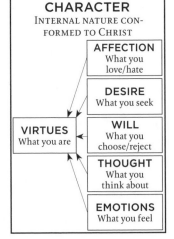

CHARACTER
INTERNAL NATURE CONFORMED TO CHRIST

AFFECTION What you love/hate

DESIRE What you seek

VIRTUES What you are

WILL What you choose/reject

THOUGHT What you think about

EMOTIONS What you feel

SECTION INTRODUCTION: ACTION

I KNELT DOWN BY THE weathered headstone in the corner of the ancient graveyard in central Kentucky. The graveyard was small and poorly cared-for, with grass and weeds running amuck, and many of the headstones broken in half or vandalized. The small stone I was inspecting seemed older than all the others, and I was fascinated by its smooth face. I could not read a single letter that had been formerly engraved on that stone, but the sensitive tips of my fingers could still make out the slight indentations where the inscription had been carved so many years ago. From the dates on the surrounding stones, it seemed to have been made sometime between 1850 and 1875, but I couldn't be sure. The wind, rain, sand, and other effects of time had erased forever the words the tombstone maker had inscribed to commemorate that long-forgotten life.

But actually, the events of that life are not forgotten. As a matter of fact, there is a perfect record of every careless word, every kind action, every cup of cold water given to help a servant of the Lord, every sinful deed, every expenditure, every prayer (whether heart-felt or hypocritical), every penny given to the poor, every sarcastic comment, every hymn sung. The words of that perfect historical record are written in a heavenly book, from which no erasure is possible. All the actions of that person are etched in God's record book for eternity.

The final test of godliness is action. It is such a true indicator of the actual state of our souls that Christ will be able to judge everyone on the face of the earth by his full record of all we said and did. Many people go astray on this point, but the Bible is clear: we will most certainly not be **saved** by our works, but we will most certainly be **judged** (assessed) by our works.

> And I saw the dead, great and small, standing before the throne, and books were opened. Another book was opened, which is the book of life. The dead were **judged according to what they had done** as recorded in the books. The sea gave up the dead that were in it, and death and Hades gave up the dead that were in them, and each person was **judged according to what he had done.** (Revelation 20:12–13)

> God **"will give to each person according to what he has done."** To those who by persistence in doing good seek glory, honor and immortality, he will give eternal life. But for those who are self-seeking and who reject the truth and follow evil, there will be wrath and anger. (Romans 2:6–8)

These are two of the most important passages about Judgment Day, and both teach the same thing: judgment is based on works. According to John 5:27, it is the unique privilege of Jesus Christ to judge the entire human race. And Jesus is a perfect inspector; he will be able to tell the quality of the tree by the fruit that comes from it (Matthew 12:33).

God desires to see good works lived out by our bodies in space and time, and these works are fully recorded in his heavenly books. He wants us to obey him gladly, so that his will is done on earth as it is in heaven. Jesus spoke this parable to make it plain that our relationship is displayed by what we finally choose to do with the commands of our Father.

> "What do you think? There was a man who had two sons. He went to the first and said, 'Son, go and work today in the vineyard.' "'I will not,' he answered, but later he changed his mind and went. "Then the father went to the other son

and said the same thing. He answered, 'I will, sir,' but he did not go. "Which of the two did what his father wanted?" "The first," they answered. (Matthew 21:28–31)

The key question Jesus will ask us is, "Which of you has done what my Father commanded?" Our works, done in history, recorded in God's perfect heavenly books, will speak for themselves.

Ultimately, Jesus links our love of him to our works of obedience. It's as simple as this—if we love him, we will obey him. He made this abundantly clear to his disciples by repeated statements made the night before he died:

- If you love me, you will obey what I command (John 14:15).
- Whoever has my commands and obeys them, he is the one who loves me (John 14:21).
- If anyone loves me, he will obey my teaching (John 14:23).
- He who does not love me will not obey my teaching (John 14:24).

The bottom line is plain: a true Christian life is a life of action, of consistent activity, defined by the highway of holiness laid out in God's commands. If we belong to Christ, he has truly set us free (John 8:36). But true freedom means we will run along the pathway of holiness: *"I run in the path of your commands, for you have set my heart free"* (Psalm 119:32).

In this section, I will argue that a spiritually mature Christian will lead an active lifestyle of **habitual obedience** to the commands of God. This active lifestyle begins with the presentation of their body to God as a living sacrifice, with each member of the body given over to God in active service to his will. I will then argue that sanctification (holiness) is both negative and positive, consisting of things we **must not** do in the body, and things we **must** do. Concerning things we must not do, I will speak of purity in four key arenas: sexual purity, speech purity, relational purity, and purity in lawful pleasures. I will also address the negative topic of how a mature Christian deals with their own sin, how we must respond when we do what we ought not to do, or when we fail in some responsibility God has entrusted to us. I will speak of the private humbling and the public works of repentance that God works in us when we have sinned. Concerning positive actions, what we **must do**, I will break our active life of service to Christ into seven essential patterns of habitual obedience: worship, relationships, spiritual disciplines, ministry, mission, stewardship, and work.

Since the commands of God extend to all of these arenas (positive and negative), Christians should consider themselves spiritually immature if they are neglecting any of these responsibilities. By the Spirit, God is continually working toward the goal of full obedience to all his commands, in all his children, all the time. He will work these works in us until the day we are glorified and each of these is perfected in us.

CHAPTER 17

HABITUAL OBEDIENCE

FOR THE SEVENTY-FIFTH TIME THAT day, the concert pianist plays the difficult passage in the Chopin concerto, his ear telling his brain what his fingers don't want to know: it's still not perfect. The tempo was right, but the accents on each note still, after two hours of practice, sound wrong. The tiny muscular movements of his fingers, controlled by the brain through nerve paths, still need to be better trained. Repetition alone can accomplish the burning in of the patterns that would satisfy his ear. Once the patterns have been established, they will have to be engraved deeper and deeper in his body, just as a diamond stylus must repeatedly trace out the lines the engraver seeks to write permanently on the steel plate. Soon the pianist will sit down at Symphony Hall to play this piece and others in front of a thousand classical music lovers, and he must be able to play it perfectly, relying on the programming of his body that these seemingly endless repetitions will produce. So the pianist plays it again, and again, always thinking, "Just one more time."

That same evening, an exhausted basketball player stands alone in a dimly-lit gym on the other side of the city. He's dripping with sweat and driven by determination as he toes the free throw line, bounces the basketball exactly four times, bends in a precise way at the waist, flexes his knees, holds the ball with his fingertips, focuses on the rim exactly fifteen feet away, bends his knees and releases his 536th free throw of the evening. As it rips through the net and lifts his percentage slightly to an 89% success rate for the session, he slowly trudges over to retrieve the ball, and then throw it for the 537th time. His goal? Simple: the next time he stands alone on the free throw line with less than a minute to go and his team trailing by two points, he won't miss one of two free throws as he did last week.

At the same time, in a fifth-story apartment in the same city, a woman serves a hot meal to her husband, a meal she has labored over for almost an hour. She is a new Christian, and he is not a Christian at all. As he looks at the meal, he sneers and takes his frustrations out on his wife: "You always make the same lousy meals!" She is naturally hot-tempered, and for years she has trained herself for such a time as this, trained herself to do the wrong thing. She has practiced as much as the pianist and basketball player on how to repay evil for evil, how to escalate a conflict with a harsh word. Like him, she is an expert in sin. And where water has flowed before, more times than anyone but God could count, it will most surely flow again—unless the Holy Spirit intervenes. But he does intervene, calling to mind a new Scripture she'd learned just that morning: *"A gentle answer turns away wrath, but a harsh word stirs up anger"* (Proverbs 15:1). Instead of doing the natural thing, something she's practiced for decades, pouring out a mixture of anger, pride, viciousness, and defensiveness, instead she gently and kindly says, "Honey, if there's something else you'd like for dinner, I'd be happy to make it for you." A new path is laid in her heart, holding out great promise for the future. But it will take seemingly endless repetition until she can by instinct do what the Savior would have her do.

HABITS OF HOLINESS

Habits. The body is trained by them, by repetition, day after day, for good or for evil. The key to a lifestyle of godly actions is habitual obedience, unlearning habits of wickedness and learning new habits of obedience. We are erasing lines of wickedness which sin has deeply engraved on the steel plate of our soul, and beginning to etch (however lightly) a new pattern, in the image of Christ. Romans 6:19 teaches this plainly: *"Just as you used to offer the parts of your body in slavery to impurity and to ever-increasing wickedness, so now offer them in slavery to righteousness leading to holiness"*.

Habitual obedience is the key to a godly lifestyle, because habits have the power to be used either for sin or for righteousness. Our old pattern was to offer the parts of our bodies to our old master, sin, with the result of "ever-increasing" wickedness. This is accomplished by habit, by repetition. The Greek phrase is literally "in slavery . . . to lawlessness into lawlessness."

A mature Christian has engraved very deeply certain lines of habitual obedience, and is constantly laboring to engrave them even deeper by repetition. As he grows in his knowledge of the Christian life, he will also seek to engrave new lines of righteousness in areas he's never before attempted. The engraving pen must move over the same lines again and again to make the slightest mark on the steel plate of his soul, for patterns of righteousness cannot be established overnight. Sadly and painfully, however, he must also somehow erase the old lines of wickedness, unlearn habit of selfishness, anger, laziness, lust, pride, and greed.

The soul is trained for good or evil with every movement of the will and every action of the body. We can **train** ourselves for godliness (1 Timothy 4:7); by constant use of spiritual resources we can **train** ourselves to distinguish good from evil (Hebrews 5:14); God can **train** us for godliness through painful discipline for sin (Hebrews 12:11). Or, conversely, we can **train** ourselves to be experts at lust and greed (2 Peter 2:14). All four of these verses use the same Greek word, *gymnazo* (train), from which we get the word gymnast. In the New Testament era just like today, it related to athletic training. It proves that the soul can be trained through habit to be either godly or ungodly.

The tablet on which our habits are progressively engraved or from which they are progressively erased is the body, especially including the brain. Therefore, a godly Christian lifestyle consists very much in training the body to act in righteousness, and to refrain from wickedness. Righteousness and wickedness in daily life are completely defined by the word of God, by obedience or disobedience to the commands of God.

THE COMMANDS OF GOD
DEFINE GODLY ACTIONS

I am here arguing for the sufficiency of Scripture in defining godly living in the body. When it comes to pleasing God in actions, obedience to God's commands is everything. We cannot do anything well-pleasing to God that he did not first tell us to do. God doesn't sit on his throne and say to his children, "Surprise me! Come up with something that will delight me!" Even apart from the theological fact that our omniscient God cannot possibly be surprised, we should understand that God doesn't desire to be surprised by our good works. He wants to lead and he wants us to follow. He must be the initiator, and we the responders. And as the hymn "How Firm a Foundation" puts it, "What more can he say than to you he hath said?" God has commanded holiness, and we must obey. God has commanded daily righteousness, and we must obey. Nothing we do in life, even in our modern technological world with its constantly developing electronic and computer advances, is not adequately described, either commanded or forbidden, in Scripture. 1 John makes this very clear through repeated statements:

> We know that we have come to know him if we obey his commands. The man who says, "I know him," but does not do what he commands is a liar, and the truth is not in him. But if anyone obeys his word, God's love is truly made complete in him. This is how we know we are in him: Whoever claims to live in him must walk as Jesus did. (1 John 2:3–6)

Those who obey his commands live in him, and he in them. (1 John 3:24)

This is how we know that we love the children of God: by loving God and carrying out his commands. This is love for God: to obey his commands. And his commands are not burdensome, for everyone born of God overcomes the world. (1 John 5:2–4)

So the sum of the matter for us in daily life is habitual obedience to God's commands as recorded in Scripture. We cannot at any given moment do any better than obey God's commands; obedience alone describes a lifestyle of godly actions.

OBEDIENCE IN THE BOOK OF ROMANS

True saving faith produces physical obedience to the commands of God. The book of Romans makes this insight the bookends of the entire epistle:

- through [Christ] we have received grace and apostleship to bring about **the obedience of faith** for the sake of his name among all the nations (Romans 1:5, ESV);
- [God has chosen to reveal the gospel] to bring about **the obedience of faith** (Romans 16:26).

It was by Adam's disobedience that the world fell into bondage to sin (Romans 5:19), and this bondage to sin is characterized by disobedience to God's commands (Romans 1:30; 11:30–32). It is actually impossible for the natural man to obey God, to submit to his law (Romans 8:7). In fact, in the mystery of God's wisdom, God has in some manner consigned the entire human race to disobedience so that he may have mercy on all (Romans 11:32). Conversely, it was by Christ's obedience that we were saved (Romans 5:19). And the greatest, clearest outward evidence of saving faith is a lifestyle of obedience to God's law. Paul speaks glowingly of the clear obedience of the Romans as evidence of their conversion:

"Everyone has heard about your obedience, so I am full of joy over you" (Romans 16:19).

The keys to a lifestyle of obedience to God's commands are 1) the spiritual union we have with Christ by faith, and 2) the gift of the indwelling Holy Spirit. Without those two spiritual realities, a lifestyle of habitual obedience would be impossible. But Romans 6 clearly establishes the first—our union with Christ in his death and resurrection; and Romans 8 clearly establishes the second—the power of the indwelling Spirit to orchestrate habitual obedience to the laws of God. By these two gifts, the Christian is able to develop entirely new habits of obedience to God's all-encompassing commands, and thus leave a permanent record of good deeds that will glorify God for all eternity.

CHAPTER 18

THE BODY AND ITS WORKS

AS WE COME TO THE topic of action in the Christian life, we are talking about the movement of the body in God's physical universe. We are talking about signals given from the brain to move certain muscle groups to accomplish things in this world. The body is the vessel of action by which we human beings make an impact on the physical world in which we live. There is a tremendously close link between our character and our body's actions. As a matter of fact, we cannot really say that we will to do something if we do *not* do it, when given the opportunity. Thus, if power and opportunity are given to us to speak a word of encouragement, or give money to the poor, and we do not do it, we cannot rightly say that we willed it.

All our actions are therefore the natural outflow of our character. We love, we desire, we choose, we think, we feel, we are, therefore we do. We never act except as a reflection of our inner nature. And God desires that we act righteously in his world.

DUALISM IS REJECTED

The topic of the body is a fascinating one in the Bible and in the history of human philosophy and religion. Many Greek philosophical systems were dualistic, and posited that the physical world is evil: an emanation of evil spiritual beings called "demiurges." They believed that the true God was free from physical existence, physical drives, physical desires, and physical passions. Therefore, to be saved from this evil world, these philosophies taught that we had to become more and more detached from our bodily existence. This dualistic philosophy was behind the trouble in the Colossian church, to which the Apostle Paul wrote his epistle. There, some false teachers were mingling elements of dualistic Greek philosophy with Jewish legalism and asceticism to produce a hybrid religion that was not Christianity at all. These false teachers denied the incarnation of Christ, and sought to escape bodily lusts by rules and regulations: *"Do not handle! Do not taste! Do not touch!"* (Colossians 2:21). So also many Eastern religions and pseudo-Christian cults have had the same dualistic disdain for the body. For example, the Shakers cult believed the human body was evil, and thus forbade simple touching between the sexes, never mind marriage. Obviously, their movement eventually died out!

FIVE-FOLD PROOF OF GOD'S ESTEEM OF THE BODY

But the Bible has a much healthier view of the human body, one that is essential for us to understand in order to live godly lives in this world. First of all, the Bible teaches that the body is **not** inherently evil, and that God is deeply concerned about the body, not merely trying to save us out of it. Five key doctrines establish this view: creation, the incarnation of Christ, the resurrection of Christ, the indwelling of the Holy Spirit, and the general resurrection at the end of the world.

At creation, God fashioned a physical universe by the word of his power. This included specially creating a man's body from the dust of the earth and a woman's body from the rib of the man. After finishing the creation of the physical universe, God declared all of it "very good." (Genesis 1:31). This destroys the false teaching that the physical universe was made by evil demiurges and that God had nothing to do with the physical universe.

Secondly, when God sent his Son into the world, it was by an incarnation, the enfleshment of his only begotten Son: *"the Word became flesh and made his dwelling among us"* (John 1:14). The word "flesh" is a striking statement: a clear indication that the body itself, with its muscles, tendons, blood vessels, nerves, intestines, etc., is still a good gift from God, despite our sin. The idea that God abhors the physical body and desires to free us from it is made preposterous by the fact that he sent his Son *"in the likeness of sinful flesh to be a sin offering"* (Romans 8:3). If the body itself were evil, Christ would never have taken on human flesh. In Colossians, Paul focuses greatly on Christ's physical body as the instrument of our redemption: *"But now he has reconciled you by Christ's physical body through death to present you holy in his sight, without blemish and free from accusation"* (Colossians 1:22). There, Paul doubles up the Greek words for body (*soma* and *sarx*) to intensify the physical nature of Christ's atoning work.

Thirdly, Christ's resurrection stands forever as proof that God has a saving purpose toward the human body. If the body were evil, and God simply desired to save us from it forever, why would Christ re-enter the body that was laid in the grave? But the bodily resurrection of Christ, the same body that was wrapped with linens and laid in the cave rising to live forever, proves that the body itself is good and that God intends to redeem the body and make it a holy habitation to last for all eternity. The physical nature of Christ's resurrection could not have been made clearer than his statement to his stunned disciples in the upper room: *"Look at my hands and my feet. It is I myself! Touch me and see; a ghost does not have flesh and bones, as you see I have"* (Luke 24:39). Jesus still has flesh and he will have it forever.

Fourthly, the indwelling of the Holy Spirit in the bodies of redeemed saints while they still live on earth proves that God delights in the body and considers the body central to his salvation plan: *"Do you not know that your body is a temple of the Holy Spirit, who is in you, whom you have received from God?"* (1 Corinthians 6:19). The fact that Christ himself is dwelling in our physical bodies by his Spirit is put in the most graphic terms in that same passage, as Paul is calling on the Corinthian Christians to flee sexual immorality and not unite themselves with prostitutes: *"Do you not know that your bodies are members of Christ himself? Shall I then take the members of Christ and unite them with a prostitute? Never!"* (1 Corinthians 6:15).

Fifthly, the human body is elevated to eternal significance by the doctrine of the general resurrection. Every single human being on the face of the earth will rise from the grave, to spend eternity in a body either in heaven or hell: *"Multitudes who sleep in the dust of the earth will awake: some to everlasting life, others to shame and everlasting contempt"* (Daniel 12:2); *"Do not be amazed at this, for a time is coming when all who are in their graves will hear his voice and come out—those who have done good will rise to live, and those who have done evil will rise to be condemned"* (John 5:28–29). For Christians, God's special crafting of a resurrection body, a body which will never grow weary, feel pain, or die, a body which will be equipped to serve him for eternity in a New Heaven and New Earth, is final confirmation of the incredible significance of the human body in God's redemptive plan.

THE BODY OUR ONLY VEHICLE FOR EARTHLY OBEDIENCE

Furthermore, we know that it is only by our physical bodies here on earth that we can obey his commandments to serve him in our generation. It is our hands that we extend to the poor and needy; it is our feet that carry us to the lost to evangelize them; it is our mouths that speak the word of life to them so they may believe; it is our eyes that weep for the suffering of the world, our ears that listen to the word of God. The body is vital to the two infinite journeys, vital to what God desires to do in and through us. Therefore it is vital for us to esteem it properly, to care intensely about what we do with our bodies.

BUT . . . THE BODY IS A CURSED BATTLEFIELD WITH SIN

However, the New Testament also has a realistic and somewhat negative view of our life in the body at the present time. Our bodies are now under the curse of sin, and are therefore in a lowly state. Our bodies are now "bodies of sin," because our bodies are affected by our unregenerate state. Romans 6:6 states, *"for we know that our old self was crucified with him so that **the body of sin** might be done away with, that we should no longer be slaves to sin."* Our sinful identity in Adam died when we came to faith in Christ, but we still have the body of sin that we had when we were that old person. There is a physical effect to our career in sin. It does not just go away, but instead has a momentum to it. By sinning, we build up habits and tendencies which continue to pull at us even after we come to salvation in Jesus. This is the body of sin.

The Bible describes the body of sin in other terms as well;:

- In Romans 6:12 it is called a *"mortal body,"* or a body that is constantly dying and destined to die.
- In Romans 7:24 it is called the *"body of death."*
- Genesis 3:19 declares that this body is "of the dust" and "earthy." It states, "b*y the sweat of your brow you will eat your food until you return to the ground, since from it you were taken; for **dust you are** and to dust you will return.* 1 Corinthians 15:47 says, *"The first man is from the earth, **earthy**; the second man is from heaven* [NASB]."
- 2 Corinthians 4:7 says that our bodies are like "jars of clay."
- Philippians 3:21 declares our bodies to be "lowly." The word used here means bodies of humiliation.

Other passages refer to the earthly body as an "earthly tent." This means that the earthly body is impermanent, in the same sense that the pegs of a tent can be pulled up and moved. Second Peter 1:13 says, "*I think it is right to refresh your memory as long as I live in the **tent of this body**.*" Also, 2 Corinthians 5:4 says, "*for while we are in **this tent**, we groan and are burdened, because we do not wish to be unclothed but to be clothed with our heavenly dwelling, so that what is mortal may be swallowed up by life.*"

There is in all this a present ambivalence toward the body, because the body is a battlefield against sin. In Romans 7:22–23 Paul speaks of this: "*For in my inner being I delight in God's law; but I see another law at work in the members of my body, waging war against the law of my mind and making me a prisoner of **the law of sin at work within my members**.*" This gives the idea that our body is in mutiny against the city of truth being established in our character. Because of this, the body is also viewed as constantly dangerous, and needing to be subjected to discipline. In 1 Corinthians 9:27 Paul says, "*I beat my body and make it my slave so that after I have preached to others, I myself will not be disqualified for the prize.*" Paul is in one sense suspicious of his body. He thinks that if his body wants something, it is probably not good, and so then he will subject his body to discipline.

Therefore we constantly care for the body's needs, but we must not give in to its lusts. This is certainly a delicate balance. Ephesians 5:28–29 addresses wives and husbands: "*In this same way, husbands ought to love their wives as their own bodies. He who loves his wife loves himself. After all, **no one ever hated his own body**, but he feeds and cares for it, just as Christ does the church.*" You should comb your hair, shave, feed yourself when hungry, scratch your skin when it itches, relieve your arms when they are weary, and in other ways care for your body. Part of being a Christian is taking good care of your body, even though it will end up decaying in the grave. However, all the while we must keep our bodily drives under subjection so that they do not end up destroying the very body from which they arise. As Romans 6:12 states, *"Therefore do not let sin reign in your mortal body so that you obey its lusts."*

At the end of this struggle awaits future glory. Philippians 3:21 says, *"[Christ], by the power that enables him to bring everything under his control, will transform our lowly bodies so that they will be like his glorious body."* The doctrine of our glorious resurrection bodies must always stand before us as a fountain of hope.

A PATHWAY OF PREPARED WORKS

As we have said, God doesn't sit on his throne and say, "Surprise me!," but rather, as Psalm 119:4 says, *"You have laid down precepts that are to be fully obeyed."* In the same way, God doesn't leave to chance and to our imaginations the specific paths our obedience will take, but rather ordains good works for us in advance. He then sovereignly orchestrates daily life circumstances, acting as a matchmaker between his children and the good works he wants us to delight in and to do. Ephesians 2:10 teaches this marvelously: *"For we are his workmanship, created in Christ Jesus for good works, which God prepared beforehand, that we should walk in them"* (Ephesians 2:10, ESV).

Paul says that "we are his workmanship," his masterpiece. In the Middle Ages, trade guilds dominated the economic life of society. Craftsmen were organized into these guilds to guarantee the quality of their workmanship. Apprentices, frequently the sons of the guild members, were trained by master craftsmen in the nuances of the craft. For example, a master silversmith would train his son in how to make a silver pitcher until he could perform every step of the process by memory. Then he would further hone his son's artistry until he felt his son was ready to become a master craftsman himself and set out on his own. In order to put his shingle up as a master silversmith, however, the apprentice had to submit a "masterpiece" to the guild for inspection. He would craft a silver pitcher of his own and present it for inspection. All of the basic skills, coupled with his own personal artistry, would be evident in this one masterpiece. According to Ephesians 2:10, we are God's *poiema* (from which we get the word poem), God's workmanship, specially shaped and crafted by his skill and artistry. God does not submit his masterpieces to any guild, however, or to any judgment higher than his own discerning eye.

And according to Ephesians 2:10, like the silver pitcher, we are crafted for a purpose, for specific good works. We are not meant to be ornamental, sitting in a display cabinet like a fine Italian vase. God intends us to be useful in his Kingdom, and he thus ordains good works for us to do. Ephesians 2:10 says God prepared those good works in advance. This concept boggles the mind, as we glimpse the complexity of God's sovereign plan unfolding in Church history.

I believe the verse implies that God both prepares us for the good works and the good works for us. Perhaps the best illustration of this is in Acts 10, where we see God working both sides of the equation in bringing the gospel to the Gentiles for the first time. He prepared the Roman centurion Cornelius to receive the gospel by sending an angelic messenger telling him to send to Joppa for Peter (Acts 10:1–8); then he prepared Peter to do the preaching by giving him a vision of a sheet being let down from heaven with unclean animals, and by commanding Peter to eat food that had been previously unclean and forbidden for him (Acts 10:9–16). I think this stands as a paradigm for all the good works which God ordains for us to do. The works God prepares in advance are essential to the Kingdom advance, as well as to our own personal progress in Christ. This is the stuff of the two infinite journeys: the works display and consummate our progress in sanctification, while they push us on to new levels of Christlikeness. Meanwhile, it is by these good works that the Kingdom is advanced to the ends of the earth. The Greek word translated "prepared in advance" in Ephesians 2:10 is used in only one other place in the New Testament, and that is Romans 9:23, where God speaks of his purpose in predestination, saying he did all of this *"in order to make known the riches of his glory for vessels of mercy, which he has **prepared beforehand** for glory—even us whom he has called, not from the Jews only but also from the Gentiles"* (Romans 9:23–24, ESV). Just as God prepared us beforehand for glory in heaven, so he also prepared beforehand good works for us to do.

And these good works really make up the whole course of our daily lives. Ephesians 2:10 says he prepared these works in advance for us to "walk" in them. I envision, therefore, a road of glory stretching out before us, every step of the way prepared ahead of time by God, specific good works that only we can do. No one can do anyone else's good works for them; we cannot hire substitutes to take our place in these works. We can choose to step off the glorious path of good works through disobedience, and on Judgment Day I believe we will weep when we see all the opportunities we wasted. But mysteriously, God's overall plan cannot be derailed by our disobedience. Mordecai spoke confidently about this to Esther concerning her role in working deliverance for the Jews: *"If you remain silent at this time, relief and deliverance for the Jews will arise from another place, but you and your father's family will perish. And who knows but that you have come to royal position for such a time as this?"* (Esther 4:14).

A mature Christian, therefore, awakes every day knowing that God has orchestrated a series of good works that will carry him or her through the whole day. And occasionally, God may call on him or her to a radical new direction of ministry, beginning a whole new path of good works:

1) A godly woman in Port-au-Prince, Haiti, steps from an early morning quiet time, to a prayer-walk through the rubble-filled streets of the city, to a day full of service at

an orphanage (including teaching English, making lunches, cleaning and bandaging a scraped knee, hugging a crying girl, encouraging a weary Haitian pastor, praying for an unreached people group in China, mopping up a spill), to a weary walk home, to a solitary dinner while reading the Bible.

2) A Christian legislator in Washington, D.C. steps out in faith to argue boldly for a law restricting funding for abortions, knowing that his bold stand may cost him the next election.

3) A believing couple who own a chain of small businesses take their vacations every year in India, teaching missionaries there how they can use small business start-ups as a platform for ministry.

4) A senior in college decides to forego plans for medical school and to trust the Lord for funds to enable him to go on a short-term mission trip to a college campus in the Persian Gulf.

5) A single mom in downtown Detroit, recently converted through the prayers and witness of a godly aunt, learns how to live by the Spirit her grueling daily life providing for and raising her two young children.

6) A wealthy British investment banker identifies his spiritual gift as giving, and begins a pattern of sacrificial and wise donations to evangelical ministries throughout the United Kingdom, eventually impacting ministries to the lost and poor in over twenty nations around the world.

Here are a variety of golden pathways of good works, and these brothers and sisters walked in all of them by the power of the Spirit. Every day, each one of them rises to walk in today's path of good works. Tomorrow, there will be another path, slightly different. At that point, today's opportunities will be gone forever, but by the grace of God they live in God's record book, each of them waiting to be fully rewarded in the New Heaven and New Earth.

CHAPTER 19

THE PRESENTATION OF THE BODY

IN THE SPRING OF 1194, during the third crusade to the Holy Land, crusader Henry of Champagne went to a mysterious castle in the rugged mountainous region of the Nizari in Syria to meet with Abu Mansur, the notorious "Old Man of the Mountain." This man was the leader of the most dreaded commandoes of that era, the Assassins, who were specially trained to sneak into enemy fortresses and assassinate a king or other key leader on whom a contract had been settled. Abu Mansur welcomed Henry and entertained him with a lavish feast. At the end of that feast, to prove the unswerving loyalty of his soldiers, Abu Mansur summoned two men and commanded them to fling themselves from the ramparts of the castle. Without hesitation, these two men obeyed, and hurled themselves down to their deaths.[38]

Now this story rightly horrifies our modern sensibilities. But the fact is that the most loving and gentle emperor in the history of the world, Jesus Christ, commands his subjects to do something vastly more difficult. Not just once, but possibly hundreds of times a day, he commands us to die to our self, to sacrifice ourselves for his glory. He summons us forward and commands us to lay down our lives, to "die" before angels and demons, before friends and foes. The perfection of the Christian life is this: a constant death, what Paul calls, in a mysterious paradox, "a living sacrifice": *"I appeal to you therefore, brothers, by the mercies of*

God, to present your bodies as a **living sacrifice***, holy and acceptable to God, which is your spiritual worship"* (Romans 12:1, ESV). This is the primary action of the godly Christian life. This is what Christ calls on all of his disciples to do every day: to present our bodies to God as a living sacrifice. A far greater thing he demands than anything any commander has ever asked of one of his soldiers, for it is a living death, offered countless times over the course of our lives. Other than the sacrifice of his own Son, it is the costliest thing God ever demanded of anyone, and only this pattern of life leads to heaven. All other physical obedience hangs on this first act, and it hangs continuously on it.

CHRIST BIDS US COME AND DIE

We have been trained to think of a human life as ultimately precious, the most valuable thing in the world. This mentality arises from the Judeo-Christian worldview, and is mostly right. However, four factors change the equation. First, the Bible teaches that there is something of infinitely greater worth than a human life, and that is the glory of God. Secondly, we have seen from the gospel that the Father was willing to pour his own Son out unto death, a bloody and painful death on the cross, in order to save us from our sins. Thirdly, we learn from Scripture that the doctrine of the resurrection means that this world is not all there is, and that death is not the end of our existence. Fourthly, we also learn from Scripture that seeds that fall into the ground and die are the very ones that produce much fruit (John 12:24).

These four factors help explain a perplexing verse in Scripture. I once went to a funeral in which there was a puzzling reference printed in the bulletin, laying out the Scripture passages to be read that morning. The puzzling reference was Romans 8:31–35, 37–39. What had happened to Romans 8:36? I was immediately intrigued as to why this verse had been excised from the funeral, deemed somehow unworthy of being read publicly. So I flipped open my Bible and read these words: *"As it is written, "'For your sake we are being killed all the day long; we are regarded as sheep to be slaughtered.'"* (Romans 8:36, ESV). At once I understood: the family of the deceased didn't want to think of people being killed, not to mention being "slaughtered," and so they cut it from the service.

But the Lord wants us to face the fact that, in this hostile world dominated by Satan's dark power and by people who are serving his dark purposes, God's people will often be thought of as sheep for the slaughter. And amazingly, the slaughter of God's people has been instrumental in the advance of the gospel. As Tertullian said to the enemies of the church, "We conquer in dying. . . . The oftener we are mown down by you, the more in number we grow. The blood of Christians is seed."[39] God tenderly watches over his suffering people and powerfully uses their Christ-like deaths to advance his Kingdom.

So God sometimes calls on us to die, to be sheep for the slaughter. It was Dietrich Bonhoeffer, the German pastor who died as a martyr at the hands of the Nazis, who stated plainly, "When Jesus calls a man, he bids him, 'Come and die!'"[40] Jesus had stunned his disciples in Caesarea Philippi with the revelation that he was going to be arrested, tortured, and killed in Jerusalem, and on the third day, be raised to life. Peter, speaking undoubtedly for all of them, took Jesus aside and began to rebuke him: *"Never, Lord, this shall never happen to you."* Jesus rebuked Peter, saying *"Get behind me, Satan, you are a stumbling block to me. You do not have in mind the things of God but the things of men"* (Matthew 16:23). Then Jesus turned to all his disciples and gave them a very plain command, from which Bonhoeffer and all generations of faithful Christians have taken their marching orders: *"If anyone would come after me, he must deny himself and take up his cross and follow me. For whoever wants to save his life will lose it, but whoever loses his life for me will find it"* (Matthew 16:24–25).

LEARNING TO DIE DAILY

This death march following Jesus is to be a daily shouldering of the cross (Luke 9:23). In Jesus' day, if you saw a condemned man carrying a cross surrounded by a detachment of Roman soldiers, it was a fair assumption that this was the last action of his life, and that, unless he lingered overnight, this would be the last day of his life. But Jesus calls on all his disciples, throughout all generations and in all nations, to die daily. So he is clearly referring to a spiritual death we must die.

Therefore, this was the central drive of Paul's sanctification as well. He wrote in Philippians 3, verses 10–11: *"I want to know Christ and the power of his resurrection and the fellowship of sharing in his sufferings, becoming like him in his death, and so, somehow, to attain to the resurrection from the dead."* When Paul wrote "becoming like him in his death," he was thinking of a daily process whereby he could live out the mentality of servanthood which Paul had spelled out so gloriously in the previous chapter, the humble self-sacrifice of Christ that saved our souls.

A LIVING SACRIFICE

Nowhere in all the New Testament, however, is the theology of self-sacrifice so clearly laid forth as in the book of Romans, and the culmination is in Romans 12:1. After Paul has unfolded the mysteries of the gospel for eleven glorious chapters, he now turns to practical matters, to the application of the gospel to the daily lives of Christians. He will give sweeping commands touching every area of life. He will speak of their spiritual gifts, of their love for one another, of their handling of money, and their submission to government authorities. He will address the issue of dealing properly with "debatable issues" with other Christians, and the topic of missions to the unreached peoples of the world. In all of these topics and others, he will call on the Roman Christians to act, to serve God in this physical world. But all of it hangs on this one concept: the presentation of the body as a living sacrifice, holy and pleasing to God. Without this, none of our service will be done with the right heart attitude, and will thus not be acceptable as "spiritual worship."

PRESENTED TO GOD

So what, exactly, does it mean to "present" your body, holy and pleasing, to God? The Greek word translated here is fairly common, but in this context it has to do with presenting yourself to a king, standing ready to do his bidding. Jesus used the same Greek word poignantly in Gethsemane at the moment of his arrest, urging Peter to put away his sword. Peter was ready to fight six hundred or more Roman soldiers who were there to arrest Jesus and take him to trial. Jesus told Peter: *"Do you think I cannot call on my Father, and he will at once **put at my disposal** more than twelve legions of angels?"* (Matthew 26:53). In effect, Jesus was telling Peter that if he were trying to escape being captured, he would turn to his Father in prayer, not to Peter's sword. If his Father sent the twelve legions of angels, they would be put fully at Christ's disposal. This is the same Greek word that Paul uses in Romans 12:1 for "present." The 72,000 angels would be dispatched to their commanding officer, King Jesus. And whatever the King told them to do, they would instantly obey, with great pleasure. That is how angels obey. The Lord's Prayer says, *"May your will be done on earth as it is in heaven."* How do the angels obey? They obey completely, promptly, and joyfully. So must we.

So, if the twelve legions were in fact dispatched to Jesus, one can imagine them standing fully at attention like perfect soldiers, ready, willing and able to obey him. If he commanded the angels to kill the six hundred or more soldiers that came to arrest him that night, those men would be dead within seconds. That is how the angels have always been. They stand ready in heaven, ready to do whatever Almighty God asks of them. In the same way, we should present our bodies to God, standing at attention before him, ready to do his bidding, whatever it may be. Like the angels who would have been dispatched to Jesus, so we are to dispatch our bodies to the King for his service.

This is the first and greatest act of Christianity. Some might argue that it is not an act at all, but a disposition of the mind, and with them I would not quibble. However, since it regards a presentation of the body for service, I think it is the foundation of every holy and godly action in life. Thus our bodies are to be "holy," says Paul, pure from sin and set apart unto God. In this way, our bodies will be seen as fully pleasing to God, ready to do his pleasure.

All of this is presented in much more detail in Romans chapter 6. Frankly, Romans 12:1 is merely a restatement of the key principles of sanctification Paul laid out in Romans 6. There, having clearly explained, in great detail, justification by faith alone apart from works of the law, having established how secure we are in God's lavished provision of grace, having proven that, *"where sin abounds, grace abounds all the more"* (Romans 5:20), Paul has to refute the typical human response to grace, which is: "Let us sin as much as we can so that grace may abound more and more!" The whole purpose of Romans 6 is to refute our faulty tendency to use the security of grace as a license for sin.

One of the key principles Paul establishes there is that, on the basis of our spiritual union with Christ, we died to sin and can never live in it again. But beyond that, we have an obligation clearly before us: *"Therefore do not let sin reign in your mortal body so that you obey its evil desires. Do not offer the parts of your body to sin, as instruments of wickedness, but rather offer yourselves to God, as those who have been brought from death to life; and offer the parts of your body to him as instruments of righteousness"* (Romans 6:12–13). Here we see the same principle, stated both negatively and positively. Negatively, do not let sin reign in your mortal body, because sin is no longer your master. Therefore, do not offer the parts of your body to sin. Positively, offer yourself to God, and offer the parts of your body to him. The behavior of the body is sure proof of the master who is ruling. We have two possible masters: God or sin. At every moment throughout the day, the Christian is faced with a critical choice: who shall rule me at this moment? Who is my master? A Christian must present himself again and again to his/her true master, God, by continually presenting the members of the body as instruments of righteousness. If not, then the Christian is really presenting himself/herself to sin as if still its slave, and he/she is presenting the members of the body as instruments of wickedness.

MEMBERS OF THE BODY

What does Paul mean when he speaks of the "members" or our bodies? In a very literal sense, it means any part of the body—our hands, arms, feet, eyes, mouth, ears, etc. Paul uses this expression metaphorically to speak of our being different parts of Christ's body, the church, in Romans 12: *"Just as each of us has one body with many members, and these members do not all have the same function, so in Christ we who are many form one body, and each member belongs to all the others"* (Romans 12:4–5). In a parallel passage in 1 Corinthians 12, Paul gets specific about such organs as the eye, the ear, the hand, and the foot.

So, at least, we are to present our hands, mouths, feet, and eyes to God as instruments of righteousness. How do we do this? In Romans 10, Paul speaks of the feet that carry messengers of the gospel across mountain ranges, rivers, oceans, and deserts to bring the saving light of Christ to the lost: *"And how can they preach unless they are sent? As it is written, 'How beautiful are the feet of those who bring good news!'"* (Romans 10:15). Raymond Lull, the courageous missionary to the Saracens in the thirteenth century, presented his feet to God as an instrument of righteousness when he overcame his fears and boarded the ship that carried him to

Tunis. So also Dr. Paul Brand presented his hands to Christ as a surgeon, specifically looking after the degenerated bodies of lepers in India. George Whitefield presented his mouth to Christ as an instrument of righteousness every time he drew breath and preached to the tens of thousands who flocked to hear him, even to his dying day. And every Christian martyr who has ever died for the gospel presented his or her body completely to Christ, who poured it out entirely as a drink offering.

So, the "members" we present to Christ have at least to do with the parts of our physical bodies that God will use to accomplish his purposes on this physical earth. But I think it extends to our minds as well, our internal selves. This we have already covered in the Character section, but I think we must "consider ourselves" dead to sin but alive to God in Christ Jesus, and thus be certain that our minds are fixed on the things of God, that our hearts are in love with the things of God. Our affections, our desires, our wills, our thoughts, our emotions are themselves to be presented to God as instruments of righteousness.

This presentation must happen literally moment by moment in the Christian life; it is certainly done once for all time at conversion, but must be reenacted again and again, countless times, in the journey of sanctification. Every time a temptation comes, we are brought to the fork in the road: sin stands beckoning left, and Christ stands beckoning right. It is impossible not to choose one or the other. We either present ourselves to Christ and our members to him to serve his purposes, or by default we have chosen to obey sin.

HERE I AM!

The essence of presentation is saying "Here I am! I am yours to command!" Again and again in the Bible, when God calls a godly man, the man answers in exactly this manner (all emphasis mine):

- Some time later God tested Abraham. He said to him, "Abraham!" "**Here I am**," he replied. Then God said, "Take your son, your only son, Isaac, whom you love, and go to the region of Moriah. Sacrifice him there as a burnt offering on one of the mountains I will tell you about." (Genesis 22:1–2)
- Then he reached out his hand and took the knife to slay his son. But the angel of the Lord called out to him from heaven, "Abraham! Abraham!" "**Here I am**," he replied. (Genesis 22:10–11)
- And God spoke to Israel in a vision at night and said, "Jacob! Jacob!" "**Here I am**," he replied. "I am God, the God of your father," he said. "Do not be afraid to go down to Egypt, for I will make you into a great nation there." (Genesis 46:2–3)
- When the Lord saw that he had gone over to look, God called to him from within the bush, "Moses! Moses!" And Moses said, "**Here I am**." (Exodus 3:4)
- Then I heard the voice of the Lord saying, "Whom shall I send? And who will go for us?" And I (Isaiah) said, "**Here am I**. Send me!" (Isaiah 6:8)

THE EXAMPLE OF CHRIST

But no godly man or prophet has ever said "Here I am, send me" with more purity and courage than Jesus Christ. Jesus was in a constant state of readiness before his Father, always ready to listen and to do his Father's will. This disposition of Christ's soul was predicted in some key places in the Old Testament. Psalm 40 is a powerful prediction of Christ's obedience, quoted also in Hebrews 10:

> Sacrifice and offering you did not desire, but my ears you have pierced; burnt offerings and sin offerings you did not require. Then I said, "**Here I am**, I have come—it is written

about me in the scroll. I desire to do your will, O my God; your law is within my heart." (Psalm 40:6–8)

This passage clearly displays Christ's attitude as a servant. God has "opened" Christ's ears, either simply opened them to hear his commands, or pierced them as one would do to a servant who loves to do his master's will and yearned to stay permanently obedient to him (Exodus 21:6). Jesus said to his Father before the world began, "Here I am, send me." God's law was perfectly written in his heart, and he perfectly and constantly presented his members to the service of God's will. He was the "Servant of the Lord" in Isaiah 52–53, whose willingness to offer himself and all his members to the Father's will saves our souls. Christ's spirit of willingness to listen and then to offer himself was predicted in Isaiah 50:

> The Sovereign Lord . . . wakens me morning by morning, wakens my ear to **listen** like one being taught. The Sovereign Lord has opened my ears, and I have not been rebellious; I have not drawn back. **I offered** my back to those who beat me, my cheeks to those who pulled out my beard; I did not hide my face from mocking and spitting. (Isaiah 50:4–6)

This is obedience; it is how Christ saved us from sin, and it is to this same obedience that Christ now calls us. Before his incarnation, Christ presented himself to his Father to offer his body as an atoning sacrifice for our sins. During his days on earth, he arose morning by morning and listened to his heavenly Father, then daily offered himself fully to his Father's will, even to the point of death on a cross.

So also Christ now calls all of his disciples to listen to his call morning by morning and to offer ourselves to him, and to offer the parts of our bodies to his service. Full submission to his will is what this living sacrifice is about, and it is intrinsic to the sweetest call he ever made:

Come to me, all you who are weary and burdened, and I will give you rest. Take my yoke upon you and learn from me, for I am gentle and humble in heart, and you will find rest for your souls. For my yoke is easy and my burden is light. (Matthew 11:28–30)

The word "yoke" relates directly to Christ's Kingly authority, for repeatedly in the Old Testament that is how the word was used, usually in a very negative sense of domination by a harsh king or a tyrant (1 Kings 12:4, Isaiah 9:4, Isaiah 14:25, Jeremiah 27–28). Jesus commands us to bow our stiff necks at last under his yoke, but he is no tyrant. Our old master, sin, was the worst tyrant the world has ever seen. But Jesus' yoke is easy and his burden is light. Full, glad obedience to Christ's moment-by-moment commands results in "abundant life" (John 10:10). Only by continual submission to this new Master, Christ, will we break our habitual allegiance to our former master, sin. By this new submission alone will we craft the good works that God will reward eternally.

CHAPTER 20

PURITY FROM SIN

THE NEW TESTAMENT CONSISTENTLY PRESENTS holiness in both a positive and a negative light, as well as with both an internal and an external aspect. Holiness is essentially separation: separation from evil and separation to God. The internal separation from evil and to God we have already discussed in the Character chapter—it has to do with affection for God and hatred of sin, desire for righteousness and desire to be free from wickedness, choosing what is right and rejecting what is evil, thinking properly of ourselves and of life so that our hearts are freed from the influence of sin. These internal aspects of the battle for holiness we have covered in detail.

But now we face the external aspect—bodily actions. Here we come to the fruit on the tree of character. Jesus said, *"Make a tree good and its fruit will be good, or make a tree bad and its fruit will be bad, for a tree is recognized by its fruit"* (Matthew 12:33). Our actions in holiness must therefore also be separated: separated *from* sins, separated *to* God in specific ways. Separation from sins, from specific patterns of sin, is essential to spiritual maturity. Because this is so essential, there are many negative lists of sinful behavior throughout the Bible. Of the Ten Commandments, all but one, *"Honor your father and mother"* (Exodus 20:12), are negative, prohibiting something:

1. You shall have **no** other gods.
2. You shall **not** make any idols or worship any idols.
3. You shall **not** take the name of the Lord in vain.
4. You shall **not** do any labor on the Sabbath.
5. Honor your father and mother.
6. You shall **not** murder.
7. You shall **not** commit adultery.
8. You shall **not** steal.
9. You shall **not** bear false witness.
10. You shall **not** covet.

So also in the New Testament, holiness is taught both negatively and positively. In Romans 6, Paul makes the negative aspect clear in a theoretical sense: *"Therefore **do not** let sin reign in your mortal body so that you obey its evil desires. **Do not** offer the parts of your body to sin, as instruments of wickedness"* (Romans 6:12–13). We see the same thing in Ephesians 4:22–32. In verses 22–24, Paul teaches the Ephesian Christians to be holy by putting off the old and putting on the new. This sets up the good-evil pattern of the commands that follow:

Positive	**Negative**
	[25] Therefore each of you must put off falsehood
and speak truthfully to his neighbor, for we are all members of one body.	
	[26] "In your anger do not sin": Do not let the sun go down while you are still angry, [27] and do not give the devil a foothold. [28] He who has been stealing must steal no longer,

Positive

but must work, doing something useful with his own hands, that he may have something to share with those in need.

Negative

²⁹ Do not let any unwholesome talk come out of your mouths,

but only what is helpful for building others up according to their needs, that it may benefit those who listen.

³⁰ And do not grieve the Holy Spirit of God, with whom you were sealed for the day of redemption.
³¹ Get rid of all bitterness, rage and anger, brawling and slander, along with every form of malice.

³² Be kind and compassionate to one another, forgiving each other, just as in Christ God forgave you.

Therefore, a mature Christian understands that the Christian life is warfare against sins, against specific practices that manifest the sin nature, and that are forbidden by God. The negative aspect of holiness is clearly spelled out in these prohibitions, and a mature Christian puts these sins to death.

Paul specifically names the acts of wickedness that must not be part of a Christian's life in various places in Scripture:

> They have become filled with every kind of wickedness, evil, greed and depravity. They are full of envy, murder, strife, deceit and malice. They are gossips, slanderers, God-haters, insolent, arrogant and boastful; they invent ways of doing evil; they disobey their parents; they are sense-less, faithless, heartless, ruthless. (Romans 1:29–31)

> The acts of the sinful nature are obvious: sexual immo-rality, impurity and debauchery; idolatry and witchcraft; hatred, discord, jealousy, fits of rage, selfish ambition, dis-sensions, factions and envy; drunkenness, orgies, and the like. (Galatians 5:19–21)

Christian maturity consists in a life increasingly free from these evil deeds of the flesh.

MORTIFICATION OF THE DEEDS OF THE BODY

It is evident from these verses that specifically naming sinful practices is essential to our holiness. Personal holiness, then, con-sists in **not** doing these things, in putting them to death by the power of the Spirit. This warfare against actual bodily deeds is of the essence of sanctification. If we are not following the Spirit in this mortification (putting to death) of these deeds, we are not children of God: *"For if you live according to the flesh you will die, but if by the Spirit you put to death the deeds of the body, you will live. For all who are led by the Spirit of God are sons of God"* (Romans 8:13–14).

In other words, to be a "son of God" means to follow the Spirit into daily battle against these practices, as we've already noted above. The great Puritan theologian John Owen, in his classic *On the Mortification of Sin*, spoke of this battle in poignant terms:

> The choicest believers, who are assuredly freed from the condemning power of sin, ought to make it their business all their days to mortify the indwelling power of sin.

> You must mortify! You must make it your daily work. You must be constantly at it while you live. Cease not a day from this work! **Be killing sin, or sin will be killing you!**[41]

We mortify sin primarily by starving it, by resisting it consistently, ever weakening its habitual grip over our bodies. Christian maturity is impossible without this continuous act of spiritual warfare.

PURIFYING OURSELVES AS HE IS PURE

The negative, external aspect of holiness is this: there are specific actions from which we must be pure, in which we must not indulge. The word "pure" is a word of perfection, and is therefore only a goal. Jesus said *"Blessed are the pure in heart, for they will see God"* (Matthew 5:8). We have already seen that it is impossible for any sinner to be clean in the holy sight of God apart from the blood of Christ. In Christ, however, every Christian is justified and thus seen to be perfectly pure in God's eyes. Sanctification is the ongoing work of Christ in our internal hearts and in our external behavior to make us as pure as he is.

During the footwashing in John 13, Jesus spoke very clearly both to our present status as already clean and our need for ongoing purification: *"A person who has had a bath needs only to wash his feet; his whole body is clean. And **you are clean**, though not every one of you"* (John 13:10). Later that same evening, Jesus said the same thing again: *"You are already clean because of the word I have spoken to you"* (John 15:3). Yet in both cases, we who are already clean still need to be cleaned. We who have had a bath through faith in Christ still need to have our feet washed.

The mystery of sanctification is that, while it is God who cleanses us through Christ, yet we are most certainly required to purify ourselves as well. We are to be active in fleeing pollution and purifying our minds, hearts, and bodies from habits of sin already engraved in our lifestyles: *"Everyone who has this hope in him purifies himself, just as he is pure"* (1 John 3:3). There is both a work of protection from pollution that could enter from the outside, and of cleansing of defilement that has already entered in the past. We see both aspects in the two verses just quoted. John tells us that our hope of final perfection, of becoming like Christ for we shall see him as he is (1 John 3:2), is the solid ground under our feet for a work of ongoing purification from that which is already impure within us. So also James tells us that we must guard against new forms of defilement that come from living surrounded by the pollution of the world.

FOUR KEY ARENAS OF PURITY

Having studied the various lists of prohibitions for Christians in the New Testament, I would like to focus on four major arenas Christians must fight for separation from sin: sexual purity, speech purity, relational purity, purity in lawful pleasures.

1). SEXUAL PURITY

Few areas have the power to destroy with as much devastating power as sexuality. It is clearly a tremendous weakness in the armor of our souls. Because of the significance and sacredness of sex, Satan has concentrated much of his effort at polluting us in this one arena. A mature Christian will never underestimate this issue, knowing from biblical history, church history, and perhaps from personal acquaintance some who have lost everything of value because of sexual transgression. Therefore, mature Christians are constantly vigilant lest they should fall sexually: *"Flee from sexual immorality. All other sins a man commits are outside his body, but he who sins sexually sins against his own body"* (1 Corinthians 6:18).

As a man, I have found Job's example of purity and self-protection extremely helpful. Job was a holy man, blameless and upright in his generation. Yet he felt a need for extra protection in this terrifyingly dangerous area of lust and adultery: *"I made a covenant with my eyes not to look lustfully at a girl"* (Job 31:1). He went on to speak in graphic terms of the effects of sexual sin, of adultery, of sleeping with another man's wife. Knowing that Almighty God sees his ways and counts his every step (Job 31:4), knowing that God would most certainly judge sexual sin, he says, *"It is a fire that burns to Destruction; it would have uprooted my harvest"* (Job 31:12). Just as a Kansas wheat farmer would scream with terror at waking one morning to find his harvest uprooted, all of it lying flat on the ground to rot, so a Christian man should recoil in horror at the effects of sexual sin: the ruin of a happy marriage, the loss of the respect of his children and all his friends, the spoiling of any evangelistic effects he might have had on his coworkers, a future of loneliness and bitterness.

Likewise, a Christian woman must guard her own heart from adultery, from the lure and excitement of a new relationship, from intimacy with a man who is not her husband. She must consider anything which causes her to lose respect for her husband and to see him poorly in comparison with some other man to be the voice of the devil. She must guard her heart from the enticements of romantic novels and movies, and learn to be content with the man God has provided for her. Furthermore, a mature Christian woman will understand the power of her body, the allure of her beauty, and dress modestly (1 Timothy 2:9). She will be careful to analyze each outfit for its modesty, and she will err on the side of caution rather than on the side of lust-inducing worldly fashion.

Here I must speak a specific warning against the evils of pornography, whether on the internet or in movies or printed material. This danger has grown greater and greater over the last two decades, and is a murderous threat against the hearts of Christians all over the world. God's command is clear: *"Beloved, I urge you as sojourners and exiles to abstain from the passions of the flesh, which wage war against your soul"* (1 Peter 2:11). Pornography is Satan's bombing run over the souls of Christians. We must be pure from it.

Too many Christian men and women have been destroyed by sexual sin. It is a dangerous thing, with the power to destroy households, churches, mission agencies, lives. So, caution must be exercised at all times. However, mature Christian people still must embrace the gift of sexuality and not forbid marriage or act as though married life is somehow impure: *"Marriage should be honored by all, and the marriage bed kept pure, for God will judge the adulterer and all the sexually immoral"* (Hebrews 13:4).

2). PURITY IN SPEECH

According to James, no member of the body causes so much pain, so much anguish, as the tongue, and no member is so hard to control. Therefore, a certain sign of Christian maturity is purity of speech: *"If anyone is never at fault in what he says, he is a perfect man, able to keep his whole body in check"* (James 3:2). The reason the tongue is so difficult to control is that it is a reflection of the state of the heart. Jesus said, *"out of the overflow of the heart the mouth speaks"* (Matthew 12:34). Because the Christian heart is divided, sometimes submissive to God, sometimes submissive to sin, therefore the tongue is divided: with the same mouth we both praise God and curse people! (James 3:9–10).

Therefore, it is essential for a Christian to learn how to control his tongue. It is astonishing how much the Bible has to say about sins of the tongue. The book of Proverbs has at least 142 proverbs that directly address matters of the tongue, and probably more than that. One proverb in particular speaks to me of the need for special caution in speech: *"the tongue has the power of life and death, and those who love it will eat its fruit"* (Proverbs 18:21). How powerful must be this small organ with the power of life or death!

Thus, Scripture gives us this prayer: *"Set a guard over my mouth, O Lord; keep watch over the door of my lips"* (Psalm 141:3). I get the image of a prison guard at a maximum security federal penitentiary. The guard's primary task is to ensure that no prisoners escape incarceration past his station. He is constantly vigilant over his post, using guard dogs, barbed wire, watch towers, search lights, and gun emplacements. He is trained to distinguish between prisoners that must not escape, and visitors that must be permitted to pass through and return to the outside world. So the "guard over the door of my mouth" must be able to distinguish between words that must never be said, and those words which may be sent out into the outside world.

Another powerful image for me is that of an expensive water filtration system, such as would be used in the manufacture of pharmaceuticals or semiconductors requiring ultra-pure water. The normal city water is piped into the filtration system, but then all particles, sediment, dissolved metals, bacteria, and other contaminants are systematically removed, resulting in water purified to an exacting specification. I look on Ephesians 4:29 as the ultimate "word filter" in the entire Bible. Anything that does not meet the specification laid down in that one verse must be filtered out from my speech: *"**Let no** corrupting talk come out of your mouths, **but only** such as is good for building up, as fits the occasion, that it may give grace to those who hear"* (Ephesians 4:29, ESV). The word structure "Let no . . . come out . . . but only . . . " is a word filtration system. What is filtered out is *"corrupting talk"*, what is permitted are words that *"may give grace to those who hear."*

Words that corrupt include: arguing (2 Corinthians 12:20, Philippians 2:14); blasphemy (1 Timothy 1:13, 20); boasting (James 4:16, 1 John 2:16); coarse speech (Ephesians 5:4); complaining (Philippians 2:14, 1 Peter 4:9); cursing (James 3:9–10); deceit (1 Peter 3:10); disrespect (Acts 23:5); false doctrine (1 Timothy 6:3); filthy joking (Ephesians 5:4); flattery (Romans 16:18); foolish talk (Ephesians 5:4); gossip (Romans 1:29); insults (Matthew 5:22); lies (Colossians 3:9); mockery (Galatians 6:7); rebellion (Titus 1:10); slander (Titus 3:2, 1 Peter 2:1); threats (Ephesians 6:9, 1 Peter 2:23); words of unbelief (Hebrews 3:19, cf. Numbers 13:31–33), and the like.

Words that give grace include: the gospel message (Romans 1:16); right doctrine (Titus 2:1); scriptural exhortation (Hebrews 3:13) and encouragement (1 Thessalonians 5:11); praise (Hebrews 13:5) and thanksgiving (Colossians 2:7) to God; prayer (Philippians 4:6); godly counsel (Proverbs 27:9); practical daily life issues (Proverbs 1:3); small amounts of talk of earthly pleasures (James 1:17); large amounts of talk of heavenly pleasures (Colossians 3:1–2), etc.

One more filter the mature Christian sets up over his mouth is a word-count filter: *"My dear brothers, take note of this: Everyone should be quick to listen, **slow to speak** and slow to become angry"* (James 1:19). A person who won't shut up, even if saying true and generally helpful things, has an inflated view of his own wisdom and the importance of his own perspective. *"When there are many words, transgression is unavoidable, but he who restrains his lips is wise"* (Proverbs 10:19, NASB).

Therefore, a spiritually mature Christian speaks relatively few words, but those words are precious, Scripture-saturated, ministering grace to everyone who hears. He has learned how to filter out hurtful, corrupting patterns, and to speak only words of grace. Though no Christian will ever do this perfectly, yet mature Christians show their maturity by the purity of their speech.

3). PURITY IN RELATIONSHIPS

Sin has the effect of isolating human beings from each other. After murdering his brother, Cain was exiled from human society and had to make his own way apart from his family. This is the result of all relational sins: it leaves husbands estranged from their wives, parents from their children, former friends or church members from each other, employers from employees. It leaves us lonely, cold, and isolated in the world.

A mature Christian strives constantly to love others as himself, in obedience to the second great commandment. In order to do this, he must purify himself of all defiling attitudes and behaviors. In this section, there is no need to unfold the need for absolute sexual purity, for we have already covered that. So also have we covered in the Character section all the internal dispositions, attitudes, and thoughts that are appropriate for godliness, such as a loving disposition (affection), humility, self-denial, etc. Here I want to speak of habit patterns that defile relationships, and that are specifically singled out in the New Testament as dangers.

In the "acts of the flesh" listed in Galatians 5, Paul lists fifteen sinful behaviors that show the power of the sin nature still residing in Christians. Remarkably, eight of them have to do with relationship-destroying actions rooted in pride and anger: *"hatred, discord, jealousy, fits of rage, selfish ambition, dissensions, factions and envy"* (Galatians 5:20–21). At the core of all of these is the root sin of pride. Pride is the swelling of self that it seems was the cause of Satan's original fall from purity (Ezekiel 28:17). Arrogant humanity has followed Satan's pride, self-will, and selfishness, and most relational sins flow from this. Pride is the root cause of all wars, all marital squabbles, all lawsuits, all luxury and all poverty, all addictions, all parenting struggles, all church splits, all vaunting ambition: basically, all trouble between human beings.

Consider how sweet all human relationships would be if pride and selfishness were entirely absent, and each of us only thought about the needs and interests of others. The joy of the Christian hope is that, in the New Heaven and New Earth, we will actually enjoy precisely those kinds of perfected, pure, selfless relationships, with a multitude of people greater than anyone can number, and from every people group on earth (Revelation 7:9) and every era of church history. For eternity, we will be in complete harmony with these brothers and sisters, and there will be no factions, no dissension, no envy, no bitterness, no revenge, no plots, no relational defilement whatsoever.

Since this is our future, it is required that Christians purify from their lifestyles any habit pattern that harms relationships. A mature Christian gives special attention to anger, since it is almost always born from the parents of pride and selfishness. James commands us to get rid of anger, calling it "moral filth" (James 1:19–21).

A spiritually mature Christian will also purify himself of unforgiveness and all of its connected sins. In the Parable of the Ten Thousand Talents (Matthew 18:21–35), Jesus likened our forgiveness before God to the forgiving of a multi-*billion*-dollar debt owed by a servant to a king. He then showed us how repugnant someone's behavior is who, after having been forgiven so much, then chokes another man who only owed him the equivalent of several *thousand* dollars. The parable ends with the king throwing the unforgiving servant in jail to pay his debt. The lesson of the parable was driven home by Christ with a dire threat, if we refuse to forgive: *"This is how my heavenly Father will treat each of you unless you forgive your brother from your heart"* (Matthew 18:35).

A mature Christian will purify his heart from all bitterness, rage, and anger (Ephesians 4:31), and from the defiling actions that result. He will strive to keep his life free from broken relationships due to unforgiveness. He will abstain from revenge, hostility, power plays, cliques, backbiting, and other such sins that destroy relationships.

4). PURITY IN LAWFUL PLEASURES

At no time in the almost two thousand years of church history have Christians had so many lawful diversions from the work of the Kingdom, and (seemingly) so much time with which to enjoy them. This I can say with absolute certainty when it comes to the majority of American Christians, for no age in history has enjoyed such widespread affluence, so much leisure time afforded by labor-saving devices, and so many creative ways to feed our ever-growing hunger for sensory indulgence and entertainment. I add this word "seemingly," because time is no more abundant now than it ever was, and no less precious. One of Satan's great tasks in Western Christianity is to convince us that the time and money lavished on us is ours to spend on ourselves, and that— simply because we no longer need to wrestle so clearly with the ground so that it produces the food we need to stay alive—all the surplus time exists solely for our self-gratification.

Since Satan is so active in this area, purity in the enjoyment of lawful pleasures is a paramount issue in our generation. In this section, I do not speak of purity from illicit pleasures, like sexual gratification outside of marriage, drunkenness and other forms of chemical intoxication, etc. Rather, I speak of those good gifts given by God for us richly to enjoy, but from which we must constantly guard our hearts, lest we become ensnared by them. The tendency of our restless hearts is to take created things and lift them up to fill a role that was meant for God alone, but this is idolatry: it is in fact "idolizing" these things (Romans 1:25).

In this matter of the enjoyment of lawful pleasures, there are two extremes to which we are constantly tempted to go. On the one hand, we are tempted by deny all sensory pleasure by believing that the physical body is intrinsically evil. On the other, we are tempted to indulge in God's gifts to the point of gluttony and enslavement.

Concerning the first pattern, this is the route of the ascetics. Scripture reveals that God is exceptionally generous, and he created a world full of things he meant for us to enjoy: *"Every good and perfect gift is from above, coming down from the Father of the heavenly lights, who does not change like shifting shadows"* (James 1:17). But throughout history, the church has been plagued by false teachers called ascetics, who have taught that physical pleasure is evil and that we must not indulge in any sensory pleasures lest we be damned. Paul attacked this false teaching most vigorously in several places. In his letter to the Colossians, Paul spoke against false teachers who were commanding, *"Do not handle! Do not taste! Do not touch!"* (Colossians 2:20–23). In 1 Timothy 4:1-5, Paul warned against those who taught *"doctrines of demons,"* and who went so far as forbidding people to marry and commanding them to abstain from food which God created delicious, purely for pleasure. He summed up his warning by this statement: *"For everything God created is good, and nothing is to be rejected if it is received with thanksgiving"* (1 Timothy 4:4).

Enjoying the physical world is precisely what God intended when he made our five senses. God created an almost incalculable array of foods, each with distinctive flavors matched to specific regions of taste buds on the tongue, to give pleasure to the palate. In the same manner, God created breathtaking beauty on earth—soaring mountains, lush valleys, rushing whitewater, churning ocean waves, mighty oaks, soaring eagles—and designed the eye to take in the colors. And even the most proficient *parfumier* in Paris has not studied completely all the myriad fragrances that are locked into the countless species of flowers. Truly these gifts were designed for the senses, and it is foolish heresy to deny that God intended them for our pleasure. But they were meant to be received as from the hand of God, and enjoyed in his presence with thanksgiving, not away from him and as if he didn't give them.

The pleasures of life extend far beyond this, however. There are the delights of relationships—marriage, the parent-child relationship, siblings, close friendships, etc. God also gives us the delight of productive labor, of producing useful things with our hands or minds (Ecclesiastes 5:15–18). And the ingenuity of humanity has created many other pleasures as well, none of which are intrinsically evil, but are good gifts from God through our creative ability. Here I speak of art, music, games, literature, sports, plays, movies, hobbies: things which delight and engage the mind, stimulate the senses, challenge the body, and bring various kinds of pleasure.

All of these are good gifts from God. But every single one of them can become a trap into which we can fall, or a form of bondage in which our hearts can become ensnared, if we are not vigilant. Perhaps the most important verses addressing our need for purity in lawful pleasures are found in 1 Corinthians: "*'Everything is permissible for me'—but not everything is beneficial. 'Everything is permissible for me'—but **I will not be mastered by anything**. 'Food for the stomach and the stomach for food'—but God will destroy them both*" (1 Corinthians 6:12–13).

The great danger is that lawful pleasures can somehow take control of our hearts and enslave us. What did Paul mean, "I will not be mastered by anything"? The Greek word here implies an exercise of authority, as a master over a slave. The human heart is made for pleasure, but that pleasure was meant to be God-focused. The idea is that lawful pleasures can grow and grow in the heart, taking an inordinate place that God never intended. They can cause a new form of bondage that enslaves the Christian simply due to of the formation of habits. This enslavement to some otherwise valid pleasure actually can cause us to become idolaters: thinking, dreaming, yearning, and working only for that pleasure. That good gift from God, meant only to enhance and sweeten our lives, becomes instead the reason we live, the focus of our thoughts and energies.

In the book of Proverbs, God uses honey to symbolize lawful pleasures, and gives beautifully balanced wisdom concerning its use. On the one hand, God commands us to partake with thankful hearts: *"Eat honey, my son, for it is good; honey from the comb is sweet to your taste"* (Proverbs 24:13). When God lays out a good gift, it is folly not to partake of it. But that is not all that Proverbs says about honey, however. There is a built-in danger to honey if we over-indulge: *"If you find honey, eat just enough—too much of it, and you will vomit"* (Proverbs 25:16). Here God commands us to eat honey, but to do it in moderation. If we cross the line and overindulge, we will have to endure the painful and humiliating process of vomiting. This danger of over-indulgence is repeated a few chapters later: *"It is not good to eat too much honey, nor is it honorable to seek one's own honor"* (Proverbs 25:27). God makes far more honey than we can eat in a lifetime, and he puts far more in our path than is good for us to ingest. We must learn how to eat honey with thankfulness, and also when to stop eating, lest we vomit.

There is another danger to over-indulgence of honey, and that is a sated palate that comes to loathe the very gift of God for which he ought to be praised: *"He who is full loathes honey, but to the hungry even what is bitter tastes sweet"* (Proverbs 27:7). If we over-indulge in the good gifts of God, we will eventually become weary of them and grow to despise them. If we have enough wealth and leisure time, and glut ourselves constantly on all the good things we have come to love in life, we will eventually find ourselves in bondage to earthly pleasures—but they will no longer bring us any pleasure at all.

In C.S. Lewis's classic work on Satan's strategies for temptation, *The Screwtape Letters*, the elder demon Screwtape is giving his young apprentice demon, Wormwood, a lesson on tempting humans with pleasure. He cautions Wormwood about the whole matter of pleasure in the first place:

> Never forget that when we are dealing with any pleasure in its healthy and normal and satisfying form, we are, in a sense, on the Enemy's (i.e. God's) ground. I know we have won many a soul through pleasure. All the same, it is his

> invention, not ours. He made the pleasures: all our research
> so far has not enabled us to produce one. All we can do
> is encourage the humans to take the pleasures which our
> Enemy has produced, at times, or in ways, or in degrees,
> which he has forbidden.[42]

Having established the "danger" of pleasure to the demonic cause, Screwtape then gives Wormwood the recipe for "success" (i.e. temptation leading to sin):

> An ever increasing craving for an ever diminishing plea-
> sure is the formula. It is more certain; and it's better style.
> To get the man's soul and give him *nothing* in return—that
> is what really gladdens our Father's (i.e. Satan's) heart.

Now certainly, we see the effects of this formula in the pathetic lives of spiritually lost addicts of all kinds: drug addicts, alcoholics, sex addicts, tyrants, etc. None of these people genuinely delight in the thing they yearn for the most. They actually hate what enslaves them. But they can't break the bondage, and so they go right on doing, every single day, something which they loathe.

So it is with lost addicts. But it is wrong for a Christian to think such bondage could never happen to him or her. Our hearts are truly "prone to wander," and since we generally wander after what pleases us, it is frequently lawful pleasures that Satan can use to bring us into a form of practical bondage, though we cannot be enslaved by sin ever again. By capturing our pleasure with something created, then enlarging that pleasure beyond healthy boundaries, we render ourselves worthless for the Kingdom of God, and stop making progress in the two infinite journeys.

So, the lover of food becomes a glutton; the wine drinker becomes the drunkard; the model train hobbyist invests thousands of dollars and thousands of hours on his hobby; the lover of sea shells seeks to collect as many as possible; the movie lover builds a collection of hundreds of DVDs or watches ten movies a week on the movie channel; the investor becomes consumed with managing his stock portfolio; the real estate expert spends all his time, effort and money researching, purchasing, and selling properties; the pleasure in a career becomes the driven ambition of a workaholic; the stimulation of a computer game becomes an addiction, keeping an ordinary person awake till three in the morning finishing the game.

So God commands wisdom and balance in the matter of lawful pleasures. Love your spouse, play with your children and grandchildren as they grow, sit with your aging and ailing parents while there's time, enjoy your job, dabble in a hobby, watch a game or two, see a movie, own some things, eat your favorite entrée with relish. But watch yourself closely lest any of these things take over and become the master, rather than the servant, of your soul.

Finally, and more darkly, a Christian must study his lawful pleasures to see if any of them inevitably lead to sinful patterns. If making use of the internet invariably leads a man to seek out lustful images, if eating chocolate invariably leads a woman to gluttony, if sipping wine invariably leads someone to drunkenness, if downloading a movie from Netflix invariably leads to compromise, if pursuing a legitimate new business or investment opportunity invariably leads to greed or pride or self-centeredness or taking advantage of others or neglecting God or one's family, then we must heed Jesus' radical advice: *"If your right eye causes you to sin, gouge it out and throw it away. It is better for you to lose one part of your body than for your whole body to be thrown into hell"* (Matthew 5:29). Any lawful pleasure that leads to sin must be done away with, radically cut out, for the good of our souls.

The biblical term for purity in lawful pleasures is *self-control*, and it is last of that beautiful array of virtues Paul calls the *"fruit of the Spirit"* (Galatians 5:23). Only by the Spirit can we maintain purity while enjoying all the lawful pleasures with which God has filled this world.

SUMMARY

The actions of a mature Christian must be pure, free from defilement of any kind. In this chapter we have looked at four key areas of purity: sexual, relational, speech, and lawful pleasures. It is only as we keep ourselves pure in these areas that our lives will be pleasing to God.

CHAPTER 21

DEALING PROPERLY
WITH SIN

DESPITE THE FACT THAT CHRISTIANS have been given *"everything we need for life and godliness"* (2 Peter 1:13), that we are *"no longer slaves of sin"* (Romans 6:6), that Jesus has made us *"free indeed"* from sin (John 8:36), that if we *"resist the devil, he will flee"* from us (James 4:6), that we have impenetrable spiritual armor from God (Ephesians 6:11–17), and therefore never need to sin again, the fact of the matter is, *"we all stumble in many ways"* (James 3:2). As we have noted, Romans chapter 7 makes it plain that we will be struggling with sin the rest of our lives—not just struggling and overcoming, but struggling with the shame of actually doing the very things we hate (Romans 7:15).

However, a mature Christian knows how to respond to sin, and does so quickly. I heard once that sin is like mud, and we are to be like spiritual cats, who, having fallen into the mud immediately spring up and begin cleansing ourselves, rather than spiritual pigs who wallow in it and spend the rest of the day covered in it. A mature Christian knows that sin is not his home, and though he may fall into it, he doesn't take up residence there.

Basically, dealing properly with sin involves a vertical and horizontal aspect: vertically, the Christian must deal with God over his sin; horizontally, the Christian must deal with others that the sin has affected.

CONFESSION OF SIN

Having understood the law of God from Scripture (Knowledge), having been convicted of specific sin by the indwelling Holy Spirit (Faith), and having repented from that sin and grieved over it (Character), a Christian begins acting against it (Action) by confessing their sin to Almighty God. Confession involves agreeing with God over the sin, speaking back to God the names of the sins involved, and dealing honestly with God over what has offended him. From the very beginning, the shame caused by sin has caused sinners to want to hide from God and each other, and to cover over their sin. Adam and Eve covered themselves with fig leaves, and, upon hearing God approaching, hid from him. Sin must be covered, but only God can cover it effectively. Confession involves *uncovering* sin before God, making known to God openly what he already knows fully: *"He who conceals his sins does not prosper, but whoever confesses and renounces them finds mercy"* (Proverbs 28:13).

For over a year, King David resisted confessing his sin with Bathsheba because he had hardened his heart, and did not want to face the consequences of his evil actions. So he covered his own sin through self-deceit. But God sovereignly pressed on him, until at last he was ready to confess. Psalm 32 tells the story of the worst year of David's life. During that year, the baby conceived by his adultery was born, but David's spiritual life seemed to be dead. While David *"kept silent"* about his sin (verse 3), his *"bones wasted away"* and he groaned all day long (verse 3). God's *"hand was heavy"* upon him (verse 4), and his strength was *"sapped as in the heat of summer"* (verse 4). The only remedy was to acknowledge and confess his sin to God (verse 5), and allow God to cover it. Thus did David write, *"Blessed is he whose transgressions are forgiven, whose sins are covered"* (verse 1). The key to this experience of forgiveness was confession of sin.

The Apostle John gives us the greatest encouragement to confess our sins to God when he writes, *"If we confess our sins, he is faithful and just and will forgive us our sins and purify us from all unrighteousness"* (1 John 1:9). Isn't it amazing that God is "just to forgive" our sins? At one time, God's justice was our greatest fear—for if we received full justice from God for our sins, we know we would have deserved hell. But now that Christ has suffered for all of our sins, it would actually be unjust of God **toward his Son** to make him suffer for sins and then not forgive them. So what greater inducement could there be for us to confess our sins and let God cover them in Christ's blood and cleanse us from their defilement?

When confessing sin, a mature Christian seeks to root out everything his conscience has against him. Like digging a tick out of his thigh, he will not want to leave any part unconfessed, lest spiritual infection result from his laziness. So, with the light of the Holy Spirit, he will probe his soul and his actions honestly and confess what needs to be confessed: *"Search me, O God, and know my heart; test me and know my anxious thoughts. See if there is any offensive way in me, and lead me in the way everlasting"* (Psalm 139:23–24).

A mature Christian is also willing to face other people and confess sins to them as well, where needed. His pride will not stop his deep desire for holiness and reconciliation: *"confess your sins to each other and pray for each other so that you may be healed"* (James 5:16). This is the horizontal aspect of confession, and it is essential to keeping relationships healthy.

MOURNING AND FASTING FOR SIN

One aspect of the healthy Christian's emotional life is grieving over sin, as we've already mentioned in the section on emotions. However, this grieving takes some very physical forms, affecting our actions in some very significant ways. It certainly can be wrenching, time-consuming, and painful to meditate on our own sins until we feel genuine grief. It is even more difficult to pour out that grief in actual mourning: weeping, wailing, fasting, and other displays of mourning for sin. This runs so contrary to our shallow, fun-loving age. We deal lightly with sin and tend to minimize it. But a mature Christian recognizes that failure to mourn over sin is a guarantee to repeat it. So a mature Christian readily obeys James' command to mourn:

> Come near to God and he will come near to you. Wash your hands, you sinners, and purify your hearts, you double-minded. Grieve, mourn and wail. Change your laughter to mourning and your joy to gloom. Humble yourselves before the Lord, and he will lift you up. (James 4:8–10)

Fasting is also seen to be a display of grief and mourning, for Jesus linked the two. When asked by John the Baptist's disciples why he and his disciples didn't fast, Jesus answered, *"How can the guests of the bridegroom mourn while he is with them? The time will come when the bridegroom will be taken from them; then they will fast"* (Matthew 9:15). Thus did Jesus link fasting with mourning. So the Lord commands sinners in Israel, *"Even now,"* declares the Lord, *"return to me with all your heart, with fasting and weeping and mourning. Rend your heart and not your garments"* (Joel 2:12). Therefore, a mature Christian will occasionally fast as a display of grief over sin, seeking not to pay for sin by good works, but rather to prepare his heart for future godliness.

FRUIT IN KEEPING WITH REPENTANCE

Having dealt with God directly over the sin, having repented and confessed, having grieved and prayed, now the mature Christian is zealous to produce fruit in keeping with the repentance the Holy Spirit has worked. When John the Baptist came preaching in the desert of Judea and administering water baptism in the Jordan River, his message was: *"Produce fruit in keeping with repentance"* (Matthew 3:8).

Fruit in keeping with repentance is essential to a life of saving faith. Just as James taught in James 2:26 that faith without deeds is dead, so also is repentance without its connected fruit. The life of genuine repentance is costly, and it involves drastic actions. When convicted by the Holy Spirit of sin, the godly man or woman will take powerful actions to bring forth fruit in keeping with repentance. We see evidence of this throughout the Bible: a heart genuinely convicted of sin and repentant will act boldly to make it right; conversely a hypocrite will have feelings of regret over sin,; they may make promises concerning it, but will not produce the fruit (actions) that genuine repentance inevitably produces.

Perhaps the most stunning example of repentance in the Bible is that of Manasseh, perhaps the most wicked king that Judah ever had. This man had involved himself in all of the most detestable practices of the pagan nations that God had specifically forbidden. He tragically rebuilt all of the high places that his godly father, Hezekiah, had destroyed, and actually built pagan altars in the temple of the Lord. Even worse, he sacrificed his own sons in the fire of Ben Hinnom, and he practiced sorcery and divination. He was thoroughly evil, and one might have expected that there was no hope for him. But God sent the Assyrian army, and they captured Manasseh and deported him to Babylon. There Manasseh experienced one of the most astonishing conversions in the Old Testament: *"In his distress he sought the favor of the Lord his God and humbled himself greatly before the God of his fathers"* (2 Chronicles 33:12). God was moved by Manasseh's prayer and restored him to his throne. Then Manasseh brought forth abundant fruit in keeping with repentance:

> He got rid of the foreign gods and removed the image from the temple of the Lord, as well as all the altars he had built on the temple hill and in Jerusalem; and he threw them out of the city. Then he restored the altar of the Lord and sacrificed fellowship offerings and thank offerings on it, and told Judah to serve the Lord, the God of Israel. (2 Chronicles 33:15–16)

So also in Ephesus, after Paul preached the gospel, many who practiced sorcery and divination heard the word, and they were convicted and repented of their sins. They brought the scrolls they used for sorcery and burned them publicly, and their total value was calculated at fifty thousand drachmas—an amount as much as six million dollars today! (Acts 19:18–19). The burning of the paraphernalia of sin represents a vital element of true repentance, and this "burning" means ridding yourself of anything that causes sin. In the section on lawful pleasures, we already discussed Jesus' command concerning cutting off your right hand or gouging out your right eye if they cause you to sin (Matthew 5:29–30). If someone finds that using the internet invariably causes lust or gambling or gossip or time wasting, and if they don't make effective changes (either by canceling the internet service or by putting filters and safeguards that effectively remove the danger), they haven't truly repented of that sin. If someone finds that using credit cards inevitably results in overspending, and if they don't make effective changes (either by cutting up the card or by making themselves accountable in its use), they haven't really repented of that sin. If someone who is dating a non-Christian hears a sermon about the danger of mixed marriages and is convicted by the Holy Spirit that they must break off the relationship, but they fail to do it, they haven't repented of that sin.

MAKING RESTITUTION

So also our sinfulness puts us in the need of humbling ourselves and asking forgiveness of others, and seeking to make restitution for our wrongs. Zacchaeus is a good example of this aspect of repentance. As a chief tax collector, he had become fabulously wealthy by taking excessive taxes from his countrymen, cheating them to profit himself. But when conviction and salvation came to his heart, he knew what he had to do:

Zacchaeus stood up and said to the Lord, "Look, Lord! Here and now I give half of my possessions to the poor, and if I have cheated anybody out of anything, I will pay back four times the amount." Jesus said to him, "Today salvation has come to this house, because this man, too, is a son of Abraham." (Luke 19:8–9)

Jesus' reaction shows how important these actions were in demonstrating the reality of repentance and salvation. Making restitution for wrong is not very popular these days. Our culture is exceptionally proud, and people rarely deal properly with the effects of their sin on others. Athletes or Wall Street investors who have been caught cheating rarely give back their earnings, or "come clean" with the effects of their sin. Politicians who make racial slurs or slanderous comments hurtful to many people use vague language like, "If I have offended anyone, please know that it was not my intention to cause any pain."

Genuine repentance produces many actions of humbling and of dealing painfully and properly with the effects of sin. Mature Christians do not shrink pridefully from this responsibility.

ETERNAL VIGILANCE

In 1790, Irish orator John Philpot Curran spoke his most famous words: "The condition upon which God hath given liberty to man is eternal vigilance." The phrase has come into American popular culture as "Eternal vigilance is the price of liberty," frequently attributed to Thomas Jefferson. What Curran spoke concerning freedom from political and military tyranny, the Bible speaks of in terms of ongoing freedom from sin. Paul put the concept this way: *"Therefore let anyone who thinks that he stands take heed lest he fall"* (1 Corinthians 10:12). The context is very significant. In 1 Corinthians 10:1–11, Paul has been sternly warning the Corinthian church about presumption and sin, based on Israel's history. In verses 13–14, he goes on to speak of temptation and of the way of escape that God gives us so that we don't have to sin. The lesson is this: just because you are part of the community of faith, don't presume on the grace of God by living a life of sin.

My application of this concept from Paul is more detailed. After a Christian has sinned, they should study what happened, how they reacted, what temptations the devil used to deceive them, and what actions led to the sin. Then the Christian should be doubly vigilant about that sin in the future, knowing that a pattern of sin can be established quickly. If a Christian confesses some outburst of anger, they should focus on that anger and pray against it, and be careful of that area of weakness. So also, a prideful statement should lead to vigilance in the area of pride; a lustful action should be met with vigilance over lust; etc. Without this kind of vigilance toward sin, we have learned nothing from the experience and may soon be repeating it regularly.

CHAPTER 22

WORSHIP

"OH!"

That's it: a single word, of one syllable, in the greatest theological writing in history, the book of Romans. Paul wrote over seven thousand words to explain the mystery of the gospel, and perhaps the point of it all comes down to a single word of wonder, a word of awe, a word of astonishment, of self-forgetfulness . . . a word of worship:

> **Oh**, the depth of the riches of the wisdom and knowledge of God! How unsearchable his judgments, and his paths beyond tracing out! "Who has known the mind of the Lord? Or who has been his counselor?" "Who has ever given to God, that God should repay him?" For from him and through him and to him are all things. To him be the glory forever! Amen. (Romans 11:33–36)

There really is no other purpose for the word "Oh!" than to express emotional response to some external stimulation. In this case, it is the greatest stimulation possible: the truth of God as revealed in the gospel of Jesus Christ. Worship begins with God's self-revelation, and it exists in our response to that self-revelation. And that response is the culmination of all the internal work God does in us to bring it about: knowledge resulting in faith resulting in character resulting in worship. God reveals, we know, we believe, we love, and we worship.

Worship is the goal of God's whole work of redemption. John Piper makes this very clear at the beginning of two of his greatest books, *Desiring God* and *Let the Nations Be Glad*. At the beginning of *Desiring God*, he reworks the Westminster Shorter Catechism's statement in an unforgettable way: "The chief end of man is to glorify God BY enjoying him forever."[43] Piper goes on to restate this in another way: "God is most glorified in us when we are most satisfied in him." The whole direction and purpose of the Bible and of redemptive history is to transform us, body and soul, so that we will eternally glorify him by being perfectly satisfied with him: *"You make known to me the path of life; in your presence there is fullness of joy; at your right hand are pleasures forevermore"* (Psalm 16:11, ESV). This is the final destination of the internal journey: perfect happiness in the presence of God, eternally in the New Heaven and the New Earth.

The final destination of the external journey is the same for a countless multitude from all the people groups on earth. So, in the first words of *Let the Nations Be Glad*, Piper states

> Missions is not the ultimate goal of the church. Worship is. Missions exists because worship doesn't. Worship is ultimate, not missions, because God is ultimate, not man. When this age is over and countless millions of the redeemed fall on their faces before the throne of God, missions will be no more. It is a temporary necessity. But worship abides forever.[44]

From this, we can see how central worship is, since it is in worship that both the internal and external journeys find their perfect fulfillment. We have already covered the internal aspects of worship in the Knowledge, Faith, and Character sections. Since this is the Action section of this book, it is reasonable for us to concentrate our comments here on the actions of worship. We cannot worship what we do not know; knowledge itself is not enough for us to worship now, we must have faith. Faith will be completely unnecessary in heaven, for *"we shall see him as he is"* (1 John 3:2). But without faith now, it is impossible to worship God, for as we've seen, faith is the vision of the soul. By faith we "see" now what we will see later by our eyes. But knowledge and faith merely produce a heart ready to worship. Worship originates in the affections, in our deep love for God. It kindles itself in desire, a yearning to see God, to be with God, to be totally absorbed in God. It prepares us for action in the will: because God is worthy of worship we will to obey him, to present our bodies to him for his service. Worship fills our thoughts with truth, with concepts that we mull over and savor and understand deeply. Worship moves us emotionally, so like Paul, we can say "Oh!" to the depths of God: His person, his attributes, his actions in history, and his purposes for the future.

Without these internal things occurring, we will not truly worship God. All the actions of worship without the knowledge-faith-character precursors are pure hypocrisy, as Jesus poignantly proclaimed to the Pharisees: *"You hypocrites! Isaiah was right when he prophesied about you: 'These people honor me with their lips, but their hearts are far from me. They worship me in vain; their teachings are but rules taught by men.'"* (Matthew 15:7–9)

John Piper argues persuasively that the actions of worship **must** flow from the heart preparation or it means nothing: "Almost everyone would agree that biblical worship involves some kind of outward act. The very word in Hebrew means to bow down. Worship is bowing, lifting hands, praying, singing, reciting, preaching, performing rites of eating, cleaning, ordaining, and so on. But the startling fact is that all these things can be done in vain. They can be pointless and empty."[45]

SPIRIT-EMPOWERED WORSHIP

It is the special glory of the Holy Spirit to move his people to worship. The indwelling Spirit takes the truth of Scripture and lays it out in our hearts, then ignites it that our souls may ascend to God in true worship. Spirit-empowered worship is the special joy and privilege of the Christian: *"For it is we who are the circumcision, we who **worship by the Spirit of God**, who glory in Christ Jesus, and who put no confidence in the flesh"* (Philippians 3:3). The Spirit moves us to love God, to cherish him, to trust fully in Christ, and to approach Almighty God and present an offering of worship. The Spirit is the One who enables us to worship in spirit and truth, as Jesus taught the Samaritan woman in the most important passage in the New Testament on worship: *"Yet a time is coming and has now come when the true worshipers will worship the Father in spirit and truth, for they are the kind of worshipers the Father seeks. God is spirit, and his worshipers must worship in spirit and in truth"* (John 4:23–24). I think the English translations do well not to capitalize the word "spirit" in these verses, for I think true worship comes from the human heart upward to God, our minds believing the truth and our spirits moved by what we have seen of God. A mature Christian is consistently led by the Spirit of God into passionate worship based on the truth of Scripture.

WHEN SHOULD WE WORSHIP?

Let's organize our times of worship into three main categories: **private worship** and its actions, **daily life worship** and its actions, **corporate worship** and its actions.

PRIVATE WORSHIP

The foundation of private worship is regular intake and meditation on the word of God. The key to this is the daily quiet time, a time regularly set aside for spiritual disciplines. I will discuss spiritual disciplines separately in a section dedicated to that purpose. Here I just want to say that a mature Christian lives a life of personal worship to God. He rises early in the morning to praise and give thanks to God for his salvation. He pores over Scripture to find ways to praise God, and he personally delights in what the Scripture teaches him of the nature, names, acts, and purposes of God. His private worship life is the foundation of his public worship life, for he is no hypocrite, no whitewashed tomb, doing everything for others to see.

At the core of this private worship is the daily struggle to stimulate our sluggish souls to fervent worship. We don't usually arise passionate and fervent to worship and serve an invisible God. Rather, there are times when we must provoke our souls to respond appropriately to invisible truths: *"Praise the Lord, O my soul; all my inmost being, praise his holy name. Praise the Lord, O my soul, and forget not all his benefits"* (Psalm 103:1–2); *"Praise the Lord. Praise the Lord, O my soul. I will praise the Lord all my life; I will sing praise to my God as long as I live"* (Psalm 146:1–2).

The Psalmist works on his soul so that he may praise the Lord. So also a mature Christian labors daily on his soul so he can have a healthy life of private worship.

In all of this, the mature Christian prepares his soul to seek the Lord day after day; he arrays the instruments of personal worship (Bible, daily devotional, hymnal, a quiet place, etc.), and more importantly, he prepares his own heart for the battle it will be to keep worshiping through all the ups and downs of the day. Without conscious preparation of the soul, we will not worship God properly:

- [speaking to King Jehoshaphat] Nevertheless good things are found in you, in that you have removed the wooden images from the land, and have **prepared your heart** to seek God. (2 Chronicles 19:3, NKJV)
- So Jotham became mighty, because he **prepared his ways** before the Lord his God. (2 Chronicles 27:6, NKJV)

- For Ezra had **prepared his heart** to seek the Law of the Lord, and to do it, and to teach statutes and ordinances in Israel. (Ezra 7:10, NKJV)

A mature Christian knows it will be a battle against spiritual forces of evil in the heavenly realms and against his own weak flesh to maintain a worshipful demeanor all day long, and he prepares his heart for that battle.

DAILY LIFE WORSHIP

Worship occurs any time the greatness of God pierces the veil of our soul's dimness and the shaft of divine light causes us to say "Oh!" in wonder and amazement. Anything that moves us, anything about which we marvel and turn back to God in praise, is true spiritual worship. Thus does worship flow through the daily life of the mature Christian, and the mature Christian is "walking with God" so actively by the power of the Spirit that "every good and perfect gift" (James 1:17) is a cause for instantaneous worship. Perhaps it is in looking at the face of his newborn daughter, saying "I praise you, O Lord, for she is fearfully and wonderfully made!" Perhaps it is in walking through a forest in the fall and looking at the magnificent glowing foliage, watching a single red oak leaf make its fluttering final journey from a lofty tree branch to the ground beneath. Perhaps it is in seeing the Colorado Rockies glowing at sunset, or studying the perfect symmetry of a simple wildflower, or looking at the splendor of the Milky Way through a quality telescope. Spiritual maturity includes a healthy worship life at every moment, expressing wonder, thanks and praise to the God who rules all these things.

So also as the mature Christian makes his way through the day, he or she is calling to mind memorized Scriptures, meditating on biblical truth and stimulating himself to worship. She is praying "without ceasing" (1 Thessalonians 5:17), and much of that prayer is worship and thanksgiving to the God who never changes. In this way, the mature Christian seeks to practice the presence of Christ all day long and to give him glory.

CORPORATE WORSHIP

There is a simple standard that a mature Christian refuses to violate: if we are physically able, we must assemble with other Christians for corporate worship. This is commanded very plainly by God: *"And let us consider how to stir up one another to love and good works, not neglecting to meet together, as is the habit of some, but encouraging one another, and all the more as you see the Day drawing near"* (Hebrews 10:24–25). The word "neglecting" in the Greek is actually a little stronger, more like "forsaking." It implies a conscious choice to stop assembling together with other Christians for corporate worship. The decision for an able-bodied person to stop going to corporate worship is devastating for the soul. It is usually a masking sin that covers the real issue: the person is drifting away from Christ (Hebrews 2:1). A mature Christian realizes that he needs to continue in corporate worship, for accountability, for ministry, for opportunities to serve others, for stimulation to love and good deeds, for enriched worship, for many other reasons besides. We need each other!

A mature Christian also knows the responsibility we have to stimulate others to worship. If a brother or sister is cold toward God, it is our responsibility at least to pray for that person; but also with wisdom to seek to "stimulate them to love and good deeds" (Hebrews 10:24) in the area of warm-hearted worship. Perhaps the most striking verse related to this issue is this one: *"Oh, magnify the Lord with me, and let us exalt his name together!"* (Psalm 34:3). When we pray fervent and Bible-saturated prayers of worship in the hearing of our brothers and sisters, we are magnifying God to them. When we preach Christ-exalting, Spirit-anointed, and scripturally rich sermons, we are holding up a telescope to the souls of the congregation so that their breath can be taken away when they catch a clear glimpse of some aspect of God's character. When we listen to sermons intently, leaning forward in our seats, taking careful notes and turning the pages of our Bibles at the appropriate times, we are honoring God's word and stimulating others to worship. When we close our eyes, singing fervently, with tears streaming down our faces at the grace God has so richly shown us in Christ, we are helping our brothers and sisters to glorify God with passion. This responsibility a mature Christian takes seriously, so he or she does not enter the sanctuary on Sunday mornings unprepared or lightly.

WHAT KINDS OF ACTIVE WORSHIP?

So how do our bodies act out our worship? Were we totally paralyzed, we could certainly still worship God in the inner recesses of our souls. However, God gave us bodies and there are reasonable acts of worship that will accompany a healthy, mature Christian life.

One of the most common acts of worship is singing. Because of the astonishing goodness of God in Christ, Christians are commanded to sing praise to God. Now we are not commanded to sing well or beautifully beyond the talent he's given us, but singing is part of a heart offered to God in worship: *"Speak to one another with psalms, hymns and spiritual songs. Sing and make music in your heart to the Lord, always giving thanks to God the Father for everything, in the name of our Lord Jesus Christ"* (Ephesians 5:19–20).

Scripture also reveals many other physical responses of worship. Here are just some: standing (Nehemiah 8:4), kneeling (Psalm 95:6), bowing down (Psalm 5:7), falling prostrate (1 Chronicles 29:20), shouting for joy (Psalm 118:15), speaking words of praise (Psalm 78:4), speaking words of thankfulness (Psalm 100:4–5), lifting hands (Psalm 63:4), covering the face (1 Kings 19:12–13), leaping for joy (Luke 6:23), dancing (2 Samuel 6:14), playing musical instruments (Psalm 150:3–5). All these and many others are actions of the body done in conjunction with worship. When the heart worships, the body moves!

SUMMARY

The life of a mature Christian is one rich with praise and worship of Almighty God. A mature Christian man or woman is delighted to spend eternity in the presence of God, giving him honor and glory for his salvation. Worship begins in a heart that knows, believes and delights in spiritual truth as revealed in the Bible. From a heart prepared for worship comes a river of sacrificial praise, in a wide variety of actions and at various times: alone in the morning quiet time, throughout the day informally, and during corporate worship. Like everything else in the Christian life, this rich offering of worship is empowered and directed by the indwelling Holy Spirit, and it is deeply satisfying to the Christian.

CHAPTER 23

SPIRITUAL DISCIPLINES

IT MUST HAVE BEEN A strange sight, one cold night in a mostly abandoned hockey rink in Norway. It was September of 1979, and some hockey players with the letters "USA" on their uniforms were skating up and down the ice in the dark, doing a brutal skating drill that had most of them on the verge of collapse. Their coach, Herb Brooks, was preparing them for the Olympics at Lake Placid, and he'd been disgusted with their lackluster performance that evening—a tie against Norway's second-best national team. So he decided to punish them with "Herbies," repeatedly making them skate up and down the ice in starts and stops, continuing long after the rink janitor had turned off the lights. Little did they realize that this grueling night of seemingly endless repetitions was building a foundation that would result in their shocking victory over the greatest hockey team in the world— the Russians—five months later. And as they completed their 4–3 victory on February 22, 1980, what was most noticeable was how the Americans were consistently skating better than the Russians, beating them to the puck, seemingly tireless as the last few minutes drained away. The discipline of that long night of skating in a darkened rink in Norway five months earlier had helped make this hockey miracle come true.

SPIRITUAL DISCIPLINES

Discipline is absolutely essential to success in the Christian life as well. Twice the Apostle Paul used athletic analogies to make this point in his epistles. In his day, the version of the Olympics was called the "Isthmian Games." A victor's crown in these games was very prestigious, and athletes would make supreme sacrifices to obtain it. Paul likened his own discipline of his body to those rigors: *Every athlete exercises self-control in all things. They do it to receive a perishable wreath, but we an imperishable* (1 Corinthians 9:25). Paul refers to the astonishing discipline of an athlete exercising self-control in all things: strictly watching his diet, sleep, and leisure so that he can give full attention to athletic training. Little has changed in two thousand years. Modern Olympic athletes must be extremely disciplined over every detail of their lives, or they have no chance of winning the gold medal. They must especially focus on the specific aspects of their own sport to gain the highest level of skill possible. In the same way, excellence in the Christian life requires discipline, strict training, specifically in the area of personal spiritual development.

Another key passage from Paul appears in 1 Timothy 4:

> Train yourself to be godly. For physical training is of some value, but godliness has value for all things, holding promise for both the present life and the life to come (1 Timothy 4:7–8).

Paul there commands Timothy to train himself to be godly. As we noted earlier, the Greek word translated "train" is *gymnazo*, from which we get the word "gymnastic." Here Paul directly contrasts the physical training an athlete undergoes to the training needed for godliness. He commands us to train ourselves for godliness with the same relentless purpose that a skilled athlete uses to develop his technique.

So how do we "train ourselves for godliness?" Here we come to the matter of spiritual disciplines. A mature Christian invests in certain habit patterns on a daily basis that prepare him/her for maximum fruitfulness in facing the day's challenges. A Christian stores up the riches of God's word and the sweetness of fellowship with God in prayer. Simply put, a mature Christian has a daily devotional life, a regular pattern of Bible intake, personal worship, and prayer. Bible reading and prayer are the two legs by which we make progress in the internal journey, and a mature Christian will not let a day go by without time spent in each discipline.

FOLLOWING CHRIST'S EXAMPLE

In this commitment, we are to imitate our Lord Jesus Christ. We get a glimpse of some of Jesus' habits of personal piety in the Gospels. For example, in the first chapter of Mark's Gospel, we learn of Jesus love for an early morning prayer time with his Father: *"Very early in the morning, while it was still dark, Jesus got up, left the house and went off to a solitary place, where he prayed"* (Mark 1:35). He continued this habit throughout his busy ministry: *"Jesus often withdrew to lonely places and prayed"* (Luke 5:16).

Jesus' prayer life prepared him daily for his perfect works of service to God. He stressed that he did nothing apart from the expressed will and command of his Father, and the indication is that Jesus arose early every morning and prayed, to get his marching orders from his Father. Isaiah's prophecy captures this:

> The Sovereign Lord has given me an instructed tongue, to know the word that sustains the weary. He wakens me morning by morning, wakens my ear to listen like one being taught. The Sovereign Lord has opened my ears, and I have not been rebellious; I have not drawn back. (Isaiah 50:4–5)

"Morning by morning," the heavenly Father wakened Jesus and spoke his words and his will into the willing ears of his perfect Son. With this private time, Jesus gained "an instructed tongue" filled with messages from God to sustain those weary and burdened by sin. And, as we noted earlier, Jesus obeyed whatever his Father told him to do. So Jesus testified that all of his words and works came directly as a result of what he heard from his Father: *"Don't you believe that I am in the Father, and that the Father is in me? The words I say to you are not just my own. Rather, it is the Father, living in me, who is doing his work"* (John 14:10). The cumulative weight of evidence is that Jesus woke early every morning, went to some solitary place and prayed. During that time, he heard clearly from his Father what he was to do that day, and he went and did it.

Similarly, we see two other aspects of Jesus' spiritual disciplines in his time of testing in the desert: Scripture intake and fasting. The scriptural side of Jesus' devotional life comes out in the three passages from Deuteronomy he quotes to resist the temptation of the devil. The first of these was Deuteronomy 8:3, which Jesus quoted to refute the temptation to use his miraculous powers to benefit his own life: *"The tempter came to him and said, "If you are the Son of God, tell these stones to become bread." Jesus answered, "It is written: 'Man does not live on bread alone, but on every word that comes from the mouth of God'"* (Matthew 4:3–4). This was more than just the right verse to crush the temptation Satan hurled at him. It also showed the preciousness of "every word" that came from the mouth of God. Though we have no direct evidence that Jesus read the Bible every day in his morning quiet time, he must have had a regular pattern of Bible intake. The preciousness of the Scripture to Jesus is also in evidence when we consider that Jesus had memorized all three of the passages he used in the desert. God's word he had hidden in his heart that he might not sin against the Father (Psalm 119:11).

Concerning fasting, the forty day fast of Jesus in the desert is clear evidence of his life of total self-control over his appetites. Jesus did not fast as mourning for sin, but he fasted in conjunction with his prayer life and the time of testing in the desert. We do not see Jesus fast again in the New Testament, but his willingness to fast is plainly established at the beginning of his ministry.

A DAILY QUIET TIME

A daily quiet time is the foundation to progress in the Christian journeys. Therefore, a Christian should "train for godliness" by consistency in this area. Following the example of Jesus, I think the best time for a quiet time is early in the morning before the business of the day overtakes us. To make certain this happens, we need to set our alarm early enough to allow for a rich time in the Word and in prayer. But if we deprive our bodies of sleep too regularly, we will be sleepy during our devotion times and throughout the day. So we need to go to bed a little earlier to maintain the same length of sleep time the body needs. This requires sacrifice, since evening is a time in which our desire for relaxation and voluntary pleasures may tempt us to stay up too late.

BIBLE INTAKE

It was Christ who likened Scripture to food when he said, *"Man does not live on bread alone, but on every word that comes from the mouth of God"* (Matthew 4:4). One thing is for sure, we cannot survive spiritually without a steady diet of Scripture any more than we can survive physically without a steady intake of nourishment. There are many ways of taking in the Scriptures. A steady diet of good preaching in a local church is indispensable. Modern technology also makes excellent sermons and other scriptural resources available by internet with great ease. Many solid Christian books are saturated with Scripture texts and are readily available. The basic idea is that, like believers in the early church, Christians should *"devote themselves to the apostles' teaching"* (Acts 2:42) daily.

Despite the value of these resources, the primary source of biblical intake must be our daily reading and personal study of the Bible. Our Bible intake should be both broad and deep. A common way of speaking of a person who gets too immersed in the details of an issue is "He can't see the forest for the trees." The big picture (forest) gets lost in the details (trees) that make it up. However, a Christian needs to give attention to both the big picture of the whole Bible story (forest) as well as the details of particular passages (trees). The spiritual discipline of reading through the entire Bible in a year, year after year, will help a person maintain a sense of the sweep of redemptive history, as well as continue their ongoing training in biblical theology (the study of the unified message of the whole Bible, Old and New Testaments together). George Mueller read through the Bible *twice* a year, for over fifty years! Over one hundred times, each chapter of the Bible flowed through his mind, helping transform him into the image of Christ. This must have had a major impact on the shaping of his heart and the empowering of his ministry.

MEDITATION AND MEMORIZATION OF SCRIPTURE

At the same time, it is beneficial to focus intently on key passages and know them deeply. George Mueller gave a poignant testimony to the value of deep meditation on Scripture, and how it flowed into prayer for him. His goal in his daily time in the Word and in prayer was to strengthen his inner man, and to get into a happy state in which he could serve the Lord with gladness:

> I saw more clearly than ever, that the first great and primary business to which I ought to attend every day was, to have my soul happy in the Lord. The first thing to be concerned about was not, how much I might serve the Lord, how I might glorify the Lord; but how I might get my soul into a happy state, and how my inner man might be nourished. . . .

> The most important thing I had to do was to give myself to the reading of the Word of God and to meditation on it, that thus my heart might be comforted, encouraged, warned, reproved, instructed; and that thus, whilst meditating, my heart might be brought into experimental, communion

with the Lord. I began therefore, to meditate on the New Testament, from the beginning, early in the morning. . . .

As the outward man is not fit for work for any length of time except we take food, and as this is one of the first things we do in the morning, so it should be with the inner man. . . . Now what is the food for the inner man? Not prayer, but the word of God; and here again, not the simple reading of the word of God, so that it only passes through our minds, just as water runs through a pipe, but considering what we read, pondering over it, and applying it to our hearts.[46]

Meditation on Scripture is essential to gaining a deep understanding of the truth of its words. Without meditation, the words of our daily reading can flow through our minds like water in a pipe and make no impact. But by means of meditation, we give the word a chance to settle in our minds and do its work.

Psalm 119 is a potent manual on scriptural meditation, producing ever-increasing insight and understanding. My favorite prayer for insight when coming to the Bible every day for my quiet time is Psalm 119:18: "*Open my eyes that I may see wonderful things in your law.*" The "seeing of wonderful things" in God's law is a mental "sight" which can be called "illumination," and it is the special work of the indwelling Holy Spirit.

But these moments of illumination don't come without labor on our part. So meditation on God's word is essential to attaining the deeper knowledge, insight, and understanding we crave. Psalm 119 contains almost half of all the references to meditation in the Bible, and is therefore the primary handbook for learning how to meditate on Scripture to gain insight. I found a fascinating couplet of verses in that magnificent Psalm. Let me put them side by side so you can see the full impact:

- Psalm 119:99: I have more insight than all my teachers, for I meditate on your statutes.

- Psalm 119:27: Let me understand the teaching of your precepts; then I will meditate on your wonders.

Verse 99 teaches something we would expect: "I meditate, therefore I have insight." Verse 27 reverses the order and therefore surprises us: "I understand, therefore I meditate." Verse 27, because it was surprising to me, was worth some meditation in its own right. "Why does the Psalmist ask God for understanding *in order that he might meditate?* Then it hit me: meditation on Scripture is hard work (see Psalm 119:148, *"My eyes stay open through the watches of the night, that I may meditate on your promises"*), and we probably won't keep doing it if we get nothing from it!

An illustration may help us understand. Suppose you had an eccentric old uncle in Arizona who died and, in his will, left you an abandoned silver mine. Let's say you flew out there to investigate your new property. You went to the nearby town and told the townsfolk about the will, and they laughed. They said, "That old mine has been abandoned for years . . . no one has been up there even to look around . . . and as far as we know, no silver ever came out of that hole in the ground." Let's say you rent a pick-up truck, drive to the base of the mountain, climb up to the entrance and past the old plywood and 2x4s blocking the entrance . . . you poke around for two hours with a flashlight. Now, let's say you find nothing but spiders and dust. Will you be motivated to ever go back in that hole again? No, you will try to sell the mountain and get something for your trouble.

But let's say after ninety minutes, you suddenly notice a small tunnel leading off the main tunnel and it seems different than the others. So you crawl in about a hundred feet, and suddenly your flashlight shines on some shiny substance on the wall; your heart beat faster, you take your trowel and, with building excitement, dig some of the shiny rocks into your bucket. You take the rocks to the assay office in town and, with a look of amazement, the assayer says, "This is silver, my friend." Now let me ask the same question again: will you be motivated to ever go back in that hole again?

Once you start discovering new things through meditation, you will go down into the tunnel again and again for more silver. By the hard work of careful Bible meditation, you will mine out the building blocks of a new civilization within your heart—a City of Truth built over the years.

Memorization is one of the simplest ways to ensure long term meditation. By memorization, we hide God's word in our hearts that we might not sin against him (Psalm 119:11). I think it is only by memorization that we can practically meet Christ's condition in John 15:7: *"If you remain in me and my words remain in you, ask whatever you wish, and it will be given you."* How can Jesus' "words" (plural) remain constantly in us if we don't memorize them?

And I believe it's best to memorize extended portions of Scripture, even whole chapters and books. I have written a booklet on memorization called "An Approach to the Extended Memorization of Scripture," and in it I speak of the many benefits of memorizing long passages.[47] Here the "forest" and the "trees" can both bless the heart: by memorizing the whole book of Ephesians, for example, you can have a grasp on Paul's entire argument, along with the details of each verse.

PERSONAL PRAYER

Along with consistent Bible intake, we must have a healthy prayer life as well. Bible reading is God speaking to us; prayer is us speaking to God. The conversation is the essence of the spiritual journey of sanctification. Perhaps more books have been written about prayer than any other spiritual discipline, so there's no need for me to go into great depth here. In this section, I am urging a pattern of focused, concentrated, uninterrupted prayer: *"But when you pray, go into your room, close the door and pray to your Father, who is unseen"* (Matthew 6:6). Of course, there is immense value to *"praying without ceasing*" (1 Thessalonians 5:17), weaving prayer throughout the day as needs arise. I think it's fine to pray while driving to work, or while waiting for people to come for a meeting, etc. Jesus certainly wove prayer through his daily life, thanking God when the disciples returned after their fruitful mission trip (Luke 10:21), praying for God to raise Lazarus from the dead (John 11:41–42), etc. But Jesus also withdrew to solitary places and did nothing but pray. So also a mature Christian knows the value of times of concentrated prayer, and doesn't try to shortchange them.

If anyone complains that their lives are too busy for extended times of prayer, they should consider the example of Daniel, who was the second most powerful man in the Medo-Persian Empire. He never neglected his duties, but was diligent in everything he had to do. Yet he still prayed three times a day, down on his knees, thanking God and asking God for help (Daniel 6:10–11).

Prayer comes in various types. For years I have used the A.C.T.S. acronym to help me be thorough in my prayers: Adoration, Confession, Thanksgiving, and Supplication. I have also made a prayer notebook, a three-ring binder with these four areas sectioned off. I have sheets for each area—an attribute sheet to help me praise God, a listing of various types of sins to help in my confession, a two-sided sheet of various blessings for which God deserves thanks, and a prayer list of people who need my prayers. I also have Paul's prayers copied out so I can pray like he did for his disciples, based on Ephesians 1, Ephesians 3, Colossians 1, Philippians 1, and other sample passages. And I have blank sheets at the back of the notebook in which I can record specific prayer requests and keep a record of God's faithfulness.

Prayer life is the barometer of the health of the Christian soul. Some years ago, I came across a sermon by Jonathan Edwards, and the title alone convicts me greatly: "Hypocrites Deficient in Private Prayer."[48] It challenges me to be faithful in my personal prayer life. Mature Christians are **not** "deficient in private prayer," but sometimes I can be. It is a point of maturity for me to grow constantly in my prayer life. John Bunyan said something very profound about prayer: "Prayer will make a man cease from sin, or sin will entice a man to cease from prayer." [49] If we are not praying as we should, it could be that some area of sin has sapped our strength. And if we are cherishing some secret sin in our hearts, God will not hear our prayers (Isaiah 59:1–2).

Peter pointed out two things that could destroy our prayer lives: 1) *"The end of all things is near. Therefore be clear-minded and self-controlled so that you can pray"* (1 Peter 4:7). If we are too wrapped up in the things of this world and have forgotten that the end is near, if we have given in to temptation or enjoyed the lawful pleasures too much, we have lost our self-control. Our prayer life will suffer accordingly. 2) *"Husbands, in the same way be considerate as you live with your wives, and treat them with respect as the weaker partner and as heirs with you of the gracious gift of life, so that nothing will hinder your prayers"* (1 Peter 3:7). If I as a husband have forgotten to be loving and gentle with my wife, and have not treated her with respect, our prayers will be hindered (both individually and together).

OTHER SPIRITUAL DISCIPLINES

Though the two primary disciplines of Bible intake and prayer are central, there are many habitual practices which can help spiritual growth. A rich devotional life must also include personal worship, as we have already mentioned above. Times of singing and praising God privately are essential to maintaining our joy in the Lord. Other spiritual disciplines such as solitude, various types of fasting, silence, journaling, etc. are helpful in the Christian life. Don Whitney has written an excellent book on this topic and I commend it to you.[50]

CHAPTER 24

FAMILY RELATIONSHIPS

FEW CHRISTIAN THINKERS IN THE 20th century had the impact of C.S. Lewis. He is probably best remembered for such literary works as *The Chronicles of Narnia* and *Mere Christianity*. But he was also a skillful and powerful preacher, and on June 8, 1942 at the Church of St Mary the Virgin at Oxford, he preached probably the most influential sermon of his life, "The Weight of Glory." In that memorable message, Lewis argued that there are no insignificant human beings, and thus there are no insignificant human encounters. The sermon gets its title from the concept that every single human being you meet will spend eternity either in abject torment or in indescribable glory, and hence, we must bear the "weight" of our neighbor's possible destiny in mind at all times:

> It may be possible for each to think too much of his own potential glory hereafter; it is hardly possible for him to think too often or too deeply about that of his neighbor. The load or weight or burden of my neighbor's glory should be laid daily on my back, a load so heavy only humility can carry it, and the backs of the proud will be broken. . . . It is in the light of these overwhelming possibilities . . . that we should conduct all our dealings with one another, all friendships, all loves, all play, all politics. There are no ordinary people. You have never talked to a mere mortal. Nations, cultures, arts, civilization—these are mortal, and their life is to ours as the life of a gnat. But it is immortals

whom we joke with, work with, marry, snub, and exploit—immortal horrors or everlasting splendors.[51]

This concept is true, and vital for a mature Christian to keep in mind. But that does not mean that every human relationship is equally significant, or that we bear equal responsibility for the "weight of glory" of a janitor at an airport from whom we ask directions to a rest room that we do for the weight of glory of our spouse, our parent, our child, or a fellow church member.

In this and in the next two chapters, we are going to look at the issue of how a Christian should relate to other human beings in the world. God has placed each Christian in a network of relationships, and each is to be redeemed for God's glory, lived in light of the two infinite journeys. But these relationships fall in a series of concentric circles emanating outward from the individual believer. The most significant in life is the marriage relationship; secondly, the parent-child relationship; thirdly, the relationships with other Christians in the body of Christ. Beyond these, there are an array of relationships with varying levels of responsibilities. The Christian is called upon to be a godly employee (and sometimes, employer), a godly citizen (and sometimes, government official), and a godly human being to the rest of the world, as providence allows opportunities.

In this chapter, I will discuss the highest level of committed relationships in life: those in the family, especially marriage and parent-child. In two later chapters, I will briefly cover our responsibilities to other Christians under the heading of "ministry", and our responsibilities to the outside world under the heading of "mission." In all these levels of relationships, Christian maturity consists in habitual obedience to God's all-sufficient commands to live for his glory.

MARRIAGE

Marriage is the first human relationship that God established, taking priority over all other relationships. It is the most important social relationship in the world. Both the church and the nation are only as strong as the marriages that sustain them. The stronger the marriages, the stronger the church and the nation will be. Because of this immense significance, it should not surprise us that Satan exerts some of his most concentrated efforts on this critical relationship. In the United States, many of the "hottest" hot button issues the church faces center around the husband-wife relationship. Divorce, homosexuality, gay marriage, feminism, pornography, and spouse abuse are all Satanic attacks on the primary relationship God instituted.

Since marriage is under such Satanic attack, it is vital for godly Christians to saturate their minds with what the Bible says about marriage, so that we can fight Satan's schemes, *"demolish[ing] arguments* and *tak[ing] captive every thought to make it obedient to Christ"* (2 Corinthians 10:5). Mature Christian husbands and wives will give concentrated daily attention to their marriages, seeking to fulfill their Christ-ordained responsibilities. Without sweet, Spirit-induced harmony at home, it will be impossible for the husband and wife fully to walk in all the good works God has for each of them, and they will be increasingly disqualified from his service in vital areas. But if by the Spirit they are fruitfully obedient here, God will put their home on display as a powerful gospel outpost, a way-station of rest, a launching pad of Kingdom weapons (children) for generations to come.

The clearest pattern for mature Christian marriage comes from the analogy of Christ and the church set up in Ephesians 5:21–33. In that vital section of Scripture, the wife is commanded to submit to their husbands in everything (v. 24) *"for the husband is the head of the wife as Christ is the head of the church, his body, of which he is the Savior"* (v. 23). In a moment, Paul will describe how a husband is to imitate Christ in godly headship. But amazingly for the wife, the greatest pattern of submission ever displayed is that of Christ to his heavenly Father. Christ obeyed his Father in everything the Father commanded him to do (John 14:31, 15:10; see also Romans 5:19, Hebrews 5:8, and Luke 22:42). As we have already learned, the essence of sanctification, of Christian maturity, is Christlikeness in everything. Paul says, "*as the church submits to Christ, so a wife should submit to her husband in everything*" (v. 24). But the only way she can do this is to follow Christ's example of total obedience to the Father. So we might also say, "As Christ submitted to his Father, so a wife should submit to her husband in everything." Her wifely submission is both an act of obedience to Christ, and is empowered by his submission to his Father.

Likewise, the husband must imitate Christ in his headship of his wife. The grammar in Ephesians 5 is plain. It is not that the husband *ought to be* head of his wife, or that he *might become* head of his wife; he *is* head of his wife. It is a position God established plainly at the beginning of humanity in Genesis 1–2, and no power on earth can overturn it. The real question for a husband, then, is what kind of head will he be? He could be a foolish head, a lazy head, an angry head, a negligent head, a drunken head . . . but he will be head still. Ephesians 5 says he ought to carry himself toward his wife as Christ does toward the church. The pattern is set up especially in his self-sacrifice for her: "*Husbands, love your wives, just as Christ loved the church and gave himself up for her*" (v. 25) As we have already seen, love is essentially cheerful self-sacrifice for the benefit of another. The epitome of love on earth ought to be the Christian husband toward his wife.

A husband must invest himself in the overall well-being of his wife, her ongoing needs. He is to provide for her body (food, clothing, shelter) through his labor; he is to care for her needs whenever she is weak or ill. And he is to give himself fully to the overall development of his wife, especially her spiritual development. As

Christ seeks to cleanse the church, *"washing her with water through the word,"* so also a husband should seek to disciple his wife and help her to grow to spiritual maturity. This is even more the case when we consider the topics of this book, the fullness of sanctification: Knowledge, Faith, Character, Action. There is a lot to do, and it is the husband's responsibility to his wife to see that she develops toward maturity.

R.C. Sproul spoke very plainly to husbands concerning their role in the development and growth of their wives:

> In the Ephesians passage, it is clear that the husband is called to be the priest of his home. The man is responsible for the spiritual well-being of his wife. Her sanctification is his responsibility. There is probably no male task that has been more neglected than this one.[52]

A mature Christian husband will take the ongoing spiritual maturation of his wife as his personal responsibility, will meet with her regularly, plan with her, pray with her, and above all, study the Bible with her so that he may present her to Christ ready for her true, eternal wedding day.

Likewise, a godly wife who supports her husband in his life and ministry will receive the same rewards he gets on Judgment Day. If even the giving of a cup of cold water to a messenger of Christ will never lose its reward (Matthew 10:42), how much more the daily thoughtful, skillful work of a godly wife, who provides countless meals for her husband, washes his clothes, keeps his home orderly, prays for him, encourages him in his struggles, blesses him with wise counsel, nurses him to health when he's sick. How Christlike is this servanthood, and how guaranteed is such a godly wife of eternal rewards from Almighty God!

Above all, a godly wife desires to help her husband make progress in the two infinite journeys. She sees their relationship in the light of eternity. She is not her husband's discipler, nor his pastor, nor his master in any way. But there is no human being on the face of the earth with as much influence over a man as his wife. This influence can be used for good or evil. Solomon's foreign wives led his heart astray from devotion to the eternal God (1 Kings 11:4); Job's wife said to him in his time of greatest affliction, *"Are you still holding on to your integrity? Curse God and die!"* (Job 2:9); Lot's wife longed to go back to Sodom and Gomorrah (Genesis 19:26). But the godly wife of Proverbs 31 is a rich fountain of blessing to her husband: *"Her husband has full confidence in her and lacks nothing of value. She brings him good, not harm, all the days of her life"* (Proverbs 31:11–12). These words find their highest fulfillment in a New Covenant marriage in which a Spirit-filled wife seeks every day to help her husband in his internal journey of sanctification, praying for him to develop in knowledge, grow in faith, become strong in character, and fruitful in action. She also seeks to bless him in his external journey of ministry and mission, giving him godly counsel, fervent prayer, and heart-felt support in whatever God leads him to do for the Kingdom of Christ.

PARENT-CHILD

The second most important human relationship on earth is the parent-child relationship. From the very beginning, God established procreation as a central part of his plan for the human race, to fill the earth with the knowledge of his glory as the waters cover the sea (Habakkuk 2:14). For this reason God blessed Adam and Eve, and said to them, *"Be fruitful and increase in number; fill the earth and subdue it"* (Genesis 1:28). The link between God's blessing and the children that would come as a result is unmistakable. So also Psalm 127:5 says a man is blessed if he has many sons. In this day rife with abortion, materialism, child-abuse, and poor parenting, the fact that children are a blessing from the Lord cannot be stated often enough. It was precisely because God desires godly offspring that he makes the husband and wife one flesh (Genesis 2:24, Malachi 2:15).

But now that Adam has sinned, and with him the entire human race, offspring will not be godly without the work of grace in their hearts, so parents see their role in the lives of their children primarily in terms of God's plan of salvation. Their primary responsibility is to bring their children to a saving knowledge of Christ. To this end they pray, teach the Bible daily, give godly counsel, discipline sin, set a good example, involve them in a good church, challenge them to serve others, and in general *"bring them up in the training and instruction of the Lord"* (Ephesians 6:4).

A godly father takes his children's salvation as primarily his responsibility. Certainly, a godly mother plays an indispensable role in the evangelism and discipleship of their children, as Lois and Eunice did in Timothy's life (2 Timothy 1:5, 3:15). And clearly a godly mother has a major role in instructing the children spiritually in the book of Proverbs (Proverbs 1:8, 6:20, 31:1). But a father must oversee that process and be clearly the head over it. It must be seen clearly that he is walking with Christ and that his wife is instructing them under his headship and leadership in the home, not apart from it. So many men do what Adam did in his original sin: they stand idly by while their wives transact significant spiritual business (Genesis 3:6). A father must make the evangelism and discipleship of his children one of the central purposes of his life.

To this end, the most important thing a father can do is saturate the lives of his children with the word of God. Knowledge primes the pump for everything spiritual; knowledge feeds faith, faith transforms character, and character results in action. So a godly father enriches his children with the word of God. He sets a good example by speaking the word of God consistently. Charles Spurgeon spoke of a man's blood being "bibline."[53] A godly father makes life itself bibline. He leads in daily family devotions, and simply the image of dad there with the Bible open in his lap, instructing his children, will make an indelible mark on their souls. However, a godly father goes far beyond this, following the pattern laid out in Deuteronomy 6:

> These commandments that I give you today are to be upon your hearts. Impress them on your children. Talk about them when you sit at home and when you walk along the road, when you lie down and when you get up. Tie them as symbols on your hands and bind them on your foreheads. Write them on the doorframes of your houses and on your gates. (Deuteronomy 6:6–9)

The steps are all there. Practically speaking, a godly father will display a deep love for the word of God, keeping the commandments of God on his own heart. Then he will "impress" them on his children. The word literally means "sharpen," as a sword or arrow tip is whetted by repetitious motion (Deuteronomy 32:41). In the same way, a father will engrave the word of God deeply in his children's hearts by creative repetition, weaving the Bible into everyday life.

Similarly, a godly mother will seek to support the father's leadership by teaching the children the word of God as well, filling her heart with wisdom that pours forth in daily life situations: *"She speaks with wisdom, and faithful instruction is on her tongue"* (Proverbs 31:26). The faithful instruction on her tongue is biblical through and through.

The primary goal of both father and mother is plain: to bring their children to repentance and faith in Christ. The primary tool for this is Scripture, of course: *"from infancy you have known the holy Scriptures, which are able to make you wise for salvation through faith in Christ Jesus"* (2 Timothy 3:15). But along with a steady stream of biblical instruction from both father and mother, so also is a pattern of godly discipline when the children sin:

He who spares the rod hates his son, but he who loves him is careful to discipline him. (Proverbs 13:24)

Folly is bound up in the heart of a child, but the rod of discipline will drive it far from him. (Proverbs 22:15)

Do not withhold discipline from a child; if you punish him with the rod, he will not die. Punish him with the rod and save his soul from death. (Proverbs 23:13–14)

Moreover, we have all had human fathers who disciplined us and we respected them for it. How much more should we submit to the Father of our spirits and live! Our fathers disciplined us for a little while as they thought best; but God disciplines us for our good, that we may share in his holiness. No discipline seems pleasant at the time, but painful. Later on, however, it produces a harvest of righteousness and peace for those who have been trained by it. (Hebrews 12:9–11)

When a child sins, a godly father or mother will take the time to train his or her heart, bring the child to see the sin in light of eternity, and to see the absolute need for repentance and faith in Christ.

Godly parents never lose sight of the big picture at three levels: 1) God's glory as the center of the parent-child relationship; 2) the full individual salvation (justification, sanctification, glorification) of each of their children; 3) the passing on of a multigenerational view of godliness. Busy parents easily lose sight of these, especially the third. But a multigenerational view of godly children, grandchildren, great-grandchildren, and future generations beyond that, is biblical:

I will open my mouth in parables, I will utter hidden things, things from of old—what we have heard and known, what our fathers have told us. We will not hide them from their children; we will tell the next generation the praiseworthy deeds of the Lord, his power, and the wonders he has done. He decreed statutes for Jacob and established the law in Israel, which he commanded our forefathers to teach their children, so the next generation would know them, even the children yet to be born, and they in turn would tell their children. Then they would put their trust in God and would not forget his deeds but would keep his commands. (Psalm 78:2–7)

In Psalm 78, the psalmist stands in a line of at least five generations: forefathers, fathers, the psalmist and his generation, the next generation (the psalmist's children), and children yet unborn. Too many American parents forget the need to train this multi-generational view into their own children.

One other aspect of the parent-child relationship worth mentioning here is the ongoing need for adults to honor their aging parents. The commandment *"Honor your father and mother"* (Exodus 20:12) does not expire when children grow up, marry, and start their own families. Jesus upheld the command well beyond that, as we see in Matthew 15:4–6 when he addressed the issue of *corban*: i.e, gifts devoted to God that no longer need to be used to support aged parents. Based on Christ's understanding of that commandment, we are to continue to honor our parents in very practical ways long after we are grown.

THE LIMITS TO FAMILY LOYALTY

One last word on the family before we move on: though our responsibilities to our family are the highest of any human relationships, yet the sovereignty of God in giving the New Birth is such that we cannot guarantee that our spouses, our children, or our parents will be believers. God may save only one of a married couple, resulting in a mixed marriage, the outcome of which is uncertain (1 Corinthians 7:16). Similarly, it may be that, despite the best efforts of Christian parents, their own children may end up as enemies of their faith (Matthew 10:35–36); so also God may save the children of non-Christian parents. Our highest loyalty, then, must be to Christ, and to those who obey God by grace. These two statements by Jesus put the family into eternal perspective:

> Anyone who loves his father or mother more than me is not worthy of me; anyone who loves his son or daughter more than me is not worthy of me. (Matthew 10:37)

> Someone told [Jesus], "Your mother and brothers are standing outside, wanting to speak to you." He replied to him, "Who is my mother, and who are my brothers?" Pointing to his disciples, he said, "Here are my mother and my brothers. For whoever does the will of my Father in heaven is my brother and sister and mother." (Matthew 12:47–50)

SUMMARY

The most important relationships on earth are family relationships—especially the husband-wife and the parent-child relationships. Godly Christians recognize this, and are faithful to carry out their God-ordained roles in submission to his commands. The ultimate, multigenerational, vision of family-based evangelism and discipleship will remain the most powerful vehicle on earth for consummating the two infinite journeys we have spoken about in this book, for no other relationships can approach the intimacy and effectiveness promised by the blessing of God at the beginning of the human race. However, mature Christians realize that only the sovereign grace of God can finally consummate the intended purpose of these relationships—a countless multitude from every tribe on earth, worshiping Christ for his salvation.

CHAPTER 25

MINISTRY TO CHRISTIANS

IN 1630, THE MUSLIM EMPEROR of India, Shah Jehan, lost his beloved wife Mumtaz in childbirth. Overpowered by grief, Shah Jehan was determined to perpetuate her memory in immortality, so he decided to build his beloved wife the finest sepulcher ever—a monument of eternal love. The sad circumstances which attended the early death of the empress—who had endeared herself to the people—inspired all his subjects to join in the emperor's pious intentions. After twenty-two laborious years, and the combined effort of over twenty thousand workmen and master craftsmen culled from all over India, as well as Asia and Europe, the complex was finally completed in 1648 on the banks of the river Yamuna in Agra, the capital of the Muslim empire in India.

The graceful structure was built as a perfect fusion of Muslim and Hindu styles, with four minarets and a tranquil reflecting pool. It glistened in the sunlight, since it was built almost entirely of white marble. The army of skilled craftsmen intricately inlaid the walls with the most precious gems in the world; one flower, carved in its walls and only one inch square, was inlaid with sixty different materials, so perfectly meshed that they feel smooth to the touch like glass.

This incredible building was named by the emperor the Taj Mahal, and it stands today as an enduring testimony of the love of one man for his wife; it is perhaps the most exquisite building in the world. But however spectacular it is, it is nothing compared to the most magnificent building project in history: the construction of the Church of Jesus Christ.

BUILDING THE CHURCH OF CHRIST

For over two thousand years, the magnificent Church of Jesus Christ has been in construction. This structure is rising, generation after generation, to be an eternal testimony to the love of Christ for the church, a love which infinitely outstrips the love of any earthly husband for his bride.

Two key passages speak of this magnificent building project. The first is 1 Peter 2:4–5, which likens Christians to *"living stones [which are] built into a spiritual house"* in which spiritual sacrifices are constantly offered to Christ. These *living stones* are people rescued from every tribe, language, people and nation, who are quarried out from Satan's dark realm, then shaped, dressed, and prepared to perfection by the power of God, and put into place in a wall of the temple, to bring glory to God forever. The second key text on the establishment of this spiritual temple is in Ephesians 2:19–22. Here Paul speaks of a spiritual building which *"rises to become a holy temple in the Lord."* The constant building of this structure is highlighted with the verb tense in verse 22: *"And in him you too **are being** built together."* I believe this has reference to both of the infinite journeys: the external journey of Kingdom advance and the internal journey of sanctification. As the church makes progress in each of these ways, it is *"being built together"* to become an eternal dwelling place for the living God.

The book of Revelation pictures this *"dwelling place"* not as a temple but as a city, the *"New Jerusalem."* This is the bride of Christ, radiant with the glory of God (Revelation 21:1–3). This glorious dwelling place, where God and redeemed humanity will dwell together eternally, is the same as the spiritual temple being built in Ephesians 2 and in 1 Peter 2. The question before us is this: how does this glorious structure get built?

GOD BUILDS THE CHURCH
BY OUR GOOD WORKS

First of all, we must be very clear about who builds this glorious structure. The building of the Church is the central work of history. Therefore, it is the Triune God who builds the Church, and to him alone be the glory! Hebrews 11:10 says God is the *"Architect and Builder"* of the eternal dwelling place: He crafted its plans and he is carrying them out. In Matthew 16:18, Jesus says, *"On this rock I will build my church."* So it is Jesus who is building his Church day after day, year after year, generation after generation. And 1 Corinthians 12 speaks clearly about the power and will of the Holy Spirit in building up the church according to his own purposes (1 Corinthians 12:11). So it is the Father, the Son, and the Holy Spirit together who build the church.

But the Scriptures also reveal that God does this by means of good works done by his people. These good works come in two different patterns: specific good works done as part of a regular pattern of spiritual gift ministry, and general good works done by all Christians as opportunity arises. By both of these types of good works, the church is built up to be like Christ:

> It was he who gave some to be apostles, some to be prophets, some to be evangelists, and some to be pastors and teachers, to prepare God's people for **works of service**, so that the body of Christ may be built up until we all reach unity in the faith and in the knowledge of the Son of God and become mature, attaining to the whole measure of the fullness of Christ. (Ephesians 4:11–13)

This vital passage speaks of the manner in which God uses his people to build up the church through good works. Amazingly, it is the Body that builds **itself** up in love, **as each part does its work** (Ephesians 4:16). The goal of the spiritual maturity of the church is accomplished by God's people doing their appointed works of service—both in spiritual gift ministries and in general good works.

SPIRITUAL GIFT MINISTRIES

Having established the unity of the worldwide Church of Christ in the strongest possible terms in Ephesians 4:1-6, Paul turned to the issue of its diversity: *"But to each one of us grace has been given as Christ apportioned it"* (Ephesians 4:7). This diversity is not so much about race or gender or socio-economic issues, which are addressed beautifully in other places (see Revelation 7:9, Galatians 3:28, 1 Corinthians 1:26, James 2:1-5). No, here the diversity has to do with function in the growing "body of Christ." It has to do with diversity of "spiritual gifts," and the ministries that come from those gifts. Spiritual gifts are special abilities given to each Christian for building the Church to maturity.

In Ephesians 4:7, Paul calls these spiritual gifts "grace[s]," saying that various forms of "grace" are given to **each one of us**, and that this grace is given **as Christ apportioned it**: literally, *"according to the measure of Christ."* The picture is that Christ ponders each one of his children, and graciously gives them a role to play, equipping them for that role by a measure of his grace. Every single Christian, then, has a spiritual gift ministry laid out for them to do.

In Ephesians 4:11-12, he focuses on the primary ministries necessary for beginning the flow of good works that build up the Body of Christ: apostles, prophets, evangelists, pastors, teachers. All of these gifted people have one thing in common: they directly minister the word of God to the people, and the ministry of the word of God prepares believers for every other service there is in the Church. Just as we have said, knowledge produces faith, faith transforms character, and character produces action. So if the works of service are to be done by God's people, then the apostles, prophets, evangelists, pastors and teachers must minister the word of God, "*to prepare God's people for works of service so that the body of Christ may be built up*" (Ephesians 4:12). However, it is not only the ministry of the word that builds up the church to maturity, but it is **all** the "works of service" that accomplish this growth.

Paul goes into far greater detail in 1 Corinthians 12–14, laying out a careful theology of spiritual gifts there. In 1 Corinthians 12:12–20, he uses the analogy of a human body to make his point: "*The body is a unit, though it is made up of many parts; and though all its parts are many, they form one body. So it is with Christ*" (v. 12). Just as the body has a wide array of parts with different functions, so it is in the church of Christ—each Christian is gifted by God and is indispensable to the overall health and function of the Body.

Part of spiritual maturity, then, is to discern one's own role in the Body of Christ, and be faithful to do that ministry. Discovering one's own spiritual gifts, developing them, and then using them with great perseverance and skill are essential parts of the healthy Christian life. This is precisely the topic Paul addresses in Romans 12:1–8. After his stirring command to present our bodies to God as living sacrifices in Romans and to be transformed by the renewing of our minds, Paul shows the outcome: "*Then you will be able to test and approve what God's will is—his good, pleasing and perfect will*" (Romans 12:1–2). Many Christians go to this verse to address the issue of "discovering God's will for my life," meaning "Whom should I marry?", or "What job should I take?", or "Which car should I buy?" As important as these issues are, the context of Romans 12 argues that Paul is speaking of discovering and approving of your own spiritual gift ministry:

> For by the grace given me I say to every one of you: Do not think of yourself more highly than you ought, but rather think of yourself with sober judgment, in accordance with the measure of faith God has given you. Just as each of us has one body with many members, and these members do not all have the same function, so in Christ we who

are many form one body, and each member belongs to all the others. We have different gifts, according to the grace given us. (Romans 12:3–6)

In other words, if we present our bodies to God as living sacrifices, willing to do whatever his will is for us, and if we study the Word of God so carefully that our minds and hearts are transformed, we will be able to "test and approve" God's perfect and pleasing will for us, namely, our role in the Body of Christ. Then we will be able to think of ourselves properly by faith, to discover our own pattern of service in the body, and to be faithful to do those good works with great skill and perseverance:

If a man's gift is prophesying, let him use it in proportion to his faith. If it is serving, let him serve; if it is teaching, let him teach; if it is encouraging, let him encourage; if it is contributing to the needs of others, let him give generously; if it is leadership, let him govern diligently; if it is showing mercy, let him do it cheerfully. (Romans 12:6–8)

Spiritual gifts enable Christians to minister to other Christians, building them up to full maturity in Christ. In the very process of serving others and helping them make progress in their internal journeys, we ourselves are making progress in our own. Behold the wisdom of God!

A spiritually mature man or woman, then, knows what his or her spiritual gifts are, and they have been using them for years. They have carefully developed a life of ministry around those gifts, and have seen years of fruit in those efforts. While some spiritual gift ministries can be used to bring others to faith in Christ, many of those ministries are meant for the encouragement, strengthening, and growth of existing Christians.

GENERAL MINISTRIES OF LOVE TO THE BODY

A spiritually mature person also recognizes their responsibility to build up the Body of Christ in other ways than just by means of spiritual gifts. For example, a gifted teacher of the word of God will spend much—but not all—of his ministry time preparing and teaching excellent Bible lessons to the people of God. Some of his ministry time he will spend building up the Body of Christ in other ways. Perhaps he will speak a word of encouragement to a dejected new Christian who is struggling with fear in evangelism. Perhaps he will give sacrificially to a mission offering. Perhaps he and his wife will open their home to have international students over for a meal and to share the gospel with them. Perhaps he will attend a two-hour prayer meeting focused on unreached people groups, and pour out his heart in prayer for a missionary team sent out to try to plant churches among them. Perhaps he will help organize his small group's fall kick-off picnic. And yet he will not say that he has the spiritual gift of encouragement, giving, hospitality, evangelism, prayer, or administration. He just sees these as general good works that God gave him an opportunity to do. These are general responsibilities of all Christians, whether they are "gifted" in those areas or not. And these efforts do build up the Church by the power of the Spirit.

C.J. Mahaney's list of "one another" passages from the New Testament shows how comprehensive are our responsibilities to each other in the Body of Christ:

- Be at peace with each other (Mark 9:50)
- Love one another (John 13:34)
- Be joined to one another (Romans 12:5)
- Be devoted to one another (Romans 12:10)
- Honor one another (Romans 12:10)
- Rejoice with one another (Romans 12:15)
- Weep with one another (Romans 12:15)
- Live in harmony with one another (Romans 12:16)

- Accept one another (Romans 15:7)
- Counsel one another (Romans 15:14)
- Greet one another (Romans 16:16)
- Agree with each other (1 Corinthians 1:10)
- Wait for one another (1 Corinthians 11:33)
- Care for one another (1 Corinthians 12:25)
- Serve one another (Galatians 5:13)
- Carry one another's burdens (Galatians 6:2)
- Be kind to one another (Ephesians 4:32)
- Forgive one another (Ephesians 4:32)
- Submit to one another (Ephesians 5:21)
- Bear with one another (Colossians 3:13)
- Teach, admonish each other (Colossians 3:16)
- Encourage one another (1 Thessalonians 5:11)
- Build up one another (1 Thessalonians 5:11)
- Spur one another on (Hebrews 10:24)
- Offer hospitality to one another (1 Peter 4:9)
- Minister gifts to one another (1 Peter 4:10)
- Be humble toward one another (1 Peter 5:5)
- Confess your sins to one another (James 5:16)
- Pray for one another (James 5:16)
- Fellowship with one another (1 John 1:7)[54]

Each one of these deserves fuller treatment than I can give here. Suffice it to say that a healthy life of ministry by a mature Christian to other Christians involves all of these areas at different times, as the need arises and as the Spirit leads. However, there are three key responsibilities that mature Christians focus on within the Body of Christ for maximum fruitfulness: intercession, discipleship, accountability. Let's look at each briefly.

INTERCESSION

Paul's life of intercessory prayer is exemplary, and worthy of careful study. So our brother Don Carson has done precisely that in his excellent book, *A Call to Spiritual Reformation: Priorities from Paul and His Prayers.*[55] We have already discussed (in the Knowledge section of this book) some aspects of how Paul prays for other Christians. However, a careful study of all aspects of Paul's prayers, and his request for prayer, is an excellent starting place for Christians who want to shoulder each other's burdens in fervent, consistent, intercessory prayer. What we learn from such a study is how spiritually-focused, consistent, and fervent were Paul's prayers for the churches and for individual Christians. A clear example of this is found in Colossians 1:

> And so, from the day we heard, we have not ceased to pray for you, asking that you may be filled with the knowledge of his will in all spiritual wisdom and understanding, so as to walk in a manner worthy of the Lord, fully pleasing to him, bearing fruit in every good work and increasing in the knowledge of God. (Colossians 1:9–10)

We ought to pray for each other like that! Too often we fail to pray for each other, or when we do, our prayers are weak, sporadic, and focused too much on this world.

Paul clearly commanded all Christians to be faithful in prayer for each other: *"And pray in the Spirit on all occasions with all kinds of prayers and requests. With this in mind, be alert and always keep on praying for all the saints"* (Ephesians 6:18). Mature Christians make this a consistent part of their lives. A subset of this is praying for each other's ministries, especially for those in strategic ministries of missions to unreached people groups. After Paul has spoken to the Roman Christians about his plans for upcoming mission work in Spain, taking the gospel to those who've never heard of Christ, Paul says solemnly: *"I urge you, brothers, by our Lord Jesus Christ and by the love of the Spirit, to join me in my struggle by praying to God for me"* (Romans 15:30). Spiritual maturity means shouldering the burdens of the ministries of other choice servants in the Lord, so that Christ's Kingdom can advance.

DISCIPLESHIP

One of the most important ministries which mature followers of Jesus can be involved in is that of mentoring disciples. One doesn't need to be a pastor or teacher to do this vital task. Jesus is the ultimate example of this discipleship ministry, gathering around him twelve men to train and prepare for future ministry. The Apostle Paul did the same with many young men, including Timothy. The essence of this ministry is helping to shape young disciples according to the patterns laid out in Scripture.

As we saw earlier, there are two basic patterns for discipleship, and all disciples must conform to these patterns. The first is the pattern of doctrine (right thinking), and the second is the pattern of behavior (right living). Like the coins struck by that pattern, all bearing the exact same imprint, so also all disciples of Christ are to be conformed to two patterns to achieve Christlikeness:

> Sound doctrine: *What you heard from me, keep as the* **pattern** *of sound teaching, with faith and love in Christ Jesus.* (2 Timothy 1:13)

> Godly lifestyle: *Join with others in following my example, brothers, and take note of those who live according to the* **pattern** *we gave you.* (Philippians 3:17)

Christ's strategy for worldwide disciple-making is to have this dual pattern reproduced from more mature Christians to less mature Christians, multiplied exponentially generation after generation. Paul urges this spiritual multiplication on Timothy, out to four generations of disciples: *"And the things you have heard me say in the presence of many witnesses entrust to reliable men who will also be qualified to teach others"* (2 Timothy 2:2). Paul to Timothy,

Timothy to "reliable men," and "reliable men" to "others." This is God's strategy for worldwide Kingdom advance.

Mature Christians embrace their role in this spiritual discipleship, taking on younger Christians and training them in the faith. Older men are to teach younger men; those especially qualified to do this are recognized as elders in the church (1 Timothy 3:1-7, Titus 1:5-9, 1 Peter 5:1-4). Older women train younger women in the pattern of Titus 2:3-5. By making themselves available to God for mentoring and discipleship, older Christians help younger Christians in their internal journeys, and bring the Church of Jesus Christ closer to its final goal of heavenly glory.

ACCOUNTABILITY

Finally, mature Christians understand their accountability for the spiritual welfare of other Christians, especially those in their local church. Our church covenant says, "We will watch over one another in brotherly love." The murderer Cain, when asked by God, "Where is your brother, Abel?" answered literally, "Am I my brother's guardian?" (Genesis 4:9). In Christ and in the local church, that is precisely what we are called to be for each other.

There is a negative side to this role, and that is guarding each other from our own indwelling sin: *"See to it, brothers, that none of you has a sinful, unbelieving heart that turns away from the living God. But encourage one another daily, as long as it is called Today, so that none of you may be hardened by sin's deceitfulness"* (Hebrews 3:12-13). The author to the Hebrews is urging that local church to watch over each other's hearts, lest they wander into sin. Sin is so deceitful, and we need loving brothers and sisters to call our attention to our own blind spots and danger zones. So also a mature Christian knows how to restore someone gently and humbly who has been wandering from the truth (Galatians 6:1, James 5:20; cf. also 1 John 5:16).

There is also a positive side to this mutual accountability, and that is stimulating brothers and sisters in Christ to be maximally fruitful. This is clearly taught in Hebrews 10:24–25: *"And let us consider how we may spur one another on toward love and good deeds. Let us not give up meeting together, as some are in the habit of doing, but let us encourage one another—and all the more as you see the Day approaching."* The NIV translation is a bit off in verse 24: the Greek literally says "Let us consider one another . . ." Our "considering" should focus on people: "one another." Our consideration of one another should be deep and personal, and be led by prayer, the light of Scripture, and the wisdom of the Spirit. We should ask "Lord, how can (so and so) best serve you at our church? What are they good at? How can they store up treasure in heaven and glorify you?" Having considered that person in the light, the mature Christian then "spurs" them to love and good deeds, like a cowboy's jangling spurs give incentive to the horse to move. We are a Body together, and we are responsible to be sure each person is actively involved in ministry, serving the Lord until the final day.

SUMMARY

The most important work going on in the world today is the building of the Church of Jesus Christ. Spiritually mature Christians recognize this, and spend their lives in works of service to build up the Body of Christ. Our ministry to other Christians follows two basic patterns—specific good works done as a pattern governed by spiritual gifts, and general good works all Christians do for one another. This is the love God commands for us to show to one another, by which the world will know we are Christ's disciples (John 13:35).

CHAPTER 26

MISSIONS TO NON-CHRISTIANS

ON DECEMBER 26, 2004, A massive earthquake, of magnitude 9.3, in the center of the Indian Ocean started a tsunami, with waves cresting over one hundred feet high. As this wall of water hurtled toward the Indonesian coastlands surrounding the Indian Ocean, little children were playing in the surf. A shaky hand-held video of the final seconds of some of these unsuspecting children, taken from a hill overlooking the beach, made its rounds on YouTube. One moment these children were happily playing, and the next moment they were turning to face a huge force that would sweep them from life. Even years later, I can scarcely think of that scene without tears.

Of course, no human father would ever willingly place his child in such danger. Yet that is precisely what our heavenly Father has done with us. Jesus was well aware of the danger of leaving us in this world, so dominated by Satan and his people. For this reason, Jesus prayed for his disciples the night before his death: *"I will remain in the world no longer, but they are still in the world, and I am coming to you. Holy Father, protect them by the power of your name, the name you gave me, so that they may be one as we are one"* (John 17:11). If we could see into the spiritual world how great are the satanic forces arrayed against us, we would melt away in terror. Those forces are far more dangerous than that tsunami that swept away those little children in Indonesia.

So why does God leave us in this dangerous world? First of all, he is fully confident of his power to protect us from anything Satan can do to us (1 Corinthians 10:13, 1 Peter 1:5). And because of that, God is able to accomplish his wise purposes in us and through us: the consummation of the external journey by the completion of the internal journey of all his elect from every nation.

Consequently, what actions does God command from his children toward the unbelievers of this world? No summary I could give here could supplant that of Scripture: *"Love your neighbor as yourself* (Matthew 22:39); *Love does no harm to its neighbor. Therefore love is the fulfillment of the law"* (Romans 13:10). In both of these passages, God summarizes all horizontal commandments—from man to man—in one word—love. But how do we love unbelievers? I would like to focus briefly on seven areas: 1) evangelism, 2) cross-cultural missions, 3) prayer, 4) mercy ministry, 5) being salt and light, 6) good citizenship, and 7) love for our enemies.

EVANGELISM

Jesus put this responsibility at the top when he gave the following valuation of the human soul: *"What good will it be for a man if he gains the whole world, yet forfeits his soul? Or what can a man give in exchange for his soul?"* (Matthew 16:26). A single human soul is worth more than all the material possessions on earth. In a similar fashion, what good would it be for us to care for the bodily needs of our neighbor, and do nothing for his perishing soul? The Bible reveals that people are naturally *"dead in transgressions and sins"* (Ephesians 2:1), under the wrath of God (John 3:36). Therefore, Christ has commanded us to love our lost neighbors by seeking to labor with him in the salvation of their souls. Christ made it very plain why he entered the world: *"The Son of Man came to seek and to save what was lost"* (Luke 19:10). And he wants us to labor alongside him as he does: *"Whoever does not gather with me scatters"* (Matthew 12:30). In other words, if we are not active in evangelism, we are scattering—working at cross-purposes with the Lord. For this reason, Christ gave us five different versions of the Great Commission of making disciples of all nations: Matthew 28:18–20, Mark 16:15, Luke 24:46–48, John 20:19–23, Acts 1:8. This is the most important action a Christian can be involved with in this perishing world.

Personal evangelism is a daily commitment: a choice we must make with every encounter God gives us. Even those who preach regularly from the pulpit have to make a corresponding commitment to be daily witnesses for Christ. George Whitefield may have been the greatest evangelistic preacher in church history, pioneering the open-air field preaching that came to characterize the First Great Awakening. Though he was primarily called to preach to thousands of people, and spent most of his life doing that, he was no less committed to personal evangelism. He said, *"God forbid that I should travel with anybody a quarter of an hour without speaking of Christ to them."*[56] D.L. Moody made a personal commitment that he would never go to bed at night without having shared the gospel with someone that day. Several times, just as he was about to go to bed he remembered that commitment and that he had not yet met it that day, and he would get out of bed and go out to try to find someone to witness to.[57] The more we grow, the more that evangelism will be part of our daily walk.

For me, it is helpful to pray a three-fold prayer every day, "Lord, give me an opportunity to share the gospel with a lost person today, and give me the wisdom to see it when it comes, and the boldness to make the most of it." It is also helpful to memorize a simple gospel outline and some supporting Scriptures, so that we will be ready. We should try to make the gospel as winsome as Jesus did with the Samaritan woman at the well, asking thought-provoking questions or making fascinating statements that entice people into spiritual conversations (John 4:10). Furthermore, a spiritually mature Christian will analyze the patterns of his own life, and will thus seek to become more accessible to non-Christians for the purpose of evangelism. It is so easy for Christians to hide comfortably in a Christian ghetto, only ever interacting in meaningful ways with other Christians, and seeking to avoid close encounters with non-Christians.

God has called on us to share the gospel. Paul said *"I am obligated both to Greeks and non-Greeks, both to the wise and the foolish"* (Romans 1:14). That debt, that "obligation," could only be discharged by preaching the gospel. The verbal message of the gospel of Jesus Christ is *"the power of God for the salvation of everyone who believes"* (Romans 1:16), and it is our responsibility to share it with as many people as God brings to us providentially. No one will be saved from their sins by watching how righteously we live or how neat our yard is or how well-mannered our children are. They will be saved by hearing the gospel message with faith. And if we are not gathering sinners by that means, we are scattering.

CROSS-CULTURAL MISSIONS

The external journey of worldwide disciple-making has as its goal the proclamation of the gospel to every tribe, language, people, and nation. Christ made the completion of this task essential to his plan for the end of the world: *"And this gospel of the kingdom will be preached in the whole world as a testimony to all nations, and then the end will come"* (Matthew 24:14). Every mature Christian is actively involved in this process, cares passionately about it, and makes it a central concern of his daily life.

There are some Christians, like the Apostle Paul, who are called to be trailblazing, church-planting missionaries, going to distant lands to take the gospel to people who have never heard of Christ: *"It has always been my ambition to preach the gospel where Christ was not known, so that I would not be building on someone else's foundation. Rather, as it is written: 'Those who were not told about him will see, and those who have not heard will understand'"* (Romans 15:20–21). For those people, essential to their spiritual maturity is that they obey the heavenly call of God, and go. Each person should know clearly what God intends them to do, what are the specific good works he has prepared in advance for us to do (Ephesians 2:10). So for those people, traveling to distant lands, learning a foreign tongue, eating unfamiliar foods, braving cultural differences, facing vigorous rejection to win the lost in an unreached people group is the central, organizing calling of their lives. All other good works will revolve around that calling.

It seems reasonable to conclude that the majority of Christians do not have such a calling. Paul does not write the Roman Christians to persuade them all to leave their homes in Rome and join him as he goes to distant Spain. Rather, he asks them to help him in his mission: *"I plan to [come to you] when I go to Spain. I hope to visit you while passing through and **to have you assist me** on my journey there, after I have enjoyed your company for a while"* (Romans 15:24; blooding mine). So every mature Christian who is not called to go to a distant unreached people group still embraces his responsibility to assist those who are.

When William Carey departed England to go to India as a missionary, he told the little mission agency he had helped to form, "I will go down into the dark mine of heathenism, but you must hold the ropes."[58] The Christians who remain in their native culture must "hold the ropes" for their brothers and sisters who go, and they do this by prayer support (Romans 15:30, Colossians 4:3, 2 Thessalonians 3:1), financial support, short term missions trips, encouraging e-mails, Skype calls, etc.

Having said all that, however, a mature Christian will constantly be challenging himself to see if the Lord can use him overseas. The overwhelming needs of a world dying without any knowledge of Christ have motivated many to reevaluate their lives. Hudson Taylor, the pioneering missionary who took the gospel to the interior regions of China, was convicted to this work by the "accusing map" of China and the relative ease of the English Christians he knew:

On Sunday, June 25, 1865, unable to bear the sight of a congregation of a thousand or more Christian people rejoicing in their own security while millions were perishing for lack of knowledge, I wandered out on the sands alone, in great spiritual agony, and there the Lord conquered my unbelief, and I surrendered myself to God for this service.[59]

John Paton, Scottish missionary to the New Hebrides, was almost crushed by the constant press of the lost in the South Seas while he carried on a fruitful urban ministry on Green Street in Glasgow. This was his reaction:

> The wail and the claims of the heathen were constantly sounding in my ears. I saw them perishing for lack of knowledge of the true God and his Son, Jesus, while my Green Street people had the open Bible and all the means of grace within easy reach.[60]

A mature Christian feels this same passion for the lost, and wrestles faithfully with the question, "Am I called by God to go to an unreached people group with the gospel?" Far from assuming the answer is "No," they need ongoing, compelling evidence for reasons to stay, working among people who have so many "means of grace within easy reach."

PRAYER

One of the most significant differences between a Christian and a non-Christian is in the ongoing sense of constant dependence on God for everything. We Christians know that we must ask God for everything we need, including our daily bread. But since non-Christians have not yet understood their true position before God, since they are dead in transgressions and sins (Ephesians 2:1) as we noted, we must pray on their behalf, since they cannot do it themselves.

Though there are many things we can pray on behalf of the lost, the most significant have to do with their salvation. I want to concentrate on two biblical passages that teach this responsibility. In Romans 9:1–3, the Apostle Paul opens to us his heart of compassion for the lost among his countrymen, speaking of his *"great sorrow and unceasing anguish"* at their rejection of Christ. In Romans 10:1, he reveals how this heart of compassion pours out in prayer for them: *"Brothers, my heart's desire and prayer to God for the Israelites is that they may be saved."* A mature Christian prays for lost parents, children, relatives, neighbors, coworkers, and others in his circle. He or she goes beyond this, and prays faithfully for unreached people groups, using books like Patrick Johnstone's *Operation World* (a comprehensive prayer guide for every country on earth), and online resources like *Global Prayer Digest*[61] and Joshua Project[62], which seek to make specific people groups "come alive" for more knowledgeable prayer.

The second key passage is Matthew 9:36–38. There, Jesus is moved with compassion at the overwhelming spiritual needs of the crowds following him. He told his disciples, *"The harvest is plentiful but the workers are few. Ask the Lord of the harvest, therefore, to send out workers into his harvest field"* (Matthew 9:37–38). This should part of the regular prayer life of a Christian on behalf of the lost.

MERCY MINISTRIES

I remember well riding through the streets of Mombasa, Kenya, on my first overseas mission trip. It was the last week of a summer long trip, and we were staying in a comfortable resort, right on the Indian Ocean. Some of us wanted to see the city, so we were touring some of the poorer districts in a brand-new, air conditioned van. Never, in all my life, had I seen what was displayed to us. The more streets we drove down, the more uncomfortable

I became with the shocking disparity I saw between my lifestyle and that of the people we were viewing through the tinted glass. It wasn't long after this that I began to see that air conditioned van as a metaphor of the manner in which I was making my way comfortably through life on this suffering globe—"in the world, but not of it." I have wrestled with the customary comforts of my upper-middle class lifestyle ever since.

I have come to the conclusion that the Lord Jesus Christ does not want us to feel at ease with the issue of human suffering. Instead, he intends to test us, to probe our hearts by confronting us with poverty. In John 6, we read, *"When Jesus looked up and saw a great crowd coming toward him, he said to Philip, "Where shall we buy bread for these people to eat?" He asked this only to test him, for he already had in mind what he was going to do"* (John 6:5–6). Christ tests us by seeing if we are willing to spend ourselves on behalf of the poor as he did. Among the actions Christ commands of us in our interactions with the world is the ministry of mercy—the alleviating of the temporal suffering of people, as he gives us opportunity.

It is Christlike to be moved with compassion when we see the suffering of widows, orphans, the poor, the oppressed, those crushed by natural disasters, and the like. The Bible has a great deal to say about such compassion, and the physical deeds that should come from it:

- Is not this the kind of fasting I have chosen: to loose the chains of injustice and untie the cords of the yoke, to set the oppressed free and break every yoke? Is it not to share your food with the hungry and to provide the poor wanderer with shelter-- when you see the naked, to clothe him, and not to turn away from your own flesh and blood? (Isaiah 58:6–7)
- He who is kind to the poor lends to the Lord, and he will reward him for what he has done. (Proverbs 19:17)

- Jesus answered, "If you want to be perfect, go, sell your possessions and give to the poor, and you will have treasure in heaven. Then come, follow me." (Matthew 19:21)
- Religion that God our Father accepts as pure and faultless is this: to look after orphans and widows in their distress and to keep oneself from being polluted by the world (James 1:27).

Western Christians are the richest Christians in the history of the church. We should be using some of our wealth to relieve the sufferings of the poor.

There are an array of complicated issues to resolve when speaking of mercy ministries, and resolving them all is worthy of a lengthy book in its own right. Let me just mention a few themes. In the Parable of the Good Samaritan, Jesus defined loving our "neighbor as ourselves" in terms of physical care for a suffering stranger (Luke 10:30–37). In his account of Judgment Day in Matthew 25, Jesus separated the nations into sheep (believers) and goats (unbelievers) based on how actively they fed the hungry, gave drink to the thirsty, welcomed the stranger, clothed the naked, and visited the sick and imprisoned in their distress (Matthew 25:31–46). Of course, Jesus was speaking there of ministry to his own people, saying, *"Whatever you did for one of the least of these brothers of mine, you did it for me"* (v. 40). But this doesn't mean that we should only help Christians—the Good Samaritan passage rules that attitude out. Rather I take it to mean that we do this mercy ministry always in the light of eternity, hoping that all the people we help will in the end prove to have been Christ's elect, and that our mercy ministry may have been instrumental in bringing them to faith in Christ. Giving to the temporal needs of non-Christians is complicated by the fact that, in some cases, their sinful neglect of work may disqualify them from conscientious aid (2 Thessalonians 3:10). Finally, many have pointed out how damaging poorly reasoned and lavish aid can be to those we are trying to help.[63] While there is no easy answer to these complex issues, it is clear that God desires us to be consistently generous to the poor and needy.

SALT AND LIGHT

Another pattern of actions which Christ commands us to embrace toward the outside world is that of being "salt and light": *"You are the salt of the earth . . . You are the light of the world"* (Matthew 5:13–16). By this, Jesus means for us to have an effect on the surrounding world of exposing and retarding the spread of evil. Salt was a preservative, a desiccant that dried up moisture and prevented the multiplication of bacteria that defiled the meat. So Christians are meant to stand up for righteousness in the non-Christian world. In the same way, light exposes evil and makes all things visible (Ephesians 5:11–13). Christians are to expose the evil of the world by the purity of their lives and the boldness of their words, so that evil cannot run amok so quickly and destroy the order of society, and make the peaceful spread of the gospel impossible (1 Timothy 2:2).

For some Christians, this may mean a life ministry of social action, such as William Wilberforce of England, using his position as a member of Parliament to fight a twenty-five year battle against slavery in the British Empire. In our modern era, a major social issue is abortion, and Christians can and should use their influence to crush this legalized evil. There are many other social issues that are worthy forums for displaying the glory of God and the values of the Kingdom. Christians can retard evil by working to get an unjust city ordinance overturned; by speaking out against the unfair treatment or criticism—or mocking sarcasm— of someone in a group they are in; or simply by speaking up against someone taking the name of the Lord in vain or spreading a crude joke. Though evil will only get worse in this world (2 Timothy 3:1, 13) and can only be finally destroyed by the glorious coming of Christ (2 Thessalonians 2:8, Jude 14–15), yet the active retarding of evil as a sign of the Kingdom to come is a vital work of the church in this age.

GOOD CITIZENSHIP

Concerning our relationship to the government and to our secular nation, Christians really are between two worlds: we are citizens both of heaven and of earth. God desires Christians to be good citizens of the secular government, submitting gladly to God-ordained authority whenever it doesn't conflict with the commands of God. The clearest passage on this in the New Testament is Romans 13:1–7, which begins with these words: *"Everyone must submit himself to the governing authorities, for there is no authority except that which God has established. The authorities that exist have been established by God"* (Romans 13:1). Other passages teach the same basic lesson—submit to the rulers (1 Peter 2:13–17). Some Christians from the Anabaptist heritage (e.g. the Amish) have refused to participate in secular affairs in any way, refusing to serve as elected officials, on juries, or in the military, etc. These issues are matters of conscience for every person to resolve for himself. However, the example of Daniel as a godly magistrate in a pagan context is helpful for those whose consciences allow their participation. All Christians, in any case, must be faithful to pay their taxes and to show proper respect to God-ordained authorities. We are also commanded to pray for those in authority, that they may be saved, and that we may live peaceful, godly lives (1 Timothy 2:1–4).

However, it is essential for Christians to remember constantly that *"our citizenship is in heaven"* (Philippians 3:20), and that ultimately there is no truly "Christian" nation on earth, for the *"Lord is angry with all nations"* (Isaiah 34:2). The Apostle Paul enjoyed the benefits of his Roman citizenship and consistently taught submission to the authority of Caesar, while at the same time rejecting the pagan aspects of that government. His is a powerful example to follow.

LOVING OUR ENEMIES

One final theme is sadly worth noting in this chapter, and that is the command that Christ gave us to love our enemies. As we are active in all these other areas in the world—evangelism, missions, prayer, mercy ministry, salt and light, and citizenship—our convictions are going to bring us into conflict with the children of the devil (John 8:44). Jesus made this promise: *"In this world you will have trouble"* (John 16:33). Paul linked our trouble to our bold ministry: *"In fact, everyone who wants to live a godly life in Christ Jesus will be persecuted"* (2 Timothy 3:12). The more faithful we are to Christ, the more persecution we should expect. A Christian who gets along well with everyone and never experiences persecution may not be challenging the satanic grip on the status quo; he may be tame milk-toast, no threat to Satan's dark reign. A faithful Christian should expect to have enemies.

Jesus has commanded us plainly to love our enemies: *"But I tell you who hear me: Love your enemies, do good to those who hate you, bless those who curse you, pray for those who mistreat you"* (Luke 6:27–28; see also Matthew 5:43–48). He himself set an example that we should follow, by his loving demeanor toward men who were killing him: *"When they hurled their insults at him, he did not retaliate; when he suffered, he made no threats. Instead, he entrusted himself to him who judges justly"* (1 Peter 2:23). So also Christians throughout history have died gloriously, loving enemies who were soon to become eternal brothers and sisters in Christ. Stephen prayed for his hate-filled murderers with his dying breath, *"Lord, do not hold this sin against them"* (Acts 7:60). Christians died in the Roman era with such dignity and Christlike love that Tertullian said "the blood of the martyrs is the seed of the Church."[64] So too, in the modern context, even Christians who are not called to be martyrs still can turn the other cheek and answer kindly when slandered (1 Corinthians 4:13). This has every bit as much power now to convert our enemies as it did during the era of the Roman Empire.

SUMMARY

Christ has left his church in enemy territory, surrounded by Satan's kingdom and his people. He did this to achieve his purposes in the world: the rescue of the elect from the kingdom of darkness to the kingdom of light. Christians are called on to engage the non-Christian world in seven important ways: evangelism, cross-cultural missions, prayer, mercy ministry, salt and light, citizenship, and love for our enemies.

CHAPTER 27

STEWARDSHIP

"WHAT DO YOU HAVE THAT you did not receive?" (1 Corinthians 4:7). This profound question cuts to the root of the issue before us in this chapter—stewardship. The fundamental concept that everything we have in life comes from God and will go back to God, with an accounting, is the essence of stewardship. This chapter brings us to one of the most uncomfortable topics for the pseudo-convert and for the immature Christian. These people always cling to their wallets as the last stronghold of their pagan way of life. The foreign god *Mammon* (money) is one of the chief rivals to the true God of the Bible. And for this reason: "the Bible's Author and Editor . . . devotes twice as many verses to money (about 2350 of them) than to faith and prayer combined."[65] Jesus spoke more about money than he did about heaven and hell. In the end, if our wallet is not truly converted, neither are we; and if our wallet is not being progressively sanctified, neither are we.

WHAT IS A STEWARD?

A steward is a servant who manages someone else's property. As we noted above, everything we presently possess is given us in stewardship by God, and God will expect an accounting for it all on Judgment Day. Many of Jesus' parables spoke of this reality and underscored our role as stewards. All of the following parables are based on the essential truths of our stance before God as stewards: the Parable of the Talents (Matthew 25:14–30), the Parable of the Unforgiving Servant (Matthew 18:23–35), the Parable of the

Faithful or Unfaithful Servant (Matthew 24:45–51), the Parable of the Ten Minas (Luke 19:11–27), the Parable of the Vineyard (Matthew 21:33–43), the Parable of the Dishonest Manager (Luke 16:1–12). In each of these parables, the scenario is basically the same: an authority figure (king, master, homeowner, etc.) entrusts a servant (steward) with something valuable, departs so the steward is in charge and empowered to make decisions, then returns and calls the steward to account for the possessions the master entrusted. The steward's standing, and rewards or punishment, are based on their faithfulness in managing the master's possessions. This is the essence of stewardship.

STEWARDS OF WHAT?

Stewardship relates to anything that God entrusts to us to use for his glory. When most Christians think about stewardship, they think first and foremost about money and material possessions. In one sense this is appropriate, as we've already noted. Godly stewardship of money is an incredibly accurate barometer of the state of our hearts. If by faith we are living for the future world, our giving patterns will show it. We will use our money to invest for eternity.

However, we should consider ourselves stewards of more than just our money and possessions. We are also stewards of our bodies (and health), our time, our opportunities, our gifts and talents, the earth, our national advantages, and any other temporal resource God gives us. All of these come under the rubric of stewardship, those things for which we will give an account on Judgment Day.

THE PROPER PERSPECTIVE

Randy Alcorn has given us an immeasurable blessing by writing his book *Money, Possessions, and Eternity*.[66] Alcorn says rightly, "The key to a right use of money and possessions is a right perspective— an *eternal* perspective. . . . The everyday choices I make regarding money and possessions are of eternal consequence."[67] Alcorn's basic message is that money is a gift of God to be invested in the advancement of Christ's Kingdom, but is a dangerous snare of the devil when not so invested. One of the key points of the book is, "you can't take it with you, but you can send it on ahead."[68] By this he means that, by being faith-filled people in this present age, we will generously invest our earthly wealth in God's work; God will account that gift to our heavenly ledger book and we will be rewarded accordingly on Judgment Day. We "send it on ahead" every time our faith moves us to use our money and possessions for Christ's work. We will never lose our reward. Jesus taught this principle in many places, but perhaps most clearly in Luke 12:

> Sell your possessions and give to the poor. Provide purses for yourselves that will not wear out, a treasure in heaven that will not be exhausted, where no thief comes near and no moth destroys. For where your treasure is, there your heart will be also. (Luke 12:33–34)

Faith-filled, generous giving on earth is actually stored up in heaven in "purses . . . that will not wear out." This kind of faith perspective is essential to spiritual maturity, and it makes Christian giving a daily adventure in investing in eternity.

LESSONS FROM JOHN WESLEY

Church history is full of the accounts of people whose faith freed them from covetousness and greed (which is idolatry), and enough to give with supernatural generosity. Early in his ministry, John Wesley visited a debtor's prison, where he learned that one shilling could release a person from prison and set them free. He never looked on money the same way again. As his income increased from book sales and salary raises, he determined to live at the same level his whole life and to give the rest away. One year, his income was slightly over £1,400, and he gave away all but £30. He felt that, with increasing income, a Christian's standard of *giving* should increase, not his standard of living.[69] When he died, his earthly possessions totaled no more than a few coins, but his heavenly tally was infinitely richer. He said very poignantly, "I value all things only by the price they shall gain in eternity."[70]

FAITHFUL IN LITTLE MEANS
FAITHFUL IN MUCH

Money is "very little" in God's sight, though the world often goes to war to possess it. But what is much in God's sight is how we manage the "very little" that we have:

> Whoever can be trusted with very little can also be trusted with much, and whoever is dishonest with very little will also be dishonest with much. So if you have not been trustworthy in handling worldly wealth, who will trust you with true riches? And if you have not been trustworthy with someone else's property, who will give you property of your own? No servant can serve two masters. Either he will hate the one and love the other, or he will be devoted to the one and despise the other. You cannot serve both God and Money. (Luke 16:10–13)

Handling money properly here and now means many things. It means giving generously to the work of God. Randy Alcorn calls tithing (giving a tenth to God) the "training wheels of Christian giving."[71] He argues that tithing is an Old Covenant principle for giving, and in every other case the New Covenant life is a great improvement and enlargement of the Old Covenant life. Therefore, a tithe should just be the start of what a Spirit-filled Christian gives. Paul's command to give cheerfully whatever God leads us to give (2 Corinthians 9:7) is the best principle. But the drive in stewardship should always be toward greater and greater generosity in Christian giving.

A mature Christian "sends it on ahead" by investing in eternity. He makes sacrifices in his present daily life—with both necessities and pleasures—so he can store up treasure for eternity. He invests sacrificially in his local church, as well as in other ministries that are advancing the Kingdom of God. He invests wisely by researching these giving opportunities and taking each one to the Lord in prayer. He does all of this by faith, fully expecting to be rewarded for his good stewardship by the master. When the time comes, he yearns to hear this commendation: *"Well done, good and faithful servant! You have been faithful in a few things; I will put you in charge of many things"* (Matthew 25:21, 23).

OUR FINANCIAL RESPONSIBILITIES

Handling money properly also means caring for the basic ongoing needs one's own family: *"If anyone does not provide for his relatives, and especially for his immediate family, he has denied the faith and is worse than an unbeliever"* (1 Timothy 5:8). By this we mean such necessities as food, clothing, and shelter: *"but if we have food and clothing, we will be content with that"* (1 Timothy 6:8). Pleasures and wants beyond that may well be gifts of God, *"who richly provides us with everything for our enjoyment"* (1 Timothy 6:17). But they can also be snares into godless covetousness and love of money, which can ruin our souls: *"For the love of money is a root of all kinds of evil. Some people, eager for money, have wandered from the faith and pierced themselves with many griefs"* (1 Timothy 6:10). A mature Christian will constantly guard their heart from wandering from the faith through love of money and possessions.

Handling money properly also means saving money for the future as God leads: *"Go to the ant, you sluggard; consider its ways and be wise! It has no commander, no overseer or ruler, yet it stores its provisions in summer and gathers its food at harvest"* (Proverbs 6:6–8). Of course, there is a great danger here of becoming like the rich fool in Christ's parable, who stores up abundance for himself to enjoy for years to come, not realizing that he is to die that very night and has done nothing to store up for eternity (Luke 12:16–21)

American Christians, so richly blessed by God, sometimes act the role of the rich fool. They pour huge amounts of resources into retirement accounts so they can live comfortably in their retirement years pursuing their own interests. What is this but building bigger barns, and laying up good things for years to come? Satan's world system teams up with our fleshly selfishness to teach us an overpowering lie: "These resources are mine to do with as I please; they have come to me to make my life comfortable and pleasant to me." The rich fool made that mistake, and it cost him his soul.

Another practical issue of stewardship is the maintenance and care of existing possessions:

> I went past the field of the sluggard, past the vineyard of the man who lacks judgment; thorns had come up everywhere, the ground was covered with weeds, and the stone wall was in ruins. I applied my heart to what I observed and learned a lesson from what I saw: A little sleep, a little slumber, a little folding of the hands to rest—and poverty will come on you like a bandit and scarcity like an armed man. (Proverbs 24:30–34)

The sin of laziness leads to waste of the Lord's possessions; it is a bad witness, and an arrogant presumption on the future. Thus a spiritually mature person will keep his house, car, clothing, and other vital possessions in good repair, ready for future use for the Master.

OTHER REALMS OF STEWARDSHIP

As we've already noted, there are many other realms of stewardship not usually thought of under that title. It isn't just our money or our possessions about which we will give the Master an accounting.

Our bodies are a matter of stewardship, in that God expects us to *"feed and care for them"* (Ephesians 5:29). Paul reminds the Corinthian Christians that their bodies are a temple of the Holy Spirit (1 Corinthians 6:19), and uses that fact to encourage sexual purity. He mentioned that those who sin sexually sin against their own bodies (v. 18), and therefore had the physical health of the Corinthians in mind as well as their spiritual health. Therefore, a mature Christian looks on staying in good physical condition, eating well, and exercising consistently as a part the responsibility of a good steward. Many American Christians are given to gluttony, and to the obesity that comes as a result. Also, due to the ironic busyness of a basically sedentary life, many do not make time for regular exercise, and so get out of condition. A mature Christian looks after his health in all areas.

Our time is a matter of stewardship, for we will not be here forever and we must *"redeem the time because the days are evil"* (Ephesians 5:16). "Redeeming the time" implies that the time must in some sense be bought back from captivity, rescued from waste by energetic effort. Time is brief and unspeakably precious. I will speak more of this in a moment.

Our physical talents are a matter of stewardship, whether athletic, musical, artistic, intellectual, or any other talent. If we have an ability, we should use it for the glory of God, and we will give him an account. In the movie *Chariots of Fire*, Eric Liddell was a young man blessed with many talents. He was preparing to be a missionary in China, but he was also one of the fastest men in the world. He was trying to juggle a lot of duties, but finally had to focus on perfecting his running to get ready for the Olympics. His pious sister was worried about the effect his dedication to running would have on his future life as a missionary, so finally Liddell shared with her his reasons for his training: "God made me for many things—for China, yes. But he also made me **fast**. And when I run I feel his pleasure. To not do it would be to hold him in contempt."⁷² This was a man with a steward's mentality about his physical talents.

Opportunities that come to us through the providence of God are also matters of stewardship. When we sit next to a stranger on an airplane, we should assume that the time is ordained by God either for witnessing or a ministry of encouragement to a fellow believer. So also when there comes a chance to serve in some unique way, or hear a gifted Bible teacher, or go on a short-term mission trip; all of life's marvelously varied "chance" occurrences are measured out to us providentially by God, and we will be held accountable for each one.

Positions of power are also matters of stewardship. If we hold a position such as pastor, elder, deacon, chairman, president, representative, general, CEO, chief of police, head librarian, king, prime minister, or any other position, we should never forget the lesson that God gave Nebuchadnezzar: *"the Most High is sovereign over the kingdoms of men and gives them to anyone he wishes and sets over them the lowliest of men"* (Daniel 4:17). Leadership is a steward-ship for us, temporarily ours until the day we give it up. And on Judgment Day, we will give an account of what we did with it.

We should also see our ministry for the Lord as a stewardship. That is precisely the language the Apostle Paul used of his minis-try to the Gentiles: *"assuming that you have heard of the stewardship of God's grace that was given to me for you"* (Ephesians 3:2, ESV); *"for if I do this of my own will, I have a reward, but not of my own will, I am still entrusted with a stewardship"* (1 Corinthians 9:17, ESV). This stewardship called from Paul the highest level of devotion that he could give, and Paul gave it all his life. So also is our ministry for the Lord: our evangelism, our mission work, our protection of the gospel from doctrinal perversion, and our patterns of service to Christ are all matters of stewardship before God.

Finally, and in a more general sense, all Christians are stew-ards of the earth and all its created resources. The earth was entrusted to us at creation, as we have already noted. God created man, male and female, and commanded them to *"fill the earth and subdue it and rule over it"* (Genesis 1:28). More specifically, he put Adam in the Garden *"to serve it and protect it"* (Genesis 2:15). Our sin has clearly cursed the earth; not just in that God subjected the earth to futility (Romans 8:20), but that in our greed and self-ishness, we have ruined the beauty of the earth. In 1991, during the first Gulf War, Saddam Hussein ordered his fleeing troops to dump five million gallons of crude oil into the Persian Gulf and set on fire. This immense environmental disaster lasted for years after the war was over, and marine and avian life around the Gulf has still not fully recovered as of this writing. This is just one of many ways that human sin has directly destroyed the ecology of our beautiful planet. The book of Revelation says that judgment is coming for this sin: *"The time has come for . . . destroying those who destroy the earth"* (Revelation 11:18). Christians should love the earth, its natural beauty, its fragile ecosystems, and seek to preserve them as an act of worship to God and an act of faith in the future New Heaven and New Earth of which we will be heirs. This does not mean embracing the political agendas or eastern religions of Earth- or Gaia-worshiping activists; nor does it imply that we should spend inordinate amounts of our time in politi-cal struggles to change environmental laws (though for some Christians it might). The principle of stewardship of the earth does mean, however, that we should not purposefully pollute or litter, and that we should work to cherish and love the creation that God entrusted to us.

CHAPTER 28

WORK

A CERTAIN MILLER FROM A nondescript village wanted to make himself appear important. So he boasted to the king that his beautiful daughter could spin straw into gold. The king called his bluff, and locked his daughter in the tower with a room full of straw, ordering her to spin the straw into gold by morning, or else face a horrible death. As the hapless girl sat there in despair, suddenly a strange dwarf appeared, and offered to do the magical deed. He had the power to spin the straw into gold. But in order for him to do this, she had to agree to give him her firstborn child.

This is how the strange and somewhat eerie children's story "Rumpelstiltskin" goes. For me, it is a striking illustration of the incredible power of faith to transform even the most menial tasks and the most ordinary days into gold, and for all eternity. Apart from faith in Christ, our deeds are said to be no more than *"wood, hay, and straw"* (1 Corinthians 3:12). When they are tested on Judgment Day for their quality, they will burn up and we will suffer loss (v. 15). However, anything done by faith in Christ, for the glory of God, will survive the fire of Judgment Day and will last for all eternity. In this way, faith transforms straw and makes it gold.

The final arena of positive Christian action for us to consider is our work. This includes our careers and our daily chores. It includes labors of our bodies and of our minds. Though our earthly labors may seem insignificant, nothing could be further from the truth; God actually delights to use our work to advance his Kingdom.

REDEEMING THE TIME

Though certainly not originally intended this way, the story of Rumpelstiltskin can be seen as a parable concerning the power of human labor to turn something worthless into something of immense value. As a Christian, I see it directly connected to the concept of "redeeming the time." In Ephesians 5:16, Paul says we must be *"redeeming the time, because the days are evil"* (Ephesians 5:16, KJV). As we have already noted, the word *redeem* used here literally means to "ransom" or "buy back." The image is of a slave market in which, for the payment of a price, a captive can be set free. In some sense, then, every moment of the day is like a captive, needing to be rescued through the payment of a price. The price for rescuing every moment is Spirit-empowered labor. In effect, every minute comes to us as straw, worthless, fit only for burning. Apart from Spirit-empowered labor, those minutes will be wasted. But by the Spirit, we can actually transform the straw of earthly minutes into the gold of deeds done for Christ. They will then last for all eternity, rewarded on Judgment Day.

DO IT ALL FOR THE GLORY OF GOD

For this reason, a mature Christian seeks to glorify God in whatever work his hand finds to do, no matter how insignificant the task may seem to be. Though his moments on a given day may be reduced to making photocopies, or weeding a garden, or picking up his boss at the airport, or getting the car inspected before the deadline, yet even these things can be done to the glory of God:

> Whatever you do, work at it with all your heart, as working for the Lord, not for men, since you know that you will receive an inheritance from the Lord as a reward. It is the Lord Christ you are serving. (Colossians 3:23–24)

So we are to spin straw into gold by following the Spirit, moment by moment. By the Spirit-led labors of ours hands and of our minds we are storing up treasure that will last forever. Of course, I am not here arguing against rest and relaxation, or against sleep. God humbles us by making such bodies and minds as these that easily get weary and regularly need rest. But rest and relaxation, like the honey we mentioned earlier, must be taken in appropriate doses. Too much and we are ruined.

One of the central figures in the book of Proverbs is the sluggard, who ruins his life by his unwillingness to work. It starts innocently, just by sleeping in. But soon it leads to wholesale destruction, with his property totally ruined, as we saw in the last chapter (Proverbs 24:30–34). This lazy man is so listless, he can't rouse himself out of bed: *"As a door turns on its hinges, so a sluggard turns on his bed"* (Proverbs 26:14). He constantly makes imaginative excuses against doing any work: *"The sluggard says, '"There is a lion outside!" or, "I will be murdered in the streets!"'"* (Proverbs 22:13). He can barely lift his own food to his mouth: *"the sluggard buries his hand in the dish; he will not even bring it back to his mouth!"* (Proverbs 19:24). He has become worthless through self-indulgent laziness.

These Proverbs may seem like harsh indictments against any rest or recreation at all. Obviously, God desires that we rest (Psalm 127:2 says God grants sleep to those he loves), and that we recreate (or else why did Jesus recline at table and feast with his friends: John 12:1–2). But just like with the threat of money, we must be vigilant against the alluring siren call of a life of comfort, ease, and recreation. The recreation industry in America is growing exponentially. This includes the multi-billion-dollar movie industry, as well as computer games, sporting goods, hammocks, and recreational vehicles. If we are not careful, we can begin to look on work as an annoying interruption in a life of fun, pleasure, and ease.

A THEOLOGY OF WORK: FROM
GENESIS TO REVELATION

We were created for work, and work itself is a gift of God. Work predates the Fall of Adam, as we have already noted. Certainly Genesis chapter 1 presents the incredible labor of God in creating the heavens and the earth. God labored for six days, and crafted an immense universe filled with the works of his hands. Human beings, created in his image, were created to do work after his pattern.

To the human race was given the awesome responsibility to fill the earth, rule over it, and subdue it (Genesis 1:28). The word *subdue* implies wrestling with the earth, but since this command was given before the Fall, that wrestling would have been astonishingly fruitful all over the world.

In Genesis 2, the text names four rivers—the Pishon, Gihon, Tigris, and Euphrates—that flowed from the Garden of Eden and the lands that awaited Adam once he ventured forth from Eden (Genesis 2:10–14). This passage gives a sense of the incredible adventure of discovery and fruitful labor that awaited Adam and Eve and their children. In due time, they would have made boats and traveled down those four rivers to discover the natural resources (gold, resin, and onyx) of the land of Havilah. It would have taken immense toil to bring these things forth, but the toil would have been blessed by God and sweet to the laborer.

So also the command of Genesis 2:15: "*The Lord God took the man and put him in the Garden of Eden to work* (lit. serve) *it and take care of* (lit. protect) *it.*" To Adam was given the responsibility to bring from the Garden of Eden all of the full potential of the seeds that God had crafted on the third day of creation (Genesis 1:11–12). The skill of bringing forth the shrubs and herbs mentioned in Genesis 2:5 would be taught by God (Isaiah 28:24–29), but it would be man's labor in the fields that would achieve the blessed harvest.

From all of this evidence, there can be no doubt that fruitful labor, blessed abundantly by the hand of God, would have characterized humanity's life on an earth free from the curse caused by Adam's sin. Thus it is a false doctrine that teaches that the curse placed on Adam as a result of his sin was that he would have to work. No, it was that his work would be cursed and ultimately futile because of a cursed earth and his own inevitable death:

> To Adam he said, "Because you listened to your wife and ate from the tree about which I commanded you, 'You must not eat of it,' Cursed is the ground because of you; through painful toil you will eat of it all the days of your life. It will produce thorns and thistles for you, and you will eat the plants of the field. By the sweat of your brow you will eat your food until you return to the ground, since from it you were taken; for dust you are and to dust you will return." (Genesis 3:17–19)

From that day until this, humanity has labored under this curse from God. This is the great lament of Solomon in Ecclesiastes: *"Meaningless! Meaningless!" says the Teacher. "Utterly meaningless! Everything is meaningless. What does man gain from all his labor at which he toils under the sun?"* (Ecclesiastes 1:2–3). Death stands over all our projects and seems to mock them, as though they are worthless.

When I was in a missionary in Japan, we lived near the sea on the island of Shikoku. One day, I took my two little children to the beach and the three of us labored for an hour, building "the best sand castle in history." It was quite elaborate, with a high outer wall, multiple ramparts, guard towers, a moat, a drawbridge, several smaller buildings inside the wall, etc. My son thought for sure it would stand forever! I knew better. As a matter of fact, the very next day I passed that same beach, but saw only a nondescript lump where the massive sand castle had been just one day before.

So it will be with the physical effects of all our labors, for God is going to destroy this present world to make way for the New

Heaven and New Earth: *"The heavens will disappear with a roar; the elements will be destroyed by fire, and the earth and everything in it will be laid bare"* (2 Peter 3:10). But that does not mean our labors are worthless. Not at all! On the contrary, our works will remain in the record book of God, if they were done by faith for his glory.

The theology of Christian work is perfected in the life of Jesus Christ. Jesus' example of diligence in being about his Father's work sanctifies all work for all Christians throughout all time:

- "My food," said Jesus, "is to do the will of him who sent me and to finish his work." (John 4:34)
- Jesus said to them, "My Father is always at his work to this very day, and I, too, am working." (John 5:17)
- I have testimony weightier than that of John. For the very work that the Father has given me to finish, and which I am doing, testifies that the Father has sent me. (John 5:36)
- As long as it is day, we must do the work of him who sent me. Night is coming, when no one can work. (John 9:4)
- "Are there not twelve hours in the day? If anyone walks in the day, he does not stumble, because he sees the light of this world." (John 11:9)
- I have brought you glory on earth by completing the work you gave me to do. (John 17:4)

In these statements, we see an incredible focus in Jesus. There was no time to waste, and at every moment he was focused on doing the work God had assigned him to do. Modern Christians, besieged by innumerable distractions, have to fight at every moment to keep focused on the work God has assigned us to do. In North Carolina, where I live, the biggest sporting event of the year is the NCAA men's basketball tournament, called "March Madness." In recent years, ESPN has offered constant streaming of daytime games directly to your computer at work, so you don't have to miss a moment of any game you care about. What's so amazing about this is that ESPN is actually shamelessly advertising this capability, showing workers at the office dressed up in face paint and cheering their teams rather than working diligently on their tasks.

Christ had perhaps three years in which to change history; three years in which to cure people; three years in which to teach multitudes about the Kingdom of God; three years in which to do the works of the One who sent him. At the end of that brief time, Jesus died. On the third day, God raised him from the dead. He then had forty days to train his newborn church to prepare it for the works God would assign to them. Then, when the forty days were over, Jesus ascended to the sky, his time on earth finished. There was not a moment to lose.

We see a similar dedication in the Apostle Paul, who frequently spoke of his own labors for Christ:

- You yourselves know that these hands of mine have supplied my own needs and the needs of my companions. In everything I did, I showed you that by this kind of **hard work** we must help the weak, remembering the words the Lord Jesus himself said: "It is more blessed to give than to receive." (Acts 20:34–35)

- To this very hour we go hungry and thirsty, we are in rags, we are brutally treated, we are homeless. **We work hard with our own hands.** (1 Corinthians 4:11–12)

- In beatings, imprisonments and riots; in **hard work**, sleepless nights and hunger . . . (2 Corinthians 6:5)

- Are they servants of Christ? (I am out of my mind to talk like this.) I am more. **I have worked much harder**, been in prison more frequently, been flogged more severely, and been exposed to death again and again. (2 Corinthians 11:23)

- To this end I **labor**, struggling with all his energy, which so powerfully works in me. (Colossians 1:29)

- For you yourselves know how you ought to follow our example. We were not idle when we were with you, nor did we eat anyone's food without paying for it. On the contrary, **we worked night and day, laboring and toiling** so that we would not be a burden to any of you. (2 Thessalonians 3:7–8)

This is an overwhelming body of evidence of the incessant labors of the Apostle Paul for the Kingdom of Christ. And his labors were a mixture of practical work for money (tentmaking) and spiritual work in the gospel. From Acts 20:35 and 2 Thessalonians 3:7–8, we get the clear picture that Paul worked diligently with his own hands (almost certainly making tents) so that he could meet the financial needs of his traveling companions, who had left everything to follow Paul as he followed Christ.

Jesus and Paul set very clear examples before us: joyful labor in the Lord. And no task was beneath them. Jesus' example of the footwashing (John 13:1–12) showed that he was willing to do the lowliest of tasks. No Christian can ever refuse to do some work because they think it too demeaning. Christ has removed that excuse forever.

So, from the foundation of the world, God himself worked. He created man to work. Jesus worked. Paul worked. So must we. And in this theology of work, we find immense dignity. The straw of every moment—serving God and others—can be spun into gold. This occurs even when doing the homeliest of tasks: *"So whether you eat or drink or whatever you do, do it all for the glory of God"* (1 Corinthians 10:31). A Christian learns how to eat and drink to the glory of God, even though that particular meal will go into the stomach and then pass out of the body (Matthew 15:17). So also a Christian learns how to wash dishes, mow the lawn, paint a fence, make a bed, do laundry, cook a meal, rake leaves, and take out the trash to the glory of God. Anything that does not come from faith is sin (Romans 14:23), but anything that does come from faith and is led by the Spirit is eternal. This is how we spin straw into gold.

And in heaven, we will work as well. Though we cannot be specific about this, it is clear that the New Heaven and New Earth will not be a place of idleness, but of creative labor for the glory of the Lord: *"No longer will there be any curse. The throne of God and of the Lamb will be in the city, **and his servants will serve him**"* (Revelation 22:3). The removal of the curse is not an end to work, but rather a promise that the work we do in service to God will be richly blessed.

ALL HONORABLE WORK IS "SACRED"

A mature Christian view of work, then, begins with the premise that Christ is Lord of all, and thus can be glorified in all things. Abraham Kuyper, the Dutch Reformed scholar, professor, and church leader, who served as prime minister of the Netherlands from 1901–1905, defended his involvement in politics with a famous quote worthy of much meditation: "There is not a square inch in the whole domain of our human existence over which Christ, who is Sovereign over all, does not cry: 'Mine!'"[73] If this is true (and the Bible teaches that it is), then there are no forms of honorable work in which a Christian cannot glorify God.

Early in church history, there came an unbiblical dichotomy between the sacred and profane realms. "Sacred", it was claimed, had to do only with directly spiritual work, done by professional clergy (priests) in their service to Christ; "profane" had to do with secular work, done by laymen in the pursuits of their trades. Eusebius, writing in the fourth century A.D., upheld this unbiblical distinction:

> Two ways of life were given by the law of Christ to his church. The one is above nature, and beyond common human living. . . . Wholly and permanently separate from the common customary life of mankind, it devotes itself to the service of God alone. . . . Such then is the perfect form of the Christian life. And the other, more humble, more human, permits men to . . . have minds for farming,

for trade, and the other more secular interests as well as for religion. . . . And a kind of secondary grade of piety is attributed to them.[74]

From this hierarchy of piety came a class of professional clerics, including the pope, cardinals, bishops, monks, priests, nuns, all of whom gave their full time in spiritual service of God. Below them on the "ladder of piety" were the secular people: princes, knights, tradesmen, farmers, housewives, serfs, pages, and everyone else.

With the coming of the Protestant Reformation, all of this changed forever, at least among those who embraced reformation doctrine. Martin Luther emphasized the "priesthood of all believers," and worked out consistently a doctrine of labor. Look at this series of quotes from Luther on the issue of "secular" work:

> When a maid cooks and cleans and does other housework, because God's command is there, even such a small work must be praised as a service of God far surpassing the holiness and asceticism of all monks and nuns.[75]

> Seemingly secular works are a worship of God and an obedience well-pleasing to God.[76]

> Your work is a very sacred matter. God delights in it, and through it he wants to bestow his blessing on you.[77]

William Tyndale, and the English Puritans who followed him, worked out this doctrine of the sacredness of all honorable work more consistently than any other movement in church history:

> William Tyndale: [If we look externally] . . . there is difference betwixt washing of dishes and preaching the word of God; but as touching to please God, none at all.[78]

> William Perkins: The action of a shepherd in keeping sheep . . . is as good a work before God as is the action of a judge

in giving sentence, or a magistrate in ruling, or a minister in preaching.[79]

The Puritans developed the doctrine of a Christian's vocation, or calling, as being their sacred offering to a sovereign God, who sanctifies all of life with his holy presence and blessing:

> William Perkins: A vocation or calling is a certain kind of life, ordained and imposed on man by God, for the common good. . . . Every person of every degree, state, sex, or condition without exception must have some personal and particular calling to walk in.[80]

> Richard Steele: He that hath lent you talents hath also said, "Occupy until I come!" How is it that you stand all day idle? . . . Your trade is your proper province.[81]

The rewards a Christian should expect from their professions should not lead them to greed or vainglory, but rather to a heavenly mindset, their hearts set on the future blessings from God on Judgment Day. All Christians should serve at their jobs, then, with an eye to the blessing of the Master who gave them the employment:

> William Perkins: They profane their lives and callings that employ them to get honors, pleasures, profits, worldly commodities, etc., for thus we live to another end than God hath appointed, and thus we serve ourselves, and consequently neither God nor man.[82]

> Cotton Mather: Oh, let every Christian walk with God when he works at his calling, act in his occupation with an eye to God, act as under the eye of God.[83]

Of course, the great danger of such a heavenly mindset and a high level of work ethic from a consistent worldview is that the work will be done exceptionally well, and thus be all the more valued on earth. This will inevitably mean earthly prosperity and, with it, the danger of idolatry. John Cotton sought to oppose this tendency in his life by teaching what Christian maturity would produce:

> There is another combination of virtues strangely mixed in every lively holy Christian, and that is diligence in worldly business and yet deadness to the world; such a mystery as none can read but they that know it. . . . Though he labor most diligently in his calling, yet his heart is not set upon these things, he [knows how to use his wealth wisely] when he has got it.[84]

What a goal in our careers! To so labor that we give everything we have to excellence in our employment every moment of the work day, yet be dead to the earthly treasures that will get piled upon such excellence: wealth, praise from men, power, etc.

A mature Christian seeks to glorify God with all his labor, whether in menial daily chores or in a career. A mature Christian will feel the pleasure of God in all his tasks: whether a scientist doing an experiment for a pharmaceutical company, or a janitor cleaning a toilet in a public washroom, or a journalist writing an article for a newspaper, or a missionary learning a language, or a pastor preparing a sermon, or a college student studying for an exam, or a housewife cleaning the dishes. All godly work is sacred.

THE K-F-C-A CYCLE, UNDERSTOOD AND APPLIED

A PATHWAY TO CHRISTIAN MATURITY

KNOWLEDGE
FACTUAL AND EXPERIENTIAL
SPIRITUAL INFORMATION

FACTUAL
Gained from the Scripture

EXPERIENTIAL
Gained from living in God's world

Leads To

→

Romans 10:17
So faith comes
from hearing,
and hearing
through the
word of Christ.

FAITH
ASSURANCE OF AND COMMIT-
MENT TO SPIRITUAL TRUTH

- Certainty that specific invisible spiritual realities are true
- Assurance that hoped-for specific good thing promised in scripture will certainly come true
- Conviction that specific sin in me, and that God hates it and will judge people for such sins
- Reliance on Christ as all-sufficient savior, refuge, provider, shield
- Reception of spiritual guidance and knowledge

**Leads
To**
↑
Psalms 119:100 I have
more understanding
than the elders, for I
obey your precepts.

**Leads
To**
↓
Ephesians 3:16-17
...that Christ may
dwell in your hearts
through faith.

ACTION
EXTERNAL LIFESTYLE OF
HABITUAL OBEDIENCE

1. Presentation of Body to God
2. Personal Holiness
3. Seven-fold obedience to God's commands

   1. Worship   5. Mission
   2. Spiritual   to Non-
      Disciplines   Believers
   3. Family   6. Stewardship
   4. Ministry to   7. Work
      Believers

Leads To

←

Matthew 12:23
Either make the
tree good and

CHARACTER
INTERNAL NATURE CON-
FORMED TO CHRIST

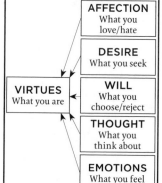

AFFECTION
What you love/hate

DESIRE
What you seek

VIRTUES
What you are

WILL
What you choose/reject

THOUGHT
What you think about

EMOTIONS
What you feel

415

CHAPTER 29

AN ENGINE FOR GROWTH

THUS FAR, WE HAVE SIMPLY described what spiritual maturity looks like. In effect, we have captured a snapshot of a spiritually mature man or woman in midstride. When I was a student at M.I.T., I used to delight in a series of pictures along the wall of the Infinite Corridor, the long hallway that connected several of the main buildings. The pictures were wall-sized enlargements of pictures taken by Dr. Harold Edgerton in the 1930's and 40's using strobe-light photographic techniques. One in particular showed a drop just entering a pool of milk and making a splash that looked like a crown. The amazing techniques of strobe photography took high-speed occurrences and portrayed them frozen in time.

But real life is all about motion, about constant change. When Thomas Edison invented the first motion picture machine, the Kinetoscope, in 1892, he devised a way to capture motion with a series of still photographs, one taken a split second after the last, then shown in a rapid series before the human eye, creating an illusion of movement. By this technique, the technology was established which ultimately gave rise to the motion picture industry and Hollywood. Sanctification is not about a static definition of four major areas of the Christian life, but rather about constant change. It is not a still photograph, but a constantly changing motion picture.

A FOUR-STROKE ENGINE DRIVES
SPIRITUAL GROWTH

In this chapter, I am going to argue that growth to Christian maturity happens when knowledge increases faith, faith transforms character, character produces action, and action promotes knowledge. I will argue that this constant cycle produces an upward "spiral," which leads to Christlike maturity.

In 1876, a German engineer developed a machine that would change the history of transportation, of commerce, of warfare, and indeed, of the world. His name was Nikolaus August Otto, and his machine was known as the internal combustion engine. The basic principle of the internal combustion engine was a cycle of four strokes which would be endlessly repeated. This cycle, which was called the "Otto cycle" after its inventor, was used to drive a shaft; this cycle would eventually power automobiles, boats, motorcycles, airplanes, generators, and many other devices. The four-stroke cycle is this: 1) intake (a fuel-air mixture is sucked into the cylinder), 2) compression (the piston compresses the mixture by decreasing the volume in the chamber), 3) ignition (a spark ignites the fuel mixture, causing an explosion), and 4) exhaust (the fumes from the explosion are driven out of the chamber). At the end of the exhaust cycle, the piston comes to the top of the cylinder to begin the cycle again. In this fashion, internal combustion engines have driven all manner of vehicles billions of miles in the last century.

Of course, a driver motoring along the road does not generally think about this four-part cycle—it just goes on and on, whether he is aware of it or not, and the vehicle makes progress. So it is with the engine that drives sanctification. Without us being conscious of it occurring, knowledge (factual and experiential) produces faith, faith transforms character, character results in actions, and actions give greater opportunity for growth in knowledge.

Is it always this way? Logically, I would argue it is, if we understand each of the four elements properly. Does faith ever produce godly action directly without affecting the character? No, for how can we act godly without our hearts consenting? So, even though we can logically conceive of reversing the cycle or leaving a step out, it doesn't work that way in real life. Let's see if we can defend my idea from Scripture.

KNOWLEDGE INCREASES FAITH

"The apostles said to the Lord, 'Increase our faith'" (Luke 17:5). "Immediately the boy's father exclaimed, 'I do believe; help me overcome my unbelief!'" (Mark 9:24). These two verses record words which sprang from the hearts of believers. Both of them were built on a foundation of existing faith, and both were focused on one thing: the growth of faith. Far more importantly, both were addressed to the Lord Jesus Christ, and were the petition of spiritual beggars who know that growth in faith is a gift of Christ as much as was their initial saving faith.

Just as it is God who gives faith (Ephesians 2:8–9), so it is God who gives growth in faith. There is nothing mechanical or guaranteed about it. God doesn't owe growth to anyone, but he does it as an act of his grace to his children. But *how* does that increased faith come? Here I will argue that it comes on the basis of true spiritual knowledge, gained from the Scripture and from experiences that he crafts for that purpose.

BIBLICAL KNOWLEDGE INCREASES FAITH

According to the Bible, spiritual knowledge is the basis of all faith in Christ: simply put, we cannot believe what we do not know. And this knowledge is of the invisible spiritual world that surrounds us but which cannot be discerned except by the revelation of God. Therefore, God's word is foundational to all faith, as the Apostle Paul stated so plainly: "*so faith comes from hearing, and hearing through the word of Christ*" (Romans 10:17, ESV).

The Word of God is also the food of growing faith, as Paul asserts in Galatians 3:1-6. In that key passage, Paul rebukes the Galatian Christians for seeking to grow in the Christian life differently than the way they first began:

> O foolish Galatians! Who has bewitched you? It was before your eyes that Jesus Christ was publicly portrayed as crucified. Let me ask you only this: Did you receive the Spirit by works of the law or by hearing with faith? Are you so foolish? Having begun by the Spirit, are you now being perfected by the flesh? Did you suffer so many things in vain—if indeed it was in vain? Does he who supplies the Spirit to you and works miracles among you do so by works of the law, or by hearing with faith just as Abraham "believed God, and it was counted to him as righteousness"? (Galatians 3:1-6, ESV)

The origin of their faith was the vivid proclamation of Jesus Christ crucified (v. 1). The proclamation was the **factual** basis of their faith, and they believed what they heard. Then **experientially**, they immediately received the gift of the Holy Spirit as a seal proving their justification. All of this was given as a gift by God simply by *"hearing with faith"* (v. 2). Then Paul asks the key question for our study: *"Having begun by the Spirit, are you now being perfected by the flesh?"* (v. 3). In other words, Paul asserts that the Christian life is perfected the exact same way it begins. Sanctification, like justification, is by faith, and faith is based on factual and experiential knowledge.

So it is for us today. We grow in faith by growing in spiritual knowledge. We grow in spiritual knowledge factually by saturating our minds in the Bible (by personal spiritual disciplines, hearing good preaching, reading good books, etc.) and experientially by putting ourselves in situations in which we are trusting God for more and more.

EXPERIENTIAL KNOWLEDGE INCREASES FAITH

We have already assigned the primary place to the Word of God for the formation of faith in the human heart. But I believe that life experience prepares the human heart to believe, and that after saving faith has come, life experience feeds faith and gives it opportunity to grow.

Life experience, rightly interpreted by the Word of God, is foundational to saving faith. One of the clearest scriptural links between experience and faith is in Psalm 22:9: *"Yet you are he who brought me forth from the womb; you made me trust when upon my mother's breasts"* (Psalm 22:9, NASB). While David was a newborn infant nursing comfortingly at his mother's breast, he learned by experience what it means to trust another being for life and sustenance. The capacity to trust was formed in David's heart before he transferred that capacity to the invisible being proclaimed in the Scriptures. Nursing was pre-evangelism for David! The lessons learned by experience paved the way for saving faith later. David learned how to trust his mother by experience before he learned to trust God by Scripture.

The link between life experience and the development of faith is made in other places in Scripture. By faith David killed Goliath, and became powerful in battle, routing a pagan Philistine army (Hebrews 11:32, 34). But by the time he fought the Philistine, his faith had been developed by experience: by killing a lion and a bear while watching his father's sheep. David learned from experience that the Lord is powerful to deliver him from danger, and he applied that knowledge to the impending battle with Goliath (1 Samuel 17:32–37). Experience fed David's faith.

We see the same thing again in the New Testament concerning the disciples' struggling battles to grow in their faith in Christ. Christ clearly expected their experiences with his miracles to be a firm foundation for their faith in him as Messiah. The night before his death, Jesus said to his disciples: *"Believe me that I am in the Father and the Father is in me, or else believe on account of the works themselves"* (John 14:11, ESV). This is amazing! Yes, *"faith comes by hearing"* (Romans 10:17), but Jesus expected faith to come by *seeing* his miracles as well. This expectation on the part of Jesus comes out clearly when the disciples forgot to take bread with them in one of their journeys across the Sea of Galilee. This error on their part was significant, but it occurred after the two miraculous feedings: the feeding of the five thousand (Matthew 14:13–21) and of the four thousand (Matthew 15:32–39). Their argument among themselves about forgetting to bring the bread proved their unbelief, and Jesus rebuked them for it:

> Aware of their discussion, Jesus asked, "You of little faith, why are you talking among yourselves about having no bread? Do you still not understand? Don't you remember the five loaves for the five thousand, and how many basketfuls you gathered? Or the seven loaves for the four thousand, and how many basketfuls you gathered? How is it you don't understand that I was not talking to you about bread?" (Matthew 16:8–11)

Mark goes even further than Matthew and links their failure to understand the lesson of the loaves to hardness of heart: *"they had not understood about the loaves; their hearts were hardened"* (Mark 6:52). Christ clearly expected the experience of living through these miracles to have been a basis for the faith of the apostles.

So it is today. God still acts in history, and his sovereign control over all events is still observable and a strong basis for faith. Throughout church history, men and women have undergone abundantly rich or exceptionally trying circumstances, and have found that each of these has shaped their faith and strengthened it (1 Peter 1:6–7). As we've noted, George Mueller saw God answer over fifty thousand specific prayers in his life, keeping a meticulous record of them in one notebook after another. Thus he developed a confidence in the promises and provision of God that soared above that of most people in church history. By living through a Nazi concentration camp, Corrie ten Boom developed a deeper maturity than if she had never gone through that experience. By living through the death of her husband, and then living with the people who killed him and seeing them eventually come to Christ, Elisabeth Elliot saw her faith strengthened in ways not possible by any other route.

When you sit in the presence of aged warriors for Christ and listen to their tales of God's faithfulness, you are listening to the effects of faith bolstered by experience. If you had had the privilege of talking to Adoniram Judson on April 12, 1850, as he lay dying on the French ship *Aristide Marie*, and if you had asked him about his life, he would have spoken of promises fulfilled in space and time, in experience. You would have been standing in the presence of an incredible faith bolstered by years of experience. If you had lived in Smyrna in A.D. 155 and had been able to hear Polycarp refuse to deny Christ, you would have heard him say: "Eighty-six years have I been serving him, and he has done me no wrong; how then can I blaspheme my King who saved me?"[85] His eighty-six years of walking with Christ were the basis for his courage in facing death at the stake. Each of those experiences were filtered and interpreted by the perfect Scriptures, but having survived that scriptural scrutiny they became a rich treasure trove from which daily faith could draw sustenance.

In summation, faith grows on the basis of an ongoing intake of Scripture and a stream of rich experiences of joy and suffering in God's world. Both of these, under the powerful influence of the Holy Spirit, will cause faith to grow mighty in the heart.

FAITH TRANSFORMS CHARACTER

The next key step in the growth process is the power of faith to transform character. I believe that a good and noble heart is

formed inside a person only by faith. It is because a person believes the promises of God that their heart is transformed and
made ever-increasingly Christlike. The stronger the faith, the
more Christlike the character.

There are many verses which strongly link faith to the transformation of the heart. At the very beginning of the sanctification process is the purification of the heart from sin's dominion.
In Peter's statement at the Jerusalem Council about the circumcision question, we see the direct connection between faith and the
change of heart essential to justification.

> God, who knows the heart, showed that he accepted them
> by giving the Holy Spirit to them, just as he did to us. He
> made no distinction between us and them, for he **purified
> their hearts by faith**. (Acts 15:8–9)

This is a vastly important statement for our purpose. It is faith
that purifies the heart from sin at initial conversion, and it will
be faith that continues this purification work throughout the
Christian's life. This growth in purity by faith is called sanctification. One of the clearest passages showing knowledge as the basis
of faith, and faith as the power of sanctification is in 1 John 3:

> See what kind of love the Father has given to us, that
> we should be called children of God; and so we are. The
> reason why the world does not know us is that it did not
> know him. Beloved, we are God's children now, and what
> we will be has not yet appeared; but we know that when
> he appears we shall be like him, because we shall see him
> as he is. And everyone who thus hopes in him purifies
> himself as he is pure. (1 John 3:1–3, ESV)

Factual knowledge initiates this whole process. John is writing about spiritual facts, things we know are true in Christ: the
greatness of the Father's love for us in Christ, our adoption as

God's children, our estranged relationship with the world, and our future perfection effected by seeing Christ himself at the Second Coming. These spiritual facts have been proclaimed in the gospel and written in the Scriptures. For Christians, we *know* they are true **by faith alone**. The link between faith and hope here is so close, I see them as almost synonymous: *"faith is the assurance of things hoped for"* (Hebrews 11:1). Therefore, I believe John's statement, *"everyone who has this **hope** in him"* is effectively the same as *"everyone who has this faith in him."* And what does this faith produce? The ongoing self-purification from sin known as sanctification. Thus faith produces godly character.

Another such passage is 1 Peter 1:13–2:3. In this extended section of his epistle, the central exhortation from the Apostle Peter is this: *"Just as he who called you is holy, so be holy in all you do; for it is written: 'Be holy, because I am holy'"* (1 Peter 1:15–16). The biggest enemy to this holiness is evil desire: *"as obedient children, do not conform to the evil desires you had when you lived in ignorance"* (v. 14). In order to battle these pervasive evil desires, we have to be ready for internal action: *"therefore, prepare your minds for action; be self-controlled; set your hope fully on the grace to be given you when Jesus Christ is revealed"* (1 Peter 1:13). The battle for holiness, then, comes down to hope: setting our hope fully on grace to be given us in the future. As we have already noted, the setting of full hope on future grace is the core of saving faith. Peter, like John in the passage just studied, speaks of hope rather than faith here, but the disposition of soul is the same. Later in the passage, he will shift the focus openly to faith, and will put faith and hope side by side: *"through [Christ] you **believe** in God, who raised him from the dead and glorified him, and so your **faith** and hope are in God"* (1 Peter 1:21).

A final passage that teaches the power of faith to transform character is in Paul's marvelously rich prayer for the Ephesian Christians:

I pray that out of his glorious riches he may strengthen you with power through his Spirit in your inner being, so that **Christ may dwell in your hearts through faith**. And I pray that you, being rooted and established in love, may have power, together with all the saints, to grasp how wide and long and high and deep is the love of Christ, and to know this love that surpasses knowledge-- that you may be filled to the measure of all the fullness of God. Now to him who is able to do immeasurably more than all we ask or imagine, according to his power that is at work within us, to him be glory in the church and in Christ Jesus throughout all generations, forever and ever! Amen. (Ephesians 3:16–21)

There are more truths packed into these few verses than I can unfold in twenty chapters. But I want to focus on this: the power of God is working within our hearts to enable us to glorify him by being like him. This is the power of sanctification, though the language is a little different than usual. Paul speaks of God's power within us three times in these six verses: power through his Spirit in the inner being (v. 16), power to grasp the infinite measure of God's love for us in Christ (v. 18), and the inconceivably great power of God at work within us which will produce glory in the church and in Christ Jesus throughout all generations (v. 20-21). Thus the power of God within our hearts is the topic of the prayer.

Now, Paul knows God's power will be at work in the Ephesians whether they know it or not. But he also wants them to know about that power, and to trust in it, and to believe in it, so that 1) Christ will dwell in their hearts by faith; 2) they may be filled to the measure of all the fullness of God; 3) God would be glorified in his church. The key to all this is the Ephesian Christians' faith in the power and presence of God. It is by faith that Christ will dwell in their hearts, and it is by Christ dwelling in their hearts that they will be filled to the measure of all the fullness of God. Christ "dwelling in our hearts" means that we are strongly conscious of his presence, power, nature, and Kingly commands for our lives. It is by faith that the invisible Jesus becomes powerfully real and active in our hearts. And this presence of Jesus in the heart of a Christian is what enables us to become more and more like God ("*filled to the measure of all the fullness of God*"). Faith transforms character.

CHARACTER PRODUCES ACTION

From the beginning of creation, God ordained an unbreakable connection between the nature of the tree and the fruit that came from it. "*Then God said, "'Let the land produce vegetation: seed-bearing plants and trees on the land that bear fruit with seed in it, according to their various kinds.'"* (Genesis 1:11). Jesus applied this spiritually to assessing the hearts of teachers of the Word: "*by their fruit you will recognize them*" (Matthew 7:16).

More pointedly for the issue of growth in the Christian life is this dynamic verse: "*make a tree good and its fruit will be good*" (Matthew 12:33). In order for a human being to produce good fruit (actions), he must **be** good first. If the heart is purified by faith (Acts 15:9), then it is capable of producing good fruit. And if the heart is increasingly conformed to Christ, it is increasingly capable of doing works that are pleasing to him. Thus I am arguing that Jesus would say, "Make a tree better and its fruit will be better." This is the theory of the matter—that increasingly Christlike character produces increasingly Christlike works.

If we want to have a rich treasure of good works that we can present to God for reward on Judgment Day, we will need a heart transformation. Actions that are done contrary to the dominant bent of the heart are actually hypocrisy—play-acting—and God hates such "good works." Giving alms to the poor while announcing the actions with trumpets on the street corners is no good work at all, since it is done from an impure and earthly motive. But actions done by faith, from the goodness of a regenerate heart, are well-pleasing to God, and reap an abundant harvest of righteousness.

The more our heart is conformed to Christ, the more abundant will be our harvest. Jesus spoke of this harvest in the Parable of the Seed and the Soils. The soil that produced "*a hundred times what was sown*" (Luke 8:8) represents "*those with a **noble and good heart**, who hear the word, retain it, and by persevering produce a crop*" (Luke 8:15). This is amazing, because the Scripture reveals that "*the heart is deceitful above all things and beyond cure. Who can understand it?*" (Jeremiah 17:9). So no one naturally has "*a noble and good heart.*" But by the power of regeneration in Christ, and by the transformation worked internally in sanctification, we can have a "*noble and good heart*" which is able to produce a crop. In Matthew's account of the same parable, there is a wide variety of the abundance of the harvest: "*a hundred, sixty, or thirty times what was sown*" (Matthew 13:8, 23). I believe the size and worth of our harvest will be directly proportional to the purity of our hearts, to the degree to which we have been sanctified after the pattern of Christ. Thus, ever-increasing Christlikeness in character will produce ever-increasingly Christlike actions.

ACTION PROMOTES KNOWLEDGE

The final link in the cycle driving us toward spiritual growth is that between action and knowledge. This is simply common sense, but it is also supported richly from Scripture. We have defined "knowledge" as "factual and experiential spiritual information." Thus it stands to reason that, the more we read, memorize, and study the Bible, the more we will grow in knowledge. And the more obedient we are in our actions, the more experiences we will have of God's faithfulness. Habitual obedience fuels an ever-increasing storehouse of spiritual knowledge.

Any pattern of godly action (habitual obedience) will strengthen our knowledge of spiritual things. The action of memorizing a book of the Bible will result in a far greater knowledge of the contents of that book than before. Instead of wasting all those hours, a Christian who invests time habitually in memorizing Scripture will be constantly building the City of Truth within his heart. And a man who carries on a faithful prison ministry for twenty-five years without missing a single Monday evening Bible study (we have such a man in our church), at the end of that twenty-five years of stepping out in faith will have a much stronger experiential knowledge of God than he did before he started. This much is common sense: actions put us in a position to increase our knowledge, thus resetting the cycle for even greater growth.

However, it is always best to support our views from texts of Scripture. And the relationship between obedience and increasing knowledge is strongly made in a number of texts. Psalm 119, for example, has this cycle clearly described: understanding of God's law promotes obedience, and obedience promotes understanding of God's law.

UNDERSTANDING PROMOTES OBEDIENCE:
- Give me understanding, and I will keep your law and obey it with all my heart. (Psalm 119:34)

OBEDIENCE PROMOTES UNDERSTANDING:
- I have more understanding than the elders, for I obey your precepts. (Psalm 119:100)

In other words, this is a cycle for spiritual growth centered on the word of God: the more we understand of God's word, the more we will obey; the more we obey, the more we will understand.

Jesus made this concept much more personal. Basically it comes down to this: God is like an investor who wants to try out a new portfolio manager. So he gives him a small sum to manage for a year. If good things happen, he will invest more, because the manager has proven himself skillful and diligent. So it is with spiritual truth. All spiritual truth is revealed by God to human hearts. If God reveals truth and we obey it, he will reveal even more; if God reveals truth and we do not obey it, why should he reveal any more? Jesus made this plain after the parable of the Faithful or Unfaithful Slave (Luke 12:42–48). At the end, he said this:

> That servant who knows his master's will and does not get ready or does not do what his master wants will be beaten with many blows. But the one who does not know and does things deserving punishment will be beaten with few blows. From everyone who has been given much, much will be demanded; and from the one who has been entrusted with much, much more will be asked. (Luke 12:47–48)

The "much" that is entrusted in this case is insight into the master's will. Whenever the master reveals his will to his servants, they are under obligation to obey and act accordingly. The more faithful they are with the insights they have been given, the more will be entrusted to them.

He also said the same to his disciples in John 14 the night before he was crucified: *"Whoever has my commandments and keeps them, he it is who loves me. And he who loves me will be loved by my Father, and I will love him and manifest myself to him"* (John 14:21). To "have" Jesus' commandments means to know what they are, to have them stored up in our minds; this is factual knowledge, and for us it can only come by the Bible. However, it is clearly not enough merely to "have" Jesus' commandments: we must also obey them. And if we meet the two conditions, having **and** obeying Jesus' commandments, we reveal that we truly do love Jesus; and as a result, God the Father will love us and God the Son will *manifest* himself to us. This word "manifest" implies a rich kind of self-revelation of God to the obedient Christian. At that point, one of his disciples asked, *"But, Lord, why do you intend to show yourself to us and not to the world?"* Jesus answered, *"If anyone loves me, he will obey my teaching. My Father will love him, and we will come to him and make our home with him"* (John 14:23). So clearly, an ever-increasingly intimate relationship with the Father and the Son is based on ever-increasing obedience. This is the cycle I am advocating: knowledge promotes faith, faith transforms character, character bears fruit in action (habitual obedience), and action (habitual obedience) will result in ever-increasing factual and experiential knowledge of God.

Another example of this comes in Jesus' teaching at the Festival of the Booths in John 7. After listening to Jesus preach, the crowds were amazed and asked "Where did this man get such wisdom without having studied?" Jesus answered: *"If anyone chooses to do God's will, he will find out whether my teaching comes from God or whether I speak on my own"* (John 7:17). In other words, habitual obedience to God's will results in ever-increasing knowledge of the origin of Christ's teaching. This may have more to do with faith (i.e. obedience will result in assurance), but it still passes through knowledge first.

A prime Old Testament example of this is seen in Malachi concerning the tithe: *"'Bring the whole tithe into the storehouse, that there may be food in my house. Test me in this,' says the Lord Almighty, 'and see if I will not throw open the floodgates of heaven and pour out so much blessing that you will not have room enough for it.'"* (Malachi 3:10). If in the New Covenant, a believer trusts God for the privilege of giving sacrificially for the advance of the gospel to an unreached people group, and then sees the hand of blessing in his life abundantly over the next five years, did not his obedience to the prompting of the Spirit produce in him a far greater sense of the faithfulness of God?

Anything we do in obedience to the commands of God puts us in the immediate position of growing in grace and in the knowledge of Christ. Obedience promotes knowledge.

AN UPWARD SPIRAL WHICH BECOMES A PYRAMID

Thus we have argued for a cycle: knowledge promotes increased faith, increased faith transforms character, transformed character bears fruit in action, and increasingly obedient action feeds growing knowledge. However, it would not do to see this as a two-dimensional cycle, like a dog chasing its tail and never seeming to go anywhere. One of my favorite artists is M.C. Escher, who mystified the eyes of the beholders of his art by seeming to break the rules of perspective. One of the strangest prints he ever did is called "Ascending and Descending." It shows a monastery in which monks are on a square staircase, some of the monks going up, and some going down. The ascending monks are constantly passing the descending monks on the staircase, but none of them ever get anywhere. The staircase goes around and around in a square, making no progress anywhere.

I reject such a static view of the knowledge-faith-character-action cycle. Rather, I think this is precisely how we follow the pattern of progress Paul spoke about in Philippians 3: *"forgetting what lies behind and straining forward to what lies ahead, I press on toward the goal for the prize of the upward call of God in Christ Jesus"* (Philippians 3:13–14, ESV). The *"upward call of God in Christ Jesus"* is a call to ascend morally higher and higher. Our sanctification cannot build a stairway to heaven as in Jacob's dream (Genesis 28:12) on which we could ascend to heaven by our own moral progress. As we have already said time and time again, only the perfect righteousness of Christ is sufficient for heaven. But I do believe there **is** an *"upward call of God in Christ Jesus,"* and it is the pressing on daily for Christlike perfection. It is done through this knowledge-faith-character-action cycle.

So, in this way we "ascend," becoming more and more Christlike in our daily lives. But the cycle is not merely a spiral. Rather, since each of the four legs of the cycle are completely pointed to Christ, I find it helpful to conceive of the four legs coming together to form a pyramid. It is knowledge **of Christ**, that this cycle is seeking to achieve; it is faith in **Christ**; it is character conformed to **Christ**; it is action patterned after **Christ**. These are not four separate disciplines or four separate skills, like a decathlete learning ten different events. They are completely integrated in Christ.

So, I envision a spiral pattern around four legs of a pyramid, coming to a point called "Perfect Christlikeness." Recently, a French architect named Jean-Pierre Houdin has proposed a theory that the Great Pyramid of Khufu in Egypt was built 4500 years ago by means of internal ramps that spiraled upward from corner to corner until the top stones were set in place.[86] This picture captures the image in my mind of spiritual growth by knowledge-faith-character-action. Each corner represents one of these ramps—knowledge, faith, character and action. They ascend together, in cooperation, to a focal point—Christlikeness.

 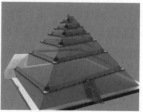

Houdin's internal ramps [Pictures used by permission]

SUMMARY

As we follow Christ in this infinite journey, we are called to make constant growth in each of these four major areas: knowledge (1 Peter 2:2, 2 Peter 3:18), faith (Luke 17:5, 1 Thessalonians 3:10, 2

Thessalonians 1:3), character (1 Thessalonians 3:12, 2 Peter 1:5–8), and action (1 Thessalonians 4:1). This growth is pictured as upward toward heaven (Philippians 3:14), and it follows this pattern: knowledge promotes faith, faith transforms character, character bears fruit in action, and action feeds knowledge. We may not always be conscious of this "four-stroke engine" and the rhythm it makes toward our final destination, but that is what is happening all the time.

Our four-fold growth focuses on a single goal: total conformity to Christ. The image I have in my mind is that of a pyramid, a glorious ascent of ever-increasing Christlikeness in all four areas. Though we will never reach perfection in this life, yet the progress we make is greatly glorifying to God, and a down payment he makes in our souls guaranteeing the full inheritance at the moment of glorification.

CHAPTER 30

CASE STUDIES: THE K-F-C-A CYCLE AT WORK

SO HOW DOES THIS MARVELOUS four-stroke engine of sanctification actually work in real life? If we are convinced logically that knowledge promotes faith, faith transforms character, character bears fruit in action, and action feeds knowledge, can we see this in Scripture? And can we see it in everyday life? The purpose of this chapter is to bring sanctification theory down to daily practice in various scenarios, so that we can approach daily life with a passion for growth and fruitfulness. My approach will be to identify the fruit of godly action in various real-life scenarios, and then support the K-F-C-A cycle from Scripture in each of these cases.

PERSONAL WORSHIP

One verse, Psalm 28:7, shows the flow from knowledge through faith through character into the action of worship better than any else I have found: *"The Lord is my strength and my shield; my heart trusts in him, and I am helped. My heart leaps for joy and I will give thanks to him in song"* (Psalm 28:7). **Knowledge factual and experiential:** Any statement that begins "The Lord is" is a statement of spiritual fact. So, this is knowledge: "The Lord is my strength and my shield." In other words, David is saying, "the Lord provides me with ongoing sustaining power in my life and he protects me from all harm." These spiritual truths come only from the Bible and they are borne out in experience; David read them from the word of God, and he saw them lived out in his daily life. **Faith:** Next, we see David asserting his faith in the Lord: "my heart trusts in him." That is faith, an active reliance on the protection and provision of God. **Character:** Next, David reveals the character trait of joy: "my heart leaps for joy." Not just a small sensation of happiness, but a heart overflowing, leaping with joy. **Action:** But all of that ferment cannot, simply cannot remain bottled up. Our bodies must get involved, and David's certainly did: "I will give thanks to him in song."

Another statement from John Piper shows that flow well, and I will take the liberty to superimpose the "knowledge-faith-character-action" matrix on his quote about worship:

> The fuel of worship is a true vision of the greatness of God [Knowledge]; the fire that makes the fuel burn is the quickening of the Holy Spirit [Faith]; the furnace made alive and warm by the flame of truth is our renewed spirit [Character]; and the resulting heat of our affections [Character] is powerful worship, pushing its way out in confessions, longings, acclamations, tears, songs, shouts, bowed heads, lifted hands and obedient lives [Action].[87]

Every time we *"worship the Father in spirit and in truth"* (John 4:24), we are displaying the K-F-C-A cycle, or we are acting as hypocrites, whose hearts are cold and distant from God and who worship him in vain (Matthew 15:9). Every new fact we learn about God from the Bible and every experience we have of God in life is a fitting starting place for worship. Faith picks up the truth thus gained and makes it intensely personal—not merely that such and such a verse teaches such and such a thing about God, but that God himself is telling me personally this about himself. Faith opens the eyes of the heart to the reality of the invisible realm that surrounds the worshiper, moving him to a new level of personal awareness and active trust. The heart is then moved to respond with love, an intensified sense of interpersonal affection and warmth. The worshiper is kindled with feelings of desire, and soon emotions begin to flow. It isn't long before the body is moved to action in the various ways John Piper describes above.

INTERCESSORY PRAYER

The prayer warrior begins with the commands of Scripture, such as *"always keep on praying for all the saints"* (Ephesians 6:18), and with the experience of daily life surrounded by such overwhelming need. He also has the abundant example of prayer in the Bible, of Paul's many prayers for the churches in the New Testament, and of the incredibly varied and potent prayers of the Psalmists. He also lives life surrounded every day by overwhelming needs, and he learns to feel the weight of those needs by experience. Thus his **knowledge** is the starting point for his prayer life.

Moved by the Holy Spirit, his faith takes this knowledge and makes it personal and spiritual. It is God himself who is beckoning him to join what he is doing in the world by praying for specific people and specific needs. He is praying according to the revealed will of God because he is praying Scripture into each situation. He has a vivid sense of the efficacy of prayer because of the reality of God's sovereignty and of God's love, and he is fully confident that his prayers will be heard and will transform the world. He is willing to trust God to do what is most for his glory and for the joy of his elect people. Thus does his **faith** make his prayer life powerful and effective.

The prayer warrior's heart is thus drawn into the act of prayer, and his love for God and for the person he's praying for is deepened immensely. He desires God's glory and goodness to flow into that person's life, and he chooses only what is according to the will of the Father. His emotions may well be kindled at this moment, deeply moved over the condition of the person while praying for him. This is the **character** of the Christian prayer warrior, a prayer offered from the heart. All of these first things are internal, and some prayer warriors have been known to wait a long time in the presence of God before uttering a single word of prayer.

Dr. John Wilbur Chapman, a great Presbyterian evangelist, was conducting a series of evangelistic services in April of 1911 in London, England. The meetings started slowly until a man known simply as "Praying Hyde" came to ask for God's blessing on those services. Dr. Chapman recalls the power of prayer in the following episode:

> The audience was exceedingly small, but almost immediately the tide began to turn, the hall became packed, and in my first invitation fifty men accepted Christ as their Savior. As we were leaving I said, "Mr. Hyde, I want you to pray for me." He came to my room, turned the key in the door, dropped on his knees and waited five minutes without a single syllable coming from his lips. I could hear my own heart thumping and his beating; I felt hot tears running down my face. I knew I was with God. Then with upturned face, while the tears were streaming down, he said, "O God," then for five minutes more, at least, he was still again. And then when he knew he was talking with God there came from the depths of this heart such petitions for me as I had never heard before. I rose from my knees to know what real prayer was.[88]

"Praying Hyde" was the nickname for a powerful man of God named John Hyde, a missionary to India. He knew the value of heart preparation before prayer. Though there is no indication he ever spoke of "knowledge-faith-character-action," that is what was going on to prepare his heart before he ever uttered a word of prayer.

The final step of prayer is actually to pray, to make the request known to God. We may kneel, we may weep, we may cry aloud, we may pace back and forth, we may lift holy hands, we may do many **actions** in expressing his prayers to the Father. These actions are vital, as are the words we speak in prayer. Christ asked blind Bartimaeus, *"What do you want me to do for you?"* (Mark 10:51). Everyone knew exactly what this poor blind man wanted, but Jesus still made him vocalize his need. Yet for all of that, the true prayer happened in the heart before it reached his mouth, for the heavenly Father knows what we need before we ask (Matthew 6:8). For this reason, John Bunyan said "When thou prayest, rather let thy heart be without words than thy words without a heart."[89]

EVANGELISM

The K-F-C-A cycle applied to evangelism is seen most plainly in 2 Corinthians 5. Paul speaks of the link between **knowledge** and evangelism in verse 10–11: we know that every one of us will appear before the judgment seat of Christ; *"since then we know what it is to fear the Lord, we try to persuade men"* (v. 11). Paul also speaks of **faith**, when in verse 7 he says *"we walk by faith, not by sight,"* and in verse 9 he says, *"we make it our goal to please him."* The lifestyle of evangelism comes as a direct result of this faith-filled, Godward commitment. The **character** aspect of evangelism comes in verse 14: *"for the love of Christ compels us."* This could either be our love for Christ, or Christ's love operating through our hearts. Either way, the act of sacrificial evangelism is a display of the love of Christ working through his servants, through hearts transformed by his love. Finally, the result of this is trying to persuade men (v. 11), imploring them to be reconciled to God (v. 20).

In a modern-day case study, it isn't hard to see how a single act of evangelism comes also from the K-F-C-A cycle as well. Let's take the example of a Christian witnessing to a stranger on an airplane. It begins with the **knowledge** that Christ wants us to seek and save the lost (Luke 19:10) and to be his witnesses (Acts 1:8). Scripture also has trained the believer that the gospel message alone is the power of God for salvation (Romans 1:16), and that no one can call on Christ if evangelists are not sent with the message (Romans 10:13–15). The believer also has learned by experience that we are surrounded by lost people, and that, in this age of over-booked flights, we are likely to be sitting next to a lost person on the plane. (At this point, the Christian evangelist probably trusts God in prayer for such an opportunity, but that is a separate K-F-C-A cycle I could cover another time.)

Having this knowledge in his mind is not enough, however. He must then take this knowledge as a direct command from a living God, with whom he is walking moment by moment by faith. The Holy Spirit speaks the command to witness to him, and gives him a lively sense of his presence to aid him. The Spirit also gives him a foretaste of the heavenly pleasure God will share with him by way of reward, and of the joy he may have in bringing someone to Christ that day. Along with that, the Spirit works a sense of the conviction of past sins and failures he's had, and how sinful it would be to play the coward on this flight. At the right time, the Spirit will prompt the evangelist with a specific leading, saying "This is the time—speak!" And so, by **faith** the evangelist is prepared to act.

But first, the action comes from a **character** that loves God and loves his neighbor as himself. The movement of the Spirit within his heart by faith stimulates that love, and sets in his heart the desire to obey. The will makes its choice based on the clear understanding of the scriptural truth that faith has made vivid in the eyes of his heart: to obey is better than to disobey. The feelings fluctuate since the heart is not pure, but by faith the man overcomes any fear he may have and acts courageously.

And so, out flows the **action** of evangelism. He begins a conversation, getting to know the stranger sitting in the seat next to him.

After a time, he maneuvers the conversation around to spiritual things and goes through a simple gospel outline he has memorized.

JOYFUL SUFFERING

Perhaps the most concise passage revealing the K-F-C-A cycle in joyful suffering is Hebrews 10:34: *"You sympathized with those in prison and joyfully accepted the confiscation of your property, because you knew that you yourselves had better and lasting possessions."* It begins with the **knowledge** the writer says they possessed: they knew that the possessions of heaven were better and more permanent, so therefore earthly possessions were as nothing compared to them. By **faith**, these Hebrew Christians appropriated this knowledge and made it personal—this is the *"assurance of things hoped for"* the author will mention so prominently in the next chapter of Hebrews. The author made it very direct and personal: "you knew that *you yourselves* had better and lasting possessions." It wasn't just a possible reward for some other courageous people—it was their own reward, their own inheritance. Faith had made it personal. As a direct result of this, their love for other Christians in prison was moved—they felt compassion for these prisoners; and the Hebrew Christians were actually *joyful* about the loss of their earthly possessions. These are both powerful displays of their **character**: love and emotion strengthened by faith. The resultant **actions** were clear as well: they probably ministered to the Christians in prison, thus identifying themselves as Christians; and they joyfully *accepted* the confiscation of their property. This undoubtedly was displayed by actions—facial expressions, body language, words, gestures that their persecutors probably deemed insane—but which probably resulted in some of them becoming Christians!

So many stories of joy in suffering shine radiantly from the pages of church history. During the reign of communism, a pastor in Romania was sitting at the breakfast table with his wife and six small children. Suddenly the police broke into his home to search the house and arrest him. The police asked him, "Don't you have anything to say? Have you no sorrow or regret?" The pastor said, "You are the answer to what we prayed today. We just read in Psalm 23 that God prepares a table before us in the presence of our enemies. We had a table but no enemies. Now you have come. If you would like anything that is on this table, I would like to share it with you. You were sent by God."

The man replied, "How can you say such stupid things? We will take you to prison, and you will die there. You will never see your children again." With contentment that came from God, the pastor said "We also read about that today: 'Though I pass through the valley of the shadow of death, I will not fear.'" The officer shouted, "Everyone fears death. I know because I have seen it on their faces." The pastor answered, "A shadow of a dog can't bite you, and a shadow of death can't kill you. You can kill our bodies or put us in prison, but nothing bad can happen to us. We're in Christ, and if we die, he will take us to his world."[90]

Now that Romanian pastor was not mechanically going through the K-F-C-A cycle in his mind, but it was at work nonetheless. He knew Psalm 23, by faith he believed it line by line, his heart was made supernaturally joyful at the prospect of suffering for Christ, and he spoke many words of faith to his violent persecutors.

SACRIFICIAL GIVING

The greatest scriptural passage on sacrificial giving of finances to support the needy is 2 Corinthians 8–9, revealing the incredible love of the Macedonian churches. They gave to the poor among the saints in Jerusalem (Romans 15:26) in a way so astonishing that it moved Paul deeply, and he used them as an example to other Gentile churches (such as those at Corinth and Rome).

Paul's account of their generosity in 2 Corinthians 8–9 is not written following a K-F-C-A pattern, but the tell-tale signs of this cycle are all there. The Macedonian Christians clearly had a strong

knowledge base from which their actions came. Scripturally, they knew very well that the Jewish Christians were one with them in the faith, and that they all were members of one body. They also clearly knew of the eternal rewards available for any sacrificial giving in this world for the work of God. Experientially, they were poor themselves (Paul says they gave out of *"extreme poverty"* (v. 2), and this is consistent with the regular testimony of church history: those who know what poverty and hunger is from personal experience are usually the most generous to others who are suffering.

This knowledge they drew into their hearts by **faith**, for their giving was much more God-ward than man-ward: Paul says *"they gave themselves first to the Lord and then to us in keeping with God's will"* (v. 5). It was clearly with a personal expectation of eternal reward that they were so urgent, and pleaded with Paul for the privilege of contributing (v. 4). This attitude can only come by faith in a future reward in heaven.

This display of their **character** is the main point Paul is making to the Corinthians. He says in the very next chapter, *"God loves a cheerful giver"* (2 Corinthians 9:7). It is not merely the giving, and certainly not the amount they gave: it was the joy in the giving that Paul was commending. The cheerful, loving, urgent, pleading giving of the Macedonian churches stands for all time as the standard for all Christians.

Finally, the **action** itself was consummated by the fact that the Macedonians actually gave; they didn't merely *promise* to give, as the Corinthians had done. In 2 Corinthians 9:2, Paul says that the Corinthian church had been the first to pledge money toward this relief effort. But he is clearly concerned that if any Macedonian Christians should come and find the Corinthians had not actually **acted** on their initial eagerness, both Paul and the Corinthians will feel ashamed from having been so confident (2 Corinthians 9:4). So Paul wants them to **act** on this matter, to get everything ready for his arrival, so that the gift can be given as cheerfully as was that given by the Macedonians.

So today, when a Christian woman gives money to help assist poverty-stricken Christian refugees in (for example) Darfur, she will follow the same K-F-C-A cycle displayed by these Macedonian Christians. She will **know** that God wants those of us whose circumstances have produced an abundance to share it with brothers and sisters who are suffering, for God specifically has told us that in 2 Corinthians 8:13–15: *"Our desire is not that others might be relieved while you are hard pressed, but that there might be equality"* (v. 13). She may not know by experience what it means to suffer persecution to the level that those in Darfur do, but she has lived enough in the world to understand it somewhat. By **faith** she will give to the needy secretly, "not letting her left hand know what her right is doing," therefore expecting her heavenly Father to see and reward it in heaven (Matthew 6:3). Her heart will be drawn toward the Father in the same kind of loving commitment as were the hearts of the Macedonian Christians, and she will give as an act of worship to God, out of love for God. At the same time, her heart will be knit together with the brothers and sisters in Darfur, and she will love them (**character**). But she will not love them only in word, or in theory, but, by writing the check, she will love them in **actions** and in truth (1 John 3:18).

SUMMARY

These case studies could be multiplied across the spectrum of the Christian life. These few, I think, are enough to show how consistently the K-F-C-A cycle works in hidden form in the Christian life to produce the good fruit that God demands from us, and by which he will assess us on Judgment Day.

CHAPTER 31

APPLICATION: USING THE MAP TO GROW TO MATURITY

THROUGHOUT THIS BOOK, WE HAVE spoken of an "Infinite Journey." However, from the very first chapter, I have asserted that this is a journey that we will most certainly finish by the power of God. We will not attain perfection here on earth, but in glorification, we will be perfectly conformed to Christ. And every step we make along the way that brings us closer to that ultimate goal brings great glory to God.

This book has sought to give a detailed overview of the component parts of sanctification: knowledge, faith, character, and action. Furthermore, we have sought to break each of these down even further to subcategories. The overall chart is found at the beginning of the book and can be used for constant reference. The purpose of this final chapter is to seek to put this knowledge into practice in a variety of settings.

I am very aware of how overwhelming this detailed look at all the aspects of Christian maturity can be. I do not expect anyone to be able to memorize all of the subcategories, or internalize all of the Scriptures or argumentation I have used. Rather, I desire this information to be set in front of the church as a goal for constant growth. In this chapter, I will seek to put this comprehensive map of sanctification at the disposal of 1) individual Christians; 2) parents seeking to raise their children to spiritual maturity; 3) pastors, disciplers, and missionaries, who are seeking to teach disciples of Christ to obey everything he has commanded; 4) Christian counselors, who are seeking to bring biblical wisdom to bear on weak areas in the lives of those who seek godly counsel from them.

HOW INDIVIDUAL CHRISTIANS CAN USE THIS MAP

I believe every individual Christian can look at this comprehensive map of sanctification and use it in four specific ways: 1) as a grounds for **praise** to Christ for the imputed righteousness in which we now stand and by which we will finally be saved; 2) as a means for continual **humbling** at the weakness of our present performance, so that we constantly go back to the Lord for grace; 3) as a focus for personal **prayer** for himself and for other Christians, that they would grow in specific ways in Christ; 4) as a means for **goal-setting** and **assessment** of spiritual progress for the rest of his life.

1). PRAISE TO CHRIST

This comprehensive road map is a pathetically dim reflection of the perfect righteousness that Christ actually lived out while on earth, and that the Father has now imputed to us by simple faith. Christ's **knowledge** of the Scriptures and of his Father's will revealed therein was perfect. He learned obedience from what he suffered (Hebrews 5:8), including the most intense temptation and persecution in history, and he did all this without sinning, so his experience was perfect as well. Christ's **faith** in his Father is a great mystery, but Hebrews 2:13 puts these words in Christ's mouth: *"I will put my trust in him."* As Christ was dying, he spoke these words: *"Father, into your hands, I commit my spirit"* (Luke 23:46). He entrusted to the Father everything he had come to achieve. His was the picture of frailty and weakness as he was dying. If the Father did not raise him from the dead, his work would be all for nothing. But Christ trusted the Father completely—the greatest act of faith in history. And the Father vindicated Christ's faith by raising him from the dead, and by saving his children from every nation on earth in his name. Christ's **character** is the only perfect human character in history: only his love for God and for others was pure, only his desires were perfect in the sight of God, only his will was perfectly conformed to the Father's, only his thoughts were completely the Father's, only his emotions were perfect displays of God's, only his virtues were perfect displays of the attributes of God. Finally, Christ's **actions** are the only purely holy set of human actions in history. Born "under Law" (the Law of God in Scripture, Galatians 4:4), he consecrated himself to God at every moment and obeyed every minute detail of the Law and Prophets (Matthew 5:17–18), giving his body for the will of God every day of his life. He lived a life pure from all sin, and had nothing to confess. The seven-fold path of active service he alone lived perfectly: in private worship, in spiritual disciplines, in family life, in ministry to believers, in mission to non-believers, in stewardship, and in work, his actions were constantly in perfect compliance to the word of God—He lived every moment in obedience to his Father under the Laws he had given to his people.

It is overwhelming to meditate on the perfection of Christ's righteousness, which he accomplished in space and time, walking on the guilty sod of this sin-soaked earth, surrounded at every moment by hate-filled enemies. Yet this is the perfect righteousness that is imputed to us by simple faith, our only hope on Judgment Day: *"not having a righteousness of my own that comes from the law, but that which is through faith in Christ—the righteousness that comes from God and is by faith"* (Philippians 3:9).

Go over this list carefully, and praise Christ deeply and richly for his achievement, and for his gift of righteousness imputed to your account by faith. In that righteousness you now stand, if you are a Christian, and in that righteousness you will stand for all eternity.

2). HUMBLING

It is also greatly beneficial for us to go over this detailed list of sanctification and realize that God the Father actually has commanded us to be all of this every day! We are to *"be perfect, as our heavenly Father is perfect"* (Matthew 5:48). These various areas are all substantiated by clear commands of Scripture. My big concern in this book has not been that there is too much here for us to do, but rather that I have left many things out! Therefore, this map is also here to humble us constantly, and to make us realize how far we fall short every day of the standard God has given us in Christ. We should lament our shortcomings, and yearn for a practical daily righteousness that more nearly conforms to that of Jesus Christ. We should take our failures to God in confession and repentance. And we should utterly loathe any sense of pride or self-righteousness that we may develop along the way as we actually see progress in sanctification. There is still an infinite journey ahead of us, and only by the infinite power of Almighty God will we finish that journey after we die.

To this end, we can use this map as a tool to say *"Search me, O God, and know my heart; test me and know my anxious thoughts. See if there is any offensive way in me, and lead me in the way everlasting"* (Psalm 139:23–24). And when the Lord reveals how far we fall short of his standard, we can confess our sins to him with broken hearts. This map can be used to keep us in that state which God most delights to bless: *"a broken and contrite heart, O God, you will not despise"* (Psalm 51:17). For *"God opposes the proud, but gives grace to the humble"* (James 4:6). A careful study of this map will make us ready for the grace that he alone can give, and which is essential to the next step.

3). PRAYER

The most important thing a Christian can do with this information is to bring it back to God in prayer as a spiritual beggar

(Matthew 5:3), pleading with God for transformation in all these areas. Only if God *"gives us more grace"* (James 4:6) as humble beggars will we make a single step of progress. This is so that he alone can get the glory for that progress! Below, I give a list of prayers tied to the sanctification map that you can use for yourself or for any Christian. Requests like these can and should be part of your regular prayer life:

KNOWLEDGE: SPIRITUAL TRUTH

1. FACTUAL KNOWLEDGE GAINED FROM GOD'S WORD:
- Lord, please give me a deep and accurate knowledge of your word in all its breadth and depth.

2. EXPERIENTIAL KNOWLEDGE GAINED FROM LIVING IN GOD'S WORLD:
- Lord, please providentially draw me into rich and powerful life situations that will shape me best for future service in your Kingdom.

FAITH: ASSURANCE AND CONVICTION OF SPIRITUAL TRUTH

1. CERTAINTY THAT INVISIBLE SPIRITUAL REALITIES ARE TRUE:
- Lord, please give me an ever-deepening sense of your constant presence, of the truth of your past dealings with people, of the reality of the spiritual world around me, and of the future heavenly world awaiting me.

2. ASSURANCE OF THINGS HOPED FOR:

- Lord, please give me an ever-stronger foretaste of my heavenly rewards in Christ, and an ever more buoyant hope of fruit in this world that will last eternally in the next.

3. CONVICTION OF SIN:

- Lord, please make my sins as clear and as offensive to me as they are to you.

4. RELIANCE ON CHRIST AS ALL-SUFFICIENT SAVIOR AND PROVIDER:

- Lord, please give me a much more vivid sense of reliance on Christ for everything I need in this world, and crush my self-reliance forever.

5. RECEPTION OF SPIRITUAL GUIDANCE:

- Lord, please let me learn to hear your voice and follow it, as a sheep learns to recognize the voice of its shepherd.

CHARACTER: INTERNAL NATURE CONFORMED TO CHRIST

1. AFFECTION: LOVING WHAT CHRIST LOVES AND HATING WHAT CHRIST HATES

- Lord, would you help me to love you with all my heart, and to love my neighbor as myself. And please transform my heart to love what you love and to hate what you hate.

2. DESIRE: YEARNING FOR WHAT CHRIST YEARNS FOR

- Lord, would you give me desires after your desires, and purge me of desires that are contrary to yours?

3. WILL: CHOOSING WHAT CHRIST WOULD CHOOSE

- Lord, not my will but yours be done, this instant, for the rest of today, and for the rest of my life.

4. THOUGHT: HAVING THE MIND OF CHRIST

- Lord, enable me to think as you do about everything.

5. EMOTIONS: FEELING WHAT CHRIST WOULD FEEL

- Lord, enable me to control my emotions by the standards of your Word.

6. VIRTUES: SITUATIONAL HEART ATTRIBUTES CONFORMED TO CHRIST

- Lord, may my character appropriately reveal your attributes in every circumstance.

ACTION: HABITUAL OBEDIENCE

1. MAIN ACTION: PRESENTATION OF THE BODY AS A SPIRITUAL SACRIFICE

- Lord, I now present my body to you as a living sacrifice, to be used for your holy purposes.

2. NEGATIVE OBEDIENCE: PERSONAL HOLINESS/PURITY

a. Purity from sin
  - Lord, keep me holy and pure from all sin.
b. Purity in lawful pleasures
  - Lord, help me to enjoy the sweet blessings of this world without being ensnared by any of them.
c. Proper handling of sin's occurrence
  - Lord, help me to confess all my sins to you, holding nothing back; help me to make restitution, no matter how costly.

3. POSITIVE OBEDIENCE: SEVEN KEY ARENAS
   a. Worship
       - Lord, make me willing to worship you passionately in spirit and in truth.
   b. Spiritual Disciplines
       - Lord, train me daily by Scripture and prayer.
   c. Family
       - Lord, make me faithful to my responsibilities to my family.
   d. Ministry to Believers
       - Lord, enable me to use my spiritual gifts to build up the Body of Christ.
   e. Mission to Non-Believers
       - Lord, empower me by the Spirit to advance your Kingdom in a lost world.
   f. Stewardship
       - Lord, help me to realize that all I have is yours, and give me wisdom to use my resources maximally for your Kingdom.
   g. Work
       - Lord, strengthen me to work faithfully for you, and to do everything great and small for your glory.

This is how we can be praying for ourselves and for other Christians by name. A life of faithful prayer is the key to spiritual growth, and these kinds of prayers are lined up with God's will—so God will answer them abundantly!

4). GOAL-SETTING AND ASSESSMENT

At the beginning of this book, we were inspired by William Carey's "Deathless Sermon" in which he challenged his hearers to "Expect great things from God and attempt great things for God." Carey was speaking of the external journey of Kingdom advance, but I desire to apply that same kind of kind of hope-filled optimism to the internal journey of sanctification. We should be willing to "expect great things from God and attempt great things for God" in our personal spiritual growth, by identifying weakness and seeking to grow in those areas. The comprehensive spiritual map is a tool to help in that process.

Every New Year's Day, thousands of Americans resume the habit of making (and sadly, breaking) New Year's resolutions. But while that process can be tragic for someone still enslaved to sin, it is helpful for making progress in sanctification. Even if one doesn't go to the formal length of writing out specific resolutions and seeking to keep them, yet a holy plan for godliness driven by zeal for the glory of God is a powerful tool for this journey.

So, how to proceed? Perhaps a Christian can take the list of prayer requests I just listed above and zero in on certain areas of deficiency. Under the leadership of the Holy Spirit, he will gain a sense of urgency in certain areas and begin to formulate a plan for growth. Obviously, none of us will ever attain perfection in any of these areas, and we are not free to neglect any. But that doesn't mean we can't focus our efforts in some specific areas. Now, all resolutions are made internally (in the heart) and result in some action or other. Therefore, all of the following resolutions are really actions designed to accomplish ends in each area of sanctification.

So some possible resolutions or goals based on this list might be as follows:

RESOLUTIONS FOR SPIRITUAL GROWTH
1. Knowledge: Spiritual truth
    a. Factual knowledge gained from God's word
        Resolution #1: with God's help, I will read through the entire Bible this year
        Resolution #2: with God's help, I will memorize the book of Ephesians this year

    b. Experiential knowledge gained from living in God's world

        Resolution #3: if God wills, I will expose myself more to those who are suffering by visiting a nursing home once a week

        Resolution #4: if God wills, I will go on a short term mission trip to Haiti with our church this upcoming summer.

2. Faith: Assurance and Conviction of Spiritual Truth

    a. Certainty that Invisible Spiritual Realities are True

        Resolution #5: with God's help I will grow in my sense of the fact that he sees everything I do and is with me at every moment by memorizing Hebrews 4:13 and reciting it throughout the day.

Nothing in all creation is hidden from God's sight. Everything is uncovered and laid bare before the eyes of him to whom we must give account (Hebrews 4:13).

    b. Assurance of Things Hoped For

        Resolution #6: with God's help, I will read Randy Alcorn's book *Heaven* this year, and feed my heart on the details of my future heavenly life.

    c. Conviction of Sin

        Resolution #7: with God's help, before I go to bed every night, I will pray Psalm 139:23–24 out loud, then listen to the Spirit as he convicts me of sin.

        Resolution #8: with God's help, I will enter into a solid accountability relationship this year and humbly ask my accountability partner to show me any sins gently and clearly.

    d. Reliance on Christ as All-Sufficient Savior and Provider

        Resolution #9: with God's help, I will pray about small things throughout the day that I ordinarily took for granted, and ask Christ to help me; for example, as I get behind the driving wheel, I will pray that Christ would help me get safely to my destination.

Resolution #10: with God's help, I will learn to say "If God wills . . . " before any statements concerning my future plans.

e. Reception of Spiritual Guidance

Resolution #11: with God's help, I will learn to listen to the "still, small voice" of Christ in specific forms of guidance. I will ask for specific wisdom based on James 1:5–8, and will trust God to answer.

3. Character: Internal Nature Conformed to Christ

a. Affection: Loving What Christ Loves and Hating What Christ Hates

Resolution #12: with God's help, I will seek to kindle my love for Christ to a far deeper level than ever before by meditating daily on his love for me poured out on the cross. I will work on my cold heart every morning until I am moved again by the greatness of his love and sacrifice.

Resolution #13: with God's help, when I confess my sins, I will labor to increase my disgust for them and for their vileness in God's sight.

b. Desire: Yearning for What Christ Yearns for

Resolution #14: with God's help, I will do a comprehensive Bible study, seeking to determine the answer to this question: "What do the godly desire?" Having determined the list, I will pray daily that those desires will become mine.

c. Will: Choosing What Christ Would Choose

Resolution #15: with God's help, I will learn to pray consistently in the pattern of Christ in Gethsemane: "Not my will, but yours be done."

    d.   Thought: Having the Mind of Christ

        Resolution #16: with God's help, I will control my thought-life better than ever before. I will especially seek to crush sin thoughts, and will work on my attitude, especially in trying circumstances.

    e.   Emotions: Feeling What Christ Would Feel

        Resolution #17: with God's help, I will seek to grow in daily joy in any and every circumstance based on the greatness of Christ's love for me and power in me.

    f.   Virtues: Situational Heart Attributes Conformed to Christ

        Resolution #18: with God's help, I will memorize the "Fruit of the Spirit" list in Galatians 5:22–23, and ask the Spirit to work these virtues in me moment by moment.

4.   Action: Habitual Obedience

    a.   Main Action: Presentation of the Body as a Spiritual Sacrifice

        Resolution #19: with God's help, I will begin every day by getting down on my knees and presenting my body as a living sacrifice to God with this prayer: "Here I am, yours to command today for your glory and your purposes."

    b.   Negative Obedience: Personal holiness/purity

        i.   Purity from sin

            Resolution #20: with God's help, I will identify my greatest area of rebellion and attack it with Scripture, prayer, fasting, and accountability.

        ii.   Purity in lawful pleasures

            Resolution #21: with God's help, I will monitor my eating and entertainment, seeking balance between asceticism and excess. I will occasionally

        secretly fast from food and from entertainment
to keep these things in proper perspective.

  iii. Proper handling of sin's occurrence

      Resolution #22: with God's help, I will spend ten
minutes a day in concentrated confession of
sin.

      Resolution #23: with God's help, I will get in the
habit of going to those I have sinned against and
humbly asking for forgiveness.

  c. Positive Obedience: Seven Key Arenas

    i. Worship

      Resolution #24: with God's help, I will sing a hymn
of praise every morning.

      Resolution #25: with God's help, I will prepare my
heart every Sunday morning for corporate worship by prayer, Bible reading and hymn-singing
so that I am ready to worship passionately.

    ii. Spiritual Disciplines

      Resolution #26: with God's help, I will go over all of
these resolutions daily, giving special attention
to those resolutions focused on daily Scripture
intake and patterns of prayer, especially #1

      Resolution #27: with God's help, I will make a prayer
notebook and use it daily, keeping a record of
specific prayer requests that I'm waiting on God
to fulfill.

  iii. Family

      Resolution #28: with God's help, I will lead (encour-
age) our family in daily family worship.

  iv. Ministry to Believers

      Resolution #29: with God's help, I will seek to de-
velop a consistent ministry at my local church
based on my spiritual gifts.

Resolution #30: with God's help, I will seek to encourage another believer every week in church
with some Scripture verse.

v.   Mission to Non-Believers

Resolution #31: with God's help, I will pray this
prayer every day, then act accordingly: "Lord,
give me a chance to witness today, and give me
the wisdom to see it and the boldness to make
the most of it."

[see also Resolutions #3 & 4]

vi.   Stewardship

Resolution #32: with God's help, I will increase my
giving this year to at least a tithe of my gross
income.

vii.   Work

Resolution #33: with God's help, I will oppose
pockets of laziness in my life by memorizing
Colossians 3:23.

*"Whatever you do, work at it with all your heart, as working for
the Lord, not for men"* (Colossians 3:23).

This list of resolutions is meant to be merely suggestive. With
the aid of the Holy Spirit, a Christian should make his/her own
list and follow it by his power. I would recommend that, while
seeking to be ambitious, you should also be reasonable. Focus on
fewer resolutions and make sure they actually occur before add-
ing more. But be very hopeful! These are the very things the Lord
yearns for us to do in "working out our salvation with fear and
trembling." One verse I like to use in conjunction with setting
goals and making resolutions is Isaiah 32:8: *"the noble man makes
noble plans, and by noble deeds he stands."* Another good verse for
resolutions is this: *"With this in mind, we constantly pray for you, that
our God may count you worthy of his calling, and that by his power he*

may fulfill every good purpose of yours and every act prompted by your faith" (2 Thessalonians 1:11).

Having made such resolutions, it is vital to go over them daily by prayer, and to make regular assessments of your progress. It is also beneficial to reset them regularly and address other areas of growth, perhaps yearly.

HOW PARENTS CAN USE THIS MAP

The key concept I would like to communicate to Christian parents is that it is primarily their responsibility to evangelize and disciple their own children. It is not primarily the duty of the church leaders (especially the youth group leader, etc.) to bring your children to spiritual maturity. Humanly speaking, that privilege is yours, and you must shoulder this burden with the strength the Lord gives. And what a joyous and sober privilege it is!

I am not seeking to write a book on parenting here, because there are many excellent resources available for the training of your children in the Lord. I would simply like to commend this sanctification map as a tool for your own plans for your children. Some steps may be helpful for you.

1). Be sure that you personally are growing in your own walk with Christ. Follow the first section of this chapter yourself, so that you are seeing real progress made in your own life.

2). Use the prayer list I gave in that section for your children. Take each request and match it against each child, praying that they will develop in knowledge, faith, character, and action, in all the ways described in this book.

3). Have consistent times of family devotion, preferably led by the father. This is the clearest way he can show his God-ordained spiritual leadership of the family. Go consistently through the Bible in an expository way, simply reading the text, explaining it, and applying it to their hearts.

4). Teach your children the theology of salvation, so they understand its component parts: calling, regeneration, justification, sanctification, and glorification. Make sure your lessons are Christ-centered and grace-centered. Teach the sovereignty of God in all these things, while not neglecting the commands God gives them to repent and believe in Christ for the rest of their lives.

5). Set before them the Knowledge-Faith-Character-Action chart and explain it generally to them, so they can see what still remains for them to do in personal growth. Their understanding of these things will develop as they grow older.

6). If they are old enough, help them set their own goals for personal spiritual growth by the pattern laid out above.

7). Meet with them regularly to see if they are making progress to achieve the goals they set.

Parents should prayerfully work with the Lord to see balanced development in their children. They should couple consistent biblical instruction with rich spiritual learning experiences (ministries to the poor, mission trips, evangelistic outreaches, service to other believers in the local church, etc.) to initiate comprehensive spiritual growth. Above all, they should ingrain the two infinite journeys in their hearts for the glory of God, so that these journeys are laid before them for the rest of their lives.

HOW PASTORS, DISCIPLERS, AND MISSIONARIES CAN USE THIS MAP

Christians laboring directly to fulfill the Great Commission of Matthew 28:18–20 should remember that Christ there has in mind the full development of mature disciples, not merely the making of converts. It is so easy to get caught up in the numbers game of reporting baptismal statistics, and forget that both Christ and Paul labored for people to move beyond the initial confession of faith in Christ toward full maturity in him. This comprehensive map of sanctification is a tool that pastors can use in the context of their local church ministries, that disciplers can use in their campus ministries, that church-planting missionaries can use in developing their converts, *"teaching them to obey everything"* that Christ has commanded them.

In addition to applying the Individual section listed above to themselves, and exhorting others in the church or ministry to do the same, there are some specific things pastors, disciplers, and missionaries can do with the content of this book.

1). Use this sanctification map as a guideline for developing men to be future church leaders (elders) to serve with you in the ministry of the church. 1 Timothy 3:1 says, *"If anyone sets his heart on being an overseer, he desires a noble task."* If this is so, then church leaders (pastors) should set their hearts on helping to develop future overseers. A pastor, discipler, or missionary should have a regular plan for discipling promising men, with the goal of seeing them develop into elders.

2). Set this pattern of sanctification weekly before the church in preaching. Give the church a strong sense of the infinite journey of sanctification by the applications of his sermons. Seek to find applications of expositions that relate to knowledge-faith-character-action in a set of four simple questions: what does the text want us to **know**? **believe**? **be**? **do**? Often preachers of expository sermons struggle with finding specific and timely applications for their people. These four areas give a consistent pattern of applications helpful to preachers.

3). Pastors can find good Christian books and resources for their people based on this sanctification map. Each chapter in this book could have been delved into at a much deeper level, and other godly writers have actually already done so. A pastor could put together a book table or resource center developing each of the four major areas as well as the sub-areas described in this book: books on worship, spiritual disciplines, family life, spiritual gifts, evangelism, missions, stewardship, work, etc. abound. Since a pastor probably knows the available resources better than anyone else in the congregation, this is another way he can help develop the saints in his congregation.

4).   Of course, finally, a Christian leader can use the prayer list given above to pray for his people, and to train others to pray like this as well. Spiritual growth comes only by the grace of God, and a pastor can use this spiritual map to pattern his prayer life after Paul's in praying for the spiritual growth and fruitfulness of those entrusted to his care.

HOW BIBLICAL COUNSELORS CAN USE THIS MAP

Biblical counseling is one of the great needs in the Christian church today, especially since sin's ravages have taken such a toll on individuals and families in the post-modern world. The proliferation of pornography, alcohol, divorce, abortion, materialism, and other soul-killing sins makes solid counsel from the Word all the more urgent; so also the ongoing threat from lawful pleasures that threaten to drown us in an ocean of honey, through self-indulgence.

Biblical counselors seek to address not merely the fruits of sin but its roots as well. If the counselee is actually a believer, the failure in his life will be some failure related to knowledge-faith-character-action. In the case of sins of commission, they are not merely some bad habits the counselor seeks to trim like strange fruit from the tree as if it accidentally got taped there while no one was looking. Rather, the counselor can use the sanctification map to show that the bad actions derived from heart issues.

DIAGNOSING SIN BY MEANS OF THE MAP

However, the Christian counselor can look at the opposite of knowledge-faith-character-action and diagnose all sin in this way: dullness, doubt, double-mindedness, disobedience.

Dullness is a failure of knowledge—we had ample opportunity to understand the spiritual truth the word and experience is seeking to teach us, but our minds are made dull by years of sin. Thus Jesus asks his disciples, *"Are you still so dull?"* (Matthew 15:16). Paul says of the unbelieving Jews, *"their minds were made dull,"* and he speaks of a veil covering their minds whenever the word of God is read (2 Corinthians 3:14).

Doubt is a failure of faith. Jesus hit this issue harder than any other in his dealings with his disciples: He said to sinking Peter, *"You of little faith, why did you doubt?"* (Matthew 14:31). It is precisely because we are justified and sanctified by faith that Christ takes unbelief so seriously. For myself, I believe that most Christian sin is a failure of faith, resulting in a failure of love. We generally know the commands of God. The problem is, we don't believe God enough to see the command as coming from the Throne of the Almighty Sovereign of the Universe. We then act in ways we never would if we could see him with our eyes.

Double-mindedness is a failure of character (heart). It is a matter of loving two masters, seeking to serve two masters, seeking to embrace two sources of pleasure and authority. It is seeking to mount two escalators that are going in opposite directions. So James speaks of the *"double-minded man, unstable in all he does"* (James 1:8) and warns that love for the world is the essence of double-mindedness. It is the fundamental issue of the heart, and the only cure for it is to be purified from it: *"Come near to God and he will come near to you. Wash your hands, you sinners, and purify your hearts, you double-minded"* (James 4:8).

Disobedience is a failure of action. It naturally flows from the other three, but it is good for the sinner to see it in terms of

the commands of God. All sin is disobedience, just as all godliness is obedience (Romans 6:16)

A biblical counselor or pastor—as well as an individual
Christian or parent—can take these four alliterative words and
apply them to any sinner (including himself!) to diagnose the root
cause. In so doing, sin can be pulled up by the roots, to the glory
of God and the joy of the growing Christian.

PURSUE HOLINESS FOR THE SAKE OF HEAVENLY JOY

"ONLY ONE LIFE, 'TWILL SOON be past; only what's done for Christ will last."

This is a well-known adage, and it stands over us day after day, urging us to redeem the time for the glory of Christ. What is our life? It is a mist that appears for just a brief time and then vanishes. Soon, we will breathe our last breath in these bodies. Perhaps our families will be gathered around our beds in the ICU, and we will have the privilege of knowing beyond a reasonable doubt that today is our last day on earth. At that time, our pilgrimage will have come to an end—we will have made as much progress as we're going to make in the two Infinite Journeys. At that time, our thoughts may well float heavenward to our eternal home. We will realize then that the most significant thing about us is that we have been justified by faith in Jesus Christ alone, apart from any works of the Law. The progress we have made in sanctification will not be our confidence. The people we have converted and dis-cipled will not be our righteousness. Then we will rest completely on the finished work of Christ on the cross as the full payment for our sins. Then we will know that our works, however many and however Spirit-empowered, cannot in any way pay for our sins. At that point, we will rest in Jesus alone. Then the saying will be reversed:

> "Only one life, 'tis now past. Only what's done **by** Christ
> will last."

When the Lord then calls us home, we will depart our bodies. If we are not among that mysterious final generation that will be alive on earth when Jesus returns, we will die. We will then be instantly among the company called "the spirits of righteous people made holy." (see Hebrews 12:23) By our justification, we will be qualified to join them in praising the Son of God for his perfect work on our behalf. By our glorification, we will be equipped to praise Jesus perfectly, unburdened at last by indwelling sin. Between those two moments lies our own Infinite Journey. Once safely arrived in heaven, we will give him eternal praise for the internal journey he worked in us. We were once dead in our transgressions and sins. By his grace, we were made into new creations; we saw the crucified Lord by faith and trusted him. His righteousness was credited to us and we were forgiven for all our many sins. His Spirit was poured out on us abundantly, and in that power we began to walk after the risen Christ in a brand new life. Whatever progress we made will have been done by his power and his Spirit, and he will get all the glory. But that time of making progress will be over. Whatever distance there was still to travel in our pressing on to perfection in Christ, God will instantly perform for us in glorification. But whatever distance we did travel will be reflected in our capacity for heavenly joy. Then and only then will we completely realize how eternally significant was our progress in sanctification.

Why do I say that? Because I believe the progress we will have made will affect our eternal joy: the greater our sanctification on earth, the greater our enjoyment of Christ in eternity. The measure we will have used on earth will be reflected in the measure we will be given to glorify God in heaven. If we were satisfied with a little of Christ on earth, that small measure will be reflected and perfected in heaven. If we pressed on to an ever-greater measure of holy joy in Christ, that larger measure will be reflected in heaven. Not a single redeemed person will be dissatisfied by his or her heavenly portion, but not all will have equal experience of heavenly joy. By their earthly sacrifices in personal holiness and other-worldly ambitions, some will soar above others in heavenly capacity to savor the infinite greatness of God in Christ.

Does the scripture support this idea? I think so. Take for example 1 Timothy 4:7-8: "[T]rain yourself to be godly. For physical training is of some value, but godliness has value for all things, holding promise for both the present life and the life to come." In other words, there is an eternal value to the training we do in godliness. What "promise" does such training hold for "the life to come?" Since the focus of that life is a perfect experience of worship in the presence of the Triune God, it stands to reason that the more progress we make in sanctification now, the more we will enjoy God in heaven. Jonathan Edwards believed this to be true. In his "Resolutions," made when he was merely nineteen years old, Edwards wrote this: "22. Resolved, to endeavor to obtain for myself as much happiness, in the other world, as I possibly can, with all the power, might, vigor, and vehemence, yea violence, I am capable of, or can bring myself to exert, in any way that can be thought of."[91] How can a present, earthly endeavor involving "all the power, might, vigor, and vehemence, yea violence" we can possibly muster result in greater happiness *in the other world*? It seems Edwards believed that any effort toward holy affections and genuine sanctification would serve him eternally in enjoying God, the center of his heavenly pleasures.

Thus, every time we choose to feed our hearts by the Word of God and heavenly meditation rather than to pursue worldly pleasures (even if lawful and not corrupt), we are expanding our capacity for heavenly joy. Every temptation crushed by the power of the Spirit will enlarge our capacity for heavenly joy. Every time we sacrificially give to the needy or courageously witness for Christ, we are increasing the vessel with which we will be scooping at the heavenly fountain that is Christ. The redeemed who will scoop with a cup and drink deeply will be perfectly happy. But the redeemed who scoop with a bucket will be even happier.

So, dear reader, I urge you to run with endurance the infinite race marked out in front of you. Put sin to death by the power of the Spirit! Discipline yourself for godliness! Feed your hearts on Christ by the Word of God! Serve God's people with self-forgetful abandon! Develop more and more your taste for heavenly joy! Thus your heavenly vessel will grow larger and larger, and you will look back on the progress you made by the power of Christ, knowing that you spent this brief life doing what will gain you the most eternal joy, and Christ the most eternal glory!

ENDNOTES

1   The Merriam Webster Third New International Dictionary (Chicago: G. & C. Merriam, 1971) defines "infinite" not only as "having no end" but also as "immeasurably or inconceivably great." It is in the second sense, not the first that I am using this word.

2   Mark Dever, *Nine Marks of a Healthy Church* (Wheaton, IL: Crossway, 2000), 12.

3   Oliver E. Allen, *The Pacific Navigators* (Alexandria, VA: Time-Life Books, 1980), 107–108.

4   For a concise treatment of recent attacks on justification. see John Piper, *Counted Righteous in Christ* (Wheaton, IL: Crossway, 2002).

5   Quoted by J.I. Packer, *Keep in Step With the* Spirit (Grand Rapids, MI: Baker, 2005), 92. Alexander Whyte told his Edinburgh congregation, "You'll never get out of the seventh of Romans while I'm your minister!" See J. I. Packer, *A Quest for Godliness: The Puritan Vision of the Christian Life* (Wheaton, IL: Crossway, 1990), 179.

6   Martin Luther, *Two Kinds of Righteousness* in *Martin Luther's Basic Theological Writings*, Timothy F. Lull, ed (Minneapolis, MN: Augsburg Fortress, 1989), 155.

7   Luther, *Two Kinds of Righteousness*, 157.

8   John Piper, *Don't Waste Your Life* (Wheaton, IL: Crossway, 2003), 12.

9   John Calvin, *Institutes of the Christian Religion* (Peabody, MA: Hendrickson, 2008), 1.14.20; 1.5.8; 2.6.1.

10 I have in mind the "Word of Faith" movement, which makes faith a commodity, like an amount of gold dust that is poured onto God's scales, and when there is sufficient amount, God is compelled to

give you whatever you ask. This makes God somewhat like a coin-operated vending machine.

11   Paul G. Hiebert, "The Flaw of the Excluded Middle," *Missiology: An International Review*, Vol. X, No. 1 (January, 1982), 35–47.

12   Quoted in I.D.E. Thomas, *A Puritan Golden Treasury* (Carlisle, PA: Banner of Truth Trust, 1997), 216.

13   For an excellent biography on Mueller, see Roger Steer, *George Mueller: Delighted in God* (Wheaton, IL: Harold Shaw, 1981). See also A.T. Pierson, *George Mueller of Bristol: His Life of Prayer* (Waymark Books, 2010).

14   German instructor Samuel Rodigast penned this hymn text "Was Gott tut, das ist wohlgetan" (What God does, is well done) in 1674, possibly to console a sick friend. J.S. Bach used it in his chorale cantata (BWV 99) in 1724.

15   Quoted in Christopher D. Hancock, "The 'Shrimp' Who Stopped Slavery," *Christian History and Biography* Website, *Christianity Today*, dated   January 1, 1997. http://www.ctlibrary.com/ch/1997/Issue53/53h012.html.

16   For an outstanding and very thorough extended scriptural meditation on our future heavenly blessings in Christ, I commend Randy Alcorn, *Heaven* (Carol Stream, IL: Tyndale House, 2004).

17   So why does the KJV use "evidence" to translate *elegkon*? In classical Greek usage, the sense of a debate or court trial is a common context of this word. A participant in an academic debate or a court trial would produce "evidence" in the process. The author of the letter to the Hebrews uses a very high, classical Greek style, and so the KJV translators were probably picking up on this when they chose the word "evidence" for *elegxon*. But the standard lexicon for classical Greek usages of NT words is Liddell-Scott, and that volume gives this entry: *a cross-examining, testing,* for purposes of *disproof* or *refutation,* ἔχειν ἔλεγχον to admit of *disproof,* Hdt., Thuc.; ἔλ. διδόναι τοῦ βίου to give *an account* of one's life, Plat.; εἰς ἔλ. πίπτειν to be convicted, Eur.; οἱ περὶ Παυσανίαν ἔλ. *the evidence on which* he *was convicted,* Thuc. Therefore, even the classical Greek usage of this word group is

negative; even in an academic debate, *elegxon* is used for "evidence" that the opponent is *wrong*; in a court trial, as "evidence" that the accused is guilty as charged. Therefore, the base of this word even in classical Greek is essentially the same as the NT usage: producing convincing proof of wrongdoing.

18   According to Puritan Thomas Watson, these are the six vital elements of true repentance; Thomas Watson, *The Doctrine of Repentance* (Carlisle, PA: Banner of Truth Trust), 18.

19   Dr. & Mrs. Howard Taylor, *Hudson Taylor In Early Years—the Growth of a Soul* (OMF International, 1998), 131.

20   For more on the fundraising for the Metropolitan Tabernacle, see the excellent account in Lewis A. Drummand, *Spurgeon: Prince of Preachers* (Grand Rapids, MI: Kregel, 1992), 345–347.

21   John Bunyan, *Pilgrim's Progress*, in *The Works of John Bunyan*, vol. 3 (Carlisle, PA: Banner of Truth Trust, 1991), 99–100.

22   Steer, *George Mueller: Delighted in God*, 226–227.

23   John Piper, *Future Grace* (Sisters, OR: Multnomah, 1995), 277–278.

24   D. Martyn Lloyd-Jones, *Joy Unspeakable* (Wheaton, IL: Harold Shaw, 1984), 95–96.

25   Lloyd-Jones, 80.

26   Quoted in D. Martyn Lloyd-Jones *Revival* (Wheaton, IL: Crossway, 1987), 197. Thomas Goodwin's statement comes from his exposition of Ephesians 1:13–14, *An Exposition of Ephesians Chapter 1 to 2:10* (Volume 1 in the Nichols Series, Edinburgh) 247.

27   Quoted in John Piper, *Desiring God* (Colorado Springs, CO: Multnomah, 2003), 16

28   This is made plain by the inclusion of the word *immortality* in the list. It is our own immortality we are seeking, not God's, since God is already eternal. Thus the *glory* and *honor* in Romans 2:8 are also ours. But since they are sought from the hand of God and can only be given by God, they are not sinful ambitions.

29   Jonathan Edwards, *A Careful and Strict Inquiry into the Modern Prevailing Notions of that Freedom of the Will which is supposed to be essential to*

Moral Agency, Virtue, and Vice, Reward and Punishment, Praise and Blame. In *The Works of Jonathan Edwards*, vol.1 (Peabody, MA: Hendrickson, 2000), 1–93.

30   Edwards wrote: "My idea of the sun when I look upon it is more vivid, than when I only think of it. Our idea of the sweet relish of a delicious fruit is usually stronger when we taste it, than when we only imagine it. And sometimes, the idea we have of things by contemplation, are much stronger and clearer, than at other times." Jonathan Edwards, "A Careful and Strict Enquiry into the Prevailing Notions of the Freedom of the Will," in *The Works of Jonathan Edwards*, vol. 1 (Peabody, MA: Hendrickson, 1998), 5-6.

31   http://www.quotecosmos.com/quotes/10741/view

32   The best article I've ever read on Christ's emotional life was B.B. Warfield's "The Emotional Life of Our Lord," in B.B. Warfield, *The Person and Work of Christ* (P&R Publishers, 1950). For an online version, see http://www.the-highway.com/emotion-Christ_Warfield.html.

33   Piper, *Desiring God*, 9.

34   Watson, *Repentance*, 18.

35   Ibid., 19.

36   http://www.wholesomewords.org/missions/bcarey15.html.

37   Martyn Lloyd-Jones had some of the clearest insights concerning the need for preaching to yourself to correct faulty emotions in his classic *Spiritual Depression: Its Causes and Cure* (Grand Rapids, MI: Eerdman's, 1993), 20–21.

38   Farhad Daftary, *The Assassin Legends: Myths Of The Isma'ilis* (I.B.Tauris, 1995), 74.

39   Tertullian, *Apology*, Chapter 50 in *Ante-Nicene Fathers*, volume 3, Alexander Roberts and James Donaldson, eds. (Peabody, MA: Hendrickson Publishers, 1995), 54-55.

40   Dietrich Bonhoeffer, *The Cost of Discipleship* (New York: Scribner, 1963), 7.

41   John Owen, *The Mortification of Sin* (Carlisle, PA: Banner of Truth Trust, 2004), 5.

42   C.S. Lewis, *Screwtape Letters* (New York: MacMillan, 1961), 49–50.

43   Piper, *Desiring God*, 14.

44   John Piper, *Let the Nations Be Glad* (Grand Rapids, MI: Baker Academic, 2003), 11.

45   Piper, *Desiring God*, 67.

46   George Mueller, *A Narrative of Some of the Lord's Dealing with George Muller, Written by Himself, Jehovah Magnified. Addresses by George Muller Complete and Unabridged,* vol. 1 (Muskegon, MI: Dust and Ashes, 2003), 271–272.

47   The booklet can be downloaded from our website at www.fbcdurham.org/writings.

48   Jonathan Edwards, *The Works of Jonathan Edwards,* vol. 2 (Peabody, MA: Hendrickson, 2000), 71.

49   John Bunyan, "Bunyan's Dying Sayings," in *The Works of John Bunyan,* vol. 1 (Carlisle, PA: Banner of Truth Trust, 1991), 65.

50   Donald S. Whitney, *Spiritual Disciplines for the Christian Life* (Colorado Springs, CO: NavPress, 1991).

51   C.S. Lewis, *The Weight of Glory and Other Addresses* (New York: HarperCollins, 1949).

52   R.C. Sproul, *The Intimate Marriage* (Wheaton, IL: Tyndale House, 1986), 45–46.

53   C.H. Spurgeon, "The Last Words of Christ on the Cross," *The Metropolitan Tabernacle Pulpit,* vol. 45, (Pasadena, TX: Pilgrim Publications, 1977), 495.

54   C.J. Mahaney, *Why Small Groups: Together Toward Maturity* (Gaithersburg, MD: Sovereign Grace Ministries, 1996), 23.

55   D.A. Carson, *A Call to Spiritual Reformation: Priorities from Paul and His Prayers* (Grand Rapids, MI: Baker, 1992).

56   John Gillies, *Memoirs of Rev. George Whitefield,* Sermon #20 "Jacob's Ladder"; New Haven, 1834, 535 digitized version, Googlebooks.com; http://books.google.com/books?id=DU0FAAAAYAAJ&printsec=frontcover&dq=memoirs+of+rev.+george+whitefield#PPA535,M1.

57   R.A. Torrey, *Why God Used D.L. Moody* (Chicago: The Bible Institute Colportage Ass'n, 1923), 38–42.

58   Julia H. Johnstone, *Fifty Missionary Heroes Every Boy and Girl Should Know* (New York: Fleming H. Revell, 1913), 11.

59   Dr. & Mrs. Howard Taylor, *Hudson Taylor and the China Inland Mission— the Growth of a Work of God* (OMF International, 1998), 31–32.

60   John Paton, *John G. Paton, Missionary to the New Hebrides* (New York: Fleming H. Revell, 1898), 87.

61   www.global-prayer-digest.org

62   www.joshuaproject.net

63   Glenn Schwartz, *When Charity Destroys Dignity: Overcoming Unhealthy Dependency in the Christian Movement* (Bloomington, IA: AuthorHouse, 2007); Steve Corbett and Brian Fikkert, *When Helping Hurts: How to Alleviate Poverty Without Hurting the Poor ... and Yourself* (Chicago: Moody, 2009).

64   Tertullian, *Apologeticus*, Chapter 50 in Ante-Nicene Fathers, vol. 3 (Peabody, MA: Hendrickson, 1995).

65   Randy Alcorn, *Money, Possessions, and Eternity* (Wheaton, IL: Tyndale House, 2003), 3.

66   Alcorn, *Money, Possessions, and Eternity* .

67   Ibid., xv.

68   Ibid., 104.

69   Ibid., 299.

70   Randy C. Alcorn, *The Law of Rewards : Giving What You Can't Keep to Gain What You Can't Lose* (Wheaton, IL: Tyndale House, 2003), 18.

71   Alcorn, *Money, Possessions, and Eternity*, 173.

72   *Chariots of Fire*, directed by Hugh Hudson (Burbank, CA: Warner Home Video, 1990), DVD.

73   "Sphere Sovereignty", in James D. Bratt, ed., *Abraham Kuyper, A Centennial Reader* (Grand Rapids, MI: Eerdmans, 1998), 488.

74   Leland Ryken, "Puritan Work Ethic: The Dignity of Life's Labors," *Christianity Today*, October 19, 1975, 15.

75 Cited in Leland Ryken, *Worldly Saints* (Grand Rapids, MI: Zondervan, 1986), 228, fn3.

76 Martin Luther, *Luther's Works* [American edition, 55 vols. Eds. J. Pelikan and H. Lehmann] vol. 2 (St. Louis and Philadelphia: Concordia and Fortress, 1955ff), 348.

77 Ryken, *Worldly Saints*, 228 fn3.

78 David Daniell, *William Tyndale: A Biography* (New Haven, CT: Yale University, 1994), 167.

79 Os Guinness, *The Call* (Nashville, TN: Thomas Nelson, 1998), 34.

80 Leland Ryken, *Worldly Saints*, 27.

81 Ibid.

82 Ibid.

83 Ibid.

84 Ibid, 35.

85 Eusebius, *The Church History of Eusebius*, tr. by Arthur Cushman McGiffert, in *Nicene and Post-Nicene Fathers*, Second Series, Volume 1, eds. Philip Schaff and Henry Wace, (Peabody, MA; Hendrickson, 1995), 190.

86 Jean-Pierre Houdin, *Khufu: The Secrets Behind The Building Of The Great Pyramid* tr. from French by Dominique Krayenbuhl (Farid Atiya Press, 2006).

87 John Piper, *Desiring God*, 77

88 Wilson Benton, Jr., *www.covenantseminary.edu/resource/Benton_PrayingWithPower.pdf.*

89 John Bunyan, *The Works of John Bunyan*, vol. 1 (Carlisle, PA: Banner of Truth Trust, 1991). 65.

90 Extreme Devotion Writing Team, *Extreme Devotion: The Voice of the Martyrs* (Nashville, TN: Thomas Nelson, 2001).

91 Jonathan Edwards, *Works*, vol. 1, xxi.

ABOUT THE AUTHOR

DR. ANDREW DAVIS HAS BEEN Senior Pastor of First Baptist Church (FBC), Durham, NC, since 1998. He came to faith in Christ his junior year in college. In 1984, he graduated with a BSME from MIT, and worked for ten years as a mechanical engineer. Davis received his Master of Divinity degree from Gordon-Conwell Theological Seminary in 1990 and his PhD in Church History from the Southern Baptist Theological Seminary in 1998. He was married to Christi in 1988, and they served together on the mission field in Japan for two years. They have five children. The central passion of Davis's life is the glory of God as revealed perfectly in the written word of God.

For more information about
Andrew M. Davis
&

An Infinite Journey
please visit:

Website: www.fbcdurham.org
Email: andrew.davis@fbcdurham.org
Twitter: @AndyDavisFBC

....

For more information about
AMBASSADOR INTERNATIONAL
please visit:

www.ambassador-international.com
@AmbassadorIntl
www.facebook.com/AmbassadorIntl